IMAGES OF APARTHEID

Traditions in World Cinema

General Editors
Linda Badley (Middle Tennessee State University)
R. Barton Palmer (Clemson University)
Founding Editor
Steven Jay Schneider (New York University)

Titles in the series include:

Traditions in World Cinema
by Linda Badley, R. Barton Palmer and Steven Jay Schneider (eds)

Japanese Horror Cinema
by Jay McRoy (ed.)

New Punk Cinema
by Nicholas Rombes (ed.)

African Filmmaking
by Roy Armes

Palestinian Cinema
by Nurith Gertz and George Khleifi

Czech and Slovak Cinema
by Peter Hames

The New Neapolitan Cinema
by Alex Marlow-Mann

American Smart Cinema
by Claire Perkins

The International Film Musical
by Corey Creekmur and Linda Mokdad (eds)

Italian Neorealist Cinema
by Torunn Haaland

Magic Realist Cinema in East Central Europe
by Aga Skrodzka

Italian Post-Neorealist Cinema
by Luca Barattoni

Spanish Horror Film
by Antonio Lázaro-Reboll

Post-beur Cinema
by Will Higbee

New Taiwanese Cinema in Focus
by Flannery Wilson

International Noir
by Homer B. Pettey and R. Barton Palmer (eds)

Films on Ice
by Scott MacKenzie and Anna Westerståhl Stenport (eds)

Nordic Genre Film
by Tommy Gustafsson and Pietari Kääpä (eds)

Contemporary Japanese Cinema Since Hana-Bi
by Adam Bingham

Chinese Martial Arts Cinema (2nd edition)
by Stephen Teo

Slow Cinema
by Tiago de Luca and Nuno Barradas Jorge

Expressionism in Cinema
by Olaf Brill and Gary D. Rhodes (eds)

French Language Road Cinema: Borders, Diasporas, Migration and 'New Europe'
by Michael Gott

Transnational Film Remakes
by Iain Robert Smith and Constantine Verevis

Coming of Age in New Zealand
by Alistair Fox

New Transnationalisms in Contemporary Latin American Cinemas
by Dolores Tierney

Celluloid Singapore: Cinema, Performance and the National
by Edna Lim

Short Films from a Small Nation: Danish Informational Cinema 1935–1965
by C. Claire Thomson

B-Movie Gothic: International Perspectives
by Justin D. Edwards and Johan Höglund (eds)

Francophone Belgian Cinema: Filmmaking in Wallonia since 2001
by Jamie Steele

The New Romanian Cinema
by Christina Stojanova (ed) with the participation of Dana Duma

French Blockbusters: Cultural Politics of a Transnational Cinema
by Charlie Michael

Nordic Film Cultures and Cinemas of Elsewhere
by Anna Westerståhl Stenport and Arne Lunde (eds)

New Realism: Contemporary British Cinema
by David Forrest

Contemporary Balkan Cinema: Transnational Exchanges and Global Circuits
by Lydia Papadimitriou and Ana Grgić (eds)

Images of Apartheid: Filmmaking on the Fringe in the Old South Africa
By Calum Waddell

www.edinburghuniversitypress.com/series/tiwc

IMAGES OF APARTHEID
Filmmaking on the Fringe in the Old South Africa

Calum Waddell

EDINBURGH
University Press

Dedication

This book is dedicated to the memory of my beloved mother, Helen Waddell, who passed away on 4 April 2021. She was the greatest mother anyone could wish for, raising me as a late child at the age of 40, and it pains me that she will never read this book. She will be forever missed and will never leave my thoughts.

Edinburgh University Press is one of the leading university presses in the UK. We publish academic books and journals in our selected subject areas across the humanities and social sciences, combining cutting-edge scholarship with high editorial and production values to produce academic works of lasting importance. For more information visit our website: edinburghuniversitypress.com

© Calum Waddell, 2021, 2023

Edinburgh University Press Ltd
The Tun – Holyrood Road
12(2f) Jackson's Entry
Edinburgh EH8 8PJ

First published in hardback by Edinburgh University Press 2021

Typeset in 10/12.5 pt Sabon by
Servis Filmsetting Ltd, Stockport, Cheshire

A CIP record for this book is available from the British Library

ISBN 978 1 4744 5002 7 (hardback)
ISBN 978 1 4744 5003 4 (paperback)
ISBN 978 1 4744 5004 1 (webready PDF)
ISBN 978 1 4744 5005 8 (epub)

The right of Calum Waddell to be identified as the author of this work has been asserted in accordance with the Copyright, Designs and Patents Act 1988, and the Copyright and Related Rights Regulations 2003 (SI No. 2498).

CONTENTS

List of Figures vii
Acknowledgements xi
Traditions in World Cinema xiii
Note xv

Introduction 1

1. That's ZAxploitation! South African Blaxploitation 19
2. Joe Bullet: The Unacknowledged Blaxploitation Hero 41
3. Simon Sabela: Blaxploitation Icon? 58
4. Into the Bioscope: The South African B-Scheme Explosion of the 1980s 75
5. Crime Does Not Pay: Morality in the B-Scheme 108
6. The Badass: Stickin' it to Apartheid? 125
7. For the Common Good? The ZAxploitation Buddy Movie 149
8. Be More Like Miriam: The Women of ZAxploitation 171
9. Armed and Dangerous: The Border War 190

10. A Different Kind of Gangster Cinema? Mapantsula and a State of
    'Panic' 211

Conclusion 229
Filmography 240
Bibliography 246
Online Resources 253
Interviews Conducted 255
Index 256

FIGURES

1.1	Transnational influence: Melvin Van Peebles as the original blaxploitation hero in *Sweet Sweetback's Baadasssss Song* (Melvin Van Peebles, 1971)	24
1.2	All-out war in *Doomsday* (Abie Hattingh, 1986)	29
1.3	Steve James in *American Ninja 3: Blood Hunt* (Cedric Sundstrom, 1989)	32
1.4	Ken Gampu as Joe Bullet in *Joe Bullet* (Louis de Witt, 1973)	34
2.1	A meal fit for a mafia king in *Joe Bullet* (Louis de Witt, 1973)	42
2.2	Ken Gampu in *Joe Bullet* (Louis de Witt, 1973)	43
2.3	Abigail Kubeka dances for the titular hero in *Joe Bullet* (Louis de Witt, 1973)	47
2.4	Ken Gampu returns as *Joe Bullet* in the sequel *Bullet on the Run* (Tonie van der Merwe, 1982)	56
3.1	Ron O'Neal as Youngblood Priest in *Super Fly* (Gordon Parks Jr, 1972), a notable influence on Simon Sabela's *iKati Elimnyama*	63
3.2	Simon Sabela as Lefty in *iKati Elimnyama* (or *Black Cat*, Simon Sabela, 1975)	64
3.3	Compromised by the mainstream, Simon Sabela as the Black saviour character King in *Gold* (Peter R. Hunt, 1974)	72
4.1	Two of the main faces of B-Scheme cinema, Popo Gumede (sometimes credited as Innocent Gumede, left) and Hector	

	Mathanda (right), pictured in *Fishy Stones* (Tonie van der Merwe, 1989)	81
4.2	Emmanuel Shangase (sometimes credited as Dumi or Dumisani Shongwe), another recurring B-Scheme face, and Hector Mathanda in *The Faceless Man* (Carl Bleakley, 1985)	86
4.3	B-Scheme regular Hector Mathanda runs for his life in *Beware Tiger* (Michelle Hartslief, 1986)	92
4.4	Hector Mathanda in *Ivondwe* (Louis De Witt, 1986)	94
4.5	Another fixture of the B-Scheme – Pepsi Mabizela in *Gone Crazy* (Tony Cunningham, 1980s)	96
4.6	Emmanuel Shangase/Dumi Shongwe in *Under Cover* (Tony Cunningham, 1989)	97
4.7	Crime doesn't pay in *Under Cover* (Tony Cunningham, 1989)	98
4.8	Emmanuel Shangase/Dumi Shongwe in a villainous turn opposite Zanela Nyidi in *Hostage* (Michele Hartslief, 1986)	99
5.1	Black and white working together in *Knockout Joe* (Laurens Barnard, 1984)	112
5.2	Hector Mathanda serves tea in his lavish new homestead in *The Comedians* (Japie van der Merwe, 1980)	114
5.3	Emmanuel Shangase/Dumi Shongwe up to no good in *Ransom* (Tony Cunningham, 1980s)	120
5.4	One of many repetitive scenes of characters working out in *The Boxer* – a B-Scheme film that has no boxing (Michelle Hartslief, 1986)	122
6.1	Popo Gumede sneaks up on a symbol of white authority in *Black Crusader* (Tony Cunningham, 1986)	130
6.2	Popo Gumede in trouble, as a badass for the B-Scheme in *Black Crusader* (Tony Cunningham, 1986)	131
6.3	Popo Gumede avenges his sister and father by killing another member of a local criminal gang in *Impindiso* (or *Cold Justice*, Carton Spielberg, 1980s)	134
6.4	Sol Rachilo as the title character in *Charlie Steele* (Bevis Parsons, 1984)	135
6.5	The Wild West in South Africa in *Revenge* (Coenie Dippenaar, 1986)	143
6.6A	Hector Mathanda looks on as actor Vincent Velekazi opens fire in *Umbango* (or *The Feud*, Tonie van der Merwe, 1986)	144
6.6B	Director Tonie van der Merwe, playing a victim of a shoot-out, nurses his injuries in *Umbango* (or *The Feud*, Tonie van der Merwe, 1986)	145
7.1	Ken Gampu and Michael Dudikoff are 'buddies' in *American Ninja 4: The Annihilation* (Cedric Sundstrom, 1990)	150

7.2	Nigel Davenport and Ken Gampu as an unlikely crime fighting duo in *Death of a Snowman* (Christopher Rowley, 1976)	155
7.3	Black and white team-up against criminal elements in *Run for Your Life* (Tommy Röthig, 1985)	159
7.4	Johnny Tough (Hector Rabotabi) takes on white authority in *One More Shot* (Ronnie Isaacs, 1984)	160
7.5	Actor Winston Ntshona in *The Wild Geese* (Andrew V. McLaglen, 1978)	163
7.6	White nightmare – a Black communist guerrilla takes a hostage in *Shamwari* (Clive Harding, 1982)	167
8.1A	Dominique Tyawa as Miriam in *Johnny Dlamini* (Robert van de Coolwijk, 1986)	172
8.1B	Dominique Tyawa's Miriam is a rare B-Scheme heroine who outsmarts the male characters in *Johnny Dlamini* (Robert van de Coolwijk, 1986)	173
8.2	Zep (So Mhlanga) argues with his pregnant girlfriend Caroline (unidentified actress), who later kills herself in *Zero for Zep* (Steve Hand and Laurens Barnard, 1980s)	179
8.3	Charlotte Dlamini (Lungi Mdlala) meets her bodyguard, Robert (Popo Gumede)	184
8.4	Thembi Mtshali as Pat, girlfriend of Panic and political activist in *Mapantsula* (Oliver Schmitz, 1988)	188
9.1	Actor Ken Gampu, playing a tough African dictator, in the controversial but commercial *The Gods Must Be Crazy* (Jamie Uys, 1980)	193
9.2	Arnold Vosloo as a soldier of the apartheid state in *Boetie Gaan Border Toe* (Regardt van den Bergh, 1984)	194
9.3	Vera Johns is terrorised in *Operation Hit Squad* (Tonie van der Merwe, Kathy Viedge, 1987)	196
9.4	Richard Roundtree takes aim, as a Zimbabwe liberation fighter, in *Game for Vultures* (James Fargo, 1979)	198
9.5	Hector Mathanda as a guerrilla and poacher in *Ambushed* (Tonie van der Merwe, 1988)	200
9.6	The Angolan conflict spills into Namibia in *Terrorist* (Neil Hetherington, 1978)	202
9.7	Vera Johns tries to survive in *Terrorist* (Neil Hetherington, 1978)	204
9.8	The war in Angola becomes horror film nightmare in *The Stick* (Darrell Roodt, 1988)	206
10.1	Thomas Mogotlane as Johannes 'Panic' Themba Mzolo in *Mapantsula* (Oliver Schmitz, 1988)	212
10.2	Thomas Mogotlane as Johannes 'Panic' Themba Mzolo in *Mapantsula* (Oliver Schmitz, 1988)	214

10.3	Xuma (Phinda Mazibuko) and Stella (Lungi Mkwanazi) in *Mine Boy* (Karen Thorne, 1989)	222
10.4	Xuma (Phinda Mazibuko) and Pinki (Olga Mothi) in *Mine Boy* (Karen Thorne, 1989)	224
10.5	Kliptown prostitute Pinki (Olga Mothi) awakes to money on her pillow in *Mine Boy* (Karen Thorne, 1989)	225
10.6	Peter Sephuma in *My Country My Hat* (David Bensusan, 1983), an anti-apartheid film that found its audience on the B-Scheme network.	226
C.1	Popo Gumede in *Umbango* (or *The Feud*, Tonie van der Merwe, 1986)	232
C.2	Woman meets snake in *Snake Dancer* (Dirk De Villiers, 1976)	234
C.3	Thomas Mogotlane as Johannes 'Panic' Themba Mzolo in *Mapantsula* (Oliver Schmitz, 1988), the crowning achievement of 'filmmaking on the fringe' in the old South Africa.	237

ACKNOWLEDGEMENTS

It was the most unwelcome news when I heard of the passing of South African activist and filmmaker Laurence Dworkin on 17 May 2020 from his close and cherished friend Brian Tilley. Laurence was 65 years old and had contracted COVID-19. During my research for this monograph he gave me his valuable time and offered me some incredible insights into the period it covers. My heart and thoughts go out to his friends and family. I would have been honoured to have him read this publication.

This project began back in October 2015, thanks to the friendship and influence of Paul Blom, Harry Isaacs and particularly Benjamin Cowley (with whom I have cross-checked many a minor fact and year of release), of Gravel Road in Cape Town. However, my interest in South Africa, and apartheid specifically, began when I studied the subject in the classroom under one of the most exceptional teachers I ever had: Mr Bingham at Balwearie High School in Kirkcaldy. It has been almost three decades since I saw or heard from him, but his inspiration – in a secondary comprehensive that I have otherwise less than fond memories of – never faded, and I knew one day I would visit the 'beloved country'. Thank you sir, wherever you are. In my first trip to South Africa, in 2015, I was accompanied by my friend Nana Pananon, who took a gamble and jumped on a *long* flight that began in Bangkok and then went to Hong Kong before arriving in the 'rainbow nation' with me. I owe her my thanks. Cynthia Hlanguza at Gravel Road Entertainment Group also has my deepest appreciation for her assistance during the initial stages of this monograph and

I also owe a debt of gratitude to Keyan Tomaselli and Gairoonisa Paleker, who upon hearing about this work not only encouraged me but invited me to Pretoria to screen my documentary on the 'ZAxploitation' pantheon (Covid-19 unfortunately put paid to this). There can never be a bigger honour and I will probably always feel 'academic imposter' syndrome in their esteemed company. Tomaselli has also gone to such lengths as to scan essential materials for me – for which I may never be able to express my endless appreciation. I am also massively grateful to those additional people who gave me interviews, in summer 2016, which form some of the skeleton of this book: Abigail Kubeka, Brian Tilley, Cedric Sundstrom, Christi van der Westhuizen, Clive Scott (who offered his palm-reading services as well!), Coenie Dippenaar, Darryl Els, Ian-Malcolm Rijsdijk, Karen Thorne, Litheko Modisane, Mitch Dyter, Neil Hetherington, Ntshavheni Wa Luruli, Tonie van der Merwe and Trevor Taylor. Their words offer this monograph valuable insight into the ZAxploitation period. I cannot explain how grateful I am to be working with Edinburgh University Press and, in particular, Gillian Leslie – the best publisher anyone could wish for – and I also need to express my gratitude to those at Lincoln University who have been enthusiastic about this project: Andrew Elliot, Gabor Gergely, Janice Kearns and Mikey Murray, who saw not just the potential in this monograph but in me as a colleague. The funding for my summer 2016 research in South Africa, however, came from the hard work of Professor Nick Cope and Professor Holger Briel – my former colleagues and dear, valued friends to this day. I thank you both, sincerely, for your belief in my research. The wonderful Duri Dhansay from Cape Town also warrants a credit here – not just as another valued 'trash' movie compatriot but as someone who was willing to send me some much-needed DVDs for the purpose of this project. When I think back to that long, warm and sometimes exhausting summer of 2016, I also remember how seductive Africa is – a continent of such stunning beauty and unexplainably perfect night skies that I cannot help but offer a shout out to Charles Sibanda in Victoria Falls, Zimbabwe, for no other reason than his being infectious and making me feel blessed to even be working on a project as rich as this one. Finally, I offer a thanks to colleagues Iain Robert Smith and Mikel Koven, for being there as friends and minds, Adam Marsh at the Derby Film Festival, who allowed me to bring 'Sollywood' to the attention of his audience in summer 2018, David Beckett for his outstanding proofreading and to Naomi Holwill, who has my back and my respect but who has also been so important to my motivation and dedication during this incredible research project.

TRADITIONS IN WORLD CINEMA

General editors: **Linda Badley** and **R. Barton Palmer**
Founding editor: **Steven Jay Schneider**

Traditions in World Cinema is a series of textbooks and monographs devoted to the analysis of currently popular and previously underexamined or undervalued film movements from around the globe. Also intended for general interest readers, the textbooks in this series offer undergraduate- and graduate-level film students accessible and comprehensive introductions to diverse traditions in world cinema. The monographs open up for advanced academic study more specialized groups of films, including those that require theoretically-oriented approaches. Both textbooks and monographs provide thorough examinations of the industrial, cultural, and socio-historical conditions of production and reception.

The flagship textbook for the series includes chapters by noted scholars on traditions of acknowledged importance (the French New Wave, German Expressionism), recent and emergent traditions (New Iranian, post-Cinema Novo), and those whose rightful claim to recognition has yet to be established (the Israeli persecution film, global found footage cinema). Other volumes concentrate on individual national, regional or global cinema traditions. As the introductory chapter to each volume makes clear, the films under discussion form a coherent group on the basis of substantive and relatively transparent, if not always obvious, commonalities. These commonalities may be formal, stylistic or thematic, and the groupings may, although they need not, be popularly identified as genres, cycles or movements (Japanese horror, Chinese martial arts cinema, Italian Neorealism). Indeed, in cases in which a group of films is not already commonly identified as a tradition, one purpose of the volume is to establish its claim to importance and make it visible (East Central European Magical Realist cinema, Palestinian cinema).

Textbooks and monographs include:

- An introduction that clarifies the rationale for the grouping of films under examination
- A concise history of the regional, national, or transnational cinema in question
- A summary of previous published work on the tradition
- Contextual analysis of industrial, cultural and socio-historical conditions of production and reception
- Textual analysis of specific and notable films, with clear and judicious application of relevant film theoretical approaches
- Bibliograph(ies)/filmograph(ies)

Monographs may additionally include:

- Discussion of the dynamics of cross-cultural exchange in light of current research and thinking about cultural imperialism and globalisation, as well as issues of regional/national cinema or political/aesthetic movements (such as new waves, postmodernism, or identity politics)
- Interview(s) with key filmmakers working within the tradition.

NOTE

Where I have been unable to ascertain the year of a given production, I have listed it as '1980s'

INTRODUCTION

On 29 July 2014, *The New York Times* published an article entitled 'Honoring a Filmmaker in the Shadow of Apartheid'. Written by Norimitsu Onishi, the piece explained how a director – 'Unknown among his fellow white South Africans' – had been gifted with a lifetime achievement award at the Durban International Film Festival. This recognition had come for Tonie van der Merwe's work on formulaic low budget genre films, generally inspired by glossier Hollywood templates and made in the 1970s and 1980s, that played to segregated Black cinemagoers during the period of apartheid in South Africa. In the years since his plaudit in Durban, van der Merwe has been covered in various other international press articles; his output has screened at the Berlin International Film Festival (in 2015) and, in 2019, he appeared in a short documentary for Al Jazeera television news that focused on how 'In the 1970s and 80s, the apartheid government funded a little-known film scheme aimed at Black South Africans . . .' In November 2020, an article from South African journalist Sihle Mthembu appeared, praising the director's Western *Umbango* (1986) and arguing that it 'posits something deeper about the time and era in which it was made'.[1] Surely, one would have every right to ask, such commentary points towards an important name within the country's cinema and, potentially, even as a part of global exploitation or 'B-movie' film activity?

However, in the sole mention of director/producer Tonie van der Merwe in Jacqueline Maingard's *South African National Cinema*, he is referenced only once, in regard to his role as 'one of the key players' in the industry of austerity motion pictures made for Black audiences during the 1948–1994 period of National Party rule (2007: 132). In many other studies of the continent's cinema, and in specific monographs of South African film, van der Merwe goes unmentioned entirely or the (admittedly often amateurish) work that he and many of his contemporaries made is similarly disregarded. James Murray acknowledges van der Merwe's *Ngomopho* (1975) as one of the first Zulu-language films that instigated a system of production which resulted in '120 and more' films being made 'a year by 1986' (1992: 257). These are incredible numbers that warrant further investigation; but in analysis of the country's post-1994 activity, van der Merwe's circuit, a network constructed to bring a flurry of quickly-produced genre efforts to South African townships, is castigated as 'almost entirely white directors making films for Black audiences . . . little more than propaganda for apartheid ideology' (Saks 2010: 13). Certainly, van der Merwe did himself and his brand few favours during the apartheid period – he is even quoted by Gus Silber as saying, of his ethnic viewership, '"they got nothing else to do, they make children . . . Let's face it, today our biggest problem is our black problem. The taxpayers can't support them forever"' (1992: 271).

Nevertheless, one is still compelled to ask: what *are* these obscure films that van der Merwe was involved with? What *might* they tell us about the period? Moreover, do they merely pander to the ideology of the ruling National Party or might we see aspects of Black agency that offer at least *some* indication of a wider, *specifically South African* exploitation cinema?

These were some of the questions I intended to answer when I began writing this monograph and which, I hope, are suitably analysed and discussed in the following ten chapters. Perhaps most important to address is the longstanding concept, as touched upon above, that if these films are 'just' propaganda for an authoritarian government, then they warrant their hitherto exclusion – or at least should be denied any detailed analysis – when writing about the wider pantheon of South Africa's national cinema. When author Iain Robert Smith refers to transnational adaptations of cowboy movies – 'the Roast Beef Western . . . the Curry Western' (2016: 190) – there is a sense of the whimsical in such demarcations that, for instance, an 'Apartheid Western' such as van der Merwe's *Umbango* clearly does not signify. Audrey Thomas McCluskey argues that 'domestic films that were targeted' towards South Africa's Black majority during apartheid 'were of low production value and made mainly to gain access to lucrative film subsidies by white-owned film companies' (2009: 5). Even if this were the case, and we might initially cringe at the idea of a blaxploitation cinema supported (in some cases) by a despotic government, should this also mean avoiding study of the recent plethora of 'Wolf Warrior' action heroes that have emerged from China? Given the emergence of horrifying reports about arrests, ethnic violence and purges in Xinjiang, from the

Han majority Communist Party state, and the crackdown on pro-democracy protestors in Hong Kong, it would be quite a challenge to argue that the old South Africa was (or remains) a unique case when it comes to the concept of populist filmmaking made under approval from a repressive or even racist regime.[2]

Nonetheless, few cineastes would, I imagine, argue that Chinese film – including its blockbuster genre productions such as *Wolf Warrior* (Wu Jing, 2015) – are not worth further deliberation or study. How about analysis of North Korean film? Iran? Myanmar? Venezuela? The list goes on. As such, potentially acknowledging van der Merwe as an important figure in his country's cinema, and wishing to explore his work, should not be confused with defending the regime that would subsidise the often crass and patronising films that he directed, nor his own attitude towards his audience during the apartheid years.

In fact, van der Merwe might be viewed, from the perspective of historic 'schlock merchants' working during periods of notoriously hard-fisted governance, as a figure akin to the better-known Pinoy exploitation figure Cirio H. Santiago, whose sizeable output included transporting blaxploitation emblems – including the heroines of *TNT Jackson* (1975) and *The Muthers* (1976) – into the Southeast Asian tropics during the Ferdinand Marcos dictatorship. Yet, whereas Santiago has had retrospective praise from Quentin Tarantino and seen his catalogue re-released in newly remastered Blu-rays, despite working under one of the late twentieth century's most notorious authoritarians, van der Merwe and his prolific presence as part of apartheid history have had far less attention. In the introduction to their (now hard to find) 1992 edited compendium *Movies-moguls-mavericks: South African Cinema, 1979–1991*, authors Johan Blignaut and Martin Botha state that:

> We can continue to philosophise about how films should have been made or the reasons why films were made in a particular way. But in the 90s we ought to concern ourselves with more positive issues than debating the 'hidden racism' in films of the 70s or the exploitation of tax money for 'B-grade' films in the 80s.

As such, over a quarter-century since the end of apartheid and this statement, it is worth heeding these words and returning to van der Merwe's work, and those of his contemporaries, and entering into a dialogue with a period in which a plethora of genre projects were financed (for better or for worse) because of an evident market for their release. In doing so, one can at least try to untangle a vast spectrum of low-cost filmmaking that bears its own important legacy to not just South Africa's motion picture history but that of wider, international race-exploitation and even blaxploitation cinema.

This is also, however, where my own interest and story begins. From as young an age as I can remember, my tastes in cinema have gravitated towards (admittedly sometimes obnoxious) genre fare – Cannon action cheapies, horror (and particularly slasher) flicks, classic Universal monster movies and tawdry eighties teen-comedies were a part of my life since I first had parental carte blanche at the local video rental stores. In my teens I began to seek out more controversial fare, notably the famous 'nasties' such as *Don't Go in the House* (Joseph Ellison, 1980) and *The Last House on the Left* (Wes Craven, 1972) – still banned in the UK at the time – but also thrilling gangster and kung-fu epics from Hong Kong, kaiju from Japan, foreign exploitation from France, Italy and Spain and American blaxploitation movies of the seventies. Not only did such exploration ground my interest in world cinema, and initiate my thirst for international travel, but it also led to a fascination with history – and eventually pursuing what became *The Style of Sleaze: The American Exploitation Film 1959–1977*, adapted from my PhD and published by Edinburgh University Press in 2018. It was during my writing of this project that I received an incredible offer to present my research at the SAE Institute [School of Audio Engineering] Cape Town in South Africa, organised by Paul Blom, who had previously screened my documentary output at his annual October *Horror Fest* in the city. Whilst the arrival of what would be dubbed 'blaxploitation', including most notably *Sweet Sweetback's Baadasssss Song* (Melvin Van Peebles, 1971), MGM's *Shaft* (Gordon Parks, 1971) and the similarly influential *Super Fly* (Gordon Parks Jr., 1972), has been widely chronicled in documentaries and within academic journals and monographs, it is perhaps safe to say that few film watchers of the period could have anticipated that this cycle of texts focusing on petty mobsters and suave detectives, headlined by muscular African American performers, would resonate in South Africa. I was one of them. However, at the SAE Cape Town Institute in October 2015, I was introduced to a local film buff, Harry Isaacs, who knew a gentleman called Benjamin Cowley of Gravel Road Entertainment Group, a company involved in restoring such ventures from the 1970s and 1980s. This meeting represented the gestation of the *Images of Apartheid* monograph and a subsequent successful funding bid, which allowed me to spend my summer 2016 in South Africa, conducting interviews (many of them included in this book) and research.

Initially, at least, it was from this introduction that I became acquainted with a film called *Joe Bullet* (Louis de Witt, 1973), produced by Tonie van der Merwe and originally banned by the apartheid government, and such terms as 'Sollywood' and 'ZAxploitation' (a spin on the URL domain used by Pretoria). Despite being dismissed, even recently, by Keyan Tomaselli as 'appallingly inept, exploitative and patronising' but (in the same sentence) as the key text that 'kicked off the South African blaxploitation genre' (2016: 119), *Joe Bullet* felt extraordinary. Here, at the peak of apartheid and its derogatory, demeaning Pass Laws, outlawing of interracial relationships, makeshift Bantustans[3] and townships and just a few years before the notorious Soweto riots and the imprisonment, torture and death of Steve Biko, was Ken Gampu as a big screen hero – a John Shaft-type character but in the dusty, repressive backdrop of Johannesburg. Yet, this felt just like a cheaper American blaxploitation film as well – close to the 'real' deal but without the foul language, interracial conflict, sex and gratuitous violence that one would expect from even a low-rent Rudy Ray Moore cash-in. I wanted to understand more about this film that Harriot Gavshon claimed, not without justification, 'was never meant for anything other than release to an African audience' (1983: 14). As I gained access to an increasing number of low budget South African blaxploitation texts, most of them made as part of what became dubbed 'the B-Scheme' and undoubtedly, at least in the first instance, inspired by Hollywood variants, I became drawn to how these small, often crude, improvised[4] and occasionally badly acted efforts existed in a hinterworld of wider national cinema. A national cinema that points to a brief but flourishing (and still largely *undiscovered*) exploitation industry that lasted for almost two decades. Years after first seeing *Joe Bullet*, it is now clear that previous studies of blaxploitation film, some of which have at least addressed the Filipino and Italian strains, have still never covered the full story of this period, including perhaps the most curious example of transnational adaptation . . . and from South Africa of all places.

Whilst I have defined American exploitation cinema as a stylistic movement in *The Style of Sleaze* (Edinburgh University Press, 2018), I concluded the monograph by affirming that the success of such films as *Sweet Sweetback* had invariably inspired a sort-of 'B-exploitation' wherein opportunistic directors and producers, lacking the talent and imagination of the innovating text, merely riffed on its token 'controversial' attributes until the trope finally fell prey to audience and distributor exhaustion. In the case of blaxploitation, this conclusion has been well-documented: 'It is true that Hollywood did Van Peebles one better by conventionalising his story about an urban outlaw through film after film after film' (Chaffin-Quiray 2002: 107). I also maintained in *The Style of Sleaze* that the global appeal of these trendsetting American films and exploitation demarcations undoubtedly made further research into other, similar threads of activity *abroad* essential: 'Of course, this book has focused on the American exploitation film. However, every country has seen its own emergence of marginal cinema, including the creation of similar genres as those discussed here and during similarly turbulent socio-political and censorious periods' (2018: 193). In addition, I stressed that 'Exploitation films are also evidently *of their time*' (Ibid.: 185). In the case of South Africa, what I find fascinating is not so much a deliberate stylistic similarity between texts or any sort of identifiable movement in filmmaking activity, as per the American exploitation film, but rather an assemblage of different genre cinema in dialogue with one another *and* with a wider global network of independent, low budget productions, yet retained within an indigenous (and fiercely exploitative) approach to distribution. One in which Murray has even argued that audiences were held 'captive' due to a brief trend of Black high school principals in financial alignment with white producers to extort a token payment from their pupils for mandatory screenings (1992: 257). Even by the scurrilous tactics of exploitation cinema itself, this is a unique practice within a unique filmmaking period.

This book, then, begins with what might be deemed as a loosely-defined blaxploitation cinema of the 1970s, introduced by van der Merwe and the better-known Simon Sabela, before concentrating on the predominantly Black populated films of the B-Scheme (cheap genre cinema aimed at Black viewers during the time of racial segregation in South Africa) in the 1980s. I have also focused, when appropriate, on comparable representations and demarcations that used South Africa, and even its notorious apartheid politics, for the purpose of either international distribution or to appeal to English-speaking audiences within the country. In addition, I have cast my net wide enough to include discussion of important work by David Bensusan, Darrell Roodt and Oliver Schmitz, predominantly because of their relation to the B-Scheme incentive and/or for their exploration of similar generic templates. This factor will, I hope, explain the inclusion of *Mapantsula* (Oliver Schmitz, 1988) but not, for instance, *Quest for Love* (Helena Nogueira, 1988) or *The Native Who Caused all the Trouble* (Manie van Rensburg, 1989). The parameters of this study's research – whilst still somewhat flexible – may cause some disagreement. However, this framework provides a coherent identification of ZAxploitation as a *cycle* of genre cinema – both more mainstream-orientated and produced for the townships, each existing with a crossover of ideas between one another – that gradually evolved towards increasingly more provocative presentations as the 1990s, and the conclusion of apartheid, dawned.

Tomaselli and Mikki van Zyl have maintained that 'Genres are one way in which the dominant ideas within a particular social formation are articulated and affirmed. They shield the viewer from the alternative, possibly hostile discourses, such that the only valid enunciations apart from the authorised text itself are exegesis, commentary and reinterpretation' (1992: 399). This may be the case some or perhaps even most of the time, but it is not the case all of the time – and, whether it is Kracauer's public-psyche theory regarding Weimar cinema, Robin Wood's 'American nightmare' or Cynthia Freeland's discussion of realist-horror, genre may also be read as didactic, radical and subversive, even as it presents a commercial narrative around visual spectacle. This conclusion is not to argue that ZAxploitation was, or can now be seen as, a revolutionary form of race liberation from white businessmen such as van der Merwe, but rather to propose that a cinema that began with presentations of dominant Black agency – regardless of the financial incentives – was surely, *inevitably*, going to evolve into a medium that challenged the status quo. Exploitation film, after all, is contingent on giving the audience what they want. This monograph's definition of ZAxploitation – that is, specifically, a South African cinema of (particularly race) exploitation – is thus inevitably contingent upon Black representations. This conclusion eliminates Afrikaans-language genre cinema from the study but, with this said, nearly all of the texts introduced in the following pages have been undiscussed in any previous documentation of South African film.

It is also essential to acknowledge the work by Tomaselli on the B-Scheme films that emerged with, mostly, all-Black casts from the mid-1970s until the end of the 1980s. Writing in 1988, the author maintained that – along with an absence of politics and, with few exceptions, white characters (and in some cases I am prone to disagree with the former conclusion, as I will discuss), we might see three categories of genre within these motion pictures: a) back to the homelands, b) urban-conditional; and c) authentic. It is in the second category that Tomaselli establishes we begin to see gangsterism as 'one of the major sub-themes' (1988: 73) – particularly the concept of 'crime does not pay'. Authors, including Harriot Gavshon and, more recently, Gairoonisa Paleker and Litheko Modisane, have built on Tomaselli's discussion by introducing the production histories of certain films, the financial incentives offered to the white producers and identifying troubling misrepresentations of African culture. Tomaselli's astute identification of these three categories is consistent with the films of this monograph – most of the B-Scheme output, for instance, exists within the 'urban-conditional' wherein a 'good life' for the Black characters is dependent on a narrative sense of spiritual destiny, linked to good behaviour, monogamy, marriage and even Christianity. Inevitably, this means that there are elements of ZAxploitation that reinvent some of the familiar tropes of blaxploitation for purposes and presentations that are oppositional to their inspiration.

Some analysis on this period has also emerged from a highbrow/lowbrow dichotomy – for instance, Gavshon mentions that one producer of low budget all-Black action films 'regards Roger Corman as his mentor!' (1983: 15) as if this should be taken as a negative. Writing almost a decade later, Murray belittles the investment of Cannon Films in South Africa, identifying them as the studio behind the lavish horror satire *The Texas Chainsaw Massacre 2* (Tobe Hooper, 1986), described (incorrectly) as 'low budget, low grade' (1992: 120). My own argument is that the vast bulk of the South African genre films I have viewed (including some international co-productions) have tropes in common with blaxploitation and related gangster cinema, even if the more radicalised presentations that are borrowed from the better-known American templates are stripped of their anti-white ethos, radical female protagonists or hypersexual male heroes. In other cases, for instance horror films that were aimed outside of the township networks such as *Terrorist* (Neil Hetherington, 1978) or the better-known *The Stick* (Darrell Roodt, 1988), we also see borrowing from successful foreign landmarks. Indeed, *The Stick* – despite its technical proficiency – still has a low budget, gung-ho, 'war is hell' descent into a jungle nightmare that would not be out of place on a double-bill with the trashy Italian-made Vietnam shocker *The Last Hunter* (Antonio Margheriti, 1980). This conclusion is not to degenerate *The Stick* – rather it is to maintain that one might credibly argue that *The Last Hunter* is a better film about white tragedy (and privilege) in Vietnam than many of the more acclaimed, Oscar-decorated Hollywood efforts. Subsequently, it is possible to discuss some examples of South Africa's so-called ZAxploitation as both exploitative of established formulas and presentations *but* interesting, exciting and (occasionally) even subversive in their own right.

I have also chosen to cap the findings of this study in 1990. Whilst 'In the period between 2 February 1990 and April 1994, more people were killed than during any other period in South Africa's history' (van der Westhuizen 2007: 199), the death of apartheid was clear the moment Nelson Mandela set foot as a free man and fully democratic elections were scheduled. As affirmed by Murray, the B-Scheme funding initiative was also concluded in 1990 (1992: 256). It is difficult to imagine the naively optimistic depictions of Black servitude to state and religion that comprise most of the narratives of South Africa's blaxploitation cinema interacting with the world of 'The Bang Bang Club'. As with so much exploitation cinema, the texts of this book remain rooted in a past that is now distant memory.

I have called this monograph *Images of Apartheid: Filmmaking on the Fringe in the Old South Africa* because the cinematic output of the period from *Joe Bullet* until 1990 teases us with an insight into how predominantly white filmmakers depicted the lives, politics and status of the Black majority within (after 1980) the last European colonial-settler regime on the continent, including through presentations of villainy and even aspiration. It is hardly surprising, therefore, that towards the end of the decade, these presentations also emerge as more politicised, whether intentional or not. Johan Blignaut states that 'None of our heritage other than images of apartheid and some wildlife scenes have been presented in our cinema produced in the 1980s or before' (1992: 109). In borrowing his term, I also hope that this monograph might build on this statement and lead to some fresh discussion of the 'images' within the old South African cinema. I am also aware of other genre cinema during this period in South Africa that avoided discussion of race altogether while almost always claiming to be set in America or another foreign locale. One might mention such Cannon Films irreverence as *Alien from L.A.* (Albert Pyun, 1988) or cheap slasher movies such as *The Stay Awake* (John Bernard, 1987). However, given that the majority of this book is based around an analysis of the B-Scheme blaxploitation films that emerged after *Joe Bullet*, these projects, aimed at the export market and purporting to be made and located outside of South Africa, share few, if any, identifiably relevant traits.

It must also be affirmed that anticipating a South African exploitation cinema akin to the short-lived, pseudo-documentary Mau-Mau cycle of the 1950s – described by author Kenneth M. Cameron as initiating depictions of 'the dangerous Africans' (1994: 109) – is unwise. The films that come after *Joe Bullet* are sometimes parodically self-aware, not just in regard to American blaxploitation cinema but in how Black South Africa *and* Black South Africans are depicted. This challenge means that even the commercialised, 'honourable' savage depictions of *Zulu* (Cy Endfield, 1964) are nowhere to be seen – for all accounts, these are stories about a more upwardly mobile Black class, usually living the good life in a modern state and confronted by skulduggery. Of course, given that an apartheid blaxploitation film even *sounds* ludicrous, and the existence of segregated cinemas until near the end of the 1980s affirms the dubious nature of such an undertaking, I begin my discussion of ZAxploitation by affirming that this period of activity can certainly be deemed *exploitation* – even if, purely stylistically, the majority of the productions carry minimal similarity with their American counterparts. Linda Williams describes blaxploitation as 'the overt exploitation of racialised sex and violence' (2008: 93). The films of the apartheid era, featuring predominantly Black actors, could inevitably indulge in neither.

Tomaselli has argued that:

> South Africa is a country with a scrambled periodisation regarding its path to modernity. The indigenisation argument, however, underestimates the extent to which South Africa is a modern capitalist state. The point is not that cultural or cinematic theories from other societies are inappropriate, but rather that they have a different purchase in South Africa as a partly similar and partly different society – one exhibiting a simultaneity of the modern, post-modern and even pre-modern. (1992: 341)

As such, in this case the 'exploitation film' label emerges from a financial and circumstantial perspective rather than a close, studied approach to mimicking, for instance, the experimental and frequently verité style of *Sweet Sweetback* and/or *Super Fly* (the former's agitprop approach making it a difficult proposition in a country where communist organisations were illegal). South Africa's old screen Black heroes, and gangsters, exist in a 'different purchase' indeed – their agency dependent upon their ability to succeed *within* the apartheid state, which means proving themselves as good, positive, community figures.

It is also worth noting that apartheid-era South Africa remained a Western ally for almost all of its existence. As the country began to fragment into nominally independent Black-governed Bantustans (Bophuthatswana – most famous for its Sun City resort – Ciskei, Transkei and Venda), albeit ones recognised by few governments, and the conflict with Angola dragged on, the alternative of ANC rule still continued to be viewed from the West as part of the wider Cold War story. The ANC's armed wing, MK, received shipments from the Soviet bloc,[5] and – as recently noted by Julia Lovell – Nelson Mandela had 'engaged closely with Mao's military strategies' whilst 'at least six ANC members travelled to China to study Mao's guerrilla war' (2020: 195). Acknowledging such tensions is, of course, not to defend the apartheid regime. Instead, I argue that such context assists in our understanding of *why* so many of the films discussed in this study present a clear paranoia regarding Black authority or (even worse!) a society where hard work does not result in financial betterment. It is also very likely that violent clashes which made little splash outside of Southern Africa in general – for instance the Cuban-led death squads that brutally executed anyone associated with an attempted 1977 coup in Angola against the communist-aligned MPLA government[6] – would have been at least whispered about in the white suburbs of Cape Town, Johannesburg and Port Elizabeth. In any event, such instances certainly would have been known by officials in Pretoria and by foreign governments, which perhaps explains why – per author Ron Nixon's investigation, *Selling Apartheid* (2015), the South African state used lobbyists, financial investment in foreign newspapers and other forms of hard and soft power to try and sustain its future.

Nixon's book has not been without some valid criticism[7] – however it establishes why South Africa was once viewed as such an important global figurehead: Pretoria was a nuclear power as well as a stable economy within a fast-changing continent. It was also a familiar, Western-style democracy even if only the small, white population had the right to vote. Genre trappings, then, are used throughout the films of this study – even the international co-productions, including those that tangentially critique the apartheid government such as *The Wilby Conspiracy* (Ralph Nelson, 1975) – to sustain a presentation of South Africa as a Westernised outpost of the 'dark continent'. Or, to quote from the memoir of journalist Rian Malan, 'Johannesburg lay in Africa, but that was more or less incidental. Johannesburg had skyscrapers, smart department stores, and theatres ... I didn't realise *Reader's Digest* was a foreign magazine until I was at least ten' (1991: 41). Aside from a handful of more radical films, such as *Mapantsula* or *Mine Boy* (Karen Thorne, 1989), this is also the backdrop of most South African genre cinema. Consequently, the re-imagining of Black life as similarly 'Westernised' and complacent (*Reader's Digest* in hand), across a number of low-budget projects, is – in its own way – a radical fever-dream of a South Africa that could never and probably can never exist.

What we might dub appropriation discourse, that is how other countries adapt a prominent text (typically American) into another Anglosphere, third world or foreign setting, has become increasingly popular in the academy. Recent studies, such as Iain Robert Smith's *The Hollywood Meme* (2017) and the edited compendiums *World Cinema's 'Dialogues' with Hollywood* (2007) from Paul Cooke and *Spaghetti Westerns at the Crossroads: Studies in Relocation, Transition and Appropriation* (2016) from Austin Fisher, discuss transitional adaptations – in many cases of what might be deemed 'lowbrow' films, motivated and inspired by an initial highbrow (or at least mainstream) template. Smith's study, in particular, is extremely insightful – although the author admits that by placing Hollywood 'at the centre of global film production' (2017: 4) he might be inviting controversy. Not dissimilar from Smith, however, Marwan M. Kraidy has also spoken about how electronics have 'accelerated' globalisation and notes how American media has a tendency to 'construct a monolithic hybridity' in which the United States, including its politics and entertainment industry, is positioned at the centre of the world – both in terms of economy and in terms of voice and influence (2005: 93). Building on my earlier points, what I also argue is that South African exploitation cinema is unlike any other insofar in that it takes elements of American cinema (blaxploitation) but then repositions them in terms of language, manifesto, ideology and even race and sexuality. Rather than heightening the exploitation elements of a successful trend, South African filmmakers diluted them. In addition, with apartheid being almost entirely absent from the bulk of these presentations, the cinema – perhaps the most transnational of all the twentieth century's creations – loses its own power, with few exceptions, to aptly convey any sort of cultural travelogue of place, time and identity. This aspect is also one of the most fascinating thematic traits of ZAxploitation.

Furthermore, in the case of South Africa, foreign – particularly American – support was the very lifeblood by which apartheid was permitted to breathe. Unlike neighbouring Rhodesia, which was of little strategic importance, South Africa's survival as a patchwork of supposed ethnically separated nations was foremost dependent on Washington's continued trade normalisation. As such, American cinema provides a key mode of comparison for ZAxploitation cinema. Some of the stories may well be transposed within a clearly indigenous locale – particularly those dealing with townships or the border war with Angola – but the filmmakers of many of these motion pictures have generally attempted to reclaim the basics of established Hollywood narratives and genres for a localised audience. 'Crime does not pay' is the backbone of the ZAxploitation B-Scheme pantheon – even when the films highlight a badass character who could, in an alternate universe, assist the likes of John Shaft or *Super Fly*'s Youngblood Priest. I do not want to claim that this comparative methodology is without flaws; my own perplexed reaction to *The Boxer* (Michelle Hartslief, 1986), and its rudimentary failure at achieving even the most basic cinematic professionalism, despite drawing on the popularity of Sylvester Stallone's Rocky Balboa character, should indicate this. Nevertheless, my approach is also succinct in permitting other, rarer examples of the trend to gain a well-deserved retrospective of their own, such as the experimental *Mine Boy*.

As I remain an outsider looking *into* South Africa – it is also my hope that an alternative discussion emerges relating to how a country, segregated by race and in a time of political boycott and crisis, sustained a sizeable industry of, predominantly, trashy filmmaking. My use of the word 'trash' here is, to be clear, sincere rather than reformative. For instance, Jeffrey Sconce – whose work I touched upon in *The Style of Sleaze* – invented his 'paracinema' label as an umbrella term to 'valorise all forms of cinematic trash' (including 'exploitation cinema') mentions: 'With its low-budgets, frequent incompetence, and explosive subject matter, sleazy exploitation cinema is probably the closest thing to "outsider art" possible in the capital and technology intensive world of cinema' (1995: 372). I certainly do not want to claim that South Africa's exploitation cinema needs to be seen as 'outsider art' or should even be 'valorised' – although this is an argument that author Kenneth W. Harrow makes in relation to sleazy efforts from Nollywood and other developing nations on the continent in his *Trash: African Cinema from Below* (2013). Most of the austerity-budgeted, Black-cast films of this monograph are easily defined by their lack of production values, scant care for technical competence behind the camera and monotonous, repetitive narratives. Nonetheless, to understand this phenomenon, we perhaps need to recognise that South African film producers, even during the era of apartheid, still had a financial incentive to appeal to the non-white population and, moreover, remained aware of popular exploitation and Hollywood trends.

As mentioned by academic and filmmaker Ntshaveni Wa Luruli, who grew up in Soweto, 'We watched . . . Spaghetti Westerns, B-movies, then [the] genre they call sword and sandals, gladiators and all that. B-movies – we did not know of the big stars like De Niro. We just went for entertainment. Then came kung-fu, Chinese-Hong Kong films' (2016). As such, when I say that some of these films present a trashy reimagining of (already marginal) American blaxploitation, and their tough-guy leads, I am referring to a wider lowbrow engagement and exchange. Tangentially radicalised personas from what might be dubbed a seventies inner-city 'grindhouse' culture in America (another term I deal with in this monograph) translate only so far to South Africa. Given that this very description sounds ironic, if not perverse, then the word 'trash' – to mean, quite literally, disposable, fits well, as I am unconvinced that any of these motion pictures were meant to last beyond the eventual fall of the National Party regime – and for good reason. Outwith curfews and townships, these cheapjack productions must have seemed quickly antiquated.

Imports were also of particular benefit to the South African film industry and a considerable influence on ZAxploitation. For example, in the case of Hong Kong martial arts cinema, projects that had been purchased and dubbed for the intention of global sales could be exhibited in townships on the cheap. Benjamin Cowley, the CEO and founder of the restoration house and distributor Gravel Road Entertainment Group, mentions:

> The interest in martial arts, especially because it was non-deadly forms of fighting – the use of weapons, guns and all that, was so real in the conditions they were living – these tools were used to oppress. You know, 'If I have to see guns as I walk to the school in the morning this is maybe not something I want to watch'. (2016)

Adds film curator Trevor Taylor:

> They [Hong Kong films] came in through Indian distributors. An important man called Richie Muhammed – he and his brother Rashid, also known as Robert, they loved Hong Kong cinema. Richie had a 16mm outlet down in the centre of Johannesburg called Concorde. And they were the first ones to begin bringing in Hong Kong cinema, so they made a small fortune out of the films of John Woo and before that with the Shaw Brothers. These were immensely popular. They almost took over from the Italian Western. They were hideously dubbed of course, but they had enormous audiences. (2016)

From this sort of distribution network, wherein cheap, easy-to-rent genre cinema from abroad was brought into townships and attracted profit, the South African variant emerged – beginning with *Joe Bullet*. As such, this book also approaches the foreign (re: non-American) exploitation film as a hybrid form of cinema entertainment – adaptable to different communities, no matter how (arguably) diasporic they might be.

I recognise that 'diasporic', as a term, suggests trauma – valid, I think, to the township audiences that were targeted by low budget exploitation films, such as *Joe Bullet*. However, given the old South Africa's uneasy mix of Afrikaner nationalism, historic Commonwealth immigration and multi-ethnic, multi-language communities, I don't think it is incorrect to talk of a diasporic audience in general. This is in much the way that Leon Hunt writes about *Enter the Dragon* (Robert Clouse, 1973): 'What makes the film's Hong Kong-ness problematic is the slippery, shifting sense of what constitutes "Hong Kong", not only as a colonial or post-colonial space but also a marketable, international cinematic commodity ... Hybridity is just one expression of this' (2000: 76). It is also how Gladstone L. Yearwood frames the character arc of Jimmy Cliff's iconic Ivanhoe Martin in *The Harder They Come* (Perry Henzell, 1972): 'trapped between two worlds – the persistent poverty of Jamaica's suffering underclass and an alluring metropolitan North American lifestyle' (2000: 164). It is similarly difficult to separate the characters of the ZAxploitation pantheon from the unacknowledged backdrop of township poverty when they are (typically) introduced via their comfortably middle-class, suburban, Westernised lifestyles (Tomaselli's 'urban-conditional' is a perfect description of these presentations). Of course, any identifiable South Africanness, during apartheid, is probably doomed to function along power binaries within a number of diasporas that would have had access to different forms of entertainment, information and indeed opportunity. Furthermore, given the horrors of the Boer War and Britain's scorched-earth policy as it attempted to create a new dominion in the continent, and forcefully govern the Orange Free State and the Transvaal, resulting Afrikaner nationalism and the initiation of an apartheid state certainly emerged from a traumatic history and traumatised identity. Hybridity, particularly as South Africa developed into a European enclave, is as vital to the country's identity, and cinema, as it is to that of Hong Kong. A recent study on Churchill from historian Richard Toye even reminds its readers of how problematic racial integration remained in South Africa after the second Boer War had concluded – with the British introduction of Chinese labour meeting with fierce resistance in the country in 1906 (2010: 98).

Nwachukwu Frank Ukadike mentions how, in the wake of Third Cinema, and a vaguely identifiable African cinema (including in the English-speaking parts of the continent) there emerged new indigenous filmmaking voices 'out of concern for what they regard as the understandable sociocultural and psychological impact of foreign films'. The author continues:

> Before independence (and in some cases the situation has not changed), foreigners had total control over film distribution and exhibition. They imported films into English-speaking African countries from the United States, Britain, China, Hong Kong, and India. Needless to say, the films identified ideologically and aesthetically with the sociocultural values of the producer nation – in all ramifications they are different from those of the African continent. (1994: 105)

Yet, Ukadike does not mention that key filmmakers in the specified locations were themselves also wrestling against the aesthetic and thematic complacency of the mainstream American studio system and the associated style (Ken Loach in Britain, for instance, or Tsui Hark and Wong Kar Wai in Hong Kong). In the United States itself, Van Peebles had made *Sweet Sweetback* following years of filmmaking and stage directing in Paris – during which period his style was informed by the French new wave, perhaps even more than it was by emerging cinematic traits from his own country. Texts such as *Sweet Sweetback* and *Super Fly* owe at least some lineage to such acclaimed auteur names as Jean-Pierre Melville and Third Cinema techniques, whilst also channelling their own sense of identity – which is far removed from the look, sound and tone of any comparable Hollywood gangster cinema.

The problem, perhaps, with the ZAxploitation films is that they are all, with only occasional standouts – such as *Mapantsula* and *Mine Boy* – beholden to a more traditional and old-fashioned, classic Hollywood gangster narrative of good against evil, in which the former always wins thanks to selfless, heroic acts, by Black men privileged to be middle class and urbanised. Nonetheless, I ascertain that these are still very much films of an old South Africa – and some, particularly *Joe Bullet* and its sequel *Bullet on the Run* (Tonie van der Merwe, 1982), but also *iKati Elimnyama* (Simon Sabela, 1975), *Death of a Snowman* (Christopher Rowley, 1976), *One More Shot* (Ronnie Isaacs, 1984), the Spaghetti Westerns *Umbango* (Tonie van der Merwe, 1986) and *Revenge* (Coenie Dippenaar, 1986) and the *Yojimbo* (Akira Kurosawa, 1961)/*A Fistful of Dollars* (Sergio Leone, 1964) rehash *Johnny Dlamini* (Robert van de Coolwijk, 1986), provide entertainment in their own right. Meanwhile, *Mapantsula*, *Mine Boy* and *My Country My Hat* (David Bensusan, 1983) evidence the emergence of low budget but powerful Black 'crime' stories which, unfortunately, remain internationally obscure. A global co-production, such as *American Ninja 4: The Annihilation* (Cedric Sundstrom, 1990), shot in Lesotho, also features radical depictions of overthrowing authoritarian police states, even if scholars of South African cinema have dismissed such genre projects due to their commercial, formulaic and predictably violent imagery. However, stating that such a film, made by a local director and starring the country's biggest Black star, Ken Gampu, as an armed pan-African nationalist no less, has 'nothing to do with South Africa' (Saks 2010: 35) is simply incorrect.

In Chapter 1, 'That's ZAxploitation', I introduce the term ZAxploitation and give this vaguely blanket denotation some more context and weight – arguing that it might be a useful referent to a specifically low budget and generic kind of South African exploitation film variant. In Chapter 2, 'Joe Bullet: The Unacknowledged Blaxploitation Hero', I make a case for *Joe Bullet* to be recognised as a pivotal part of the blaxploitation cycle, a worthwhile – *essential* – international and transnational variant on an established Hollywood character trope and important in its own right, being that it retrospectively should be seen as grounding a new type of cinema within South Africa. Chapter 3, 'Simon Sabela: Blaxploitation Icon?' engages with the work of the famous Black director, in particular his recently unearthed B-Scheme project *iKati Elimnyama*, and questions if this controversial project – particularly given its link to Heyns Films and the Information Scandal – might still be more radical than its production background would suggest. For further clarity, I offer a comparison between Sabela's South African action debut and his role as King in *Gold* (Peter R. Hunt, 1974), initiating the first discussion of, and comparison to, Hollywood's Africa in this monograph.

My analysis of the peak of the state subsidy initiative continues in Chapter 4: 'Into the Bioscope: The South African B-Scheme Explosion of the 1980s'. This chapter is an investigation into the B-Scheme networks and the key narrative traits that formulate the low budget and often repetitive, even monotonous, austerity morality tales, which exploded in number during this decade. Chapter 5, 'Crime Does Not Pay: Morality in the B-Scheme' analyses the most curious, recurring narrative arc of these motion pictures – namely, a male character is shown to regret having become caught up in some kind of illegal activity, or a 'big man' personality, usually a low-rent mobster or thief, gets their just desserts, in classic EC-comic book style, for having committed some dastardly deed. This guide to clean living, promoted and screened in townships to segregated audiences, is paternalistic but also curious – initiating a wider discussion of how the B-Scheme films represent ambition and achievement, the urban and the rural, with regard to South Africa's Black majority.

Chapter 6, 'The Badass: Stickin' it to Apartheid' acknowledges how the ZAxploitation cycle adapts and, in many cases, transforms the 'badass', hypermasculine persona of John Shaft and his American blaxploitation contemporaries into a more localised and diluted presentation. In Chapter 7, 'For the Common Good? The ZAxploitation Buddy Movie' the badass persona is further highlighted and debated, but this time it is within the populist structure of the Black-white buddy film, which offers some surprising depictions of interracial feuding and bonding during the apartheid era. Chapter 8, 'Be More Like Miriam: The Women of ZAxploitation' queries whether or not South Africa's low budget genre filmmaking offered audiences an opportunity to witness an alternative to American blaxploitation heroines such as Pam Grier or Tamara Dobson. In approaching this topic, I also highlight the frequent sexism of B-Scheme depictions.

I conclude *Images of Apartheid: Filmmaking on the Fringe in the Old South Africa* with two chapters which are perhaps more politically distinct due to subject matter. The border war with Angola is the subject of Chapter 9, 'Armed and Dangerous', wherein such better-known texts as *The Stick* are introduced and related to the period of their release. Trashy exploitation such as *Terrorist*, which is said to be 'based on a true story' and filmed across the expansive sand dunes of South West Africa (now Namibia) is also subjected to scrutiny. Finally, Chapter 10, 'A Different Kind of Gangster Film', offers a fresh approach on the classic *Mapantsula*, positioning the anti-apartheid story of a gangster, Panic, who is arrested, detained without trial and tortured by the local white police, as the logical conclusion of the B-Scheme – not just in terms of exploiting an already corrupt subsidy system (this time for the benefit of anti-apartheid activism) but by using such means to subvert the state's expectancy of bogus 'crime does not pay' narratives.

I recognise that, as someone not from South Africa, and somebody who never lived through the apartheid years, the liberation struggle, state of emergency and the eventual settlement, this study may raise some heckles – particularly given that my field of global exploitation cinema is prominent in how I have approached the films of this period. Nonetheless, I hope that this monograph may also be appreciated as a discussion of history and how especially troubled periods in nation-building might be re-examined from the perspective of a clutter of formulaic film activity. I also recognise the urge to dismiss the films of this book, and why this has been the case – indeed, it is difficult to recommend the majority of the motion pictures examined herein for entertainment purposes. Even so, this is still very much a study of *South African* 'poverty row' filmmaking and I think there are fascinating insights into racial power-relations, even via depictions of Black agency, throughout these otherwise forgettable stories of kung-fu heroes, gangsters and heists. Moreover, this book is also a study of global blaxploitation, a subject which (with thanks especially to recent work from Novotny Lawrence) is still finding its feet in the academy, even as regards the initial and undeniably influential American texts. Earlier mention of Cirio H. Santiago is an additional reminder, however, that foreign variants on the blaxploitation cycle remain underexamined – and I trust that my discussion of ZAxploitation will, at the very least, be accepted as emerging from an honest, scholarly interest in transnational exploitation and in South Africa itself.

When I interviewed the director Coenie Dippenaar for this study, he told me:

> Your budget could not be more than 25,000 rand at that time. We would write our own scripts but one of the things I would like to press, we were never political. We did believe in entertainment. There was absolutely no entertainment for a rural kid ... we were reaching 15 to 20,000 students a month ... On completion the government would pay you X amount of money. (2016)

Here we have the fascinating dichotomy of ZAxploitation: a white filmmaker, claiming to not make a 'political' film, and yet well aware that the end product would be screened to solely Black audiences, segregated in a township. The politics, therefore, are inherently within the representations and these are, predictably, inseparable from the period.

As such, forward we go, into the bioscope of ZAxploitation ...

Notes

1. See: '"Umbango", South Africa's first western was part of Apartheid's scheme to keep township dwellers docile' | Arts (news24.com) – www.news24.com/arts/culture/umbango-south-africas-original-western-20201116
2. I also refer to author Sabine Hake's fascinating monograph *Popular Cinema of the Third Reich*, in which she maintains, of the films made during Nazi Germany's short existence, 'The more that was written about the propaganda films, the less became known – and appeared worth knowing – about these countless genre films categorised as "mere entertainment"' (2001: 2). She continues, 'the unwillingness of scholars to deal with popular cinema masks an elitist contempt for mass cultural production and their presumably passive consumers' (Ibid.: 4). Indeed, I argue that one might learn about the apartheid state's attitudes towards its black citizens from the 'mass cultural production' of the period investigated in this book, even if the presentations (with just a small number of exceptions) are within generic frameworks of crime and action.
3. South Africa's Bantustans will be known by any historian of the apartheid era. The dubiously and hastily arranged states, unrecognised by almost every country in the world, and 'nominally led by a hand-picked brutal dictator' (Dowden 2008: 413) were an attempt to deny citizenship to millions of Black South Africans. The period is defined, most famously perhaps, by the protest song 'Sun City' (referring to the location that was used for concerts by artists such as Queen in Bophuthatswana) by Artists Against Apartheid.
4. As mentioned by James Murray, 'some scripts were handwritten on a single sheet of paper and the entire production was filmed in less than a week. (Several were made in three days.) The actors and actresses were chosen in part for their ability to ad-lib and make up the script as they went along' (1992: 259).
5. See: Johnson 2010: 33.
6. And *this* event only came to light, in such detail, thanks to the recent efforts of Lara Pawson. See: *In the Name of the People: Angola's Forgotten Massacre* (I. B. Taurus, London, 2016).
7. See: Vale (2015) Book review: *Selling Apartheid – South Africa's Global Propaganda War* – at: www.theconversation.com/book-review-selling-apartheid-south-africas-global-propaganda-war-49380

1. THAT'S ZAXPLOITATION!
South African Blaxploitation

In their introduction to the monograph *To Change Reels: Film and Culture in South Africa*, authors Isabel Balseiro and Ntongela Masilela talk about 'the unfolding of film culture' in the country 'within a series of stages that have yet to give rise to a national cinema' (2003: 1). Both Balseiro and Masilela equate the development of this culture, which by the time of the 1970s had helped to make South Africa the most prosperous filmmaking presence on the continent, with the rise of modernity. It was also the fast pace of European modernity in South Africa – encouraged by immigration towards the end of the nineteenth century and the goldrush in the Transvaal (eventually leading to the second Boer War and dominion status within the British Empire) – that inspired the well-known critical and academic work of Thelma Gutsche.[1] Gutsche would also approve the Central African Film Unit's work in the country, noting in the *Cape Times* that the morality play offered in the eighteen-minute pseudo-documentary from Rhodesia, *The Two Farmers* (Stephen Peet, 1948), 'exploited the Mr. Right and Mr. Wrong theme in an entirely different manner, both characters proving neither priggish nor incredible' (Burns 2002: 149). This positive summation of how colonial values were affixed onto two fictional Black screen farmers for the purpose of showing a (so-called) native audience the 'correct' way to approach agricultural work is, in retrospect, remarkably prophetic. As this book will indicate, forty years later and South African cinema would continue to present 'Mr Right and Mr Wrong', occasionally still in agricultural backdrops, but by this point in time the apartheid state was fighting for its very survival.

That other great, celebrated scholar of South African cinema, Keyan Tomaselli, has reflected on the writings of Masilela and Gutsche, maintaining that their arguments about modernity and the lack of Black African involvement with national film does not necessarily conclude with the end of apartheid (and settler colonialism), adding:

> Gutsche implies that film practice is one of the quintessential forms of modernity, but as Masilela observes, there could be no such thing as South African cinema under the utterly restrictive modernist conditions imposed by apartheid, a regime characterised by inequality and segregation. This is why I use the plural, 'cinemas', when discussing films made in South Africa. (2006: 7)

Tomaselli's work is essential to any scholar of South African film, particularly that of the post-war period and the peak of the National Party; however the author has not written extensively about what might be dubbed ZAxploitation. By its very terminology, an admittedly rough blanket term for a South African exploitation film industry or stylistic approach to material that we may consider provocative or salacious, ZAxploitation is a curious proposition.

Exploitation cinema itself belongs to the past – academic David Church has perhaps coined the finest term to describe the romanticising of old, cheap, often sleazy low budget genre cinema: 'grindhouse nostalgia', the title of his monograph.[2] Nostalgia for apartheid is not something that one would imagine many would admit, even those few who benefited from the system; however the cinema of this era has recently become unearthed, allowing for not just a fresh perspective on films made in the old South Africa, but on a possible new addition to studies of global exploitation. Henceforth in this chapter, the central argument will focus upon why this monograph identifies and explores a South African *cinema* of exploitation during the apartheid era, staring in 1973 and continuing through until the end of the 1980s, concluding in 1990.[3] Furthermore, in the chapters that follow, this argument will be based within the discussion of a wide spectrum of low budget genre films, most of which have gone undocumented, and which feature a mostly Black cast.

This study argues that genre is not necessarily oppositional to radicalism, but nor does it have to, or should it be expected to, conform to frameworks that have established an identifiable style or cycle of filmmaking (i.e. the racially-charged action of blaxploitation, as in this instance). For instance, Edward Mitchell addresses the conclusion of *The Harder They Come*, in which Jimmy Cliff's Jamaican gangster is gunned down by armed law enforcement on the shores of Kingston:

The harder they come, the harder they do fall. He is not an idol of the silver screen scattering baddies before him (although he clearly identifies himself with this image), nor will the military police send out 'one baaad man' to shoot it out on the empty beach. (2012: 260)

The use of 'one baaad man' is a clear reference to blaxploitation filmmaking and *The Harder They Come* was in fact initially marketed in the United States along these lines.[4] However, *The Harder They Come* is also an aesthetic and thematic mash of several varied approaches: postmodern-neorealism (even going so far as to pay homage to *The Bicycle Thieves* [Vittorio De Sica, 1948]), realist-musical, Third Cinema *and* Black-gangster film, but framed within a Jamaican vernacular that might also be viewed as radical insofar as it is both original and hitherto oppositional to enshrined presentations of screen ethnicity. The majority of the gangster-themed films of this monograph are less experimental but exist, first and foremost, as racially-driven narratives and, thus, belong within a larger international pantheon of blaxploitation-themed output – particularly including the changes that ethnic representations of the seventies inspired in Hollywood's eighties. Ironically, by generally failing to conform to representations of gun-toting, hypersexual urban heroes and heroines, these South African variants are still – ultimately – subverting an established generic framework. To argue otherwise is to assume that such subversion must only meet expectancies of liberal presentations.

In his introduction to *Film Blackness: American Cinema and the Idea of Black Film*, Michael Boyce Gillespie, drawing on writing from Mark Reid and the presupposition that cinematic representations of African American identity need to be consistent with progressive 'Marxist, feminist and psychoanalytic' readings, asks: 'How can you be willing to appreciate black film or film blackness when it is predetermined by such a prescriptive prerogative? Does any good really come from refusing to let art exceed your expectations?' (2016: 10–11). It is important to keep such a statement and proposition in mind when discussing the Black representations of the genre films made during apartheid. Indeed, some of the texts discussed in this monograph do, however surprisingly, offer interesting and even empowering images of Black heroes – but such a conclusion must not, and certainly *should not*, be misinterpreted as any attempt to re-appropriate the era into any sort of 'grindhouse nostalgia' vis-à-vis race segregated cinemas or opportunistic genre filmmaking. Similarly, this monograph proposes that representations of South Africanness in many of these films are concurrent with a paternalistic state but, nevertheless, occasionally offer agency (however compromised) to a small number of talented, charismatic actors – some of whom, such as Popo Gumede, have gone unacknowledged in previous studies of the nation's arts.

Jacqueline Maingard has chronicled a number of South African *cinemas*, establishing how different films and filmmakers have appealed to 'a varied spectrum of identities' across the decades, both during and after apartheid (2007: 178). Whilst such academic debate addresses themes of nationality and identity, a growing discourse has emerged inside and outside of South Africa in the wake of the rediscovery of *Joe Bullet*. The re-release of *Joe Bullet*, across film festivals, home video formats and other sources, as well as the re-releases of related independent productions made by enterprising, if not always competent nor indeed liberal-minded, white filmmakers, has revealed a different cinematic identity: one of genre, cheap thrills, moralising, females-under-threat and topical paranoia. This is a cinema of border wars, hostage-taking, home invasion, crime, gluttonous buffoonish mafioso, idealised Black-White friendships and, yes, even racial friction and unrest. It is through a study of this collection of texts, containing Black representations that include the urban and the rural, the criminal and the aspirational, and which share common themes and fears, that we can see the emergence and existence of a distinctly South African exploitation cinema (as opposed to cinemas): *ZAxploitation*.

Certainly, since the emergence of *Joe Bullet*, terms such as Sollywood (Haynes 2015) and ZAxploitation have begun to enter the popular lexicon. One article, from a Johannesburg newspaper, even asks if we are witnessing the rediscovery of 'Blaxploitation movies, South Africa style?' (Brown 2017). Interested historians of South African film now have the potential to address an underworld that has been kept to the fringes of scholarly research, one of opportunistic white producers, texts aimed at audiences in townships, and a circuit of popular exploitation cinema tropes. These tropes range from Spaghetti Westerns and crime thrillers to martial arts knock-offs such as *One More Shot* – and include English-language co-productions made for an international market – reimagined within a localised setting. Previously, what was available from this period was dismissed: Martin Botha, for instance, writes that 'In the 1970s, attempts were made to cultivate a cinema dealing with Black themes and geared for Black audiences' (2012: 115). However, such a proclamation also indicates an acceptance of an alternative cinema *of some kind* during the apartheid years. A decade prior, Botha and Johan Blignaut had compiled *Movies-moguls-mavericks: South African cinema, 1979–1991*, which was – before the work of Litheko Modisane and Gairoonisa Paleker – the most detailed discussion of what would become known as ZAxploitation. In its pages, author Gus Silber mentions his time with the director/producer Ronnie Isaacs:

> I am watching a movie called *Strikeback*, and the writer and producer and director is sitting next to me outlining his personal philosophy of filmmaking. 'I make pictures about the way blacks wanna be, not the way they are,' says Ronnie Isaacs, who has a body-builder's torso and a

mercurial crop of silver hair curling down to his shoulders ... 'Kind of like Sambo Rambo,' says Ronne Isaacs. (1992: 267)

Unfortunately, *Strikeback* may now be lost, but Silber unwittingly touches on the ZAxploitation formula – a 'Sambo Rambo', however derogatory the term, is a summation of the transnational nature of the form, to provide cheap cash-in entertainment to a township audience. Thus, it is by clarifying how the films of this period interact with, and even subvert, the established tropes of their more familiar, comparatively mainstream, American (usually independently made) counterparts that we see a cottage industry of exploitation cinema which is uniquely of the apartheid era, including in representations of race.

This study uses the term blaxploitation in reference to the motion pictures that emerged, mainly in the United States, following the April 1971 release of actor-writer-director Melvin Van Peebles' *Sweet Sweetback's Baadasssss Song*. Distributed in just two Detroit cinemas, word of mouth and sold-out local screenings led to national demand for bookings for Van Peebles' commercial juggernaut. Just one month after its Detroit debut, *Sweet Sweetback* was the number one film playing in the entire United States (Eshun 2005: 8). With a provocative advertising campaign ('rated X by an all-white jury' screamed the theatrical posters) courtesy of old-time exploitation distributor Jerry Gross, who had released such gruesome horror classics as *I Drink Your Blood* (David E. Durston, 1970), *Sweet Sweetback* was hugely influential. Sexually explicit, violent, racially provocative, stylistically avant-garde and starring Van Peebles himself as the silent and seductive 'Sweetback' (the character name and title being street slang for a large penis), the film also had critics debating its merits.

Almost instantly, the film was framed by some as outright exploitation[5] (a then-shocking sequence in which the character seduces and sexually pleases a white woman in front of silent onlookers was frequently discussed), and by others as a work of cinematic race-liberation. The late Vincent Canby of *The New York Times*, for instance, believed that 'Instead of dramatizing injustice, Van Peebles merchandises it' whilst *Newsweek* wondered if the director accepted 'the stereotype of black man as sexual athlete or does he use it ironically?' (Hartman 1994: 396). Recent research by Gerard R. Butters Jr has also shown that, upon the film's phenomenal commercial performance in Chicago, local Black communities feared that 'the overwhelming success of *Sweetback* would lead to a succession of clones that would warp the minds of young African Americans' (2016: 68). It is worth keeping this mixed reception in mind when discussing the cinema of ZAxploitation. Indeed, any assumption, particularly in the post-Tarantino world of pop culture 'cool', that blaxploitation was originally received with overwhelming critical accolades is incorrect.

Van Peebles' work, and also the previous year's major studio hit *Cotton*

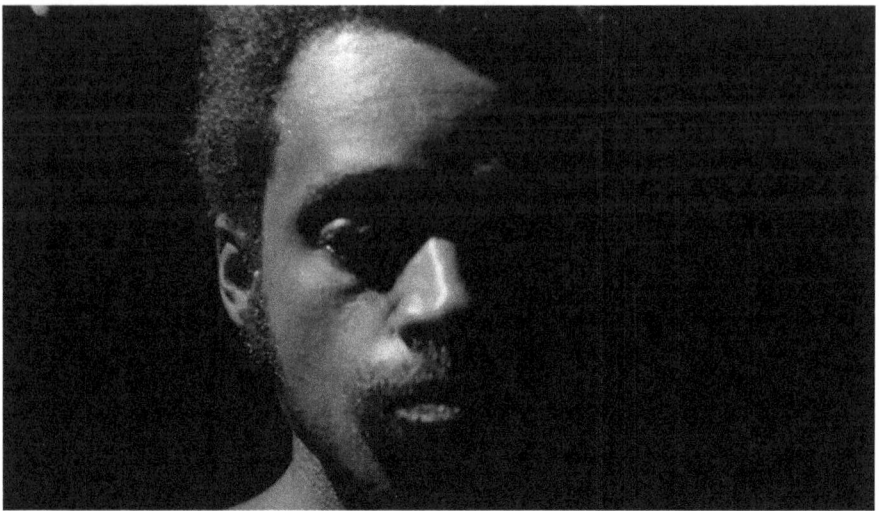

Figure 1.1 Transnational influence: Melvin Van Peebles as the original blaxploitation hero in *Sweet Sweetback's Baadasssss Song* (Melvin Van Peebles, 1971)

Comes to Harlem (Ossie Davis, 1970), have become points of key reference in studies of Black American cinema, as well as the motion pictures they later inspired – chiefly *Shaft* and *Super Fly*. In some cases, their star actors have also been retrospectively acclaimed for breaking new ground – Van Peebles for his Sweetback character, for instance, is dubbed 'something of a folk hero for the black community' by author Donald Bogle (2016: 215). The ZAxploitation actors, and their characters, however, have enjoyed little to no such discussion, despite being front-and-centre of a considerable amount of filmmaking activity (there is one exception: in Chapter 3 I note Tomaselli's early foresight regarding Simon Sabela as an important and formative figure of this period). Cedric J. Robinson would later maintain of blaxploitation: 'it degraded the Black actors, writers and directors who proved more affectionate to money than to the Black lower classes they caricatured; it degraded its audiences who were subjected to a mockery of the aspirations of Black liberationists' (1998: 1). Robinson would view blaxploitation through a Marxist prism that (one could argue) also carries an unmistakable disdain towards the notoriously profit-driven American independent film scene in general – but degradation is a strong word to use here and is probably motivated by personal taste. Robinson may just as well have attacked Hong Kong performers for popularising kung-fu violence as arguing that Richard Roundtree or Van Peebles play to 'stereotypes' of tough badass 'street' characters – after all, *that's genre*. Moreover, given that class and race are conspicuously interconnected in a number of blaxploitation films, wherein criminal activity is seen as more legitimate than brutal white police forces or corrupt bigoted politicians, it is worth remembering that the key blaxploitation films existed as part of a wider idea-exchange with Hollywood depictions of such authority figures as 'heroic' – for instance, *The French Connection* (William Friedkin, 1971).

If blaxploitation can still inspire critical retrospection from someone of Robinson's stature, years after its popularity peaked, then one needs to at least acknowledge that any attempt to retrospectively make a case for the South African variant is a challenge – particularly as the 'degradation' (or even lack thereof) is, unlike even in the American films, usually outside the control of the local actors. In approaching the various films, therefore, this study has generally constructed their presentations from the understanding that these are how the coloniser views the colonised. The same accusation could not be made of American directors such as Gordon Parks or Melvin Van Peebles.

Tonie van der Merwe, producer of *Joe Bullet*, maintains that of his recurring cast members:

> Hector Mathanda was the best actor of all [in South Africa], Joe Lopez, Popo Gumede, Ken Gampu and Abigail Kubeka … if these were Americans, they would be millionaires, winning Oscars. And not once did they complain. [Apartheid] treated them badly, like second class citizens, and they never complained about the government or the system. (2016)

Botha points to research indicating that '944 features were made during the 1980s' but laments them as being of 'mediocre value thanks to the restrictions of the A and B subsidy schemes' (2012: 123). But is it wise to shun cheap, formulaic, usually gangster-orientated genre films because of their austerity budgets and their generally apolitical perspective? Moreover, what of the actors who appeared and who should have been 'winning Oscars'? Should their efforts in 'mediocre' films be ignored? Alternatively, it could be proposed that what *one does not see* in a film from an authoritarian state is surely just as important as what *one does see*, particularly when representations in South African films made for local audiences had to be scouted and approved by the state (this factor became increasingly lax in the late 1980s – as discussed in Chapter 10). Gavshon, for instance, mentions how no film during the apartheid period could be shown 'without a certificate of approval by the Director of Publications. Although this is not serious for a filmmaker if his or her primary audience is going to be foreign, it does discourage filmmakers from making films for local use' (1991: 330). As a result, representations of race and occasionally gender are noticeably divergent between films that are designed for international display (shot in the English language) and the cheap, comparable crime thrillers that feature all-Black or predominantly Black casts (usually presented in Zulu). However, the themes are often the same – hence, to readdress an earlier point, why ZAxploitation should be considered a cinema of South Africa.

As further mentioned by Paleker:

> The differential amounts paid out to 'white' and 'black' films were in keeping with the political and concomitant economic ideology of 'separate development', and the apartheid government saw no need to expend vast resources on Africans who were not South African 'citizens'. (2010: 93)

Palekar's work comes after that of Botha and Tomaselli (it is worth noting that she also singles out Simon Sabela as a rare talent in the field) and is pivotal among more recent studies of ZAxploitation, not least because the author voices concern about the wider cultural worth of reappraising these older films within the spectrum of a supposed South Africanness. Nonetheless, the more empirical elements (such as the cheap manner in which they were made) and the frequent paternalism and dubious moralising of some ZAxploitation cinema should not necessarily invalidate the fact that Black action hero figures did provoke local censorship (as with *Joe Bullet*) and also played to audiences during a period of race segregation. Thus, to exclude Ken Gampu's *Joe Bullet* from analysis of the blaxploitation period is perhaps a contemporary apartheid in its own right; one that fails to acknowledge the (baby) steps taken in building and sustaining a badass character within a (certainly politically unpleasant but nonetheless localised) African backdrop. This more comparative approach between American blaxploitation films and ZAxploitation is also not to say that this monograph will refrain from drawing on areas in which the shadow of apartheid or the politics of the ruling National Party begin to bleed into the films' narrative. Rather, one proposes that a film such as *Joe Bullet* might benefit from being initiated into a wider academic (even paracinematic) dialogue.

Early Attempts at Race Representation

Other motion pictures attempted to connect with South Africa's Black audiences before the arrival of *Joe Bullet*, including *Jim Comes to Jo'burg* (or *African Jim*, Donald Swanson, 1950), *Zonk!* (Hyman Kirstein, 1950) and *Song of Africa* (Emil Nofal, 1951). Maingard discusses each of these films, noting them to be local productions that 'astutely exploited the growing impact on Black jazz and vaudeville of the Black social and political contexts of the 1940s period and the emerging political ideals of the time' (2007: 8). The author's use of the word 'exploit' here is interesting because each of these productions runs for under sixty minutes – akin to many of the later, cheaply-made B-Scheme films. Also of note, and documented by Peter Davis, is how *Jim Comes to Jo'burg* gained its largest local audience when the producer, Eric Rutherford, 'took a projector around the townships and showed the film in direct cinema fashion' (1996: 31). This mobile circuit would also provide the basis for distribution of later, obscure films, some made by one-shot directors and producers but often featuring a recognisable ensemble of names behind and in front of the camera. Through the interviews that were conducted for this monograph it has been established that most Black audiences of the apartheid era saw ZAxploitation cinema via this network, which lasted even beyond 1986, when the Urban Areas Act abolished the pass laws that were required for entry to the major cities and their attractions (Welsh 2000: 491).

Writing towards the end of apartheid, Murray – who was a film producer in his own right – would mention how cinemagoing was popular among township audiences, but ill-catered for: 'There is a massive and viable cinema audience in the townships and rural areas with hardly any cinemas to go to. Producers and operators of mobile units should have been encouraged to build them!' (1992: 262). Tomaselli would also note that only twenty-eight cinemas served the Black population during this period (2003: 235). As a result, the mobile networks – which would include makeshift screenings at schools – were a prolific outlet for distribution, but their emergence dated back to the early days of the apartheid state. Furthermore, they were rife for fraud and exploitation.

Producer/director van der Merwe mentions:

> There were community halls and schools and [in the townships] a demand for movies ... but you had to provide a generator and a vehicle. These mobile units expanded from there and at its height, the B-Scheme was much bigger, in turnover, than the white films. We reached seven million a month ... but it was not easy. I remember one night we showed in Kliptown and we parked the car nearby, put up our generator as there was no electricity, and then during the showing of the movie it went all black and when we went outside the generator had been stolen. So all these things had be thought about. But it was a very rewarding [time] ... You went to a school or a community hall and it was like the circus coming to town, thousands of people waiting to go inside and mobbing the actors, like they were Hollywood heroes. (2016)

Van der Merwe's comments are echoed by the director Coenie Dippenaar:

> We had premieres in schools and we invited the actors and they were heroes. Absolute heroes at that time ... We went to one show at a school where we sat amongst 10,000 pupils but we almost went back to the government and said, 'this whole system is wrong'. Later on, it was too

dangerous to go back and even check how many people were really viewing the films. This was the dilemma we had. We could not check and see what was going on. (2016)

Lest Dippenaar and van der Merwe be viewed as painting a more contemporary reappraisal of apartheid filmmaking as a positive form of distraction and/or provocation, however, it is worth referring to Murray's investigation of the B-Scheme distribution 'incentive' in schools:

> One factor that helped growth in this difficult sector of the film industry was the fact that audiences were almost exclusively 'captive'. The school principal or his school, or both, usually received a fairly large proportion of the door take of films screened. They were in a position to insist that students brought money to school on a day that had been arranged between himself, or his 'entertainment committee', for a film show. (1992: 257)

Murray's allegations help to explain why some of the uncovered B-Scheme texts appear to have been thrown together in such a rush, with haphazard narrative causality and desperate attempts to pad out the running times. Appealing to a school audience may also explain why so many of the genre films that emerged in the 1980s, from prolific names such as van der Merwe, show so little violence and were so quickly replaced with new product. As such, one has to ask if *Joe Bullet* really does initiate a heritage of South African grindhouse-grime, repackaged within a mobile fleapit.

Certainly, the era of the American grindhouse, at least as it has been reimagined in pop culture (perhaps most famously in recent series *The Deuce*), has been critiqued by Glenn Ward as 'a missed encounter with the real, and that "real" often takes the form of a chimeric "home" assembled from mediated recollections of cinema experience' (2016: 27). So too must one be careful about displacing the South African exploitation film engagement of yesteryear despite the (similar) stories of white intelligentsia (or entrepreneurs) under threat in dangerous cinemas populated by dangerous people. In the main, the South African films are not as transgressive as the better-known anarchistic and haywire cinema of sex and sleaze from America (or Hong Kong, Italy, the Philippines, Spain and so forth) even if sometimes one is presented with unexpectedly left-field imagery. Films such as *Joe Bullet* now boast lurid contemporary blurbs that engage with a purportedly rebellious past ('originally banned by the apartheid government') and poster sleeves for DVD re-releases and festival screenings draw reappraisal from academics and fan scholars (present company included). Terms such as 'Retro Afrika Bioscope' have also emerged to categorise low budget, predominantly action farces, within a catch-all sense

Figure 1.2 All-out war in *Doomsday* (Abie Hattingh, 1986)

of timely exploitation entrepreneurialism: *just like old 42nd Street*. Ironically then, particularly in spite of the past three decades of academic discussion of South African cinema, it is *postmodernity* and not necessarily modernity itself that can be seen to have brought long-forgotten apartheid-era cinema back into the public consciousness: an attempt to attach ZAxploitation to better-known, foreign cousins. 'Blood will be spilt' screams the newly designed, garish poster for the low budget actioner *Doomsday* (Abie Hattingh, 1986) from the restoration house Gravel Road Entertainment Group.

The term ZAxploitation has surfaced so recently that it is absent from all studies of the country's cinema, but a user post on the Internet Movie Database interprets it to mean:

> Exploitation genre films produced in South Africa or by the South African film industry. Most fall into one of the following categories: 1. Films by South African film makers (Some aimed at the Foreign market). 2. Co-productions filmed in South Africa (Usually on the cheap). 3. 'Darkest Africa films': The films that promote the colonial narrative of Africa as savage and exotic.[6]

Based on this description, ZAxploitation might be seen to share an identity with the 'exotic film' of yesteryear – cinema from the classic period of American exploitation cinema which, as mentioned by Eric Schaefer, 'reinforced the self-esteem of white workers in the middle and working classes through display of an abject, black primitive' (1999: 281). However, many

ZAxploitation films were not aimed at any market beyond those found in the South African townships (i.e. segregated Black audiences) and they do not – despite the quote above – 'promote' a country that is 'savage or exotic'. In fact, to the contrary, the nation depicted in the low budget South African films that emerged via the financial appeal of government subsidies is largely without much (and sometimes any) identification of time and place. For depictions of 'savage or exotic' Africa, one would be better advised to look at the more famous co-productions, partly or wholly shot on location and boasting famous star names, such as *The Wilby Conspiracy* or *The Wild Geese* (Andrew V. McLaglen, 1978).

Tomaselli and Oswelled Ureke have discussed a 'film services' approach to the country's cinema in their recent journal article 'From "African Cinema" to Film Services industries: A Cinematic Fact', noting the problems that have come from discussing motion pictures purely by geography (i.e. an imagined homogenous African filmmaking that would have some kind of continent-wide consistency) – including modes of distribution and production. In their conclusion the authors maintain:

> [P]roviders residing in particular locations are akin to cinematographic citizens and can be classified as a 'wood' hence names such as Hollywood, Bollywood, Nollywood, Zollywood and Bongowood. Although classical definitions of industry may be a misnomer when describing film sectors on the continent, a more inclusive approach would extend to these 'othered' industries. (2017: 91)

ZAxploitation, as a term (rather than Sollywood, which initiates a dubious linkage to other sub-Saharan African film industries, most obviously Nollywood), might propose that exploitation filmmaking itself is adaptable, in a commercial sense at least, to even the most unlikely communities. This conclusion would certainly include audiences across diasporic populations *within* the same nation. Whilst the bulk of the films explored in this monograph were made for local, Black audiences (there is no evidence that the B-Scheme motion pictures were popular in the Bantustans, although it is worth recording that Bophuthatswana was unique in permitting screenings of even 'soft-porn' movies[7]), they may also assume prior knowledge of wider international or local presentations. As an example, even films that played to a segregated audience might bear a clear lineage to comparable texts that were presented to the white minority during the apartheid period. As such, *Skeleton Coast* (John Carlos, 1987) – made in South Africa – is a straight-to-video effort from the old exploitation hand Harry Alan Towers that uses the unrest in Angola for its schlocky, bloody, action film violence. Tonie van der Merwe's *Ambushed* (1988), arriving a year later and featuring an all-Black cast, might be considered to exist in tandem with this and other films that engage with the Angolan conflict, exploiting a market that a small number of producers presumed existed, particularly local. However, van der Merwe's low budget film is aimed at townships, whilst the glossier *Skeleton Coast* is not. As such, even the filmmaking that took place during the ZAxploitation years, as well as the stories that resulted (including those films engaging with the same issues), was dictated by race. Nevertheless, *the cinema* – stripped down to its bare essentials such as themes, genre, concept and characters – is not dissimilar.

Blacks-ploitation?

Roy Armes mentions that 'Filmmaking in Africa by Africans is fundamentally a postcolonial activity' (2006: 3). ZAxploitation might also be seen as a difficult proposition to bring into any discussion of indigenous cinematic identity, even when, as with the *Joe Bullet* sequel *Bullet on the Run*, the local actor Ken Gampu gets a credit as 'Assistent [sic] Director' or a filmmaker such as Simon Sabela is calling the shots (see Chapter 3). ZAxploitation films were funded by, and almost always made by, the white settler minority (or white foreigners working in South Africa) and commonly with government backing. With this said, the very idea of what, as worded by Stephanie Dunn, might be called 'the ghetto action film' (2008: 2) making its way to any foreign diaspora surely seemed unlikely because of the very urban American settings and 'lingo' (although both Italy and the Philippines briefly embraced the trend) of blaxploitation itself.

Nonetheless, to ascertain that ZAxploitation is a cinema without *any* African, and particularly South African, characteristics would be unfair. One is, of course, cautious of sounding naïve, paternalistic or indeed outright ridiculous – for instance, by refuting Western influence on the continent, author Kenneth M. Cameron seems to be making a case *for* the practice of female genital mutilation when he comments that John Shaft's Ethiopian love interest in *Shaft in Africa* (John Guillermin, 1973), by refusing such a procedure, 'gives up virginity and ... her culture' (1994: 153).[8] As such, by stressing the South African elements of ZAxploitation, this study is referring, first and foremost, to the clear, identifiable visual mediation of landscapes, scenarios and places (particularly townships) that can only be of the country. Tomaselli and Ureke have discussed how – as an example – the co-production *King Solomon's Mines* (J. Lee Thompson, 1985) has been missing from studies on Zimbabwean cinema:

> An analysis that discounts those productions from the 'African cinema' corpus on the basis of race and origin of finance, therefore, misses the many benefits that accrued to black Africans who featured in the films as service providers of numerous capabilities. (2017: 80)

Similarly, the choice of this book to include some international co-productions – entirely or partly shot in or around South Africa – is largely based on genre corpus.

ZAxploitation, as with any exploitation, has repetitive, recurring formulas that ultimately provide an essential insight into an alternative, identifiable cinema of the apartheid years. The film *Black Crusader* (Tony Cunningham, 1986), for instance, has a scene that puts a heroic Black character up against a disreputable, but powerful, white character – not unlike the Hollywood co-production *American Ninja 3: Blood Hunt* (1989), from South African director Cedric Sundstrom. A cheap crime film spin-off such as *Knockout Joe* (Laurens Barnard, 1984) acknowledges illicit diamond smuggling (shades of the later Hollywood epic *Blood Diamond* [Edward Zwick, 2006]) – whilst a decade earlier Roger Moore starred in *Gold*, which also focuses on criminal elements exploiting and illegally transporting South Africa's natural resources. As cheap as the South African B-Scheme films might be, then, they do not emerge from a bubble, but rather from a clear attachment to other, successful presentations. In other motion pictures, a film such as *Shaft* is a clear influence on the main character and his narrative mission.

As discussed by Novotny Lawrence, *Shaft* was the catalyst for a number of shoot-em-up films, led by African American casts, in which 'a crime is committed, which prompts the hero/heroine's search to discover the perpetrator and reveal his/her motives' (2005: 85). Although Lawrence recognises *Cotton Comes to Harlem* as a formative text in American blaxploitation film, he also admits that its 'narrative structure follows the same pattern as traditional detective films' (2008: 29) and that '*Cotton* serves as an additional example of

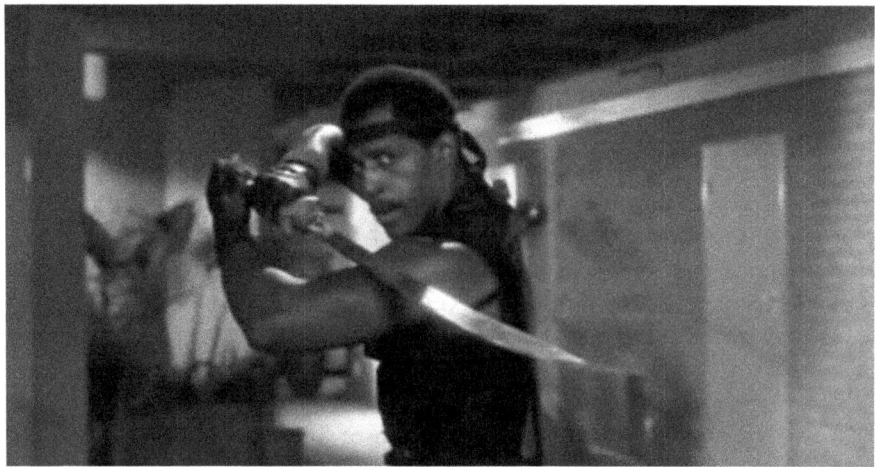

Figure 1.3 Steve James in *American Ninja 3: Blood Hunt* (Cedric Sundstrom, 1989)

genre hybridisation' (Ibid.: 36). This aspect is important because, stripped of their Black characters, several blaxploitation films follow repetitive detective narratives – including with a 'surprise' twist ending/reveal of villainy at the end (i.e. *Lady Cocoa* [Matt Cimber, 1975], *Friday Forster* [Arthur Marks, 1975]). Whilst the performers would be distinct, at least for the era, due to their ethnicity and occasional nods to 'brotherhood' and 'communities', *Shaft* and the films it inspired – such as *Hammer* (Bruce D. Clark, 1972), *Black Caesar* (Larry Cohen, 1973) and *Truck Turner* (Jonathan Kaplan, 1974) – were not as racially provocative, sexually graphic nor as explicitly anti-white as the seminal *Sweet Sweetback's Baadasssss Song*. Given this aspect, it is not too difficult to recognise how the trope, and the John Shaft character (played by Richard Roundtree) could be moulded into a figure that served other societies – even a segregated one. Thus, heroes of ZAxploitation, such as Ken Gampu's Joe Bullet, often follow the characterisation of Roundtree's iconic creation.

In discussing this aspect of transnational adaptation further, I draw on some recent commentary by Iain Robert Smith and what he calls 'The Hollywood Meme'. Looking at the genre cinema of developing societies such as the Philippines and Turkey, particularly in the 1970s and 1980s, Smith discusses how certain films would appropriate popular American blockbusters into an indigenous replica that might even satirise the Hollywood original. Also using a comparative model, Smith draws on contemporary writing about globalisation and hybridisation to investigate how these lower budgeted variants on popular Hollywood hits incorporate aspects of the latter whilst still, potentially, remaining indigenously relevant. In talking about the first South African blaxploitation film, *Joe Bullet*, such a model is useful given that the film borrows its characterisation from *Shaft* whilst basing parts of its narrative loosely on the Fred Williamson character of B. J. Hammer in *Hammer*. As with Smith's discussion of the Hollywood tropes taken and appropriated into other locales, what is fascinating about *Joe Bullet* is how it operates as an example of an 'apartheid blaxploitation' film – although the clues to its nationality and its identity are often subtle. Thus, it is doubtful that *Joe Bullet* manages to achieve the so-called 'meta-cinematic deconstruction' that author Paul Cooke sees in the transnational journey that German expressionism makes into noir and American horror in the 1930s (2007: 25). The film fails to offer its star, Ken Gampu, the same agency that Williamson or *Shaft*'s Richard Roundtree have, and the thin budget and makeshift stunt and fight work are evident, perhaps the reason for Tomaselli's initial dismissal of the (cheaply made) text as well. Nevertheless, *Joe Bullet* represents a uniquely South African attempt to reimagine such characters as those played by Roundtree and Williamson as a proverbial 'hero for the homelands'.

Smith mentions how the more recent Turkish sci-fi farce *G.O.R.A.* (Ömer

IMAGES OF APARTHEID

Figure 1.4 Ken Gampu as Joe Bullet in *Joe Bullet* (Louis de Witt, 1973)

Faruk Sorak, 2005) begins 'on a space station in which all the characters are speaking English' (2017: 34). However, one character quickly asks that they communicate in Turkish, setting the language for the rest of the film. For Smith this shows that it is not America (or Hollywood) 'that has colonised the peoples' consciousness' but rather Turkey itself (2017: 34). Language, of course, was used by practitioners of Third Cinema within a wider anti-colonial rhetoric. At the famous Resolutions of the Third World Filmmakers Meetings in Algiers, 1973, it was stated that

> [T]he language of the colonised, which is the carrier of the culture, becomes inferior or foreign, it is used only in the family circle or in restricted social circles. It is no longer, therefore, a vehicle for education, culture and science, because in the schools the language of the coloniser is taught, it being indispensable to know it in order to work, to subsist and to assert oneself. (Bakari and Cham 1996: 17)

However, a film such as *G.O.R.A.* initiates the idea that *the language* of Hollywood (in particular) need not be oppositional to indigenous presentations – including satire but even, one would presume, history. As a result, one could argue, as does Smith, that the film avoids conforming to Third Cinema dogma, especially the assumption that genre might conflict with national identity, but nonetheless maintains an identity of its own rooted in a transnational understanding of subverting mnemonic Hollywood norms.

If South African cinema has, per the writing of Gutsche, evolved from discussion of modernity, then could that modernity, as the twentieth century reached its conclusion, not also be seen to engage with more easily available foreign cinema (such as *Shaft*) than any notable indigenous political identity? If one were to answer this question in the affirmative, then we might also be offered some flexibility in seeing the genre films of apartheid outside of the very real race confines that they were produced under. As such, some of the most jarring moments in these films are those where apartheid is acknowledged via the medium of language or race-interaction. Whilst this aspect of these productions is not used to reflect on the nature of, for instance, Hollywood's transnational appeal or as a thematic rebellion against its normalisation of a sole, universal English tongue, or even on colonial influences (per *The Harder They Come*) – it is noticeable that the spectre of apartheid becomes unavoidable in a small number of key portrayals. A Zulu language film such as *The Boxer* changes to English when Black characters have to interact with white characters. In this instance, the trauma of South Africa as a nation – a diaspora of identities, enforced segregation, a paranoid white minority, Boer identity – becomes evident via the unifying language of the state (Afrikaans is never signified as a unifying language, possibly because of the additional trauma of Soweto in 1976).

In a pivotal scene in *Joe Bullet*, the dialogue switches from English to Xhosa and back to English: the heroic and statuesque Joe (Ken Gampu) walks into a party where the narrative's leading lady Beauty (Abigail Kubeka) is singing in her African language tongue. However, the language resumes into English when the two speak to one another. Unlike Smith's example of *G.O.R.A.* this brief acknowledgement of *Joe Bullet* as non-Hollywood cinema is not presented in order to satirise the commerciality of English as the language of American blaxploitation and to then reclaim a narrative of race or language liberation, but rather to conform to localised expectancies of behaviour. In other words, *Joe Bullet* wants to appear as an Americanised blaxploitation film – and yet it also confirms, in this brief switch into Xhosa and back into English, that South Africa itself is a fundamentally Westernised society in which a civilised, well-dressed Black man such as Joe Bullet can (should?) be permitted to exist and flourish without necessarily losing all traces of his own identity. This prophetic identification of the South Africa to come (even if one could argue it sustains Bullet's place in the urban-conditional) carries some impact even when viewed today. Similarly, in its sequel, *Bullet on the Run*, made almost a decade later, Joe Bullet is sent to prison for a crime that he did not commit (we later learn that he is infiltrating a gangster ring and has agreed to his incarceration). Gampu's character sits, disinterested, in a scene where the characters are taught mathematics in Tswana at a prison workshop – and is later addressed in the language by a prison guard. Outside the prison, however, the characters resort back to speaking in English – maintaining the concept that the language is the preferred source of communication and the unifying language of South Africa, while affirming where the film is from.

Other ZAxploitation films use language differently. In *Knockout Joe* the mess of settler-colonialism, war and segregation is acknowledged, however unintentionally, by having a white character interact in English with his Black counterparts and Afrikaans with his wife, whilst the Black personalities connect with one another in Zulu. Another cheapie from this period, *Run for Your Life* (Tommy Röthig, 1985) highlights a white character who interacts in English with his wife but in Zulu with his Black best friend. Such instances allow apartheid to seep into these narratives, even if it is not always explicitly acknowledged – but this use of language also allows for traditional American set-ups, most notably the blaxploitation 'buddy' film in which a white and Black partner solve crime. In the case of both *Knockout Joe* and *Run for Your Life*, criminal activity spreads across the border of South Africa and into cartels located in other unnamed African states during a period of sustained conflict in Angola and South West Africa (today's Namibia). The low budget horror film *Ivondwe* (Louis De Witt, 1986) is shot entirely in Zulu, but this means that white characters are also shown speaking the language, whilst the race-relations that are depicted do not indicate any sort of separation or infringement on movement. Whilst *Ivondwe* lapses into paternalistic depictions, it also, through this use of Zulu as a national language among races, strangely and perhaps unwittingly envisions a united South Africa.

Without such contexts, some of these cheap and formulaic films must seem, if viewed in the present day, somewhat confusing. This is further indication of why these examples conform to a rough umbrella terminology of ZAxploitation: blaxploitation adaptations, certainly indebted to aspects of Hollywood but with narratives that are sustained within the apartheid state and its immediate concerns – a *cinema* of the old South Africa. It is also worth noting the predominantly Zulu-language *Mapantsula*, a gritty and far more radical motion picture in which the lead character Panic pretends he cannot understand Afrikaans when he is imprisoned, despite the film itself having earlier (and quite subtly) established that he can speak the language. In this moment language is used as a political metaphor, with a character refusing engagement in what is deemed to be the tongue of the repressor in order to maintain dignity in a situation in which his body and life are no longer under his control. The film itself, however, might also be seen to be resisting the national language *and also* the language of Hollywood, hence its possible credentials as Third Cinema (see Chapter 10 for further deliberation on *Mapantsula*).

Smith also turns his attention to other third world genre films and notes how, in the notorious Filipino James Bond cash-in *For Y'ur Height Only* (Eddie Nicart, 1981), 'little attempt is made to localise the borrowed elements to fit the Philippines context' (2017: 89). Generally, then, it might be argued that appropriation of popular Hollywood characters, genres, or even tropes, can be seen as either resisting the established hegemonic model, by way of outright acknowledgement or postmodern satire à la *G.O.R.A.*, or taking some of the most recognisable elements to provoke commercial interest without muddying the formula too much with localism. This latter factor is nothing new of course – as fans of trashy Italian B-movies such as *2019: After the Fall of New York* (Sergio Martino, 1983), which is a clear attempt to cash-in on the popularity of *Escape from New York* (John Carpenter, 1981), or *Black Emanuelle* (Bitto Albertini, 1975), will surely attest. Similarly, the most famous moment in *For Y'ur Height Only* highlights its two-foot, nine-inch star Weng Weng escaping danger with a rocket-fuelled backpack attached to him like Sean Connery in the pre-credits sequence of *Thunderball* (Terence Young, 1965). The comedy value, for the audience, is complete only if they are aware of the Hollywood original, which has lavish production values and accomplished visual effects vs the threadbare costs of its Filipino variant. Nonetheless, I would disagree with Smith's conclusion that *For Y'ur Height Only* does not 'fit the Philippines context' – at least insofar as Bond itself was never truly Hollywood nor even British. Indeed, the character became juxtaposed with jet-set adventures and usually became *of* his exotic foreign surroundings, either challenged by them or using them to his advantage.

For Y'ur Height Only does not need to declare its Filipino locale within the narrative itself. The ethnicities and backdrops, including the tropical greenery, are front and centre – whilst the low budget location-shooting, sometimes highlighted by crumbling Metro Manila apartment blocks, indicate that this is far from the real (Hollywood) thing. Even Weng Weng's persona as a lover and seducer of beautiful women can be viewed as mocking the Orientalism of Hollywood where Asian males struggled, and still struggle, to secure sex-symbol status. *For Y'ur Height Only* does not need to explicitly acknowledge any sort of Pinoy context, because the Philippines is highlighted and moreover *used* – from ethnicity to location – to indicate a clear difference from its Hollywood counterpart. Through this difference, however, it also has appeal: fans familiar with *Thunderball* and James Bond can enjoy spotting the tributes and cheap, knock-off set pieces. In ZAxploitation, parody is almost entirely absent – and when it does appear, belatedly in *Moyo Mubi* (or *The Evil Ones*, Tonie van der Merwe, 1989), the representations being parodied are the stars themselves rather than outside Hollywood tropes. As such, South African cinema from this period, whilst showing clear transnational inspiration, also exists *within* its own structures, with its own formulas, leading men and depiction of Black life (both urban and rural).

Hence, the challenge that faces contemporary onlookers as regards much of the ZAxploitation output is not necessarily the reinvention of the blaxploitation hero for South Africa (not entirely dissimilar to Weng Weng's Southeast Asian detective), juxtaposed to localised stories and aimed at a local, Black audience. Instead, it is that the spectre of apartheid ultimately makes any, if not all, art produced in the South Africa of the 1970s and 1980s carry an additional weight. By suggesting that *Joe Bullet*, in particular, become a fixture of future studies of blaxploitation, this monograph is – to some extent – having to confront the real universe that exists behind the fictional one. At least one method to addressing this factor is the film services approach of Tomaselli and Ureke. As noted by Lawrence, 'blaxploitation films are defined as movies made between 1970 and 1975, by both black and white film directors alike, to exploit the Black film audience' (2008: 18). Lawrence correctly notes that white American producers and directors also made motion pictures to gain financial returns from a black audience. Given the stronghold of the apartheid state during the time of *Joe Bullet*'s production, one might care to argue that white capital producing a film for a Black audience was a means to at least address an ellipsis within popular representation. To critique *Joe Bullet* as a film *of* apartheid, then, would mean to overlook the comparatively flimsy representations that star Ken Gampu received from Hollywood during the same period (his role in *The Wild Geese*, for instance, amounts to little more than a glorified cameo).

Lawrence also mentions:

> There is no such thing as a white exploitation film – there is only cinema, which includes many genre films yet excludes blaxploitation films. The term 'blaxploitation' recognises the addition of blackness but marginalises the films by constructing them against whiteness and excluding them from generic categories. (Ibid.: 23)

Whilst one could argue with this conclusion, given the amount of 'white trash'/hillbilly films that were made to exploit Southern audiences in the United States throughout the 1960s and 70s,[9] (the blockbuster *Smokey and the Bandit* [Hal Needham, 1977] pays homage to this run of motion pictures), it is possible to recognise that any such blaxploitation, including the South African variant, becomes singled out because of race rather than necessarily narrative. Murray, for instance, argues that Gampu was part of what might be seen as the first South African 'ethnic' film, *Dingaka* (Jamie Uys, 1965) – because 'the vast majority of the cast were black and the story was about black people' – although the actor's role is still of the 'noble savage' in contrast to the real narrative hero, played by Stanley Baker. In contrast, *Joe Bullet* allows Gampu an agency over his character that is consistently depicted as heroic.

Of course, certain alterations are also obvious. Whereas Weng Weng could be shown in bed with glamorous, leggy women – a fundamental element of the James Bond persona, but heightened to the level of farce – *Joe Bullet* takes the blaxploitation thematic of individualism and violence but uses this to affirm an imagined South African statesman who exists outside of the confines of segregation, including a distinct lack of sexual encounters. Half a century since its release and the film remains difficult to fully understand because on the surface, at least, it does not appear to diverge too far from its own blaxploitation lineage. When Donald Bogle talks of 'tenacious buck protagonists performing deeds of derring-do, while self-righteously giving lip-service to the idea of political commitment' (2016: 218) he could just as easily be talking about Gampu's Joe Bullet or a later character, such as the provocatively-titled *Charlie Steel* (Bevis Parsons, 1984). Under closer analysis, however, and these films, as products of apartheid, become easier to comprehend and (dare I say) even appreciate. It is through an analysis of *Joe Bullet*, in the next chapter, that this study of ZAxploitation continues.

Notes

1. Gutsche's defining monograph is now sadly long out of print. See: Gutsche, Thelma (1972), *The History and Social Significance of Motion Pictures in South Africa, 1895–1940*. Cape Town: Howard Timmins.
2. See: Church, David (2016), *Grindhouse Nostalgia: Memory, Home Video and Exploitation Film Fandom*. Edinburgh: Edinburgh University Press.
3. The 'golden age' (or classic) era of the American exploitation film is defined by Eric Schaefer as lasting from 1919 until 1959. In my book *The Style of Sleaze*, I argue that an identifiable exploitation film *movement* subsequently emerged, lasting from 1959 until 1977. The approximate seventeen-year timescale of South African exploitation cinema, from *Joe Bullet* until very late-day ZAxploitation such as Cedric Sundstrom's *American Ninja 4: The Annihilation* (released in March 1990), highlights an evolution in presentations of, in particular, Black agency – although I would be hesitant to describe this as a 'movement' given the fact that the films discussed in this monograph splinter into different presentations and concerns and even occasionally share very different production backgrounds. Schaefer, Eric (1999), *'Bold! Daring! Shocking! True!' A History of Exploitation Films, 1919–1959*. Durham and London: Duke University Press.
4. See: https://www.latimes.com/archives/la-xpm-2006-dec-02-me-henzell2-story.html
5. See: Bennett, Lerone (1971), 'The Emancipation Orgasm: Sweetback in Wonderland', *Ebony*, 26, pp. 106–18, or for a more contemporary look back at the critical reception to the film: Hartmann, Jon (1994), 'The Trope of Blaxploitation in Critical Responses to "Sweetback"', *Film History*, 6:3, Indiana University Press.
6. See: https://m.imdb.com/list/ls054128531/?page=2 – as well as a Facebook page for ZAxploitation, although updates have been minimal: https://www.facebook.com/ZAxploitation/?__xts__[%2Ffacebook]
7. See 'Bringing a bit of Vegas to South Africa's Homelands' by Joseph Lelyveld in

The New York Times (1981) – archived here: https://www.nytimes.com/1981/07/19/business/bringing-a-bit-of-vegas-to-south-africa-s-homelands.html
8. I am reminded here of the exceptional Zambian film *I Am Not a Witch* (2017) from director Rungano Nyoni, which does a sublime and powerful job of documenting and satirising Western assumptions of what might be deemed local 'culture' (as opposed to exploitative practices that are outdated and abusive).
9. See also: Von Doviak, Scott (2015), *Hick Flicks: The Rise and Fall of Redneck Cinema*. North Caroline: McFarland Publishing.

2. JOE BULLET

The Unacknowledged Blaxploitation Hero

As discussed by Maingard, South African censors, from the silent period through to the height of apartheid, remained concerned about the impact of imported American cinema on the marginalised non-white citizens who 'might emulate sexual and violent images seen on screen' (2007: 51). Further detailed by J. M. Burns, these concerns were shared by the neighbouring British colonies in sub-Saharan Africa where, in regard to Westerns, 'it was not considered healthy for the people to see the gun fired' (2002: 11). That such attitudes would remain in 1973, with director Louis De Witt's *Joe Bullet* pulled from distribution and banned from any more screenings, indicates the difficulties of making films influenced by an international exploitation cycle in such a censorious state. Nonetheless, *Joe Bullet* introduced South African audiences of 1973 to a badass blaxploitation action hero, but in strange and unexpected surroundings – namely Johannesburg, although the city is never named. In describing the Joe Bullet character – played by Ken Gampu – as 'badass', I mean, per Mikel Koven, the typical persona of the American blaxploitation hero: 'being a tough-guy . . . beyond, or outside of, the law . . . they cannot be the Man, or his representatives' (2010: 17). Whilst, as noted by the author, some blaxploitation characters such as John Shaft work within the legal system, they remain self-employed and answer solely to their own whims. Ken Gampu, as Joe Bullet, is not too removed from this persona, although this study deliberates further on the badass persona, as portrayed in ZAxploitation cinema, in Chapter 6.

Figure 2.1 A meal fit for a mafia king in *Joe Bullet* (Louis de Witt, 1973)

Showing immediate understanding of the language of blaxploitation cinema, *Joe Bullet* begins with a funk theme track (with its repeated, memorable mantra of 'he's the man' it could also fit into any proverbial 'Best of Blaxploitation' CD compilations). After introducing us to two football teams (the Falcons and the Eagles), the film takes us to a university shower room where Lucas, one of the trainers, is stabbed and killed by two fake press agents who represent a mafia set-up by the name of the Vulture Gang. From here, Joe Bullet, played by Ken Gampu, is introduced (although his actual title or loyalty is never made explicit to us, one can only presume that he is a for-hire private detective) and his immediate job is to find out why the murder took place. What he discovers is a gambling syndicate that aims to fix the soccer championship final – and Joe's position is to infiltrate and compromise this devious plan, which grows to involve the kidnapping of two of the star players and the detective's girlfriend Beauty (played by Abigail Kubeka). These narrative plot points: localised crime, the kidnapping of a young woman and an athletic Black action hero, bleed into later ZAxploitation films, particularly those of the B-Scheme. In this regard, *Joe Bullet* sets up the narrative framework of the bulk of ZAxploitation: it is every bit as trendsetting within its own demarcation as, for instance, *Shaft* was to American blaxploitation.

Figure 2.2 Ken Gampu in *Joe Bullet* (Louis de Witt, 1973)

Speaking about the slasher genre and similar teen-orientated American cinema, author Richard Nowell identifies how a 'pioneer production' usually leads to a cycle of some sort:

> [A] surge in production/distribution of a film-type followed by a period of sustained production/distribution and a decline in production/distribution, a cluster is characterised by the absence of sustained production. The cluster, ostensibly an undeveloped cycle, is the product of confidence in a film-type rising quickly and evaporating suddenly after the first phase of post-hit production. (2011: 46)

This formula can also be attributed to other popular exploitation-genre trends, including blaxploitation. After the initial rush of the pioneer production, namely Melvin Van Peebles' *Sweet Sweetback's Baadasssss Song*, followed by *Shaft* and *Super Fly*, the blaxploitation boom – with only a few exceptions (such as films from D'Urville Martin and Jamaa Fanaka) – became controlled by established or up-and-coming white filmmakers and producers.

Bogle notes that 'What became most disturbing was that while these movies appeared to be Black (in concept, in outlook, in feel) and while they were feverishly promoted and advertised as such, they actually were no such thing' adding that they were 'written, directed and produced by whites' (2016: 218). Certainly, it would be difficult to argue that *Sweet Sweetback* has much in common, either aesthetically or thematically, with – for instance – later so-called blaxploitation films such as *Sheba, Baby* (William Girdler, 1975) or *Bucktown* (Arthur Marks, 1975). Indeed, the lineage of Melvin Van Peebles is no more or less apparent in these films than it is in *Joe Bullet* or *Bullet on the Run*. This conclusion, and that of Bogle, is not to ascertain that authentic portrayals of Blackness (whatever that might be) are dependent on the skin colour of the filmmaker, but rather to maintain that several films were made within the blaxploitation cycle that departed from the more radical ideology, predominantly about a resistant Black community, that *Sweet Sweetback* initiated. Michael Boyce Gillespie makes a case, for instance, that motion pictures including *Bone* (Larry Cohen, 1972) and *Coonskin* (Ralph Bakshi, 1975) were part of a small number of texts that 'exceeded what the industry, critics, and moviegoing public expected' (2016: 36), regardless of the ethnicity of the producer and/or director. Similarly, *Joe Bullet* and its sequel offer remarkable screen agency to star Ken Gampu in what could have been a career-defining role had the original film obtained an international release.

Therefore, whilst blaxploitation should be identified as a *cycle* rather than a cluster, within this cycle were clusters of *separate activity* that warrant *separate consideration*. Such clusters might include differentiating between the independent films and the studio productions and noting the Black-directed work, particularly the more experimental *Sweetback*, from the more traditional detective-crime efforts from seasoned Hollywood filmmakers such as William Girdler or Arthur Marks. Yearwood makes a similar conclusion, arguing that *Sweet Sweetback* 'is a unique film and another like it has not appeared' (2000: 89). For the author, the films that followed its success, including even *Shaft*, are seen as indebted to 'the Hollywood model as the basis for the development of black heroes' (Ibid.: 45). Fans of the form will also no doubt be aware of blaxploitation-horror such as *Blacula* (William Crain, 1972), *Abby* (William Girdler, 1972) and *Sugar Hill* (Paul Maslansky, 1974) – similarly, ZAxploitation off-shoots in other genres also exist. For example, *Friday's Ghost* (Marcel Joubert, 1980) takes the recurring trope of 'crime doesn't pay' (see Chapter 5) but transports it into a haunted house story, while *Ivondwe* has a rural 'wild man' escape from his chains and trace and stalk his brother, who works as a reverend, as part of its horror plot. Whilst genre is an ever-moving platform of definition, especially in a trend such as blaxploitation where, if the actors were not cast on the basis of race, the films themselves might be more easily placed within popular Hollywood demarcations, some standout entries in the cycle create a basis on which we can analyse, understand and compare concurrent global activity. As such, just as *Sweet Sweetback* was a *pioneering* production – leading to both a cycle and various clusters – *Joe Bullet* plays a similar part in the cinema of ZAxploitation.

The Hero Must Fall

In 1973 *Joe Bullet* had its premiere, uncertified, in the Eyethu cinema in Soweto, where it was previewed to an all-Black audience. Says Tonie van der Merwe, the film's writer and producer:

> We opened it there before it passed the censor board. That is not the way it was done, but there were special schemes [back then] so we did not break any laws. So, we were playing in Soweto and then we got told by the censor board that it had been banned outright. Later that week we got a letter of reasons for why it was banned – all sorts of reasons, a black man driving in what would be white areas, a Black man handling a gun, too much violence . . . no cuts, no nothing, it was banned completely. (2016)

As detailed by Paleker, van der Merwe saw *Joe Bullet* as a way to enter into the film business and he raised his own capital. The director 'came from a construction background and had only done some special effects for the Afrikaans filmmaker Elmo de Witt when his involvement in the black film industry began' (2010: 93). Interestingly, Tomaselli plays with this idea of a uniquely South African blaxploitation, mentioning that 'in 1974 on *Joe Bullet*, van der Merwe denied that his intention not to mix black and white actors in his films was the beginning of apartheid cinema' (1988: 81). It is also worth noting that the film does not easily fall into any of his three categories of a) back to the homelands, b) urban-conditional (which is the most likely for Gampu's character, but difficult to ascertain from the narrative) or c) authentic. As such, *Joe Bullet* is an indication of what might have been if censorship problems did not conclude its original release prematurely. It is possible to imagine further badass heroes in the Ken Gampu mould designated outside of the apartheid state and simply fighting crime within urban locations à la similar blaxploitation presentations. As such, *Joe Bullet* is not just an important South African film but – whether simply made to exploit a township audience's pockets or not – a trailblazing one as well.

Paleker notes that attempts at a Black film industry in South Africa had been undertaken before *Joe Bullet* (2010: 95) – but the few motion pictures produced (the author claims just eight) have fallen into anonymity. As such, *Joe Bullet* is our earliest insight into a Black action film that draws on clear and evident Hollywood influences. Tomaselli was one of the first scholars of South

African cinema to acknowledge (and dismiss) *Joe Bullet*, calling it 'a black James Bond … An inept film, and a financial disaster' (1988: 57) – although its lack of profits was also down to its being banned by the state. Almost three decades later and his stance had not softened, with the author maintaining:

> [F]ilms made by whites and aimed at blacks tended to be appallingly inept, exploitative and patronising, such as *Joe Bullet* (1974), which kicked off the South African blaxploitation genre. This marginalised sector of the industry literally consisted of butchers, bakers and candlestick makers. (2016: 119)

It is easy to understand Tomaselli's disdain towards *Joe Bullet* because, during a period where the author was so prolific about the state's control of the media, a motion picture that failed to even acknowledge apartheid, especially given the context of an all-Black cast, must have seemed belligerent to more liberal thinkers.

However, without wishing to deny the film its austerity budget, it should be pointed out that from a technical standpoint, *Joe Bullet* is not inept – the pace is as good as any of the less groundbreaking American blaxploitation feature films, the camerawork is serviceable, the main characters are holistic and Gampu is cleverly and consistently framed as larger than life, with the camera often capturing him from the midsection upwards. It might be a film from an apartheid state, but *Joe Bullet* – at least visually – offers a groundbreaking presentation of a Black South African hero – and it is far from patronising in this presentation (many later ZAxploitation texts, however, most certainly are). At the most minimal, Gampu is at least not presented as being 'conditionally' permitted within an urban environment – for all intents and purposes, in fact, he operates freely within such a surrounding. In his appraisal of underappreciated African cinema in *Sight and Sound* magazine, respected critic and documentary-maker Mark Cousins singled out *Joe Bullet* for attention (2017), indicating that – decades after the end of apartheid – we might now begin reappraising it within wider blaxploitation activity. Certainly, as an exploitation film, *Joe Bullet* should perhaps be more exploitative – at least of race-friction – but even here there is nothing provocative: the all-Black cast work in clearly defined roles of Mr Right and Mr Wrong, whilst South Africa as a state is simply (wisely?) not acknowledged at all.

In the mention of the B-Scheme films made by Martin Botha and Adri van Aswegen, they affirm that 'the actors and actresses were literally taken off the street and had not had any formal training in film techniques' (1992: 24). The authors do not cite examples of this approach but, as explored in the forthcoming chapters, recurring names in the films of van der Merwe, in particular, indicate that this was not necessarily common practice – at least among the

Figure 2.3 Abigail Kubeka dances for the titular hero in *Joe Bullet* (Louis de Witt, 1973)

surviving examples of the form. In regard to *Joe Bullet*, the female lead Abigail Kubeka states:

> During the apartheid years, in the industry with white artists, there was no apartheid ... We wanted to work with them and they wanted to work with us. How could we make that happen? It didn't matter. We had to. As Blacks we were not even allowed to share the stage with white artists. If it was theatre or a stage production I would act or sing behind the curtains but only my voice could be heard. That made me stronger and more determined – I wanted to show that this was my talent and that this is a career I wanted to get involved in. (2016)

To reimagine Kubeka, who is still active as a performer in Johannesburg, as someone 'literally taken off the street' is therefore to incorrectly document this era (as discussed in my analysis of *Mine Boy* in Chapter 10, some films even used local actors' groups). Whilst no one should be in doubt about the reality of apartheid as a system, introducing an unsubstantiated power binary between filmmaker and performer, regardless of race, is to do an injustice to some of the Black actors who rose to prominence in cheap, generic motion pictures. Such a comment naturally invites accusations of defending 'trash', but as maintained by Kenneth W. Harrow, 'everything the old guard of African cinema would judge inappropriate . . . is now commonly found in Nollywood' (2013: 135). Harrow argues that much of the new African cinema is formulaic, generic, sleazy and loaded with images of the defiled and defilement – which the author sees no reason not to engage with and even celebrate; 'low' art as symbolic of the art of the outsider. *Joe Bullet* might be problematic because of the apartheid state it emerges from, but as a symbol of unlikely paracinematic achievement, a blaxploitation film made under the duress of a real-world segregation, banned by a government that saw its independent spirit as a threat, it cannot and should not be easily dismissed. Even if one's defence (which *could* be made) amounts to little more than appreciating it as an anticipatory text of later trash cinema activity on the continent, for instance the farcical 'have camera, will shoot' Nollywood of *Sharon Stone* (Adim Williams, 2002), *Joe Bullet* has considerable merit.

Ken Gampu: Screen Icon

Film curator and festival programmer Darryl Els maintains:

> *Joe Bullet* is always seen as a precursor to the B-Scheme incentive. It is a different mode of production from what would come. The production values are higher and Tonie put a lot of his own money into the film. I think it is about trying something new, a new image, and that was also helped by Ken Gampu and [co-star] Abigail Kubeka, who I understand had a real hand in how the film looked and what people said and what they wore. If you look at it, it is a more cohesive film. But if you look at when the B-subsidy is in full flow, it [becomes] about a film being 70 minutes and the quality drops off quite radically. (2016)

Perhaps ironically, *Joe Bullet* does not feel entirely out of sync with its own year of release (John Shaft would even debut in a PG-rated television series in 1973, further watering down blaxploitation into a family-friendly format), let alone the wider era. The central problem that *Joe Bullet* really presents viewers with today is identifying where it comes from, where it is set and who the character might be seen to work for. Presumably to show a domineering Black character in private employment might have been contentious for the period – although a decade later, B-Scheme productions such as *Charlie Steel* would make this factor explicit.

In speaking about this aspect of *Joe Bullet*, Ian-Malcolm Rijsdijk, of the Centre for Film and Television Studies at the University of Cape Town, mentions how apartheid is seen as an abstract system or it is not there at all – it is in the background. A film such as *Joe Bullet* – it is evident because it is just not there in any form. As if that world of *Joe Bullet* exists without any sort of white power behind it. (2016)

Whilst it might be tempting to agree with Rijsdijk, especially given that *Joe Bullet* never acknowledges apartheid, South Africa or even the presence of any white characters, there are some subtle clues to suggest that the film – and especially its tough guy leading man – fits within a carefully conceived, if still admittedly vague, localised narrative and not just in the previously acknowledged introduction of Xhosa dialogue. Discussing the 'revisionist movement' that surfaced in the dramatic arts of South Africa in the 1970s and 80s, author Ian Steadman quotes the late Matsemela Manaka: 'It does not matter what language is used, what matters is whether the language communicates with the people being addressed' (1988: 128). Whilst few would want to compare the largely ramshackle work of the B-Scheme, or indeed the opportunistic blaxploitation theatrics of *Joe Bullet*, to the work of Manaka, it is worthwhile suggesting that *how* characters interact and communicate – both in language and in class hierarchies – provides insight into the cinema *of* apartheid (to borrow a term from Tomaselli).

Referring to *Cotton Comes to Harlem*, Lawrence notes how the 'narrative structure follows the same pattern as traditional detective films . . . Specifically, a crime is committed, which prompts the hero/heroine's search to discover the perpetrator and reveal his/her motives' (2005: 34). Whereas *Shaft* follows this template, so too does *Joe Bullet* – the thematic is about a hero solving a crime and battling a small gangster syndicate who operate at street level. Gampu's fictional detective is not permitted a white character to insult or offend, or a submissive white female sexual partner, but he is nonetheless given more independence than other near-contemporaries – for instance, Sidney Poitier's Dr John Prentice in *Guess Who's Coming to Dinner?* (Stanley Kramer, 1967). If Poitier's genteel character was described by Christopher Sieving as 'wholly defined within the context of white America' (2011: 93) then Gampu's Joe Bullet is at least depicted as an individual, renegade, for-hire tough-guy – the crime syndicate is afraid of him just from his reputation and he travels and works *alone* and without restriction on his movement. In addition, at least a brief nod is made to the John Shaft super-stud/Jack Johnson role that *Sweet Sweetback* initiated two years earlier: shortly after Kubeka's Beauty is introduced, a character called Jerry bemoans to her, 'I was your man Beauty, and then all of a sudden it is Joe'. Not long afterwards, Joe is referred to as 'lover boy' although Beauty also admits, 'I don't think Joe is interested in me'. Whilst this could indicate that the two have yet to sleep together, it might also point to the idea that the character played by Gampu has already moved on to his next sexual conquest à la John Shaft and his blaxploitation contemporaries.[1] The language used, and the interaction between the two actors, keeps this factor as vague as possible – perhaps on purpose.

In an interview with Gus Silber, producer Tonie van der Merwe would claim that Black audiences do not like to see sex and argued that white lovemaking was 'entirely different' from that of Black intercourse (1992: 271). Perversely, this absence of the carnal (even in explicit dialogue) means that it is possible to argue that Gampu's hero is figuratively castrated. He is the badass who cannot possibly carry out the actions of his American counterparts, thus permitting us our first real clue that *Joe Bullet* is indeed a film from the apartheid state. Linda Williams has stated that the blaxploitation genre is 'every bit as exploitative of sex as the sexploitation films it followed' (2009: 93) – but Gampu is not allowed to be a stud, he is instead indicative of how an imagined Black South African hero might amalgamate into the strict rules of apartheid society. Decency is expected of him at least insofar as a chaste personality. Notably, promiscuity later becomes a symbol of villainy in ZAxploitation – with a male 'big man' character in *One More Shot* shown to be in bed with an escort (he tells her to leave once he is finished with her) as part of the narrative establishing his dastardly persona.

The term 'big man' is aptly explained by Richard Dowden: a hard-line, authoritarian leader or rich corrupt oligarch, associated with one-party failed states in postcolonial sub-Saharan Africa, who

> likes to demonstrate how far he is from the squalor that most fellow citizens live in. He uses conspicuous displays of wealth to show that he has escaped from the ordinary life: that he is powerful and rich, a benefactor blessed by God, lord of the people whose love and obedience he takes for granted. (2008: 77)

Not only does Gampu's hero find himself battling such a thug in *Joe Bullet*, but this presentation is conspicuous across the ZAxploitation pantheon, possibly pointing to the white South African fear of a Black despot replacing a European one at the seat of high power in Pretoria. In light of the common ZAxploitation representation of a badass individualist (in this case Gampu), usually pitted against a more debauched individualist, it is worth noting that South African foreign policy at the time was to support 'big men' figures, and indeed arm them, so long as they appeared friendly to Pretoria and capitalism. Attesting to this, the government's Foreign Minister Pik Botha would, in 1992, even claim that Angola's Jonas Savimbi saw South Africa as a 'father' figure (Matloff, 1997: 128). Paternalism could not be any more explicit – and ZAxploitation certainly mediates such approaches to Black agency.

However, as discussed in the next chapter, ZAxploitation heroes (and often villains) are also usually family men, deviating from the most famous of the trend's playboy American heroes (Dolemite, Priest, Shaft, Sweetback). As much as Gampu's character is modelled on John Shaft, then, he is never shown to make a decision that involves any kind of selfless reasoning – no desire for sex, even with Beauty, no indication of where he lives (unlike with Shaft's luxurious bachelor pad), no discussion of his payment. Joe Bullet simply does good deeds because the *narrative asks him to*. It is in this aspect of the character that one could argue apartheid also surfaces – a sense that the character can be tough and individualistic, but *only to an extent*. In this regard, Gampu's Bullet anticipates the later Mr Right of the ZAxploitation pantheon. As noted by Henry Kenney, there was a 'heightened white insecurity, the sense of being submerged by an advancing black tide' in the years before apartheid took hold, which was 'solved' by the National Party's pass system and segregation laws, designed to keep the non-white population from owning property in the cities (2016: 122). Gampu's character, despite being superficially expected (at least by an audience) to work within the city given his private detective status, is never actually seen as being *of* the urban environment, perhaps because of this paranoia about free Black movement. For instance, we never see Joe Bullet actually walk the streets of Johannesburg. However, his good citizenship anticipates not just the later films of ZAxploitation and Black cinematic representations, but the premiership of Pieter Willem Botha in the eighties. Botha, responding to both domestic and international criticism, began to reform some of the most abhorrent apartheid laws – including the pass system – but the National Party 'intensified efforts to create an acceptable class of conservative black leaders' (van der Westhuizen 2007: 127). Hence, the search for a Black Mr Right did not just end at the cinema screen – with Joe Bullet himself representing a period of motion pictures that began with the post-war Central African Film Unit and led to the eventual peak of a South African cinema highlighting imagined Black heroes for an apartheid state on limited time.

Also notable is the climax of *Joe Bullet*, which takes place on top of an oil derrick – a hero and a villain fighting against one another in the shadow of colonial triumph and wealth. If *Joe Bullet* appears to be telling us anything in this conclusive sequence, it is that the symbols of white victory remain, still standing tall against tribal fighting. In this sense, Paleker's criticism that white-produced B-Scheme films fail to acknowledge 'the political, social or economic status of Africans' (2010: 97) can also be applied to *Joe Bullet*. The characters exist within their own community, with comparatively minor conflicts overshadowing the very real beast of minority rule – itself only hinted at through such symbols as the oil derrick. When Joe Bullet foils the criminal empire, it is this symbol that remains standing, an indication that Gampu's character sustains the state's authority. It is also interesting to acknowledge what *Joe Bullet* does not show on the screen: any vandalism to what could be interpreted as state identity (such as the oil derrick) – indeed, aside from a fight on a grounded train carriage, the character never interacts with any symbols of city life. This conclusion about *Joe Bullet* nevertheless takes van der Merwe by surprise:

> I don't like politicians and I never supported one – as tradition goes, we would generally vote for the ruling party [National Party]. But never did we attempt to bring forward the message that apartheid was good. Instead these were films about crime doesn't pay. There was no political motif there. There was never a message there about being a good citizen and respecting the government. (2016)

Curiously, one of the first lines in *Joe Bullet* relates to a seemingly throwaway comment at a football game: 'It seems to me they ought to play more like a team. They're inclined to be all individuals'. Here, the dialogue points to community – and whilst this could be interpreted as signalling that Black unification against apartheid is ramshackle and nothing to be feared (by whites), it is just as possible to interpret this piece of dialogue in tribal terms and as a suggestion that the Black nationals of South Africa are better off removing 'individual' aspiration for the good of the wider country (or accepting separate development in the Bantustans). This reading is supported later in the film in a scene where mafia leader and 'big man' antagonist Rocky is shown at a dinner table with a vast plate of lavish pork (in contrast, and as previously mentioned, Bullet himself never even negotiates a fee for his work). The camera focuses in on Rocky's disgusting table habits as he 'primitively' picks up and gnaws at large chunks of bright pink flesh – shown in close-up – suggesting that he is not ready for such a dignified and lavish lifestyle and casting him in the vein of (perceived) buffoon African tribal dictators such as Idi Amin and Mobutu Sese Seko,[2] the Mr Wrong characters of postcolonial rule who doubtlessly kept South Africa's whites in fear of majority rule. Those who operate for the purpose of personal gluttony – whether individual cash-gain (a lone gangster agrees to try and kill Bullet in exchange for a hefty sum) or to sustain a localised dictatorship – in *Joe Bullet* come to a decisive end.

There is also one sizeable takeaway scene that indicates that *Joe Bullet* is, indeed, a film of South Africa under apartheid – despite the blaxploitation trappings. As previously discussed, when Gampu's suave leading man first meets Beauty, she is singing in Xhosa and a party is clearly taking place – drinking, dancing, merriment . . . However, the camera cannot avoid hiding the fact that this is no more than a common living room. Not exactly the sort of surroundings in which one would expect to see, for instance, John Shaft spend a night on the town. As mentioned by actress Abigail Kubeka:

> We had social houses, where people sell liquor, and that is where people would come together. Underground politicians would go there, meet with the journalists and the musicians. Sometimes the police would come and arrest people, but usually people just paid a fine and came back. People were defiant. (2016)

This culture is most explicitly captured in *Mine Boy*, towards the end of the apartheid period. It is this 'social house' that Joe Bullet quite clearly enters – the identity of which (to paraphrase Manaka) would have been clearly addressed to an audience in South Africa, whether white or (most likely) Black, in 1973. In entering such a venue, he is also subtly maintaining his renegade nature to the audience.

Another notable aspect about *Joe Bullet* is, of course, that it features an all-Black cast, driving and walking (seemingly freely, even if the city remains largely undepicted). White authority is never present and, yet, *because* of its absence we could argue that we get some insight into a South Africa that *could be*. It is one of epidemic corruption – where even the year's biggest football game is compromised by fear, gambling, kidnapping and murder. Police are not called upon to solve the situation because the law seems to have ceased to exist. A renegade figure such as Joe Bullet is the only hope for restoring order – and yet his actual job title is never even mentioned. Whilst Johannesburg does not become a part of Joe Bullet's identity and life in the way that, as an obvious comparison, New York's backdrop, particularly the sleazy 42nd Street, becomes synonymous with the personality of Richard Roundtree's Shaft, it is difficult not to see Gampu's character as an imagined white saviour, of sorts – the acceptable face of Black militancy.

It would take decades for *Joe Bullet* to be cast back into the public conscience – with van der Merwe being awarded a special Simon Sabela award at the 2014 Durban International Film Festival, belatedly recognised as 'the most popular filmmaker among Black audiences in the 1970s and '80s' (Onishi 2014). On this, van der Merwe states:

> To me it was purely business. It was a numbers game – 32 million Blacks and four million whites. I did not think about venues or whatever. I just thought it made great sense to make a Black film and there was a demand among the Blacks for movies. So we made something that would be a Black James Bond. Ken Gampu was our number one choice as he was making movies abroad as well as at home. I got hold of Ken and we became good friends and from there I began to work on a script and a story. (2016)

As Kubeka also mentions:

> Even if you had a problem you never had a say. We were acting for money and to survive. That was our lives. It was slavery in a way. Forced to do something in a way – 'if I do not do this how will I survive?' But I also loved the career, this was my passion ... When I did *Joe Bullet*, Ken Gampu was our leading man – but it was Afrikaners who were making this. White people. We were given the script and told to act. We did not know who the sponsors were and we got those few pounds that they paid us but working on set was glorious. There was nothing wrong – there was no police. On the set it was just us, the actors and the crew ... We had a premiere [for *Joe Bullet*] in Soweto. Then from there I do not know what happened. It all went very quiet. (2016)

For van der Merwe, *Joe Bullet*'s prohibition was evidence that, despite seemingly playing the film's theatrics as safely as possible, the apartheid state was still not ready for a blaxploitation hero:

> Obviously, it was a financial disaster. Ken was my friend by that time, so I felt very bad and he was devastated especially since we planned to do some sequels. But I knew that making an expensive black movie especially in the English language was not the way forward. (2016)

For his later films, van der Merwe would almost always shoot in Zulu. A notable exception is when van der Merwe and Gampu reunited for *Bullet on the Run*, this time with the writer/producer also directing. In the interim period between the first and second *Joe Bullet* films, van der Merwe also became the premiere B-Scheme director of the apartheid period and a major figure within the mobile circuit (he did not only present and travel with his own work). Unlike the original, *Bullet on the Run* allows Gampu's character to interact with white personalities. In one scene he even narrowly escapes a shoot-out involving two white policemen. The spectre of apartheid is also more prevalent in *Bullet on the Run*: the court proceedings that find Gampu guilty of a robbery that he was not involved with are overseen by a white judge and lawyer and the jail that he is sentenced to serve time in has no Caucasian inmates. This acknowledgement of an apartheid state, however flimsy, also points to the decade between the first film, which was banned, and the follow-up. It is in this sense that we begin to see elements of a South African blaxploitation form. Tomaselli would ascertain that 'There is no attempt to stimulate a "black" film industry at all, only products aimed at blacks' (1988: 82). Certainly, van der Merwe's cinema, in particular, had little to no Black labour behind-the-scenes, aside from (during his eighties peak as a director) some script credits for his recurring actor Hector Mathanda, although he stayed loyal enough to his cast to include both Gampu and Popo Gumede in his actioner *Operation*

Hit Squad in 1987, an American co-production. Nevertheless, in this cinema 'aimed at blacks' it is possible to recognise at least some kind of evolution in the presentation of localised heroes. The Gampu that exists *outside* the city in *Joe Bullet* exists within a far wider spectrum of communities in the sequel almost ten years later.

Post-Blaxploitation and *Bullet on the Run*

Blaxploitation as a vaguely identifiable sub-section of detective cinema may have disappeared as the seventies became the eighties, but the cycle's tropes became standardised and mainstream within American film and pop culture. Black leading men, in major, big studio motion pictures or on prime-time television, particularly Eddie Murphy and Mr T – arrived only a decade after *Shaft* and *Sweet Sweetback*. Of course, screen presentations have continued to be subject to debate – Yearwood has noted how Hollywood in the seventies and eighties was 'reluctant to cast black stars without a white "buddy" as ideological chaperone' (1993: 128). Melvin Donalson has countered by arguing that such presentations of Black-white partnership were formative insofar as to 'deliberately blur racial lines in regard to the potential for interracial harmony' (2006: 56). This monograph discusses the interracial friendships of ZAxploitation cinema in Chapter 7 – ironically, one of the most potent is *Death of a Snowman*, starring Ken Gampu as a journalist who goes rogue on his newspaper editor, his white policeman best friend and other lawmen on the streets of Soweto. Outside of *Joe Bullet*, it is arguably Gampu's most impressive role during the 1970s. As such, what makes *Joe Bullet* such a vital part of South African genre cinema is that it heralds the beginning of an idea, at the very least, in which a Black leading man can dominate an action film narrative – however confined by the political situation – in a (theoretically) internationally appealing English-language production. It also initiates Gampu as a formidable action star – a South African Richard Roundtree who should, undoubtedly, be just as well-known and regarded as similarly important.

If *Joe Bullet* is mostly influenced by *Hammer* and *Shaft*, then *Bullet on the Run* is a little closer to the 'Black James Bond' personality that van der Merwe intended with the original film – in the sequel Gampu even gets to confirm that he is indeed a 'private eye'. A five-minute long opening credit sequence plays out as a cut-rate nod to Maurice Binder's iconic Bond titles, whilst a ridiculous scene in which the tall and muscular Joe Bullet is nearly asphyxiated by the villain's boa constrictor (which is feebly placed around Gampu's neck) is stolen from *Moonraker* (Lewis Gilbert, 1979). The 'undercover' aspect and the presence of a British 'M' character also indicate the lineage to the Bond mythology – although the presence of bare breasts (over the titles) and a

Figure 2.4 Ken Gampu returns as *Joe Bullet* in the sequel *Bullet on the Run* (Tonie van der Merwe, 1982)

gruesome gun fight at the end of *Bullet on the Run* show that van der Merwe may have had an eye on the more lucrative foreign exploitation film market. *Bullet on the Run* is edgier than its predecessor – although it still suffers from compromised production values – but it is surprising that the film's popcorn thrills never equated to any kind of foreign release. *Bullet on the Run* is also one of the last projects of its kind. Bigger budgeted than the later state-financed B-Scheme efforts that exploded in profile after 1986, described by Murray as of 'extremely low cost and poor quality' (1992: 259), *Bullet on the Run* offers Gampu a chance to expand on his character – including as a slightly more sexualised figure than before but also in standing with, and against, white authority. It should be affirmed that in each instance, Gampu is shown to be the most powerful figure in the film.

In later years, van der Merwe would claim that the government in South Africa did not take 'black films' (his words) seriously. There is certainly indication that, with his *Joe Bullet* films, he at least took the Black audience seriously enough to deliver entertainment on a par with global blaxploitation cinema. Nevertheless, it would be his efforts within the later B-Scheme subsidy that encouraged a new rush of cheap, often amateurish, filmmaking (Paleker 2010:

93). It is, however, in comparison to these tawdrier B-Scheme films that we can view *Joe Bullet* as being even more significant and appreciate its endurance, with contemporary festival and even DVD and Blu-ray releases, as an exciting low budget endeavour. As well as possessing clear competency in front of and behind the camera, *Joe Bullet* and *Bullet on the Run* do not overbear the viewer with dialogue on good behaviour and family living – they do, for all intents and purposes, offer Ken Gampu the opportunity to exist as an iconic action hero, one that has not yet been fully rediscovered. Whilst van der Merwe's later ZAxploitation films are discussed from Chapter 4 onwards, in the next chapter this monograph addresses Simon Sabela and his film *iKati Elimnyama*, arguably the most ambitious of all the attempts to translate American blaxploitation cinema into a South African setting.

Notes

1. Tomaselli and van Zyl note how sex has been traditionally taboo even in Afrikaans-language films as well (1992: 400).
2. The irony of the nominally democratic National Party government opposing one-party rule in Africa is that under John Vorster's 'détente' policy, the 'friendly' Malawian dictator Hastings Banda had a palace constructed for himself, paid for by aid from the South African government (Dowden 2008: 414).

3. SIMON SABELA

Blaxploitation icon?

It is a tragic irony that Simon Sabela, perhaps even more identifiable than his contemporary Ken Gampu, died in 1994 – the year that fully democratic elections were finally held in South Africa. Born in Durban in 1931, Sabela never did live to see what Tomaselli and Ureke have referred to as his 'post-apartheid rehabilitation' (2017: 76). Sabela is identified as the country's first Black film director and, even if future research produces evidence to the contrary, he is certainly the first to make cinema that was widely seen in South Africa.[1] Due to the timing of his passing, as South Africa entered an important new chapter in its history, he had little opportunity to clarify and defend a legacy that has been deemed problematic, albeit not without importance and precedence.

Tomaselli has noted that Sabela's work was 'more adventurous and accurate than those found in the "back to the homelands" category' and maintained that his projects document 'an urban-rural confusion typical of the overcrowded black townships' (1988: 72). Later writers on South Africa's genre cinema have also been cautious about integrating Sabela into wider discussion of the B-Scheme or race-exploitation films of the period. Paleker, for instance, notes how his work displays 'higher production values' and 'a degree of "cultural authenticity" not seen in the films made by whites' (2010: 96). Sabela's melodrama *uDeliwe* (1975), which was his debut motion picture, has also obtained retrospective accolades from Modisane – who notes its 'enhancement of critical engagement on black identity' (2013: 85).

Whilst this book does touch upon *uDeliwe*, the film – as a coming-of-age melodrama – does not fit into the broader ZAxploitation race/genre canon. Instead, it is Sabela's Zulu-language action thriller *iKati Elimnyama* (or *Black Cat*), in which he also stars, that this chapter explores. Unlike *Joe Bullet*, and the later B-Scheme productions of the 1980s, *iKati Elimnyama* has had some broader recognition in previous studies of South African film. Indeed, before the discovery of *Joe Bullet*, it was Sabela who was deemed to be the figure who 'reshaped' such American blaxploitation templates as *Shaft* for township audiences (Maingard 2007: 130). Towards the conclusion of this chapter, some discussion will also be introduced regarding the UK-South African co-production *Gold*, released a year before *iKati Elimnyama*, in which Sabela plays a supporting role opposite the stars Roger Moore and Susannah York. Moore, who performed in *Gold* at the same time as he was a considerable box office attraction for the James Bond franchise, would be subject to intense criticism for working in South Africa during the period of apartheid, something that he would acknowledge (without apology) in his autobiography: 'Our unit arrived in Johannesburg in September 1973 and we received a very warm welcome. The production employed a large number of local South Africans – Black and white – and we never experienced a single apartheid issue' (2008: 183). The actor's statement is clearly naïve, particularly given that he would acknowledge Black crew members had a curfew to abide by, and given that it refers to events just three years before schoolchildren were shot dead in the Soweto riots.

Through highlighting the difference between Sabela's self-directed portrayal of an action 'hero' in *iKati Elimnyama* and his participation in *Gold*, as the brave and self-sacrificing mine worker King, some interesting and possibly overlooked aspects of the former's relationship with blaxploitation also surface. Central among these is the fact that Sabela, in a film aimed at the townships of a segregated South Africa, provides a more radical portrayal of Black aspiration and independence than that of the 'magic negro' character he plays in *Gold*. This discussion, then, is not intended to disagree with the points raised by Tomaselli, Paleker and Modisane but rather to use their own valuable analysis as a skeleton for (as per *Joe Bullet*) initiating *iKati Elimnyama* into the wider blaxploitation spectrum. An analysis of Sabela's stylistic choices indicates that this was possibly even his intention in making the film.

During the 1970s, Sabela was employed by Heyns Films, a white-owned production studio that was later discovered to be 'subsidised by the Department of Information to create propagandistic imagery' (Maingard 2007: 129). Ureke and Tomaselli have noted that there is a possibility that Sabela was not aware of the film label's association with the National Party – moreover, as maintained by Modisane, in a 1978 interview Sabela openly discussed how the scripts that were chosen for him were not always to his liking (2013: 83). To what extent such grievances, or naivety about the source of his financing, allow Sabela to be reappraised as a figure who might have subverted his era, rather than played into it, particularly as a Black filmmaker, is doubtlessly up to debate. This is true especially given that the argument of this chapter, namely that Sabela was subversive enough to make *iKati Elimnyama* as a clear homage to blaxploitation rebellion, would of course be weakened if one were to assume someone of such savvy was not aware of where of his funding came from. Nonetheless, as indicated by the later example of *Mapantsula*, state support (however tangential or explicit) did not always need to equate to subservience to the government's racial line. As discussed by Maingard, planned television retrospectives of Sabela's directorial work on South African television in 2002 and 2003 involved some local controversy (2007: 133) – and when Peter Davis wrote *In Darkest Hollywood* in 1996, Sabela's films were (perhaps tellingly) given no coverage. As a filmmaker, not to mention a rare Black South African director during this period, Sabela has a remarkably and surprisingly minor presence in studies of the continent's cinema and this is perhaps because of his association with the apartheid state. Consequently, one hopes that the perspective introduced in this chapter might allow for a broader consideration of the director's achievements (including vis-à-vis one of his comparable Hollywood film roles, which indicates he was far more adept at using the language of cinema to oppose apartheid and racism in his own work than has been considered).

Filmmaker and academic Ntshavheni Wa Luruli, who grew up in Soweto, mentions:

> Simon Sabela – he was given this opportunity by Heyns films, to make Black films – about Black people in the townships or Black people in general. The first film [of his] I saw was *uDeliwe*, which made a big impression on me, as I was ten or eleven at the time and because [I was] a Black person, especially, from South Africa, speaking the language. Again, I'm talking about the impression as a young boy watching that. It was entertaining and what I saw, I was seeing myself, my surroundings, my environment, the right attitude – these people, the way they walk, the fashion, the way they dress, the way they talk, the wise guys – so, yes, I was blown away. That was very important. I later learned, actually, that the reason Simon Sabela was given an opportunity to direct was part of the government's devious scheme to keep the Blacks in the townships. That was part of the South African intelligence, although Heyns film disputed it and said they did not know they were being used. This is why the content of the stories did not deal with the situation [of apartheid] at that point of time. But for me, my angle into it, through the way I personally experienced it, is that those films had unintended consequences, which were positive, because it is from then on that Black people learned how to

write, you know – screenwriting, or learned to direct [because we wanted to be] like Simon Sabela – because before then Black people were just in front of the camera in small roles. Shooting, gaffers, all those technical professions, that did not exist before the seventies, existed. Black people did not do that [before Sabela] – and this is what I mean by unintended consequences. That opened up opportunity for Black people to be technically trained. And today that generation is still there. (2016)

Without wishing to sound overly indebted to Pierre Bourdieu and the so-called 'trash' film academics who have formulated his writing on taste into a broader discourse involving the worth of the 'lowbrow' (particularly Jeffrey Sconce), as part of a global, hybrid network of exploitation, transnationalising successful low budget generic tropes into the apartheid locale, ZAxploitation is a cinema of *representation*. Drawing on the words of Wa Luruli as well, one might argue that the central figures of these texts exist not just (or even necessarily) in the world of apartheid, but in the world of a wider idea-exchange with concurrent exploitation totems. Maingard admits as much when she compares Sabela's character Lefty, in *iKati Elimnyama*, with Richard Roundtree's John Shaft (2007: 130). Unlike *Joe Bullet*, Sabela's motion picture immediately makes its locale explicit, for instance – from some brief, but effective, travelogue documentation of township life to the opening scene, which highlights the vast motorways of Johannesburg. In this regard, we are experiencing the first ZAxploitation film that identifies itself as South African – something *Joe Bullet* refuses.

A New Black Super-Hero

In her discussion of *iKati Elimnyama*, and its relationship with *Shaft*, Maingard admits that although there 'are significant differences' Sabela still manages to reshape the 'black super-hero figure' that exists in the American prototype. Complicating this assertion, however, is the fact that Shaft *also* reshapes the figure of the silent, mute avenger from *Sweet Sweetback*'s *Baadasssss Song* – himself symbolic of a larger discourse that was both aesthetic *and* thematic. Director Van Peebles took a Third Cinema approach to his project in terms of its aesthetics, but even this proved controversial because he retained exploitation film elements – most notably graphic sex, verité violence and shocking, jarring juxtapositions. Thematically, as noted by Manthia Diawara, 'Van Peebles thematises Black nationalism by casting the Black community as an internal colony, and Sweetback, a pimp, as the hero of decolonisation' (1995: 411). As such, films like *Shaft* – and particularly the cash-in blaxploitation motion pictures that followed its success, many directed by white men, have encouraged the question: 'Can a film count as black cinema when it merely presents a blackface version of white films, or when it merely reproduces stereotypical images of black people?' (Lott 1995: 44). Sabela's *iKati Elimnyama*, however, is different because, unique amongst the ZAxploitation films, it asks the audience to identify with a petty criminal – described by Tomaselli as 'a township burglar' (1988: 72). Moreover, at least in terms of narrative, it is difficult to receive Sabela's achievement as a 'blackface version of white films' as one might say that *Joe Bullet* is *just* a detective film. This conclusion can be detailed by highlighting how *iKati Elimnyama* takes its influence from a far more radical example of 1970s American Black filmmaking.

Described by Maingard as 'a suave, wealthy businessman, with a sleek, salon car' (2007: 130), Lefty is both the hero and the villain of *iKati Elimnyama*: a successful, independent warehouse owner who, it is revealed, has gained his riches via double-crossing rival gangsters. Leading characters in the blaxploitation canon who were portrayed as antagonist and protagonist are actually not uncommon. Sweetback, the character, certainly maintained a level of provocation: he is a male prostitute, he threatens a passing woman with a knife when he thinks she might give him away to the police, he has lengthy sex with a white female to win his 'freedom' from a biker gang. However, it is really *Super Fly*'s Youngblood Priest (Ron O'Neal) who established the cycle's more ambiguous representations and who Sabela was likely influenced by. Priest is a violent, foul-mouthed drug pusher and pimp. Moreover, his unapologetically self-serving criminal lifestyle resonated with its African American audience of the time and the character became seen as a 'role model' among disenfranchised Black, urban, young men (Lawrence 2008: 67). Ed Guerrero even notes how the film inspired a 'dramatic increase in cocaine use among inner-city black youth' (1993: 97), although Priest's narrative journey is arguably not to glamourise cocaine, but to question why a racist state and its officials even care what an impoverished and ignored Black minority in America do with their bodies.

Whilst Guerrero is critical of *Super Fly*, the film's cynicism remains powerful or, as described by Mikel Koven, 'Both the cops and the mob are seen to be keeping the black man in Harlem ... As Priest says towards the end of the film, "No motherfucker's gonna own me"' (2010: 59). At the heart of *Super Fly*'s narrative is a similar story to that of *Sweet Sweetback* – the character of Priest simply wants to escape from the rundown inner-city life that he has, *despite* the narcotics and women that he treats as disposable accessories to his life as a gangster. His own revolution is not, per Sweetback, to galvanise his community, but rather to find personal sanctuary and gratification outside of surroundings that seem unlikely to change because of both corrupt and racist law enforcement and petty urban criminals living from meal to meal. It is this character arc that also becomes repeated in less impressive, but indebted, follow-up films such as *Black Caesar* and *Candy Tangerine Man* (Matt Cimber,

SIMON SABELA: BLAXPLOITATION HERO?

Figure 3.1 Ron O'Neal as Youngblood Priest in *Super Fly* (Gordon Parks Jr, 1972), a notable influence on Simon Sabela's *iKati Elimnyama*

1975). We might discuss this small grouping, at least narratively, as a sort-of *anti-hero blaxploitation* – with characters that are far removed from the more traditional heroics of John Shaft because they are *in it for themselves*.

Certainly, it is *Super Fly* and not *Shaft* that is the bigger influence on *iKati Elimnyama*. If one is to play the opening sequences of both films back-to-back, the similarity becomes strikingly apparent. So much so, that one can only presume the South African censors who had banned *Joe Bullet* were simply unaware that *Super Fly* even existed. Not only does Sabela wear a similar hat to that of Ron O'Neal's character, and an outfit modelled on the American film's famous theatrical poster, but both actors are filmed at the steering wheel of their impressive automobiles, driving alone and from the exact same side-angle point-of-view. Sabela even has a police vehicle slow down as it drives past him, with a (white) officer looking in through his car window before the car speeds away – initiating the idea, at this early stage, that Lefty is a fugitive from justice. Given the considerable drug use and sexuality of *Super Fly*, attempting to translate the film to South Africa during this time might sound futile. Nevertheless, *iKati Elimnyama* indicates that Sabela may have been a far more subversive filmmaker than he has been given credit for, particularly insofar as using visual metaphors to establish the sort of film he *wants* to be making (but cannot).

Hence, when we first meet the two Black lawmen (who will eventually kill Lefty in a shootout), one of them is shown, in close up, pouring white powder

Figure 3.2 Simon Sabela as Lefty in *iKati Elimnyama* (or *Black Cat*, Simon Sabela, 1975)

into a clear glass, which he later fills with water. The powder is nothing more offensive than aspirin, but it *stands in for* cocaine and allows anyone familiar with the *language* of blaxploitation, and the corrupt police force of *Super Fly*, to understand that the South African policemen are being depicted negatively (certainly, there is no other reason to focus on such a trivial action). Cocaine is shown, in *Super Fly*, as being coveted as much by corrupt lawmen as by the lowly Black youth they discriminate against, and Priest is smart enough to navigate not just his exit from the ghetto but to play the entire system of crooked white exploitation for his own benefit. Sabela's gangster character is also a charismatic, sly presence – and given that Maingard acknowledges how 'Hollywood gangsterism was to offer images of American culture, closely emulated in the dress style and behavioural pattern of Sophiatown street gangs' (2007: 73), it would not be far-fetched to assume that the star and director of *iKati Elimnyama* knew that his own badass portrayal – antagonistic towards the law (and thus the state) – would register in a similar manner.[2]

Indeed, it is no coincidence that later in the film the same two lawmen are shown to be in collusion with white officers (representatives of the apartheid state) who bring a Black vigilante to justice via a roadblock in the motorway. As mentioned by Peter Davis in his discussion of Sidney Poitier's iconic role in *Cry, the Beloved Country* (Zoltan Korda, 1951), 'films can carry messages that even contradict what is being said and done' (1996: 43). Given that *Super Fly*'s

Priest was perceived by some viewers as a counter-culture figure, a hedonistic gangster who outwits his fellow Black felons and also the white police force, the visual countenance of Sabela playing a South African version, indicated by the near-identical opening credits (and similar dress) is difficult to ignore. This platform also allows for a more radical reading of *iKati Elimnyama*.

It should also be established that it would be incorrect to assume that the audience for *iKati Elimnyama* had not seen *Super Fly* or other follow-up films, such as *Black Caesar*, which indicated that lawmen were just as likely to use narcotics, or profit from crime, as the Black gangsters they intended to imprison. Nor is it unlikely that *Super Fly* was 'old news' by the time Sabela was making *iKati Elimnyama* three years later. Indeed, there is a brief scene, about twenty-five minutes into the running time of *uDeliwe*, where lead actress Cynthia Shange (the former South African candidate for the Miss World competition and thus something of a superstar at the time) is escorted by her date to the famous Eyethu cinema in Soweto. On the billboard are three films – the most prominent is *Django* (Sergio Corbucci, 1966) and the others are *Upperseven* (Alberto De Martino, 1966) and *Tom Dollar* (Marcello Ciorciolini, 1967). In this moment, we can see that township audiences were not just watching cheap, dubbed imports, but *dated*, cheap, dubbed imports. According to Frank Meintjies, 'Townships and downtown cinemas steer clear of the latest movies on the circuit. Good films, by any standard, are conspicuously absent. The main themes: non-stop action, violence and of late, X-rated sex' (1992: 273). The author becomes tied-up in lowbrow/highbrow discussions, however, when he states that township audiences were simply not able to access more (perceived) quality films (the author mentions *Mapantsula* as an example), indicating that 'non-stop action' and 'violence' was somehow oppositional to political growth. However, *Super Fly*, whilst undoubtedly a violent film, is also a radical one and Sabela's decision to homage its depiction of a successful Black businessman, outplaying the police at their own rackets, is not to be taken lightly.

Distributing Blaxploitation in the Old South Africa

Modisane notes how, despite the fact *Sweet Sweetback* had been (understandably) forbidden in South Africa, a July 1974 article in *Drum* magazine detailed that American blaxploitation cinema had still made it onto the 'black circuit' in the country (2013: 89). Thus, the township circuit was not just one of legitimate distribution networks, such as the cheap imported films played in the Eyethu cinema, but one of illegitimate distribution networks as well, where a budding entrepreneur could rent imported (but banned) motion pictures and screen them to interested audiences via the mobile circuit. 'What [you could] do is hire Hong Kong films, Italian Westerns, the odd horror film or the films of Tonie van der Merwe [producer of *Joe Bullet*] to township entrepreneurs,' states the Johannesburg-based festival programmer and curator Trevor Taylor. 'They would also hire 16mm films and then hire halls in the townships [for screenings]' (2016). What makes Modisane's investigation particularly interesting is not just that *Drum* was discussing the introduction of films such as *Shaft* to township audiences in 1974/1975 (one would imagine the similarly successful *Super Fly* must have played too), but that the magazine also spoke about the popularity of Heyns Films and in particular the Simon Sabela-directed effort *uDeliwe*. In fact, *uDeliwe* was seen by an estimated 400,000 people by the end of the year of its release (Modisane 2013: 91), two million by the end of its run and at least 'one million viewers' paying to watch Sabela's other output (Tomaselli 1988: 63). Sabela, therefore, must have known that he had a rare, key localised voice by the time he began production on his next film. Given that the director also seems to assume viewers of *iKati Elimnyama* have at least some understanding of blaxploitation tropes (corrupt/bumbling police, individualistic 'badass' leading men, lavish cars, a life of hedonism)[3] it is clear that he is, despite being clearly compromised, attempting to relate a story about similar Black aspiration.

Modisane also discusses how the radio play of *uDeliwe* has a different conclusion to the motion picture directed by, and starring, Sabela. This might assert that Sabela's veiled claims to 'inappropriate' material could indicate acknowledgement of reinterpreting some of the texts he was asked to direct (2013: 81). Heyns Films, which also backed international co-productions such as *Target of an Assassin* (or *Tigers Don't Cry*, Peter Collinson, 1976), would be caught up in the Information Scandal of 1978 and Sabela's directorial career would conclude as well. In being linked to the Department of Information, *iKati Elimnyama* might be assumed to meet a standard that at least functions as propaganda for the apartheid state – and there are aspects of the film that indicate clear deviance from the blaxploitation template. Tomaselli sees Sabela's work as more authentic than those of his contemporaries in the 1970s and mentions how 'most of the gangster films' made during this period 'include ludicrous witchdoctor sequences which insensitively portray them as gruff, gross and noisy buffoons' (1988: 73). Gavshon would also remark of films 'far removed from South African reality' (1983: 14). Most of the films described by Tomaselli are frustratingly unavailable, although the author mentions actor/director/producer Clive Scott and James/Jimmy Murray as prolific filmmakers during the period, making motion pictures that carried a message of 'liberal altruistic commitment' regarding reform and reassurance but expressed 'within the system' (Ibid.: 75). Murray would later bemoan the state subsidy system (as well as noting the fact that films came, went and disappeared), also mentioning that Sabela was used to 'counter the "Americanisation of South African blacks"' (1992: 257), a factor that seems astonishing given the blaxploitation references within *iKati Elimnyama*.

Clive Scott, however, explains that the problem with the subsidy scheme was – for him – more to do with distribution than state censorship:

> I made three Black films, in Sesotho and Zulu . . . As with any filmmaker, we wanted to make films that would bring in some sort of return. In those days there was virtually nothing that Black people did [in cinema] at that time. They did do stage shows. Gibson Kente was a lovely man, he did all sorts of things in the townships, but for us as privileged whites – and we were very privileged – we made films for the white market here. That was the people who put money in the bank for you by paying to see your film . . . The Sesotho and Zulu films – we could not do this ourselves, so we had guys who used to go out with a little generator and a white sheet and you would go to a church hall in the homelands, set up the sheet [makes projector noises] and then charge people 20 cents to see the film. Then you could get a return from the government for the seats you had sold. I had a partner called Jimmy Murray and Jimmy, myself and Simon Metsing, our Black partner, we did very well out of that. The government offered an 80,000-rand subsidy for each film. It did take time and we split our cheques three ways. I don't know why we did not make more. (2016)

If the films discussed by Tomaselli, concurrent to the work of Sabela, are – as also indicated by Scott – produced with only minimal political intentions and/or with representations that do not fall within the 'authentic' category of apartheid cinema genres ('back to the homelands' etc), then perhaps we can understand why *iKati Elimnyama* might be considered unique. Indeed, most remarkable of all, Sabela creates a film that plays within the wider blaxploitation cycle but – and this is not something that could even be said of *Joe Bullet* – never feels like a mere cash-in of a successful and established trope.

Certainly, as with Gampu's Joe Bullet, Sabela's Lefty is not permitted any sort of sexual dalliances – he is married with a child – but he is nonetheless given plenty of screen time as an individual, outside of the homestead, planning and securing his own future. Moreover, his wife and child play a very minimal supporting role – Maingard indicates that such stock characters are examples of a 'diminished' female role in this kind of lowbrow cinema (2007: 133). She even points out when, after discovering his wife and daughter have been raped, 'Lefty's response does not match the severity of the situation' (Ibid.: 134). It is worth acknowledging here that female representations across the next fifteen years of low budget B-Scheme filmmaking rarely improved (I discuss this in Chapter 8). However, instead of such minimal reactions being read as the sign of either misogyny or of Sabela's lack of interest in his female characters, it might instead represent a thematic indication of the director visualising his own frustrations with the compromises that have to be made in producing a South African *Super Fly* under apartheid. One can presume that the depiction of Lefty, as a family man as opposed to a rogue badass, was enforced by Heyns Films (later B-Scheme productions also insist on these representations of tough-guy fathers and husbands). By diminishing Lefty's role as caring partner and parent, Sabela might be seen to enter into a wider discourse with his audience about portrayals – there is, fundamentally, no good reason for Lefty, as a hedonistic criminal placed within the wider blaxploitation cycle, to be married or to have a child anyway, let alone to care about their well-being. The characters of this period, be they Priest, John Shaft or Sweetback, became iconic – rightly or wrongly – partly because of their aggressive masculinity. This factor, in itself, would continue to be spoofed as recently as *Black Dynamite* (Scott Sanders, 2009). Therefore, Sabela could be interpreted as communicating a more individualistic presentation of Lefty than his home life would otherwise suggest, which is why his lack of reaction to a traumatic event is placed within the narrative (he may also be symbolising, of course, that South Africa's Black people have to accept trauma as part of their lives). Whilst having his daughter and wife kidnapped (and raped off-screen) *does* feel remarkably cold, it also permits both characters to remain on the side-lines of *iKati Elimnyama* and for the film to be almost entirely centred on Lefty himself.

Addressing the films that were made for township audiences during the apartheid period, Gavshon would state that 'self-censorship is an issue from the beginning of the process. There must be an awareness of the responsibility they carry, and the very special place they occupy within the process of cultural and ideological production' (1983: 14). This aspect is especially clear in the ending of *iKati Elimnyama*, in which Lefty is finally brought to justice and shot down. On the one hand, the death of Sabela's criminal in *iKati Elimnyama* might suggest that the director was following the typical narrative of what Gavshon describes as 'crime don't pay' (1983: 17). This is a recurring narrative arc that typifies the later, less competent work that came from the B-Scheme subsidy project and which has been commented upon by Tomaselli and Paleker as well. On the other hand, however, Sabela's focus throughout *iKati Elimnyama* is not on the 'heroic' white police force and their Black assistants, who finally bring him to justice – nor even on his mafia rivals, who are kept in the shadows (both figuratively and literally), or even on his family. It is, as mentioned, on Lefty himself. Even more than *Joe Bullet*, which at least allows its supporting characters a chance to breathe, *iKati Elimnyama* is a film almost entirely about one character. As a result, our narrative identification during the film is entirely from Lefty's perspective, and an 'unhappy ending' does not necessarily change our sympathies to him or our understanding/sympathy towards his initial desire to leave his criminal past behind him.

In another sequence spoken about by Maingard, one of Lefty's rivals has to face a small number of white policemen and – as expected – he is not given permission to rebel (even vocally) against their presence or authority. Nonetheless, one could argue that this sequence, a concluding car chase which is as thrilling as it is dangerous (it looks to have been filmed without trained stunt performers or any protection), offers more than – per Maingard – 'hegemonic control, beyond the film's enclosed black world' (2007: 131). Indeed, this sequence in which Sabela's enemy struggles to escape the clutches of the police places us quite squarely *on the side of the criminal*. Most of the chase is set-up to tease us with the idea that his escape from the apartheid state *is* possible as Sabela cuts back and forth between the troops and the criminal's car speeding down the motorway. Are we really to assume that a township audience in 1975, just one year before the Soweto riots and having already emulated the streetwear of Hollywood gangsters, was expected to cheer the sight of white lawmen setting up a barricade to stop an ambitious, charismatic Black criminal – established in the film's narrative as 'belonging' to the townships – from escaping justice? Moreover, the lack of movement from the policemen – they merely stand with rifles at the barricade, against the speed of the criminal's car – places the viewer in the thick of a frantic attempt to make a getaway and keeps the state officials anonymous. Visually, the only way for this scene to create any kind of drama is if we – as the onlookers – are willing the criminal to safety rather than the static, anonymous blockade. If our sympathies are with the lawmen, then the chase itself carries absolutely no suspense, not least of all because none of the white police officers are introduced or given any character traits. Here, Sabela's understanding of the language of cinema is especially notable.

In another telling scene, Sabela has his two, often bumbling, Black policemen (the same characters who eventually shoot him dead) arrest a pair of hoodlums, who rob someone on a dusty, ramshackle street, outside a small convenience store. Throughout his film, Sabela follows scenes of his well-dressed policemen with such juxtapositions of everyday squalor amid township life – the cinematic language is therefore clear. Lefty *could* still be subject to these conditions had he not gambled with criminal enterprise. On the other hand, the suit-wearing police officers are portrayed as privileged, even conceited – and their connection to the apartheid state, serving the white officers who provide the roadblock at the end of the film's lengthy car chase sequence, is never in doubt. In addition, the first appearance of a white police officer in *iKati Elimnyama* is only seconds after the film's title appears on the screen – when a lawman drives by Lefty on the motorway, slows down and peers through the character's car window. Sabela's subtle facial expressions indicate a mild panic and this establishes that Lefty is likely to be worth such suspicion. Whilst there is every likelihood that Heyns Films would have 'read' this, and the concluding car chase, as a reminder that 'hegemonic control' exists in the apartheid state, and that any marginalised resident seeking to try a life of crime would end up either dead or in prison, there can be little doubt that Sabela also wanted his audience to comprehend Lefty's opposition to the apartheid state. His representation, therefore, is as a rogue operative – a criminal turned legitimate businessman who must outsmart the police, his contemporaries in organised crime and even his family. In this description, and given the reminder of apartheid hegemony on his life and *lifestyle* (we see him, for instance, drinking at an upmarket bar, one which looks far removed from what audiences would have experienced in townships), Lefty as a repositioned apartheid-era version of Priest becomes ever more evident and even quite audacious.

Unlike Priest in *Super Fly*, Lefty is eventually cornered outside his house – as he 'escapes' from his bedroom window with a bag of money that he has been hiding from both the law and his wife and daughter – and shot dead. In this moment we might conclude that *iKati Elimnyama* fulfils its purpose as propaganda, of warning against a criminal life, but one is still not entirely convinced. Fred Williamson is also shot dead at the end of *Black Caesar*, and yet the world depicted in the film's narrative belongs entirely to him and his badass persona remains secure beyond the end credits. His death, (which would later be reworked for a sequel), in other words, does not necessarily distract from the enviable and lavish lifestyle that the character has been shown enjoying – especially because the other characters in the film are not permitted any heroics in their own right: *everyone is corrupt*. Similarly, whilst audiences may have had sympathy for Lefty's wife and daughter, neither the police nor the gangsters in *iKati Elimnyama* offer replacement figures. Ultimately, *iKati Elimnyama* shows how the badass blaxploitation persona of Priest in *Super Fly* could be interpreted into a compromised setting by a director who was aware of blaxploitation presentations as well as the need to placate the censorious confines he worked within. That Sabela could achieve so much, whilst everything from script to production was monitored by the state, is nothing short of astonishing, and criticising him for what he could not do seems to miss the point of embarking upon a subversive adaptation of pioneering, and transgressive, American blaxploitation cinema. It is also tempting to believe that Sabela's more domineering portrayal of Lefty may also have come from his involvement, just one year earlier, in *Gold*.

The Magic Negro

In *Gold*, Sabela plays King – a mine worker who, in perhaps the film's most famous scene, is onlooker to a violent dressing down that takes place between a Black employee and his white superior. When Roger Moore's character of Slater intervenes, he acknowledges that 'they can't hit back' – meaning the floored, Black African employee. Later in the film, Sabela and Moore attempt to save the mine from being flooded. King ultimately allows himself to die for the sake of the mine, whilst Slater makes it to safety (and wins the girl). Notes Davis: 'tradition demands the sacrifice of the Faithful Servant, for this enhances the stature of the white hero' (1996: 71). Matthew Hughey has spoken about the so-called 'magic negro' figure – a recurring on-screen Hollywood personality that surfaces in films as diverse as Disney's notorious *Song of the South* (Wilfred Jackson, 1946), *The Shawshank Redemption* (Frank Darabont, 1994), *The Matrix* (Lana Wachowski, Lilly Wachowski, 1999) and *Bruce Almighty* (Tom Shadyac, 2003). The character is one that exists to assist a larger, and narratively more important, white character arc – basically the 'Faithful Servant' persona of King, as described by Davis.

Hughey mentions:

> These films all possess a mutual resemblance regarding how the positive and progressive attributes of strong, magic-wielding black characters are circumvented by their placement as servants to broken and down-on-their-luck white characters. This on-screen relationship reinforces a normative climate of white supremacy within the context of the American myth of redemption and salvation whereby whiteness is always worthy of being saved, and strong depictions of blackness are acceptable in so long as they serve white identities. (2009: 548)

In *Gold*, Sabela fits the description of just such a character. In one telling scene, he leads a Zulu dance for a stadium full of white onlookers to appreciate. After which, Moore's Slater takes the film's heroine, Terry, back to his penthouse flat, overlooking the evening skyline of Johannesburg, and attempts to bed her (discovering his playboy lifestyle via a ruffled bed and an empty bottle of champagne, she instead leaves early). Sabela's King is permitted no such love interest and when he allows himself to be killed at the end of the film, for the greater good of saving the mine (and, by extension, allowing Moore's character to live), the sacrifice is interrupted by Slater's reunification with Terry. The white man, in the segregated country, gets the blonde, blue-eyed woman whilst Sabela's King is appreciated only insofar as his labour supports and sustains the apartheid system. This conclusion is put into its proper, obnoxious context when one understands that 'From 1911 until the early 1970s, the real wages of black mineworkers, including food, remained the same' (van der Westhuizen 2007: 67). What exactly, one must ponder, is Sabela's character even sacrificing himself *for*? 'This was a film without any political message, nor did it portray blacks or whites in any controversial manner' insisted actor Roger Moore, speaking without any apparent irony of a motion picture funded from within the apartheid state (2008: 163).

Sabela's King is very much part of a 'normative climate of white supremacy' in *Gold* – in contrast to his role in *iKati Elimnyama*. Whatever we might conclude

Figure 3.3 Compromised by the mainstream, Simon Sabela as the Black saviour character King in *Gold* (Peter R. Hunt, 1974)

from the latter motion picture's decision to have Lefty die at the conclusion of the film – at the hands of two policemen working for the official channels of state law enforcement – Sabela never permits his character to be seen as serving white identities or expectations. On the contrary, his shameless individualism knows no loyalty to anyone, even his own family unit (as this monograph will later explore, this aspect in itself is unique within the B-Scheme pantheon). Seen today and *Gold* offers audiences a reminder of apartheid as a system where Black personalities were as segregated and demoralised on the screen as they were off, but *iKati Elimnyama* at least pays some lip-service to an alternative cinema that, similar to *Joe Bullet*, could flirt with the concept of a rogue, tough, Black South African badass headlining a commercially successful action film. Koven notes how exploitation cinema uses 'topical subject matter' (2010: 12). Sabela's *iKati Elimnyama* has the trappings of a low budget exploitation film from the same period – rape, home invasion, kidnapping, crime, a badass hero and a furious car chase (predicated, no less, on a sense of race-tension). However, Sabela also appears to be making a commentary on – presumably his higher wage-paying – characters such as King in *Gold*: the proverbial magic negro that, if *iKati Elimnyama* is any evidence, he may also have held in disdain.

Following the Information Department scandal, the films that were made for Black audiences, under the B-Scheme initiative, became less ambitious than *iKati Elimnyama*, which from a technical perspective certainly holds its own with some of the lower budgeted blaxploitation variants from America. When Lefty is shot dead at the end of his solitary adventure, so too, we might conclude, was the promise of a more subversive South African blaxploitation cycle. Instead, cheap production values, frequently handheld camerawork and makeshift dialogue became the norm. This is a cinema that Ntshavheni Wa Luruli describes as made to make money. The directors were there for the money. The subsidy schemes, butchers became filmmakers overnight. It was a way of getting money quickly. People would make up a story, go to the township, make films. It was point and shoot. (2016)

South African filmmaker Cedric Sundstrom, who became one of the country's better-known international names thanks to his two *American Ninja* sequels, echoes these feelings:

By the end of 1979 [we had] the Information Scandal in South Africa, when they found that government funding – basically people were putting money into films like *The Wild Geese* or *Golden Rendezvous* (Ashley Lazarus, 1977) or *Tigers Don't Cry* – now these had international directors and they were going to be distributed by Warner Bros. or some big companies but underneath that they were financed [here]. *The Wild Geese* had Richard Harris and Richard Burton, so what they [the financiers] were doing was promoting the image of South Africa by investing taxpayers' money in these kinds of things. But to impress or to give a broader image overseas than was there, there was the cultural boycott and these things. They were paying for these big actors and directors to work here. When that was exposed, Simon Sabela and Heyns films – they suffered too because they disbanded the Department of Information. It all went down in the scandal and I think it killed the Black industry for a long time. (2016)

Nonetheless, despite the fact that genre films featuring an almost all-Black cast, aimed at a local audience, would – in the next decade – possess far lower production values than that seen in the Sabela-directed motion pictures, within such austerity motion pictures, considered lost for decades, we also see some bizarre examples of exploitation cinema. These are films that – in their own right – offer a revealing insight into white paternalism towards the Black majority during the last full decade of apartheid rule. I discuss the rise and fall of the (cheap) B-Scheme phenomenon next.

Notes

1. There was also Gibson Kente, who was imprisoned for one year for filming his stage play *How Long* (1976). When I interviewed Litheko Modisane for this monograph he explained that Kente belongs outside of what he dubbed 'Bantu films', particularly given how political his work was: 'Bantu films were not really politicised films in the strongest sense of the word. The films were being made by white filmmakers and only in the seventies did that change with people such as Simon Sabela. He was the first black filmmaker and then Gibson Kente – who was not really in the system

of Bantu films. He was an independent filmmaker and he sold films – [his work] never saw the light of day or [they] went to [Bantustan] the Transkei' (2016).
2. It might be worth noting here that the ANC's Joe Modise 'was generally assumed . . . to make money out of the drug trade . . . other high ranking ANC folk were known to be involved in the drug trade too' (Johnson 2010: 31).
3. It is worth noting, however, that the apartheid state remained an influence – Maingard notes how a supporting character in *iKati Elimnyama* is horrified to learn that his colleague's first language is Xhosa and not Zulu (2007: 133). One wonders if this is a deliberate attack on Nelson Mandela, obviously the most famous of the ANC political prisoners. However, if so, it does not necessarily permit the character to be heroic – indeed, Sabela may have used the comment to indicate the villainy of supposedly 'good' South Africans vs. his own Lefty.

4. INTO THE BIOSCOPE:

The South African B-Scheme Explosion of the 1980s

Author Ndugu Mike Ssali has discussed how the term 'bioscope' emerged in South Africa in 1898 and has remained the chosen referent for cinema, drive-in, multiplex or mobile picture-house ever since: 'In South Africa people talk about going to the bioscope and not to the cinema' (1996: 86). In recent years, the distribution company Gravel Road Entertainment Group, based in Cape Town, has begun an initiative entitled 'Retro Africa Bioscope', with the aim of restoring a number of low, *low* budget, B-Scheme films, made just a few years after Sabela's *iKati Elimnyama*, which had been considered lost. Their work has allowed for insight into a period of exploitation filmmaking that has been unavailable since the fall of apartheid – a time in which, according to Murray, 'an entire industry was based on the mobile unit distribution system' (1992: 258). Of course, not every ZAxploitation film was part of the B-Scheme – we have seen this with discussion of *Joe Bullet* – but establishing what this system was and detailing some of the productions that emerged just a few years after Sabela's groundbreaking directorial work allows for a greater clarity of the sort of production activity that proved popular, or at least prolific, in the last full decade of the old South Africa. It also, in retrospect, highlights how busy the South African bioscope was, at least in terms of quantity if not in quality. Aside from two texts that have been unavailable for inclusion in this monograph, *Lana Pirana* (1985) and *The Witchdoctor* (1985), both reappraised by Paleker in 2010,[1] this monograph represents the first time that the B-Scheme films of the 1980s have been identified in detail, and discussed, within the academy or within studies of exploitation filmmaking or South African cinema.

The B-Scheme films also permit an interesting study of other local comparisons. For instance, if we place the buddy-convict blaxploitation thriller, *Shamwari* (Clive Harding, 1982), shot in English, set in colonial Salisbury, Rhodesia[2] (now Harare, Zimbabwe) and starring South African actors Ian Yule and Ken Gampu, with the B-Scheme production *Run for Your Life* (made just three years later), also detailing a Black-white friendship, we obtain an interesting concurrency in depictions of race-relations. Whilst the former film, by being independently financed and focused on the global market, might seem to get away with more taboo material (it is certainly much more violent and the dialogue more explicit about race and the rights of the white minority in a fast-changing sub-Saharan Africa), both productions reveal a cynicism and thinly veiled paternalism towards Black South Africans. This factor is akin to Pik Botha and his claims of 'fathering' Angola's Jonas Savimbi (who had ironically been trained by Chinese Maoists, just before the onslaught of the Cultural Revolution[3]). Hence, and as established in the introduction to this study, broader discourse exists between some of South Africa's English-language ZAxploitation films that also exploit race (*Shamwari* is given more attention in Chapter 7) and the shoddier B-Scheme productions that few outside of the townships ever encountered. Not least of this is a shared interest in adapting some of the popular tropes of American blaxploitation cinema into a less racially inflammatory thematic (including in terms of visual and thematic presentation).

Prior to every Gravel Road restoration, a note appears on-screen telling us:

> The following film is one of hundreds that were produced at the height of Apartheid for African audiences with no access to mainstream entertainment. By early 1990, most of these films simply disappeared. In 2013, Gravel Road Entertainment Group launched an initiative to locate and digitally restore these forgotten films for present and future generations.

This declaration is important in the wider discussion of what might constitute an exploitation film. Paul Watson, for instance, has argued that exploitation cinema should not necessarily be separated from the birth and subsequent growth of cinema itself – arguing that just as in 'the prototypical years of cinema, it was cinema itself that was the attraction, not the fictions it projected' – the 'cinema of attractions' (1997: 74). In this regard, Watson ascertains of exploitation a 'genre not in the iconographic or narrative senses, but rather in terms of economic functioning of genre' (Ibid.: 75). The problem in Watson's discussion is that *American* exploitation, as simply *about* sordid body, race, or violent presentations, can be seen to have evolved in the 1960s and 1970s into a paradigm through which only certain kinds of stories (i.e. the hardcore Sartre-inspired sex tragedy *The Devil in Miss Jones* [Gerard Damiano, 1973]) could be told to an audience. The spectacle was still unavoidable, and often as graphic as ever, but exploitation cinema, during this period, began to move away from both the pseudo-documentary approach of old and the classical framework of Hollywood – culminating in such experimentation as the Third Cinema approach of the stylistically impressive *Sweet Sweetback Baadasssss Song*. On the other hand, most of the ZAxploitation output that forms the B-Scheme subsidy is generally focused on providing audiences with only the *distraction* of the moving image rather than projects that might be more easily placed, stylistically, within the coherent and identifiable cinematic language of low budget American blaxploitation.[4]

The South African filmmakers, aware that entertainment was in short supply within the townships of apartheid, understood that making low budget efforts which involved minimal casts and state-approved stories of good citizenship, with long credit sequences and exposition to pad out the running time, was a lucrative business. Murray notes as much, bemoaning how 'Taxpayers funded this largely opportunistic and incompetent section of the industry' (1992: 256) when addressing the B-Scheme years. Attesting to the cynicism of the era, Gus Silber quotes the B-Scheme director-producer Ronnie Isaacs as stating 'You have to give the blacks what they want. They want a picture to take them away from the humdrum of their daily existence' (1992: 268). Quality control, therefore, was secondary to profit, whilst filmmakers such as Isaacs displayed paternalistic perspectives. Consequently, this factor alone makes ZAxploitation a 'cinema of attractions' or maybe (as just aforementioned) *distractions* – but it also, in the purest sense and related mainly to the B-Scheme bulk, allows for it to be termed as a national cinema of exploitation. So much so, that Gairoonisa Paleker wonders what *is* being preserved:

> You know what concerns me about all of this? This rediscovery. This rediscovery – there are some interesting things going on and which I think we need to think about ... Gravel Road have been buying up the copyright and digitally restoring [the films]. But then when I went to see Tonie's award [at the Durban Film Festival] and I did some digging around, I discovered that SABC [South African Broadcasting Corporation] had screened some of his films and hailed them as important discoveries of our heritage. And I am thinking, 'what is going on?' Because in the process of reclamation, being said this is [part of our] lost heritage, I am afraid that what these films represent is getting lost. I understand that there are many of the filmmakers who say they created opportunities for the training of Black people and, yes, many of them got that start as a result of that. But that does not in any way mitigate the

ideological function that these films had and I am worried that in this process of reclaiming these films as a lost heritage that this part might get lost. So, is this a heritage of exploitation? A heritage of being represented as stereotypes? Is that the heritage we are reclaiming? (2016)

In the forthcoming chapters, this study offers a more detailed description of the B-Scheme motion pictures that were made during the 1980s and, in doing so, indicates how they interact with wider popular tropes of global exploitation cinema (indeed, this might be a 'heritage of exploitation'). Stereotypes certainly exist. However, what is most curious about these motion pictures is that the stereotypes are often of idealised Black citizenship – the 'correct' sort of Black African as opposed to the National Party monster: the feared guerrilla, the aspiring pan-African spokesperson, the young idealistic Marxist or small-time gangster. Writing in 1987, Tomaselli would note how

> The popular press views those who transgress or threaten dominant social norms (like drug users, criminals, soccer hooligans, homosexuals, political extremists and so on) as 'outsiders'. By casting such groups as 'folk devils', the media serve to strengthen our degree of commitment to ideas of normal behaviour, and to create a climate of opinion that supports the operations of society's sanctioning agencies. (1987: 31)

Whilst villainous presentations of soccer hooligans or homosexuals in the B-Scheme do not exist in the films of this monograph, the projects almost certainly carry the same fears as South Africa's popular press of the time. The 'folk devils' are now stereotyped as those who seek to disrupt the lives of harmonious Black families and to lead them astray, usually with wayward schemes (which can be interpreted as representing 'dangerous' philosophies – i.e. communism or similar Black liberation thought).

South Africa's original state subsidy scheme for filmmakers, which was introduced in 1956 to support Afrikaans-language cinema, has been documented by Keyan Tomaselli as 'one designed to limit the production of non-commercial films' (1988: 30). By the time of the 1970s, South Africa had a flourishing Afrikaans-language cinema – Tonie van der Merwe himself is responsible for the family favourite *Trompie* (1975) but some of this activity was also genre-orientated (and now also largely obscure if not lost entirely) such as *Ngomopho*. The country's first horror production *Jannie Totsiens* (Jans Rautenbach, 1970) is a visually interesting Polanski-style thriller about a young woman's mental decline and nightmarish visions. Meanwhile, English-language films with an eye on the global market also began to signal popular genre activity. Provocatively titled shockers such as *House of the Living Dead* (Ray Austin, 1974) and *The Demon* (Percival Rubens, 1979) gained international releases, including on

VHS, whilst the lesser-known *Livia* AKA *Amor de Assassino* (Bill Prout-Jones, 1977) draws on the giallo thrillers from Italy, for instance *The Strange Vice of Mrs Wardh* (Sergio Martino, 1971), for its psycho-sexual, murder-mystery narrative. The key to the successful distribution of some of these films was, predictably, hiding where they came from – leading to critic L. A. Morse wondering of *The Demon*: 'there is a curious mix of accents, which suggests that it has been shot in Australia or New Zealand' (1989: 248). These international-orientated efforts, alongside Spaghetti Westerns (see Chapter 6) and director Ivan Hall's low budget, martial arts films *Karate Olympiad* (1977) and *Kill and Kill Again* (1981), which comfortably exist alongside the sight of Ken Gampu in karate outfit in *Joe Bullet*, point to a substantial collection of largely undiscussed South African genre cinema.

Therefore, it should be no surprise that the B-Scheme initiative also attempted to mimic popular international trends. Escapist and often ludicrous, thanks to heavy-handed moralising and depictions of Black South Africans 'doing the right thing' to keep the state (usually reimagined as a local township or suburb) secure, these are films that come shortly after a period in which, as Murray explains, 'it would have been tragically simple for an ethnic film to disappear into obscurity without ever being screened in more than one or two local community halls' (1992: 256). Murray would later expose the fraud of the B-Scheme industry and ascertain the missed opportunity to build an ethnic cinema of less quantity but higher quality. Silber would also note how van der Merwe, prior to making *Joe Bullet* and instigating the genesis of the new South African blaxploitation cinema, was 'running a company that employed 600 blacks, whose recreation needs were met by weekly screenings of American action movies' (1992: 270). Echoing this statement, even in more contemporary writing, there has been a notable disdain towards what African cinema might be drawing its inspirations from.

Discussing the phenomenon of Nollywood, for instance, Jonathan Haynes writes:

> Almost from the moment of cinema's invention, Africa has been inserted into its global system, but on the most unfavourable terms: it has been the dumping ground for second-run 'B' movies from Hollywood, Bollywood and Hong Kong, films that are often racist and always estranged from African realities and purposes, while the formidable technical, infrastructural, and capital requirements of making and distributing films made it nearly impossible for Africans to respond in kind with their own films. (2011: 67)

As detailed in the previous chapter, dated imports were certainly screened on the mobile circuit and in township cinemas such as the Eyethu in Soweto, but there is a distinct snobbery in assuming that such a theatre was merely a 'dumping ground' for inferior, or racist, films by dictate of budget or that van der Merwe's choice of American action (presumably blaxploitation) cinema was unsuited to South Africa's majorities or even its minorities. Indeed, Mikal J. Gaines has written about how the B-films of William Castle and Roger Corman proved popular with African American audiences in the 1950s and 60s, not least of all because they highlighted narratives that could be appraised from a progressive perspective. 'Black spectators would probably have recognised the irony in seeing a white man reduced to the status of a slave, and then coerced into feeding his own kind to an alien master', says the author of Corman's *The Little Shop of Horrors* (1960) (2014: 192). Thus, whilst the inspiration of Hong Kong's classic martial arts output on films such as *Beware Tiger* (Michelle Hartslief, 1986) and the Ronnie Isaacs cheapie *One More Shot* is evident, it is difficult to conclude that this aspect should be seen from an entirely negative perspective. *One More Shot*, for instance, has a local kung-fu enthusiast called Chan and his best friend, the aptly named Johnny Tough (played by Hector Rabotabi), team-up to take down a multicultural mob of criminals – led by a white man and a number of intimidating cohorts, supported by a Black gangster called Ten-Ten and protected by an Arab millionaire who specialises in human trafficking. Despite some unpleasant stereotypes (particularly the Arab slave traders) Chan and Tough end the film in victory, pointing to the strength of a unified minority.

Cedric Sundstrom also mentions:

> Here in South Africa, with Black audiences, the [most popular] was the Western, the gangster film and definitely the Hong Kong and martial arts films. They loved these. We were in Lesotho for *American Ninja 4*, because [the star] Michael Dudikoff would not film in South Africa in case he got blacklisted. So, we were in Lesotho, and word had got around that he was in the area. Here we were, in a rural, middle-of-nowhere kind of thing, especially when you think of our locations, and this little boy came running to the set: 'Where is Michael Dudikoff?'

If anything, therefore, one may argue that ethnic heroes, from lower budgeted foreign cinema, provide a grounding for aspirational portrayals – even if it is just as 'badass' personas within the apartheid state (see Chapter 6) or as karate experts, whether Black or even white (itself, surely, initiating a multicultural dialogue that was mostly absent in Afrikaans language films from the same period). It might also be noted that the ZAxploitation films avoid some of the Orientalism of their American counterparts. Little commented upon, for instance, is the scene in *Cotton Comes to Harlem* in which an African American martial artist is degraded with the line 'when did you turn Japanese?' Similarly,

Figure 4.1 Two of the main faces of B-Scheme cinema, Popo Gumede (sometimes credited as Innocent Gumede, left) and Hector Mathanda (right), pictured in *Fishy Stones* (Tonie van der Merwe, 1989)

in *Hell Up in Harlem* (Larry Cohen, 1973), Fred Williamson's Tommy Gibbs remarks to a friend about a plan to smash a Japanese crime syndicate, 'I know you can handle some of those Japanese guys . . . Pearl Harbour on them, right?' *Cleopatra Jones and the Casino of Gold* (Charles Bail, 1975) highlights veteran Hong Kong performer Chan Shen as a Fu Manchu caricature. In contrast, for all its storytelling and technical flaws, *Beware Tiger* turns a young, Black Durban resident and his goal to complete his martial arts training in Japan into an audible character and narrative arc. With this factor established, the current chapter and those that follow refuse to accept a correlation between commercial and/or 'artier' products and quality and/or positive influence. Or, to quote André Bazin, 'maybe the notion of the B-film is open to dispute since everything depends on how far up the scale you put the letter A' (1971: 153). Speaking about the discovery of the 'lost' ZAxploitation films, Gravel Road founder and CEO Benjamin Cowley states:

> In 2013 I was fortunate enough to meet Tonie [van der Merwe] in regard to finance because he was trying to raise [money] to make another movie.

> I did not know anything about the man when I first met him but then he began to tell me about his history and about these old movies he had lying in his garage. Six movies, actually, and one of them was *Joe Bullet*. I had heard about it but never taken too much interest in it – I only knew there was an elusive *Joe Bullet* movie. Then he said that nobody wanted to watch his movies anymore. I said, "Well let me take them and see what I can do with them" and that is where we are now. Soon six movies became ten movies and then twenty movies ... this thing just grew – and we found our niche in terms of being able to digitally restore old movies. We set up the very first restoration centre in Africa, in Cape Town. (2016)

Whilst van der Merwe has been mentioned already in this monograph, particularly with regards to his production of *Joe Bullet* and his direction of the later *Bullet on the Run*, his work will be addressed throughout the monograph, particularly given his reputation as 'one of the major players' in the initiative (Paleker 2010: 93). Recently, his frequent leading man Popo Gumede went so far as to claim, 'Tonie is an icon that happened by accident' (Onishi 2014). Certainly, his lifetime achievement award at the Durban Film Festival in 2014 at least *demands* acknowledgement of his role in the industry, if not also a new appraisal that, just a decade ago, seemed unlikely. In the coming chapters, however, it is hoped that other previously unacknowledged filmmakers may also achieve a presence in future studies of South African cinema, if even just as personalities that embarked upon and profited from a number of cynical Black representations.

'Artless' Motion Pictures

Botha notes that at least 250 films were made under the B-Scheme and 'screened in churches, schools and community and beer halls' (2012: 115). The author goes on to describe the films as 'shoddy', believing that they only offer 'uniformly negative' portrayals of Black people and depictions of 'homeland life as more fitting' than urban existence (Ibid.). Paleker is similarly dismissive, if a lot more detailed, stating that 'the production values and standards of the majority of B-Scheme films cannot be deemed artistic in even the broadest terms' (2010: 94). Whilst it is difficult to deny that most of these films are 'shoddy', they do demonstrate a cinematic language that is entirely of their own, however unintentional this might be. Discussing cinemagoing in the old South Africa, Trevor Taylor mentions that:

> Twenty years ago a certain brand of film filled the tearoom cinemas, the drive-ins, the 16mm movie-hire out-lets – a brand of cinema variously referred to as B-pictures, exploitation pictures or 'crap', establishing film-

makers such as Roger Corman, Jesús Franco, Lucio Fulci and Anthony M Dawson, to name but a few. (1992: 131)

In recent years, indicating that such highbrow/lowbrow commentary is not guaranteed to stand the test of time, such directors have been given far greater attention by scholars and home video labels, to the extent that Stefano Baschiera mentions Fulci's general acceptance as a 'canonised "horror auteur"' (2016: 48). However, it is the fast-and-free approach of Spain's Jesús Franco that has kinship with the style of the B-Scheme. Whilst Franco could make films of high-quality – dubbed 'simply stunning' by Joan Hawkins – he was also, per the same author, capable of being 'sloppy . . . makes his films quickly . . . narrative continuity is totally jettisoned for the sake of affect or economy' (2008: 178). Or per L. A. Morse on *Women in Cellblock 9* (1977): 'Ridiculously cheap, shoddy, and inept' (1990: 187). It is this version of Franco, the one who could be hired to oversee woeful genre films such as *White Cannibal Queen* (1980) and *Oasis of the Zombies* (1981), that we see in many a B-Scheme effort – rushed out to meet demand but, in the process, presenting a style that is strangely, unexpectedly distinct. This 'style' might be disregarded as 'incompetent' and also 'jettisons' narrative continuity and even common sense, but it does give the various ZAxploitation benchmarks a presentation that is notably unique if also rooted in similar exploitation networks of cheap and fast turnaround, such as those of Franco.

Handheld camerawork, natural lighting, set pieces that are spoken about but rarely shown, paternalistic depictions of Black servitude to the state and lengthy opening credit sequences or long, boring B-rolls of city or township life, disco dancing, characters walking or driving, result in a cluster of films that are certainly *of* this location and this period. Watching some of the B-Scheme efforts, particularly those based around action-detective plots, can best be described as if someone remade *Shaft* but removed every moment of Richard Roundtree engaging in any exciting moments of conflict. Occasionally, however, these films *do* surprise. *Rich Girl* (Tonie van der Merwe, 1985) and *Mine Boy* are discussed in some detail in Chapters 8 and 10 respectively, whilst *Black Crusader*, *One More Shot* and *Bona Manzi* (or *Look, Water*, Tonie van der Merwe, 1989) feature Black-white antagonism and, on a narrative level, side with their heroic Black protagonist(s). Even this factor might be news to established authors on the continent's cinema. For instance, Nwachukwu Frank Ukadike mentions how the blockbuster *The Gods Must Be Crazy* (Jamie Uys, 1980) 'showed blacks and whites working or dining together' and acknowledges how this could only be depicted because Uys had shot 'most of the scenes' in Botswana (1994: 56). In actual fact, this conclusion is incorrect: even previous South African films such as *Death of a Snowman* show interaction between the races and a handful of B-Scheme motion pictures also present mixed-race friendships and rivalries. In other words, within the wider study of African cinema, much has still to be acknowledged about what the low budget, apparently apolitical, genre cinema of apartheid – its *ZAxploitation* – present as changing, even evolving, depictions of Black screen agency in and out of the continent.

Writer-director Karen Thorne, who made one of the most visually experimental B-Scheme films in *Mine Boy*, also maintains how conditions on the set of the Black subsidy productions were sometimes preferable to those in the mainstream South African film industry. She states of the television and film business at the time:

> I was so disgusted by what went on on-set, the racism and sexism and the rubbish people were making. I didn't enjoy working with the sort of people that dominated the industry at that time. Coke-snorting, fast-living, the women performing the women's roles and the men in charge and the Black people knowing their place in the pecking order. I found that disgusting, actually. (2016)

Thorne had become an anti-apartheid activist during her time at Rhodes University and when it came to making *Mine Boy*, she was becoming increasingly involved with video collectives which were documenting the sort of footage the apartheid state did not want the world to see (as discussed in Chapter 10):

> It was probably the best film school I ever experienced. We would have a week to write the script, a week to shoot the film and two weeks to edit them. We were making them for something like 50,000 rand – that was the subsidy scheme ... We were living in Joburg at the time and we travel to Limpopo, we went all over ... These were very simple stories and towards the end of that period, we started to experiment with working in communities such as Soweto and coming up with an idea for a film. The example I'm thinking of is *Mine Boy*, which is a classic coming-of-age-tale about a rural boy who comes to the big city and gets mixed up with this Shebeen Queen who takes him under her wing and he gets influenced by the bad guys. I was directing the film, but I found a lot of characters who were real Shebeen Queens and we workshopped it among the cast and made it up [that way]. And today, as much as I directed the film, I had no idea what it was about [*laughs*]. I more facilitated this group process where the actors made it. It was amazing to have the space to have that ability to work in experimental and amazing ways. (2016)

Thus, to claim that everyone involved in the B-Scheme film initiative was 'going along with government "studies" that supposedly showed that Blacks were not intelligent enough to encounter adult-orientated cinema that might confuse them or raise their ambitions' (McCluskey 2009: 5) is untrue. In some of the interviews that were conducted for this monograph, directors (including some international names who refused to participate[5]) mentioned that filmmaking in the country was generally being used a cover for fraud – a factor that, as established in the first chapter of this study, Murray exposed, relating to the B-Scheme, nearly three decades ago. Others, however, have argued that the subsidy gave some Black technicians a training ground.

Coenie Dippenaar, for instance, mentions: 'A lot of our black actors were also good on the technical side, they would handle cameras, sound and boom and things like that' (2016). Doubtlessly this was not well-paid labour, but Dippenaar's comments echo those of Ntshavheni Wa Luruli about 'unintended consequences' and how this environment led to Black motion picture professionals working in South African film. As a network, however, the B-Scheme was often a get-rich-quick formula for enterprising directors and producers resulting in poor quality output or, as Murray mentions, 'Some of the films presented were so bad that no one in his right mind could have wanted to see them' (1992: 258).

Some B-Scheme films, however, at least pay service to contemporary political concerns or controversial topics: *The Faceless Man* (Carl Bleakley, 1985), for instance, asks post-Muldergate audiences to witness a police chief embroiled in corruption. *Bona Manzi* features a Black game warden who is committed to protecting South Africa's livestock from opportunistic white poachers. *Mine Boy* engages with safe sex and abortion, and the violent *Doomsday* touches on the township unrest of the mid-1980s which resulted in 'seventy thousand police' being stationed in hot spots such as Soweto (Welsh 2000: 490). *Doomsday* even concludes with all of the gang members dead and with a reverend giving the main character his last rites. Whilst this grim scenario replays the 'crime does not pay' motif of many of the B-Scheme narratives, it also, unavoidably, points to such areas as places of danger if not explicitly revolutionary activity (although it subtly hints at this aspect). This sort of turmoil is in complete juxtaposition to many other films of the period, which present South African Black life as one that is content, humble, and usually satisfied by the presence of a loving family unit. These may have been rare exceptions, but a film such as *Doomsday* also fulfils genre requirements – it is gritty and action-packed, and its characters are given clear goal-motivation.

Furthermore, previous discussions of the B-Scheme have ostracised them as failing to convey any sense of Africana (even when van der Merwe's *Bona Manzi*, for instance, is set on a reserve for endangered rhinos and other wildlife fulfilling, however superficially, the average Joe's image of 'Africa'). Botha, for instance, introduces the harrowing, award-winning documentary *Last Grave at Dimbaza* (Chris Curling, Pascoe Macfarlane, 1974) into his brief overview

Figure 4.2 Emmanuel Shangase (sometimes credited as Dumi or Dumisani Shongwe), another recurring B-Scheme face, and Hector Mathanda in *The Faceless Man* (Carl Bleakley, 1985)

of the B-Scheme films (2012: 116) but it is unclear as to what point this fulfils. *Last Grave at Dimbaza* gives viewers a shocking insight into the nature of the apartheid state, segregated living and the grim reality of a modern, wealthy nation built on slave labour. The expository narration to the (illegally filmed) documentary strongly suggests that a cultural boycott – largely from major American and British conglomerates – might go some way to toppling the apartheid government (and, in the end, such a boycott most likely helped). To expect anything as political or provocative from films made with state-funding and geared towards a township audience, in some cases captive to what played before them, seems curious.

As cynical as most of the B-Scheme ZAxploitation films are, however, it is not helpful to retrospectively separate them from blaxploitation in general – especially when, as previously established, many of the films that emerged after the likes of *Shaft* and *Super Fly* were funded with white capital and written/directed by white filmmakers. The very existence of these spin-off films meant that American International Pictures (AIP), producers of such hits as *Coffy* (Jack Hill, 1973), found themselves targeted by offended viewers: 'an unnamed

Black militant group torched the car of Richard Zimbert, AIP vice president, while it was parked on the company lot' (Lawrence 2005: 96). Although it goes without saying that the United States in the 1970s and 1980s was not apartheid-era South Africa, it is also worth maintaining that it is doubtful that popular blaxploitation directors such as Matt Cimber, Jack Hill or Arthur Marks had any particular insight into urban, ethnic minority issues when they made their respective films in the field. Seen today, some of the dialogue in the white-directed blaxploitation films makes for uncomfortable viewing. To return to the aspect of Orientalism, a young woman of Chinese ancestry being labelled a 'sweet piece of Oriental meat' in *Truck Turner*, for instance, has not aged well. As such, it is not entirely fair to single out the South African variants for being generic or even racially naïve; but it is surely correct to critique their thematic within the wider motifs and representations that made blaxploitation popular.

Discussing comedy, Rick Altman mentions how 'we have a series of categories that have become more or less loosened from the parent genre: burlesque, farce, masque, screwball, slapstick, and so on' (1999: 51). If blaxploitation, at least following the success of *Shaft*, was 'just' a series of detective thrillers that further 'loosened' into incorporating femme-fatales such as Pam Grier, espionage, buddy-cop movies, prison narratives, race-conflict and martial arts, then there is no reason not to see the mostly all-Black films of the B-Scheme as a further demarcation within a trend that had already splintered into increasingly outlandish stories. Speaking about the lesser-known blaxploitation horror film *Ganja and Hess* (Bill Gunn, 1974), for example, authors James Robert Parish and George H. Hill quote a review from a perplexed reviewer in *Variety* of the time: 'The nudity ... is so much an element of the film that one tends to think of it as a sex film with blood' (2019: 198). Similarly, it is worth noting that the B-Scheme films also splinter into Spaghetti Westerns, horror efforts and even slapstick comedies and juvenile delinquent stories. Although the bulk of the productions that have been viewed for this project do veer towards narratives of gangsters and crime – even a melodrama such as *Ezintandaneni* (or *Orphans*, Tonie van der Merwe, 1987) contains vigilantism and a police investigation – the settings are not always ones in which a rogue tough guy or trigger-happy lawman has to resolve the narrative. As genre films, a hybrid-blaxploitation, it should also be considered that the B-Scheme projects were not made with any intention to be understood or even seen by a non-localised audience, including academics forty years later and over a quarter of a century after the fall of the apartheid system. As such, perhaps it is necessary to remain aware of their very genesis as a cinema *of* exploitation.

SEARCHING FOR IDENTITY

This book has touched upon the use of local languages in ZAxploitation and the B-Scheme films might be seen, however perversely, to follow a key aspect of Third Cinema dogma in this regard. Does, for instance, the use of the Zulu tongue necessarily indicate a South African identity? At the very least, one could argue that it offers some clarity and immediacy to viewers regarding nationality – although it is worth noting that, commenting on the Cuban zombie film *Juan of the Dead* (Alejandro Brugués, 2010), author Johnny Walker identifies it as Spanish (2014: 226). In other words, language might not be as oppositional to our own preconceived idea of what constitutes art and/ or genre, especially when it can confuse as a signifier of identity. Indeed, *Juan of the Dead* is a postmodern and arguably even post-Third Cinema example of a Cuban political satire mixed with George Romero-style blood and gore. Identifying it as Spanish, based only on the language, indicates a certain Euro-prominence that still frames popular perspectives on cinema, but so too might revisiting old ZAxploitation films and concluding that their Zulu soundtracks *are only there* to appease the B-Scheme subsidy deny them a key specification in their own right. With the B-Scheme films, we have a sense of the 'local' that is outside of the Afrikaans-language cinema of the same period, surprisingly lacking in South African cinema. Paleker has mentioned that the B-Scheme films had to be in an African language (2010: 92) but during this research some exceptions have emerged, including *Charlie Steel*, *One More Shot* and *The Priest and the Thief* (Wanna Fourie, 1980s), which is a very cheaply made (even by the standards of the time) comedy-farce. These are, however, rare.[6]

Certainly, B-Scheme stories of good citizenship and resisting criminal temptation remain in opposition to the radical concurrent African-nationalism of the ANC, not to mention any kind of anti-colonial thought. Du Bois himself would discuss how freedom is unrelated to labour so long as the opportunities afforded to the Black man, even if free from slavery or segregation, are across unequal lines:

> And after the first flush of freedom wore off, and his true helplessness dawned on the freedman, he came back and picked up his hoe, and old master still doled out his bacon and meal. The legal form of service was theoretically for daily toil in gangs; and the slave gradually became a metayer, or tenant on shares, in name, but a labourer with indeterminate wages in fact. (1903: 89)

Whilst Du Bois, one of the most prominent thinkers during the European colonial period in Africa (the house in which he died remains a key tourist attraction in Accra), is speaking about America after the Civil War, it is nonetheless relevant to attribute such compromised labour to the cinema discussed here. The idea of a 'free' Black cinema in South Africa, during apartheid, is nonsensical. The actors and, at times, scriptwriters or crew of the B-Scheme, in particular, worked within a subsidy that at least called for *a certain kind* of story; even *Mapantsula* – which was amazingly seen through until completion – had ongoing problems from the state during and after production (Gugler 2003: 91). The juxtaposition of this situation, however, is that, just as white-made American blaxploitation films would become reliant on dubious and repetitive portrayals of imagined Black militancy (usually a tough male beating up 'whitey' naively presented to equate with African American 'liberation'), the bulk of the B-Scheme stories *cannot* admit that apartheid is immoral or even 'not working'. Tomaselli would affirm that 'development of a progressive film culture . . . will remain an essential aspect of the democratic process' in South Africa (1992: 360) and there should be no doubt that seeking to identify such 'progression' in the old B-Scheme texts is ill-advised.

For instance, the Chinese and Black buddies of *One More Shot* might 'win the day' but, at the end, they are shown smiling, back in a local rural area, populated only by Black inhabitants, potentially even back 'across borders' in a Bantustan, as the local people engage in a traditional dance. This scene, more than any other perhaps, typifies what Tomaselli means by the 'urban-conditional'. With the job done, the non-white heroes are back where they 'belong', and whilst the dialogue does not acknowledge this factor, the visuals most certainly do and would perhaps relate such to the audience of the time. Presumably, *the idea* that the ethnic minorities, after defeating white gangsters, would still be shown contently back in the 'homelands' or township was enough to ensure *One More Shot* avoided censorship problems. The result of this is that the on-screen heroic Black characters exist in uneasy tension between real life segregation and storyline worlds where apartheid is only implied, if it even surfaces at all.

Ivondwe is a cheap horror film about a 'wild man' with long sharp fingernails (likely a nod to Freddy Krueger or Brazil's José Mojica Marins) which features a scene in which a local Reverend, played by Popo Gumede, meets a great white hunter. The pair converse in Zulu, with the Reverend explaining his opposition to trophy hunting. The white man welcomes his advice but admits of the local community (named on-screen as Durban), 'What irritates me the most is people complain too much'. In other words, Black and white alike can have civil interactions in the old South Africa – *just know your place and stop complaining*. Fittingly, the 'threat' of the narrative is the wild man, 'Ivondwe', a savage Black character who causes havoc when he escapes into the civilised world of Durban. City life is not, clearly, for 'this' sort of Black man (returning us to the typical Mr Wrong) – but, perversely, in the world of *Ivondwe*, it is acceptable for a man of the Church to be located in the (conditional) urban. There is no easy answer, therefore, to the compromises that the Black B-Scheme ensemble made in order to appear in cinema that mainly forbade dissent and radicalism. However, it is probably through incorporating such themes as good citizenship into their narratives that the B-Scheme films become so obviously *of* apartheid and yet their design and production methods are, outside perhaps (and this is still a slight stretch) of the more recent examples of Nollywood and related West African cinema such as Ghana's shot-on-video boom, quite unique. Discussing the Ghanaian film business, which as with Nigeria contains a number of film productions with narratives of Christian redemption (complicating, one might argue, how we choose to engage with postcolonial representations in some African cinemas), Carmela Garritano mentions the presence of 'entrepreneurial amateurs, who were paid to produce escapist rubbish for profit' (2013: 93). This comment might be attributed to the cinema of the B-Scheme, if the race-relations were not so compromised – a cinema where budgets and ambition are in short supply and, doubtlessly, low-level wages afforded to the Black cast and crew permitted a steady stream of labour. In such an atmosphere of profit, on cheap output, the chance for 'African art made for the good of the nation' (Ibid., 94) is as challenging in some sub-Saharan countries on the continent now as it was for even the privileged white filmmakers of the B-Scheme who were sustained by a system that was endemically corrupt.

Mitch Dyter, whose list of B-Scheme credits as a producer include *Gone Crazy* (Tony Cunningham, 1980s), *Hostage* (Michele Hartslief, 1986), *Ransom* (Tony Cunningham, 1980s) and *Under Cover* (Tony Cunningham, 1989), mentions:

> The government was offering a subsidy – they would pay you so many cents per ticket [sold]. But that is how it began to become corrupt ... a lot of film producers, if I can call them film producers, would make a movie with some substance in it and others would take two cameras and film a football match. That would be taken and shown to the so-called people in the locations as we called them [the townships] in those days. There were film producers who enjoyed it and others who just filmed an entire soccer match ... For [our films] we would sometimes approach these Black people who were not really actors. We would not give them a script. We would sit and tell them what to say then we would edit it. That is how we would put the whole movie together. For me and the other guys that was the exciting part. To see the end result. Some [other] people never had a script – and some would write the script on the back of a cigarette box. And you might have ten minutes of someone walking towards you because you needed to have about 60-minutes for the subsidy to kick in. (2016)

The need for a film to be almost sixty minutes long explains the substantial exposition in the B-Scheme motion pictures. It is also worth mentioning that Murray affirms that, from the mid-1980s onwards, it was actually to be a little longer: 'A new rule was immediately instigated to ensure that films for black subsidy were to run for at least 70 minutes. This made for some extremely long title sequences and even longer scenes in some films' (1992: 264). The general running time for the B-Scheme films covered in this monograph is between sixty and seventy minutes, so Dyter is more likely to be remembering correctly – although some do not even achieve this goal (Tonie van der Merwe's *Bona Manzi*, made in 1989, runs to just fifty-seven minutes). The 'padding' of running time is worth explaining further so that readers will comprehend quite how corrupt B-Scheme filmmaking could be. To give some especially absurd examples: *Fishy Stones* (Tonie van der Merwe, 1989) has a two-and-a-half-minute opening credits sequence where someone on a typewriter slowly keys out the names of the main cast and crew. Almost the entire first ten minutes of *One More Shot* contains cutaways between (presumably South) African locals performing a dance in sparsely populated land, wearing tribal attire, and two white people (unnamed and never seen again) breakdancing on a disco floor. *Run for Your Life* features no less than *twelve-and-a-half minutes* of two men jogging out to a reservoir as infuriating canned music plays on a loop. *Run for Your Life*, which only plays for a little over sixty-one minutes, also boasts an opening title sequence showing two men, in different houses, preparing for their jog by getting dressed, filling a water bottle, taking an energy pill and putting on aftershave. This runs for *seven-and-a-half* minutes. Van der Merwe's *Ukuzingela* (or *Treasure Hunter*, 1989) has several minutes of three shipwrecked white characters making their way from the sea to the sand and into the African bush, all depicted in real-time and taking up much of the first act. The B-Scheme films unravel at a pace that is uncinematic. Real-time footage of everyday events (such as putting on clothes or ordering a drink at a bar) is not the exception but the norm. Narratives, meanwhile, tend to focus on 'good' Black people, usually husbands or boyfriends but sometimes children who unravel a criminal plot on their own and show themselves to be mature beyond their years. Dialogue sounds improvised and cost-cutting stretches to using the same canned soundtrack across films. For instance, Tony Cunningham repeats the same music across his work (a monotonous electro-beat that appears to have been produced on a solitary keyboard) and even some of the same opening credits.

Regarding the paternalism that white residents of the country would frequently exhibit towards the Black majority, author Henry Kenney notes former South African Prime Minister Hendrik Verwoerd telling a 'tribal spokesman to speak to him "as a child to his father" ... He thought of blacks as children who would take a long time to grow up' (2016: 129). It is this kind

Figure 4.3 B-Scheme regular Hector Mathanda runs for his life in *Beware Tiger* (Michelle Hartslief, 1986)

of paternalism that surfaces in so many of these films – most explicitly in the films of van der Merwe that feature child heroes. *Abathumbi* (or *The Kidnapper*, 1985), *Bona Manzi*, *Ezintandaneni*, *Fishy Stones*, *Mandla* (1980s) and *Isiboshwa* (or *Prisoner*, 1989) all highlight youths who manage to curtail a criminal scheme.[7] In these films, youth aspiration and devotion to family/ friendship is rewarded within the narrative (dialogue might be about working hard at school, repeated ad nauseum for instance) – and sometimes against uneven odds. In *Fishy Stones*, the two robbers call their teenage adversaries 'mutts', 'runts' and 'brats' and carry guns, but they underestimate their young rivals and are foiled.

Mandla is a home invasion film starring the twosome of Popo Gumede and Hector Mathanda, perhaps best described as a Bud Spencer/Terence Stamp pairing with the latter usually cast as the bumbling 'comedy' sidekick to the former's 'straight' man. Here the two are convicted of robbery (after a motor- way car chase that looks unsafe and was almost certainly filmed without per- mission), escape from prison and eventually break into a middle-class house, taking two young boys hostage until their parents arrive back home. In one notably tasteless scene, Mathanda jokes about how he and his sidekick could 'eat bananas' as they find themselves wandering through some desolate fields, hungry, outside their prison cells. By comparison, the young boys are shown as smart, hardworking and devoted to their mother and father. Unsurprisingly, they help to foil the criminals. In other instances, van der Merwe's paternalism is expressed via depictions of African youths who reject European modernity. In *Isiboshwa*, for instance, three boys camp out in the woods. One of the trio gazes at the stars and says, 'This is how life was. No care and no electricity' and when his friend responds, 'Today, life is much better', he is told that, 'Now there are all sorts of evil spirits'. To foil two escaped robbers (again played by Gumede and Mathanda) in *Isiboshwa*, the boys work closely together, channelling the spirit of Shaka Zulu, and set ridiculous booby traps for the two men.

B-Scheme films also commonly conclude with the Mr Right characters being rewarded (and it is almost always *Mr* Right, not Mrs Right), sometimes even by a spontaneous act of God, for their inclination to avoid temptation (usually related to some sort of criminal means).[8] The hero of *Beware Tiger*, a twenty-something martial arts practitioner called (rather tastelessly) Dark (Hector Siswe), repeatedly tells a local drug smuggling operation that he wants nothing to do with them and will not take their money (or even join them for an alcoholic beverage) to work as a bodyguard, despite him needing the cash to complete his karate training in Tokyo. The major plot points involve Dark being asked again and again to reconsider (thus padding out the running time) At the end of the film, with the villains foiled, Dark tells his fiancée Thandi that he has won a cash prize in a local tournament that will fund his flight to Japan. This sort of revelation is common to the B-Scheme, but there is also an aesthetic strangeness in place. In other low budget genre cinema, the karate tournament would be a major set piece and we would see Dark winning (a cheap and concurrent Italian comparable from this period, *Karate Warrior* [Fabrizio De Angelis, 1987], for instance, manages to follow this basic formula). However, presumably devoid of the energy and money to stage such a comparatively lavish event, this competition is simply given lip-service in *Beware Tiger* to explain the narrative resolution. In addition, the ending, in which the Tiger infiltrates the local drug lords and their tiny office, leads to two of the villains simply running down the street, chased by the martial arts 'hero' who seeks to kill them. We never learn of their fate – again, perhaps because staging a complex and effective karate showdown was more trouble than it was worth.

This sort of cost-cutting happens throughout the B-Scheme films. In *Ivondwe*, for instance, the film concludes with Hector Mathanda's monstrous man-beast being eaten by crocodiles after a park ranger chases him into a swamp. We hear the man's screams off-screen and see his capsized boat but there is no attempt to show us the set piece itself. The audience is not even

Figure 4.4 Hector Mathanda in *Ivondwe* (Louis De Witt, 1986)

offered a 'pay-off', which makes *Ivondwe* out-of-sync with even the cheapest straight-to-VHS horror film of its era. Rape is a commonly-used plot element in the films of van der Merwe, as well as others, but – unusually for exploitation films – no attempt is made to show us the act. When the main female character is raped and killed in the township thriller *Uthemba* (Rudi Mayer, 1980), we only learn about this via the dialogue of another character after-the-fact. Reviewing *Gone Crazy*, a perplexed modern critic would discuss the uneventful conclusion that pits a local, heroic mayor against a terrorist: 'the film's climactic action sequences are boring – try not to laugh at a fight scene where almost no punches are thrown' (Foster 2018). Yet, the avoidance of major set pieces is a recurring tactic of the B-Scheme, again attesting to how these films have a strange, sometimes even surrealist, cinematic language that is uniquely their own.

The message of good citizenship is at times overbearing, particularly as it relates to marriage and aspiring for a life of peace and harmony. In the B-Scheme production *The Comedians* (Japie van der Merwe, 1980)[9], a township local called Mr Bona convinces his neighbour to lend him a magic ring to help his sick wife: 'even the traditional healers can't help' he pleads, suggesting how the director must have viewed the inhabitants' relationship with modernity. Once the ring is in hand, however, Mr Bona uses it to gain immediate riches but his greed eventually destroys him, indicating that the Black majority are not 'ready' to become consumers in their own land. 'They'll all learn their lesson,' smirks Mr Bona's neighbour and the owner and guarantor of the ring. Mr Bona and his new, small group of henchmen, meanwhile, seek to take over more land and implement rule-by-decree, thus becoming the typical African 'big man' or Mr Wrong. Van der Merwe explores a similar character arc for his Black leads in the film *Ukuzingela*, where their gluttony eventually consumes them and leads to their deaths.

Adds Litheko Modisane:

> You had a state that was at the apex of control and policing people but on the other hand you had independent [film] producers in the country. If you think about it, any system, no matter how oppressive – there will always be loopholes. So, you had people bringing them [American blaxploitation films] in from the outside. Of course, if they were to be judged by the apartheid state, they would never approve them. These films were clearly not a part of the racialised message that the state was selling. *Shaft*, for instance, was actually giving audiences of that time an image of a macho Black man with an organic, strong agency and that type of social entity is unheard of during apartheid. (2016)

Nevertheless, there also remain some comparable elements with American blaxploitation films insofar as the mode of production in the B-Scheme is concerned. For example, just as – in particular – American International Pictures had a number of performers who would become associated with their blaxploitation cinema releases, such as Pam Grier, Yaphet Kotto and Fred Williamson, the same faces emerge across the B-Scheme cinema of South Africa. The gap-toothed Hector Mathanda, who is also credited as a writer on some of his films, plays a similarly comical 'big man' character across a number of motion pictures, whilst his frequent co-star Popo Gumede (sometimes credited as Innocent Gumede) is usually given a more handsome, positive 'tough-guy' role to undertake. Gumede is labelled as a 'badass for the B-Scheme' in Chapter 6. Other notable stars include Dumisani Shongwe, typically given similar 'nice guy' roles in which he tackles local small-time gangsters, although occasionally performing as a villain when the more handsome Gumede has been available to take on the lead. The middle-aged Pepsi Mabizela is another recognisable performer who fluctuates between villainy and the more lived-in narrative 'voice of reason' (he is the older, rotund 'action' hero of *Gone Crazy*, a strange piece of miscasting). Actress Kay Magubane is frequently cast as a victim or perennial love interest/doting and hardworking wife, as seen in *Ambushed*.

Whilst the films that these actors perform in are often of evident low quality,

Figure 4.5 Another fixture of the B-Scheme – Pepsi Mabizela in *Gone Crazy* (Tony Cunningham, 1980s)

it would be wrong to disparage *their performances* as lazy or disconnected. The rotund Mathanda in particular shows himself to be a convincing comedy actor and boasts exceptional expressions and body language. Mathanda is perhaps the closest the B-Scheme cluster has to a flagship star. He is also, with Gampu and Sabela excepted, the most memorable presence from the wider ZAxploitation cycle and shows himself to be a talented character actor in even his least demanding work. His performance as the grunting, monstrous Ivondwe, for instance, sees the actor embrace the characteristics of the horror film, whilst in *The Comedians* the entire narrative is driven by his slapstick, self-referential antics. To Mathanda's credit, he is often the sole saving grace of the films in which he appears. It is certainly damning to think that the dark spectre of apartheid has denied the actor any recognition within South African cinema in general.

UNDER COVER

To further an understanding of the simplicity of the B-Scheme films, and the cynical austerity measures involved in their production, it is worth summarising

Figure 4.6 Emmanuel Shangase/Dumi Shongwe in *Under Cover* (Tony Cunningham, 1989)

the example of *Under Cover*, an attempt to mimic *Shaft* but without any comparable violent, thrilling action. The narrative of *Under Cover* – which opens with another painfully long credit sequence over a plain black background – begins and ends with the story and character arc of a young policeman called Dave (Dumisani Shongwe), who is asked by the captain of his unit to gather some dirt on a local heavy called Jack Dlomo (Pepsi Mabizela). Dave is concerned that he will be killed on duty but also vocalises that, if he comes out alive, he intends to marry his girlfriend, Princess (Sylvia Makhathini). One of Dlomo's men exposes Dave's identity and kidnaps his fiancée ('kill them both! And drop their bodies in the harbour!' insists the crime boss) before a stand-off ensues. In the end, Dlomo enters a small, cramped warehouse – whose relevance is unexplained – and is arrested at gun point by Dave's superior, the police captain. There is no concluding fight, which audiences would expect from an action narrative of this sort. The story ends with Dave and Princess safe, Dlomo arrested and one of his men dead. All sequences of robbery, battery and related violence take place off-screen and are related to us through dialogue between Dave and the police captain.

Figure 4.7 Crime doesn't pay in *Under Cover* (Tony Cunningham, 1989)

When Paleker mentions that the B-Scheme films were frequently 'cost-cutting measures' she could well have been summarising the cheapskate approach of *Under Cover*: there is not a moment of conflict until near the very end, in which a brief gun fight takes place. When Dlomo orders a man to be killed, the murder takes place off-screen – whilst even the events of criminal deals, such as a delivery of drugs, have to be related to the audience via dialogue between characters. Whilst the film works within a classical three act structure (Dave's introduction to the investigation/the investigation itself/Dave's final victory in shutting down the crime ring), attesting to a basic understanding of classical Hollywood storytelling, there is no attempt to create any suspense. Hence, part of what makes a film such as *Under Cover*, and many of its B-Scheme contemporaries, unique is this aforementioned refusal to deliver the set-pieces that their genre demands.

Further examples of this approach include *Fishy Stones*, which begins with a car chase featuring two white policemen following a pair of robbers through some parkland until the vast scrub results in their capture. We understand that the criminals have just committed a diamond heist but, once again, we never get to see the burglary. The narrative of *Hostage* introduces us to a drug baron called Michael Jackson (presumably some kind of in-joke from the cast and

Figure 4.8 Emmanuel Shangase/Dumi Shongwe in a villainous turn opposite Zanela Nyidi in *Hostage* (Michele Hartslief, 1986)

crew), played by Pepsi Mabizela,[10] who sends a token female worker to seduce his enemies. A rogue photographer captures them on camera and blackmails the lover. In one scene, Jackson boasts of a possible business proposition, 'if the money isn't enough, I'll send my girls to rob him'. For any American blaxploitation film, this would be the cue to introduce a number of scantily-clad, beautiful women. But with *Hostage* the women are never seen – either because the budget never stretched to hiring more extras or because the filmmakers never felt the mobile circuit audience would care. The sole scene in which a female character seduces a 'victim' of her scam involves absolutely no nudity, undressing or even a tease of anything salacious. Perhaps most threadbare is *Zero for Zep* (Steve Hand and Laurens Barnard, 1980), produced by *Under Cover*'s Tony Cunningham and similarly lacking in excitement. Here, the narrative, which follows a young man on a criminal rampage as he is tracked by two committed detectives, runs out of steam by simply having its young antagonist turn himself in. There is no showdown between detectives and criminal, no car chase, no suspense, *nothing*. The film merely ends with the young troublemaker opting to simply 'do the right thing' and narrating his intentions to the audience.

As further mentioned by Paleker:

> In most of the films the urban centres are shown to be unnatural to the African and the narratives suggest that habitation in these cities leads not only to moral decay, but also the destruction of traditional African lifestyles and the erosion of African cultures through exposure to European modernity (notably, and ironically, symbolized by Hollywood films). (2010: 98–9)

Whilst *Under Cover*, with its representation of a smart, tough-guy detective at work, and always one beat ahead of his adversary, does not necessarily indicate that urban centres are unsuitable places for South African's non-white populace, the B-Scheme films in general do position their characters as being honourable only insofar as whether or not they can follow the values of the society they exist within. The societies are unfamiliar but not, it should be established, always those of townships or poverty. *Under Cover* begins in what looks like a small city street and there is no indication that the characters exist outside of urbanity or as part of an urban-conditional (unless we accept the young policeman has been rewarded with this status through his commitment to his profession). As with one-woman man Joe Bullet, Dave finishes *Under Cover* by discussing his plans to marry Princess. Law and order becomes equated with doing the right thing for the state. For instance, in *Under Cover*, Dave refuses to even have an alcoholic beverage with Dlomo (this is, he explains, because he is still on duty) whilst his Captain at the police station tells him that he is being sent on the assignment because someone else has a wife and a new child and risking their lives would be morally unacceptable. As was the case for *Joe Bullet*'s buffoonish 'big man' crime-lord Rockey, *Under Cover*'s Dlomo also favours a life of despot extravagance – we see him sitting by his swimming pool or by his well-stocked private bar, with a lover called Dolly. Sexism is well-evidenced by the demeaning 'pet' names given to these briefly established female characters (see Chapter 8).

Under Cover also suffers from technical problems: there are moments when the camera, which is frequently handheld, struggles to focus on the actors and one interior scene is blighted by the hum of nearby lights, which battle to gain precedence over even the dialogue being spoken. In a short scene, calling for slow motion, the actor Dumisani Shongwe simply lessens his movements, which might be considered a moment of paracinematic 'bad movie' magic. Whereas *Joe Bullet* moves along quickly and shows some skill in the editing and filmmaking department, not to mention a strong screen presence in Ken Gampu, *Under Cover* has little indication of professional activity either behind or in front of the camera. Nonetheless, it is worth pointing out that there is nothing explicitly racist about *Under Cover*. It is paternalistic and chauvinistic:

Dave the police sergeant is the selfless, clean-living lawman whose solitary goal is to end the narrative with his safety and a wedding proposal for his girlfriend. However, one is cautious, even sceptical, of confusing this depiction of 'positive living' with racism.

Certainly, Dave does what his Captain asks him, no questions raised and the narrative rewards him for towing the line of the state but, more importantly, for not seeking any financial betterment. He is happy to complete his assignment and return to his low-key, nondescript life with his new wife (who appears to have few plans of her own) – but chauvinism is certainly not unique to the South African strain of blaxploitation. Although the American variant may have evolved to include female leads such as Pam Grier and Tamara Dobson, there is no doubting that many of the motion pictures of their period treated women as sexual prizes for their handsome leading men (including *Shaft*). It is also worth affirming that, as with *Joe Bullet*, there is little indication that South Africa plays any part in the *Under Cover* story. In later films, there are attempts to fix this by having characters discuss their cities (usually Johannesburg or Durban) or mention paying in Rand (as happens in *Beware Tiger* and *Hostage*), but several examples of the B-Scheme, such as *Under Cover*, avoid acknowledging the country at all, perhaps in the ludicrous hope that such flimsy efforts as this could eventually cross borders and achieve international sales.

Sollywood Babylon

The popularity of Simon Sabela's work with his local viewers may point towards how subtle the perceived propaganda of the Heyns Films motion pictures actually was. B-Scheme critic James Murray would also admit that Sabela's work was 'of excellent quality and content' (1992: 257). On the other hand, it is easy to suspect that the reason such vastly inferior films as *Under Cover* escaped attention until the restoration work of Cowley and his Gravel Road Entertainment Group is because they failed to capture much of the attention of the local township audience which, by all accounts, was more sophisticated than the government and the later B-Scheme producers assumed. Rudi Mayer, a director and cameraman during the period, is quoted by Murray as saying:

> Blacks don't understand film language ... This means if you show a guy going into a house, you have to show him coming out as well. If you cut from the house to a car on the highway, your audience won't know what the hell's going on. (1992: 272)

Whilst such comments explain a film such as *Under Cover* and its long, tedious establishing shots, as well as the overriding sense of paternalism in the

B-Scheme, all evidence indicates that this statement is mistaken. Indeed, it is difficult to imagine that the same Black audience which saw the thrilling car chase of *Ikati Elimnyama* (a sequence that features expert editing) – let alone the sophistication of Italian or Hong Kong imports or even the better Jesús Franco output – would have any interest in such moralising, poorly-staged and action deprived productions as *Under Cover*. It is for this reason that any attempt to find a distribution or exhibition that can be compared to the more sophisticated American 'grindhouse' circuit and the ramshackle South African mobile bioscope, per *The Guardian*'s article of 'Sollywood: the extraordinary story behind apartheid South Africa's blaxploitation movie boom' (2015), is challenging.

Austin Fisher and Johnny Walker, drawing upon American exploitation (or what some have termed 'grindhouse'; the two labels becoming almost interchangeable although the latter should really refer to the theatre of exhibition) cinema, state 'The totemic value of grindhouse cinema therefore lies in the mediated history memory of a marriage of film type, place, and experience, as much as in the professed qualities of the films exhibited there' (2016: 23). For the authors, exploitation is a site of pastness – exhibited in an imagined grindhouse (the term itself referring to space of some edge) of the 1970s that showed only wall-to-wall sleazy, gory or sexy cinema: 'Foregrounding edginess enables grindhouse cult discourse to project an image of down-at-heel or lawless audiences, while diverting attention from the middle-class cultists also sitting in the auditorium' (Ibid.: 24). It is notable that this statement does not cite the audiences who *did* frequent inner-city American cinemas, during the seventies, to see films such as *The Black Gestapo* (Lee Frost, 1975) – indeed, one suspects it was not 'middle-class cultists'. For instance, in his review of the infamous *Ilsa, She Wolf of the SS* (Don Edmonds, 1975), critic Vincent Canby of *The New York Times* mentions 'a subculture that people who do their movie-going on Third Avenue are seldom aware of . . . Such films come into town to play a first-run engagement of one or two weeks at a grubby Broadway or 42nd Street grind house' (1975: 159). Fisher complicates his own argument when he discusses how Spaghetti Westerns would be assimilated into the blaxploitation trend with such texts as *The Legend of Nigger Charley* (Martin Goldman, 1972). Describing the blaxploitation Western as 'fluid, hybrid texts', Fisher then locates them solely as (cynical) productions *of* and *for* an inner-city Black audience of the time:

> This hardheaded economic imperative was, of course, the origin and definition of the term 'blaxploitation,' and an appeal to black audiences was certainly not the same thing as black agency in the filmmaking process or an equal share of the profits for black producers. (Ibid.: 189).[11]

In this quote, which could also be seen to advocate Tomaselli and Ureke's 'film services' approach to national cinema(s), we could also argue that the means of production in ZAxploitation was not unique to the apartheid state.

In addition, we might comprehend why making claims for any reimagined South African grindhouse culture is unwise, just as assuming that a 'subculture' did not exist on 42nd Street in 1975 is not concurrent with documented (re)views. The B-Scheme films were, first and foremost, profitable *because* the township population had limited means of entertainment. Per Mitch Dyter:

> They [the state] used to have certain towns where they [the Black population] had to be out of cities – there was curfew by six in the evening. Everyone had to be back in the town, so the institutes or film producers would make movies that would interest them, and it would be in their language. And that is how it [the B-Scheme] all started. (2016)

Any such comparable subculture, as that of the old 42nd Street in New York, is simply not there in this newly imagined Sollywood.

Perhaps studies on exploitation film would benefit from further deliberation about why certain tropes and foreign adaptations emerged and travelled whilst others did not (i.e. *Joe Bullet* or the Simon Sabela productions). This is particularly relevant given that so-called cultist societies existed in countries such as South Africa. Ward, for instance, argues that 'grindhouse cinema' might have had its 'date of death' in the early 1980s (2016: 21), yet the mobile circuits and bioscopes of this study indicate a cheap, tawdry industry that was ongoing until the end of the decade in the apartheid state. The *concept* of the grindhouse might come from America, but global, low budget exploitation cinema has become more available in the digital era, initiating discussion of foreign film services and networks that have been overlooked if not entirely ignored. It is increasingly important, then, to recognise that cult cinema fans in other countries were also engaging with motion pictures that depicted similar themes and presentations, introducing hybrid elements into localised adaptations, even in foreign tongues. As such, and to bring this discussion full circle, one no more *dislikes* the term Sollywood, at least as a reference to a period of factory-like production of low budget, B-Scheme, usually Zulu-language, blaxploitation films (rather than as a mode of distribution), than one (not unlike Fisher) *likes* the use of 'grindhouse' to reference a baseless modern retrospection of cheap and sleazy American cinema accessed and appraised, now in retrospect, by local 'middle class' cineastes – but it at least signifies an era and (vaguely defined) type of filmmaking. Given the recent unearthing of South African ZAxploitation texts, the struggle to find placement for them – particularly as none crossed over to the American networks of distribution – within wider academic or fan lexicons will no doubt continue to be discussed.

Thus, to speak of the bioscope itself, at least during the apartheid era, is to speak of an indigenously South African circuit of networks, which itself was dictated by eugenics. Unlike the American grindhouse theatres, which can be replaced and repositioned to fit new narratives even today, the Zulu-language B-Scheme films of this chapter carry minimal potential for similar revisionism. Taylor mentions: 'I used to go to coloured [Indian] cinemas, and no one would challenge me. They would show cut versions of Fulci and Jess Franco. I remember [Lucio Fulci's] *Manhattan Baby* playing there, and the audience liked it' (2016). For Taylor, the cinemas that catered to South Africa's Asian population (deemed to be 'coloured' by the government during the apartheid era and afforded more rights than the Black majority, if less than Europeans) were of interest because they showed material that was not playing at the white-only bioscopes. Cheap European genre imports, such as those made by Fulci and Franco, or less costly, dubbed martial arts imports from the Far East, would have been valuable commodities in cinemas where, in general, the median income of the audience – and consequently ticket prices – would not have been comparable to the white minority.

Similarly, for South Africa's Black majority, cheap products were necessary given the inevitability of the poorer economic status of those located in the townships. Benjamin Cowley adds:

> You had trucks with [mobile] cinemas in the back of them and they would go into the townships, to churches or community centres, and set up there. Someone in Soweto told me that the cinema was this pristine sort of thing. Only a few people could afford to go to the cinema [in the townships] and some of them would just watch people arriving. People would dress up go to the cinema, it was a show and the kids would go and watch that. Often, they would be watching imported content too. It was a popular thing amongst this horrible world they were living in at the time. (2016)

In this detail, we can perhaps understand the demand or need for the flimsier B-Scheme product – cheaply made and cheaply exhibited, but also disposable after the necessary ticket sales were made to recoup investment.

Cinemas also had a responsibility to avoid showcasing anything that would offend the apartheid state. As affirmed by Taylor:

> Just about every film that was shown in the country was cut. We became very adept at watching films with bits missing but somehow one got used to it. Some of my favourite films, such as *If . . .* and *Vanishing Point*, were cut to bits. The censor board at the time, the people who were essentially at the top – and by that, I mean who were answerable to

government – were sociology professors and mainly, but not exclusively, spoke Afrikaans. And many of them loved film. (2016)

Of course, this factor means that different types of films were also *made* for different audiences and explains the Sabela motion pictures and later the need for B-Scheme productions, to fill the (few) cinemas, town halls, schools and mobile circuits of the townships. As mentioned by Paleker, whilst the state did not approve the scripts, 'final arbiter of whether a film was suitable viewing material for African audiences was the Censorship Board' (2010: 92). The financial incentive for filmmakers to make these projects was ticket stubs – returned to the government to warrant the B-Scheme subsidy – which were used to prove how many people had been to the mobile cinema unit or film theatre. It is hardly surprising that such a format was rife for corruption. Dyter, for instance, discusses how ticket stubs would be swapped with owners of more popular entertainment venues:

> There was fraud involved . . . it began to become corrupt. People would be showing matinee films at a drive-in and these were the tickets going through to the department responsible [for the subsidy] and they would look at this and say 'Wow, all these school children . . . all they seem to be doing is watching [these] movies!' But that is what they would stamp. (2016)

Cowley explains further, 'Someone could say "ten thousand people saw my movie" and then there was a stamp and a signature . . . Falsifying box office reports was how many people made money' (2016). Such statements build on Murray's initial exposé of the B-Scheme (and its own self-sufficient bioscope) during the apartheid years:

> The nearest thing to an accurate check was to visit a hall after the event and to cram as many people into it as possible. In one instance where an irregularity was suspected, the local police actually did that and found that the hall could reasonably seat 200. The daily return form in question indicated well in excess of 500. (1992: 260)

Even at the most bottom-feeding end of American exploitation, and famous carny names such as Al Adamson who re-released and re-cut the same films over and over again, there is no comparison to such chicanery as that found in the old South Africa. Nevertheless, there is no doubting that the B-Scheme, at least in terms of the *quantity* of films produced, was a roaring success.

In speaking about Hollywood representations of Africa, authors Natasha Himmelman and MaryEllen Higgins talk of how:

Crafted and reinforced by European and North American missionaries, travel writers, and filmmakers ... colonial narratives consistently referenced Africa as a dangerous or exotic territory, as the pinnacle of horror and savagery, and as the recipient of the West's benevolent, heroic humanitarianism. (2012: 3)

The ultimate irony of the B-Scheme films is perhaps that they present the exact opposite of this narrative – they depict a society of incredible charity, where criminals are easily spotted and punished for their transgressions and where good things happen to good people. There is no glimpse of a 'savage Africa' in the B-Scheme films, only a Black population living to achieve modest aspirations: marriage, a good job, a nice house and a healthy income. Anything more salacious signifies villainous behaviour. For the next chapter, therefore, this study looks at the recurring element of 'crime does not pay' and describes the perverse morality of films made during a time when an entire nation sat between international condemnation and outright civil war.

Notes

1. See: Paleker, Gairoonisa (2010), 'The B-Scheme Subsidy and the "Black Film Industry" in Apartheid South Africa, 1972–1990', *Journal of African Cultural Studies*, 22:1, pp. 91–104. In addition, Tomaselli notes that his scripts would only enter production after approval of their racial politics from an 'anthropologist' (1988: 67).
2. In some films Rhodesia would simply replace South Africa, possibly to avoid local censorship. However, the fate of Zimbabwe was important to Pretoria. As noted by Christie van der Westhuizen, the National Party believed that the friendlier Abel Muzorewa, and not the communist-associated Robert Mugabe, would win the first majority election in 1980. The South African Defence Force would organise a non-fatal operation in Zimbabwe in 1986, striking the ANC base in Harare (2007: 147).
3. As also noted by Matloff (1997: 165).
4. It is worth affirming that entertainment was also a state desire within the townships. As noted by Mangcu: 'While government-enforced segregation enabled political control of townships, it disabled social and cultural interference or any form of cultural hegemony. Those were spaces that Steve Biko and his colleagues built upon in creating a new political and cultural movement, despite the harsh political system that sought to eviscerate life itself in the townships through arrests, bannings and killings' (2012: 238). Cheap, distracting entertainment provided with the blessing of (and often ideology of) the state was how the B-Scheme emerged.
5. One foreign filmmaker, who I shall respect by keeping nameless, and who shot in South Africa against the cultural boycott, was especially forthright: 'Thank you for writing and thinking of me. I don't mind speaking about filmmaking ... but when it comes to politics and the South African apartheid, it's a subject matter that doesn't interest me, which is why I ignored the threats and paid the enormous fine to direct the film. I have nothing good to say about my experiences with the politics involving the Directors Guild and the Afrikaners. I wouldn't be a good interview and hope you will understand.'

6. I double-checked this with an email to Benjamin Cowley of Gravel Road Entertainment Group on 28 June 2020. He confirmed that the B-Scheme subsidy was also available to 'Black' films made in English: 'language was not a qualifying criterion', he told me.
7. It may be unfair to just single out van der Merwe here because other B-Scheme motion pictures such as *Umgulukudu* (or *Thieves*, Marcel Joubert, 1984) and its sequel *Thunder Valley* (Marcel Joubert, 1985) also feature young-teen heroes.
8. This idea of good 'God-fearing' Black citizens reaches its most ludicrous presentation in the films *Upondo & Nkinsela* (Bernard Buys, 1984) and *The Priest and the Thief* (Wanna Fourie, 1980s), in which both narratives are resolved by petty hoodlums convinced that 'God' himself is speaking to them and ordering them to end their wicked ways (in the former case it is a tape recorder with a mind of its own, and in the latter it is a Priest hiding behind a tree and using a megaphone).
9. Cousin of Tonie.
10. *Pepsi* Mabizela, as Michael Jackson, could be a reference to the American singer's association with the famous soft drink label.
11. It is also worth noting here that Fisher, drawing on the film's marketing ('Somebody warn the West, Nigger Charley ain't running no more') believes *The Legend of Nigger Charley* appealed to 'inner-city black markets through an antagonistic opposition to white America's most hallowed foundation myth' (2016: 181). What then of the South African variant which stages the country's old frontier as a free state for Black farmers, liquor joints and, in the case of *Umbango*, bandits who can shoot whitey dead and get away with it?

5. CRIME DOES NOT PAY

Morality in the B-Scheme

Siegfried Kracauer's public psyche theory and insightful, if still controversial, look at Weimar films in Germany would inspire further, well-known discussions about motion pictures and nation, perhaps most famously from Lotte Eisner and Thomas Elsaesser. In their own study *Film Histories: An Introduction and Reader*, authors Paul Grainge, Mark Jancovich and Sharon Monteith suggest an alternative method of understanding silent expressionist cinema, particularly given the form's relationship to periods of financial depression: '*economic success and social mobility* . . . In general terms, the possibility of improving one's fortunes is a subject that appeals to a wide spectrum of possible audiences: from working-class to petty-bourgeois, from intellectuals to white collar workers' (2007: 133). Applying this approach to the fantastic cinema of the Weimar period allows the authors to break down the aesthetic and thematic occurrences of key films and to question the relationship between class, audience and text, distinct from the more genre-orientated and life-mirrors-art epistemology of, particularly, Eisner and Kracauer. Indeed, the films of the B-Scheme that emerged in the 1980s played in townships when crime in South Africa was 'the highest in the Western World' and the apartheid state was 'the third most crime-ridden country' overall (Omond 1985: 141). The state no doubt had its own (understandable) reasons for hoping that audience and text would register with messages that opposed criminal acts and promoted clean living.

This chapter continues the analysis of the B-Scheme cinema of the 1980s, but by looking at the themes of social ambition which surface throughout the various narratives. Make no mistake: these are stories about Black aspiration within a state where only a few non-white citizens could hope for financial independence and, even then, would remain second-class inhabitants. Whilst different methodological approaches to global cinemas is inevitable, themes of economic success and social mobility cross international boundaries. As such, attempting to decipher the 'message' between the narrative arc in such presentations and the (perceived) audience, as identified by the filmmakers, allows us some insight into what a specific generic cycle (Grainge, Jancovich and Monteith focus on aspects of fantasy cinema) aspires to *say* and even *do*. The B-Scheme films, therefore, as cinema aimed at township viewers, tow an uneasy line between promoting aspiration and ascertaining that success is, ultimately, within the family unit and, moreover, available only to those citizens who prove their worth to the state. Or to put it more directly: *crime does not pay*.

In this regard, these are films of apartheid, but many of the narratives also confront aspects of South Africa itself: diamonds, multiculturalism, uprising in townships, juvenile delinquency and even the vulnerability of the country's borders. A rare example, *Ukuzingela*, even tries, clumsily, to belatedly introduce an idea of apartheid's own dubious claim to 'racial equality' to the B-Scheme narrative by initiating that Black people would be better off staying in their own communities lest they become as corrupted by capitalism as the Boers. In a roundabout way, the director of *Ukuzingela*, Tonie van der Merwe, is still – just a year before Mandela's release – advocating the same homelands/Bantustans policy that led to even F. W. de Klerk acknowledging 'the relatively successful independent state of Bophuthatswana' in his memoirs (1998: 309 – with *relatively* being the key word).

As noted by activist and filmmaker Laurence Dworkin, 'The mainstream industry was Broederbond controlled ... It was very much a Broederbond baby. The cream of the Afrikaners were all the directors of these [major South African] film companies [and] they saw the film industry as a strategic vehicle for advancing their own ideological agenda' (2016). Given this aspect of mainstream South African cinema, should anyone be surprised that far lower budgeted films, aimed at the Black majority, contained a similar voice of 'good citizenship'? Gairoonisa Paleker mentions: 'Whether the story involves a murder, gang warfare, competitive sport or gambling – and regardless of its setting either in urban townships or homeland capitals – the denouement is always a victory of good over the forces of evil and darkness' (2010: 98). The author is correct in ascertaining this; however this classic morality story of 'crime does not pay' is also a central narrative arc of blaxploitation cinema in general – witness Fred Williamson's trendsetting gangster anti-hero, Tommy Gibbs, gunned down in New York City at the conclusion of *Black Caesar*, the fate that awaits the crooked lawmen of *Detroit 9000* (Arthur Marks, 1973) and *Lady Cocoa* or the adventures of John Shaft himself.

Mark A. Reid mentions how 'black gangster films borrowed some of their elements from mainstream gangster fare, the films commonly suggesting a conventional understanding of "law and order"' (Grant 2013: 572). Inspired by the classic noir-gangster films of Hollywood's golden age (themselves compromised by the Hays Code), it is possible that even today audiences associate blaxploitation with these more traditional narratives than with the success of Melvin Van Peebles as Sweetback or the similarly avant-garde *Super Fly* (Gordon Parks Jr). Yvonne Sims states:

> *Shaft* and *Super Fly* embody the key formal and thematic features that came to define the aesthetic style of the developing blaxploitation genre, taking the model of *Sweetback*'s black male hero up against white male power into the crime or underworld action drama genre. (2006: 49)

Whilst *Super Fly*'s influence on the ZAxploitation pantheon has been established with *iKati Elimnyama*, it is *Shaft*, and the more linear detective films that it inspired, which cast a shadow over the B-Scheme productions and their narratives of crime does not pay or, per Palekar, 'a victory of good over the forces of evil and darkness'.

It should, of course, be noted that the ZAxploitation criminal empires are typical of the B-Scheme's makeshift approach. No more than a couple of well-dressed mobsters are designated to rule the local community by fear – making the showdown between hero and villain far from extravagant. *Beware Tiger*, for instance, concludes with two gangsters – the only criminal masterminds that we meet – running down the street in fear – chased by a kung-fu hitman called 'The Tiger', their entire criminal organisation now concluded. From the same director, Michele Hartslief, *Hostage* presents a local drug cartel that is managed by just three people. In one sequence, the film's hero breaks into their house, which stands unguarded. He then easily captures one of the villains. *Impango* (or *The Marked One*, although the literal translation is 'plunder' [Tonie van der Merwe, 1986]) has just three men plan the capture and kidnapping of a millionaire's wife so that she can be held to ransom and, unsurprisingly, they are foiled. For *Impango II* (Tonie van der Merwe, 1987), the exact same narrative is repeated, and the exact same character kidnapped, her attacker, joined by just one other, once again foiled at the end.

Do the Right Thing

Doing the 'right thing' in the films of the B-Scheme can be as simple as finding and returning some stolen goods (as seen in *Fishy Stones*), refusing criminal money, or stopping some local gangsters from committing further illegal acts. Sometimes, characters are guided by Christianity – appealing, one might imagine, to classic colonial fantasies about civilising the 'native' people, a perspective that remained popular at the time of the B-Scheme subsidy. Historian Frank Welsh has spoken about how 'Christian nationalism' offered 'moral strength to the doctrines of apartheid' (1998: 416) whilst, referring to P. W. Botha and his National Party, author Christi van der Westhuizen remarks of his race-based idealism, 'the South African state bore the light of Christian civilisation in darkest Africa' (2007: 122). Speaking of older cinema depicting the South African state, in this case *Cry, the Beloved Country*, Peter Davis notes 'What pervades the film is the Christian ethic as the path to both personal salvation and to the resolution of South Africa's social problems' (1996: 40).

Decades later and little had changed: in the low budget film narratives of the B-Scheme, the heroic, Black do-gooder personalities are rewarded for their positive deeds or return, content, to life with a loving wife and/or family. Films such as *Under Cover*, *Umgulukudu* (or *The Thieves* and *Black Crusader* conclude with the hero setting the date for his wedding. *Friday's Ghost* rewards its male hero with the hand of a local lady who believed she had to honour an old family promise to marry a local gangster. In some texts, God is even presented as a pivotal narrative character who determines the actions of the various personalities. *The Priest and the Thief*, for instance, is a comedy about a robber who manages to trick a local preacher and steal the donations from his Church no less than three times. Only by inheriting the wisdom of the Lord does the Priest (played by Khulikani Magubane) finally give the young drifter his comeuppance (by hiding and speaking as the voice of God via a megaphone, admonishing the petty criminal for his actions). Whilst this ending depends on accepting the thief as particularly stupid and out of his depth in the 'civilised' sphere of the Church (the Priest, on the other hand, notably and politely interacts with a white woman who is part of his congregation), the narrative arc of good citizenship is bluntly and crudely enforced. *The Priest and the Thief* is an example of Tomaselli's 'urban-conditional' demarcation: whilst the young thief is initially welcomed into the congregation, his inability to follow the religious line means that, by the end of the story, he has vowed to return to his homeland and never come back. The Priest, of course, remains part of the local suburban community.

To indicate how heavy-handed this approach to crime and its ramifications is in the B-Scheme films, one need only look to *Knockout Joe* in which the actor Isaac Xaba plays the title character (referred to as Sam in the narrative for unexplained purposes), a young police investigator. Joe/Sam [from herein Joe], who we first meet in a small dance hall, spots an opportunity to break the law when he learns about a local diamond smuggling operation. It is Xaba's expository narration, in Zulu, that drives the narrative causality and

Figure 5.1 Black and white working together in *Knockout Joe* (Laurens Barnard, 1984)

explains what is happening in *Knockout Joe*. The first time we hear his voice, he deadpans: 'In this world there is good and there is evil. But most people follow evil, believing that crime does pay'. From the start, then, the point of view of the film is clear – but the story soon splinters into unexpected directions including two different narratives. *Knockout Joe* does not fit into any of Tomaselli's three categories quite so comfortably. It is, at its heart, a clear Christian-themed film about the possibility for salvation of all races and one that does not propose any separation of ethnicities.

The first narrative features Joe as well as a white man called Max, who owns a cement company, and his Black assistant Nico. In this narrative Joe learns about Max and Nico smuggling diamonds from South Africa into an unnamed foreign locale 'across the border'. The young lawman attempts to infiltrate this scheme, with the blessing of a white friend in the police department, but instead of seizing the diamonds, the pair will take the stones for themselves. Joe dresses up as a customs officer and pulls Max and Nico aside after they drive out of South Africa, but he is also caught in the act. Some official border agents arrest him for impersonation (as with a number of B-Scheme films, this fundamentally vital plot point does not take place on-screen and we are instead told about it via the narration) and also find Max and Nico guilty of diamond smuggling. The three men are then placed in a cell together.

Narrative two, however, involves Joe – in his cell – discussing another story of Black-white 'bonding' featuring two male convicts, having escaped from prison, making their way through the African bush whilst handcuffed to one another and chased by a (white) bounty hunter. This scenario, of course, comes from *The Defiant Ones* (Stanley Kramer, 1958), an important box office hit for Sidney Poitier, but it would also be reimagined in the Philippines as *Black Mama, White Mama* (Eddie Romero, 1973), this time with two female prisoners (played by Pam Grier and Margaret Markov). *Knockout Joe* represents the second South African attempt at a transnational adaptation (following the better known *Shamwari* which is discussed in Chapter 7) and, unsurprisingly, it is less politically provocative than the Poitier original or the Filipino variant (which advocates armed revolt against authoritarianism, albeit during the period of Ferdinand Marcos and martial law). However, probably attesting to how strictly the B-Scheme films were expected to avoid provocation, given their township audience, *Knockout Joe* is also considerably less political than *Shamwari*, which was made for a South African (white) audience and an international crowd. Instead, the trope of two different races literally handcuffed together whilst under adversity is used solely to promote a story of bonding and, of course, the idea that crime does not pay.

For instance, Joe notes how the two escapees did not initially get along but became 'thick as thieves' whilst stock footage reveals a variety of African wildlife and savannah. 'Life was good for everyone in Africa' continues Joe, initiating an idea, later revisited in *The Gods Must Be Crazy* and discussed by Peter Davis as 'yearning for an idyllic simplicity in the face of an increasingly complex and stressful world' (1996: 81). Davis talks of the 'Noble savage' persona from the Uys film and this kind of exotic representation perhaps inspired *Knockout Joe*'s portrayal of a kindly local tribal King who saves both men from being killed by a bounty hunter (it potentially indicates they have found the border to Swaziland/Eswatini and this is white South Africa's interpretation of the state). The King's intervention is down to his guilt at having permitted some sanctuary to a couple of local elephant poachers. This concept of being cleansed of a past sin via a fresh good deed is not unique to *Knockout Joe* and features in other B-Scheme productions.

In Tonie van der Merwe's *Ezintandaneni*, for example, Popo Gumede plays a character involved in a hit and run accident. He does not go to the police and admit his guilt, hiding his secret from even his dear mother. The story then shows him at the bedside of his son, who is terminally ill, and who dies just days later despite his father's many prayers for divine intervention. There is supposed to be a sense of karma here (which is in bad taste), but the narrative ends with Gumede adopting the boy he hit in the car and his older sister, as

Figure 5.2 Hector Mathanda serves tea in his lavish new homestead in *The Comedians* (Japie van der Merwe, 1980)

well as falling in love with a young woman he has met through the catastrophe. He says he will spend his life with her – thus everything is considered resolved in the end. Gumede has been given a second chance as a father, and a fresh start as a husband, thanks to divine intervention.

In *The Comedians*, Hector Mathanda's buffoonish Bona is warned about using the magical ring he borrows from his kindly neighbour for gluttony. When Bona breaks his promise to act wisely, and also begins to assemble a local group to 'protect' him, he is warned by his former friend that he is following a negative path. Divine intervention strips Bona of his goods the next morning, no questions asked, and no explanation given, with the narrative then grinding to a conclusion. Similarly, heroic characters of the B-Scheme films are usually introduced with dialogue that establishes their good future under some kind of protective bubble (that can be interpreted as faith in God) that will ensure riches and success but also their survival under some sort of criminal attack. The two boys of *Fishy Stones* have a long argument about whether or not they should keep the diamonds they come across during a camping trip. It is eventually decided that they should do the right thing and alert the police. The first reaction of one of the boys is to say, 'I think we are going to be rich!' but his friend talks sense into him, insisting that they pack up their camps in the morning and alert the law to the discovered booty, because bad things happen to bad people. Without even putting up an argument, his friend suddenly sees sense and agrees, hence he can now make it to the end of the story without being killed by the gangsters looking for their stolen wares.

In *Knockout Joe* therefore a similar theme of karma and redemption is presented: the King saves the life of the exhausted white prisoner, although his Black friend later dies from eating 'contaminated food' and the long-lasting effects of a beating he obtained from the bounty hunter. We are led to believe, however, that the King has redeemed his previous guilt through his kindness to the two escapees – and the white survivor will now embark on a more positive lifestyle, having come to a resolution that his kind, and Black people, can be friends after all. Joe narrates how 'When people care for each other, no matter how much they disagree, they will always be willing to help each other'. The message can also be seen as one of racial reconciliation, the sort seen in *The Defiant Ones* and *Black Mama, White Mama*, but in this instance the circumstances, even with the best intentions, make the conclusion far more offensive. A common enemy (the bounty hunter) is enough to make segregation laws seem passé and Africa, prior to political upheaval, can be reimagined and even return – at least to a tribal tranquillity of witchdoctors, threadbare tents and Kings – if 'we' (Joe being the voice of the white filmmakers) all just learn to work together within the current status quo. It is this conclusion that is also broadened to Max and Nico – as Joe hears their stories and repeats to them, 'Crime doesn't pay. It never will'. When Max's wife visits him in prison, they speak in Afrikaans and she suggests she will leave him. Joe, once again, can only offer the patronising comment, 'Can't you see that crime doesn't pay?' If this is not laboured enough, Nico finally reveals that if he is released from the cells, 'I wanna be a priest. Teach the word of God'. *Knockout Joe* ends with a local pastor visiting the three to offer some religious guidance.

Whilst *Knockout Joe* is more overbearing than many of the B-Scheme films in regard to its message of 'crime does not pay', and it certainly has repeated religious overtones, it does indicate how the form adapts from a famous Hollywood template. In this case it is *The Defiant Ones*, however a notable link to elements of additional commercial cinema is also evident. The Noble savage portrayal, for instance – a character that exists to 'boost the central white character' (Davis 1996: 119) – is here presented merely to highlight the narrative's idealism about an 'untouched' Africa. Ironically given the brutality of apartheid, this thematic could be read in the context of the war with Angola and the theory that outside forces were responsible for destabilising the region, a belief that was not uncommon among prominent pro-apartheid figures. Gerrit Viljoen, for instance, chairman of the influential and notorious Broederbond, would remark in 1979: 'that the Afrikaner humanity "stands in sharp contrast to the cold-blooded cruelty that marks so much of the history of Africa'" (van der Westhuizen 2007: 317). The Africa that exists outside of the apartheid state, in *Knockout Joe*, is depicted as one that should be left alone, in a reciprocal détente straight from the former Prime Minister John Vorster's political handbook: we leave you, *you leave us*.

The Black-man-in-prison trope, however, is also a function of blaxploitation storytelling that includes *The Slams* (Jonathan Kaplan, 1973), *Dolemite* (D'Urville Martin, 1975) and, perhaps most famously, *Penitentiary* (Jamaa Fanaka, 1979) and its two sequels. In *Knockout Joe*, prison is not used to depict the brutality of incarceration (even the cell that the three men are filmed in is remarkably clean), despite the unnamed foreign country in which the three characters are charged and jailed, but it does permit for a modicum of conflict and discussion of future goals. *Knockout Joe* is fascinating as a hybrid exploitation film – taking from a number of sources – but also troublesome because of its absurdist, paternalistic approach to race relations, although it does mediate the presumption that apartheid might even survive as a system so long as the Black man recognises that there are plenty of decent white people who wished him no harm. With this said, there are three mixed-race friendships in *Knockout Joe* – Max and Nico, the two escapees and Joe and his police friend, although in neither of these cases do we sense that the Black personalities have either the authority or the strength to oppose their situations. However, it is likely that the film's overriding intention and message was no greater than one of Christian salvation – regardless of ethnicity. The narrative certainly makes it clear: *crime does not pay* and *Knockout Joe* is unique in featuring a trio of criminals who end the film behind bars. Hence, it is worth mentioning the manner in which other B-Scheme motion pictures introduce, maintain and exhaust this perspective of making the wrong life choices and being punished as a result.

Tonie van der Merwe's *Ukuzingela*, starring Popo Gumede, is another interesting example because, as with *Knockout Joe*, its premise is based on fractured Black-white relationships. The film begins in what is clearly a Black urban village – including the sight of a token thatched hut, hinting at a 'back to the homelands' adventure. However, van der Merwe turns his story into something less easy to define, part history lesson and part morality tale. An old man, played by a middle-aged actor wearing grey hair dye, asks his young friends to gather around and hear a story set during the (second) Boer War (this is the only ZAxploitation film, encountered during the research for this book, that acknowledges the conflict). The old man talks about being a young boy and seeing three white people, two men (one played by van der Merwe) and a young woman, swimming to land following a shipwreck and carrying a treasure chest. 'I didn't understand white people's ways at that time, they were at war, fighting each other,' narrates the old man, indicating the conflict between the British and the Boers. 'When we were growing up life was simple, we had everything in abundance, we didn't want for anything. I realised that whatever was in the box was a curse'.

Sure enough, the white characters fight over the treasure, but they all end up dying anyway. When the final man, the youngest person of the three, believes he has the chest all to himself, a poisonous snake appears and kills him. 'I thought if you were to see it, you could be overcome by greed and start killing each other. Just like the white people did,' continues the old man, who reveals that he has kept a map to the bounty. 'No Sir, that is not possible,' replies one of his small audience. 'We'd never fight among each other. We love each other and we are family. We'd split that gold equally among us'. Four Black characters, led by Gumede, then set out the next morning to find the treasure but, predictably, double-cross one another and, sure enough, they start to bicker and gradually come into physical conflict. Eventually only Gumede is left, but the same poisonous snake appears and fatally bites him just as he locates the treasure chest. Van der Merwe's statement seems to be that settler capitalism, establishing a base for mining diamonds and gold, first resulted in white-on-white violence and then Black-on-Black violence. However, *Ukuzingela* has no answers and nor does it propose any, except maybe suggesting that South Africa's Black majority should be grateful that they exist outside of the hustle and bustle of the centres of global capitalism (making it carry the message of the 'back to the homelands' films, as well as the same structure – indeed, Gumede should never have left his village).

Historian Christi van der Westhuizen notes how even the country's third-to-last white leader, John Vorster, was unable to see 'the humanity of black people' (2007: 97). However, by the mid-1980s the apartheid state had begun to at least formulate a small Black middle-class, whilst refusing political reform and suppressing, often brutally, opposition to the National Party line. Tomaselli mentions that 'The State defined as "revolutionary" *any* attempt to change South Africa away from a racially ordered society and *any* call for a more equitable distribution of wealth' (1991: 181). The confusing and disastrous nature of this approach is retrospectively so evident – a government which in the 1970s was led by someone who refused to comprehend the inhabitants of the townships as possessing basic humanity and, a decade later, a country that had finally understood the need to have some sort of class and race integration, albeit within a minority-run colonial settler hegemony. The changing nature of how exactly to deal with a Black majority, increasingly driven against the nation responsible for Sharpeville and the Soweto shootings, can also be seen in a late-day B-Scheme film such as *Ukuzingela*, where the story argues that the Boers are and were greedy for wealth and suggests that the Black audience is better staying clear of such impulses. On the other hand, by advocating that the Black man, by opening the proverbial Pandora's Box of opportunity, will fight and kill over the benefits of capitalism, van der Merwe may also be maintaining the government line of the proverbial corrupt Communist 'bogeyman'. The one who, once exposed to modernity, will refuse to share and self-destruct or, per R. W. Johnson's cynicism, where 'the nationalist elite had quickly become rich' and where South Africa's own ANC's politicians 'had no idea how to manage a middle-class lifestyle, were often broke and needed help' (2010: 18).

Van der Merwe's pessimistic and literally black/white view of South Africa's problems in 1989, the year before the release of Nelson Mandela from prison, at least indicates that a cheap B-Scheme motion picture was as capable of mediating the conflicted, paranoid mind and hapless predicament of the apartheid state as any other art that emerged from this especially troubled period. Van der Merwe would venture into similar territory with *Isiqalekiso* (or *Gold Fever*, 1980s), although this effort avoids the race-conflict of *Ukuzingela* by having Popo Gumede and Hector Mathanda fight over a small chest of Boer gold that four young teenagers discover in the Bush. In the end, Mathanda, who has taken the riches in his hands and run into a swamp to escape, is eaten by a crocodile. This is the second time that a character played by the actor has been killed in this manner (given that he was consumed by a crocodile at the end of *Ivondwe*, made by van der Merwe's *Joe Bullet* collaborator Louis De Witt). Kudos must be paid to Mathanda's thespian abilities as he simulates, as best he can, that he is being eaten by something that quite clearly is not even there and which the producers have not bothered to concoct as a special effect.

THE DO-GOODER

The do-gooder is a recurring character in B-Scheme films, adapted from the old colonial Mr Right. Joe, Max and Nico are 'do-gooders' insofar as, at the end of *Knockout Joe*, they realise that their criminal acts have doomed them to prison, and they must instead turn to the detention unit's reverend for redemption and a chance for a better future. Popo Gumede's passion for wealth in *Ukuzingela* is, of course, the opposite to this presentation – he is made to suffer and finally die for not heeding his grandfather's warnings about the perils of gluttony. In many B-Scheme films a criminal, or criminals, are thwarted by a strong-willed policeman and/or a well-meaning citizen (or two) who act solely in the interests of restoring order to the community. *Umgulukudu* features a young unemployed man (played by *Under Cover* star Dumisani Shongwe) who agrees to assist the local police in finding a kidnapper, risking his own safety in doing so – but the experience also teaches him moral responsibility. At the end of *Umgulukudu*, Shongwe's character arc is complete and he is even more interested in stopping crime than finding employment. Tony Cunningham's *Gone Crazy* follows a bitter ex-council employee who holds the city to ransom by threatening to blow up the water dam. Only the devoutly Christian Mayor and a kind, local private detective look likely to be able to bring the villain to justice. 'Everyone is a law-abiding citizen' says the Mayor of *Gone Crazy*, establishing the order of the community. The very first sequence of *Gone Crazy* concerns the Mayor and his wife sitting down to watch Christian hymns on television with their evening meal, thus establishing them as the 'right' sort of Black people in South Africa. Hardly surprising that the Mayor, and his belief in the Almighty, guide him to not just solve the crime at hand but to survive a shoot-out with only a minor wound from a gunshot and with his ever-doting wife by his side (her entire narrative arc is either to be in fear for her husband's safety or to make him and his visitors cups of coffee).

A disturbed teenager, who gets his girlfriend pregnant, causing her to kill herself, undertakes a rampage of theft (stealing some money, a motorcycle and eventually a car) and murder in *Zero for Zep*. At the end of the film, having aligned himself with two small-time criminals, he recognises he has followed the wrong path. 'I'm going to end up in prison. It's not worth it' he tells himself, before turning himself into the police. 'I deserve to be locked up', he admits to them. This resolution is closer to the narrative arc of *Knockout Joe*, where the three antagonists quickly come to their senses and realise that, as they should have known all along, crime does not pay. *Doomsday* – which was touched upon in the last chapter – is a gang war story, and more violent than most of its contemporaries, with lengthy, bloody battle scenes, some of them protracted, in a township. However, the moral perspective still comes from a local reverend who urges each side to look to God for redemption and to visit their local Church. This type of cinema belongs to the dying days of the last colonial (at least in terms of a fully settler-controlled and dominated country) visions in, *and interpretations of*, Africa. Richard Dowden has contrasted the 'most striking parallel' that 'was between the Afrikaners and the Ulster protestants' in Northern Ireland, noting the colonial lineage and the derivation from the House of Orange (2008: 403). Dowden would affirm 'Both believed that they were God's chosen people, rewarded for their faithfulness by the gift of the land they now occupied' (Ibid.: 404). It is certainly interesting and perhaps not coincidental that the B-Scheme films have recurring narratives that are focused on land rights and – most revealingly – *religious* Black men who thus deserve their urban-conditional abode, especially when up against less 'civilised' forces.

Christi van der Westhuizen also mentions that the largest Church for the white population in South Africa, the Dutch Reformed Church, had originally supported apartheid and a ban on mixed-race marriages (2007: 141), although this stance was revised via a bill that was piloted by future President F. W. de Klerk (per his memoirs) on 29 April 1985 (1998: 74). However, despite many of the films studied and made after 1985, aside from the Black hero having an Indian wife in *Run for Your Life*, mixed marriages are never shown in the B-Scheme. Nevertheless, during apartheid, the Dutch Reformed Church remained an influential voice and towed the government line for the vast bulk of the period (Welsh 2000: 415). Therefore, the presence of Black characters following Christian dogma in the B-Scheme films is a not-too-subtle signifier of their acceptance of colonial ideology and possibly even separate development.

For example, *Ransom* opens with a marriage ceremony in some scenic, sprawling gardens, but two criminals intervene and kidnap the bride. The distraught groom wonders what can be done, only to be reassured by the reverend: 'All we can do is put our faith in the Lord and wait for the police to arrive'. Later, the reverend repeats 'have trust in the Lord' and insists 'God almighty will avenge us'. As such statements seem misplaced in an action-thriller, what the dialogue instead succeeds in doing is reminding us of the stature of the Church and the relationship between Christianity and apartheid. 'Priests often turn out to be crooks. Maybe you're one too', maintains the villain of *Ransom* – his questioning of divine justice cementing his own deviance (although this comment might have spoken to township audiences on a more, presumably unintended, subversive level). Burns maintains that

> In West Africa in particular, theories that presumed innate intellectual differences between races became increasingly untenable as independ-

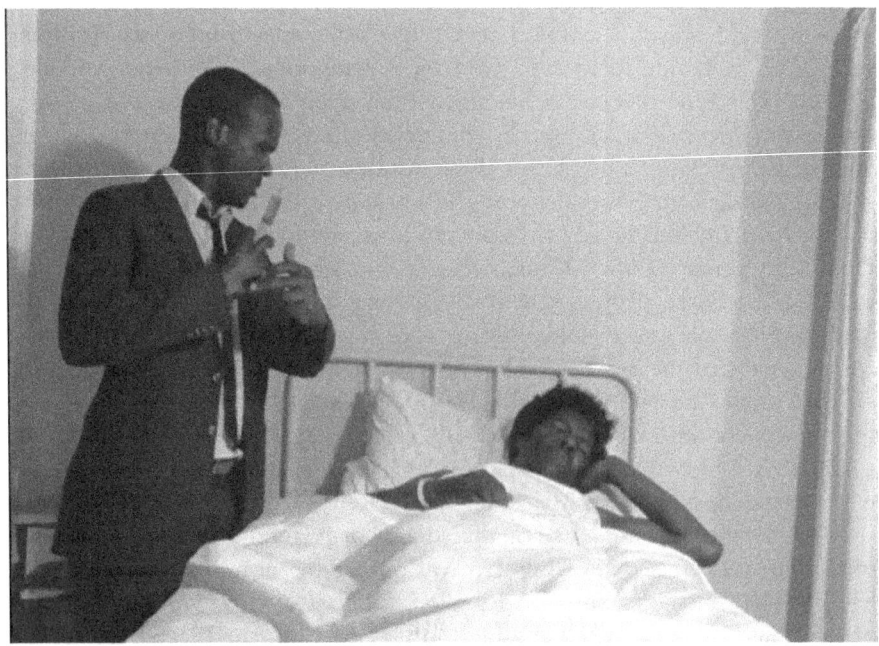

Figure 5.3 Emmanuel Shangase/Dumi Shongwe up to no good in *Ransom* (Tony Cunningham, 1980s)

ence approached. However, in Southern Africa, where the white minority sought to cling to power indefinitely, these theories retained their currency because they served to legitimatise the perpetuation of settler control. (Ibid.: 38–9)

Whilst elements of fantasy/supernatural are permitted within the B-Scheme, as with the magic ring in *The Comedians*, the mystical snake in *Ukuzingela* or a friendly spirit in *Friday's Ghost*, and Black characters are finally allowed to handle firearms – as seen in *Gone Crazy* and *Under Cover* – these are frequently 'message' motion pictures harking back to early colonial film approaches. In *Ivondwe*, for instance, the local Pastor appears on-screen to offer guidance to random characters before belatedly becoming the main focus of the story. When he finds out that his dangerous, deranged brother may be on the loose in the local town, the Pastor reassures others: 'It's a dangerous creature. Just know that the Lord is with us'. When his brother is killed and consumed by crocodiles at the end of the film, the Pastor insists that this is what God wanted. With the story concluded, and the Lord's 'work' done, everyone can finish the narrative happy.

Nonetheless, for some of these stories to promote narratives of good living and even forgiveness, they can also occasionally subvert expectations and transform themselves into a unique, farcical sort of trash cinema that has no global precedence. 'Trash' is used both pejoratively and literally – to describe product that is easy to dismiss and disregard and not just because a film struggles to be cinematic, but because it also fails at even meeting the slender demands of most basic genre filmmaking. Even more than other texts, *The Boxer* is an example of this description. So eager is director Michelle Hartslief to insist that crime does not pay, and thus justify his state subsidy, that no one – not even a solitary character – has any sort of arc that can possibly withstand even basic, rudimentary narrative scrutiny.

The Boxer introduces us to a character called Damian Phumlani (Sizwe Dlamini), who is being trained for his biggest match by Max (Hector Mathanda). Damian, his wife Judith and his best friend Qamatha spend every day obsessing about boxing, but the evening before the match a white man accidentally runs down the fighter. Damian's wife is told by a (white) doctor that her husband will probably never walk again, but a few scenes later the same medical professional is telling him to 'pull yourself together' and insisting he can be mobile in the near future if he just puts his mind to it (continuity can be remarkably haphazard in these films). Meanwhile, Max sends two disorganised, petty thugs to Damian's house to threaten him, but the two instead rape the woman (off-screen), commenting – in a manner considerably more vulgar than usual for a B-Scheme film –'Did you see that girl's breasts? Soft as cushions'. Finally, beaten emotionally and physically, Damian prays to

IMAGES OF APARTHEID

Figure 5.4 One of many repetitive scenes of characters working out in *The Boxer* – a B-Scheme film that has no boxing (Michelle Hartslief, 1986)

God that he may walk again and, by apparent divine intervention, he does. He then discovers that Max not only planned to fix his match with his opponent but had sent two men to frighten his wife and drive her into the arms of a 'real' man (meaning the portly Max). Yet Damian insists he will not kill or hurt Max as that would make him a lesser man. Instead, he insists that Max will lose his livelihood and the ability to attend matches when his misdeeds are discovered, and *The Boxer* ends with a close-up of the hero's face.

There are so many questions that arise from watching *The Boxer*: who is the random white driver who knocks down Damian and what happens to him? Why would Max believe that Judith would become his lover after being threatened by two men breaking into her house? Why did the two men, paid to enter someone's property illegally, go even further and rape an innocent bystander? Moreover, why would any narrative that builds up a character under duress (injured, learning that his wife has been raped, discovering his trusted trainer is to blame) not reward the audience with *any* sort of pay-off? *The Boxer* is so determined to show that good people do good things, even to bad people, that it defies even its own disregard for explaining random, tangentially interconnected incidents. Reimagining *The Boxer* as camp irony, a film that – per Jeffrey Sconce – represents 'the systematic "failure" or "distortion" of conventional cinematic style' (1995: 385) is difficult to accept because, against the backdrop of apartheid, there remains, even in such a flimsy failure of cinematic logic, an adherence to *good Black* citizenship that is unmistakably obnoxious. Not only does crime not pay, but any remote anger – either to a careless white car driver or thugs who have raped one's own spouse – is, it seems, wholly unacceptable. Per *The Boxer*: humanity in the apartheid state stems from a willingness to forgive that knows absolutely no bounds. In a film with a narrative that points towards revenge, but which has no on-screen vengeance whatsoever, *The Boxer* – which not only has no boxing but, like many B-Scheme films, is awash with padding (minutes of training footage; for instance two men jogging for several minutes) – is one of the most contemptible motion pictures from the ZAxploitation pantheon.

Harrow mentions that 'when African cinema is judged to be adequately serious, successfully raising social issues but failing to meet aesthetic standards, it is taken as a second-rate cinema' (2013: 29). Harrow does not focus on South African cinema, including the B-Scheme – and indeed the notion of its Africanness – but had he watched *The Boxer*, he would discover not only amateurish filmmaking but a conspicuous lack of socio-political commentary and adherence to even the most elastic of genre frameworks. Unlike the notion, per Harrow or even Sconce and his introduction of paracinema as a byword for every 'historical manifestation of exploitation cinema', that trash or the lowbrow can be readapted into some sort of positive manifesto among followers of marginal art, *The Boxer* indicates how even an amalgamation of genre – sports film, crime thriller, melodrama – fails *because of* apartheid. So established in the B-Scheme formula is the karmic sense of punishment for criminal misdeeds that in this case character actions fail to fit narrative causality or expectation and a vulgar sense of filmmaker paternalism towards Africans who have been hurt *but must never hurt back* is established. Christian values perhaps, but oppositional to a narrative containing house invasion, rape and a sleazy criminal 'mastermind'. Murray mentions that the *Rocky* (John G. Avildsen, 1976) series had been a success on the mobile circuit during the apartheid years, whilst the B-Scheme producers had responded to such popular Hollywood films with 'inferior content and extremely inferior distribution methods' (1992: 264). One can only presume that *The Boxer* is one such example. An intention to make a *Rocky*-style story of a young boxer, an outsider, rising to his game – but recentred within a gangster story – it is perhaps the most incompetent of all the films analysed in this monograph.

Benjamin Cowley, of Gravel Road Entertainment Group, maintains:

> Part of the apartheid idealism was that Black people would be separate from white people, therefore there needed to be a Black world and

there needed to be a white world. That would come through in a movie. Even back then South Africa was a melting pot of different cultures and countries ... So apartheid idealism comes through but it is not overtly there. The films that we have come across – it is all moral things ... pushing Christianity over and above tribalism or promoting values like good vs evil or crime does not pay off. If that is political, it is subjective how we interpret that [but] they were definitely movies that were made for propaganda purposes. (2016)

Good citizenship among brave, young Black men is how the B-Scheme films rewarded their characters and, presumably, hoped to promote this sense of aspirational, clean living to their audience. These are clearly stories *of* apartheid – of rejecting political motifs and avoiding armed resistance (the gang war in *Doomsday* might never be explained but, in the shadow of the very real township upheavals, it is uncomfortably exploitative if not crass) in favour of divine inspiration and the homestead. Imagining such narratives permitting singular male characters, in the vein of John Shaft or a romantic anti-hero such as Tommy Gibbs from *Black Caesar*, to surface and sustain any sort of blaxploitation 'badass' persona might seem unthinkable. However, just as blaxploitation cinema itself crystallised different presentations of Black masculinity, so too do some of the films of the B-Scheme offer their leading men opportunities to rebel and revolt against the more conservative trappings of the motion pictures explored in this chapter. This topic is explored next.

6. THE BADASS

Stickin' it to Apartheid?

To state the obvious: the badass persona is central to the American blaxploitation hero. The badass characteristic emerged from Melvin Van Peebles as Sweetback: the mute, male prostitute, on-the-run from the racist Los Angeles police force and protected by the Black community, who subsequently risk life and limb to secure his escape from the United States and into Mexico. However, as noted by author Peter Davis, depictions of sub-Saharan Africans took decades to evolve beyond that of the indigenous savage. Moreover, thanks to old colonial legends 'Cinema's South Africa was a fictional territory filled with dangerous savages that had to be quelled – in a word Zulus!' (1996: 126). Prior to the 1970s, and as discussed by Kenneth M. Cameron, it would be the Mau-Mau who would define the 'dangerous savages' of the continent, films that 'acknowledged the collapse of the British and American idea of a subservient, loving Africa' (1994: 123). What Cameron describes as the 'Dangerous African' or the 'Killer African' was already a part of Hollywood's Africa when the B-Scheme films emerged.

But what of the 'badass' African?

If *Joe Bullet* and Simon Sabela had introduced the trope into apartheid cinema, what of the cheaper, shoddier follow-up films of the 1980s? It is certainly interesting that an otherwise forgettable and family-orientated B-Scheme film such as *Isiboshwa* maintains a presentation of the 'dangerous' savage by having its three young boy leads evoke the spirit of Shaka to do battle with a pair of (blundering) thieves who they find hiding near their woodland campsite. Their 'badass' moment, probably designed as symbolic of their newly-embraced manhood under duress, is instead clumsily attached to a lineage of South African cinema stereotypes that Davis himself mentions – dating right back to the infamous blackface of *The Zulu's Heart* (D. W. Griffith, 1908).

In this chapter, focus is given to two of the more subversive B-Scheme portrayals – Popo Gumede as the vengeful farmer, David, in *Impindiso* (or *Cold Justice*, Carton Spielberg, 1980s) and as Marcus, a young professional businessman, in *Black Crusader*. Other films that are introduced include the English-language production *Charlie Steel*, which, much like *Joe Bullet* and *Bullet on the Run*, may have had an eye on the international market (the conspicuous lack of production values is no doubt the reason it never made it past the local audience). In the second half of this chapter, some discussion is given to a small cycle of Westerns that emerged from this period: *Imusi* (or *Smoke*, Carton Spielberg, 1980s), *Revenge* (Coenie Dippenaar, 1986) and Tonie van der Merwe's *Umbango* (or *The Feud*). Westerns with Black heroes became briefly prolific in the 1970s, predominantly in Italy and following the genre's second major wave under such filmmakers as Sergio Leone and Sergio Corbucci. Whilst the blaxploitation Western has been described as a cycle that 'inherits and utilises certain of the classical Hollywood Western's ideological and racial associations' (Fisher 2016: 184), the B-Scheme Western uses pastness – which should be assumed as prior to the (second and possibly the first) Anglo-Boer War – as a cipher through which to develop more coherent Black protagonists (i.e. characters who exist, narratively, outside of apartheid and thus can be presented as considerably more heroic than usual).

Whilst the South African Westerns might be seen to nominally avoid contemporary politics by setting their action in a period before apartheid, a gangster film such as *Charlie Steel* falls into the 'private dick' character category made popular by *Shaft*. Steel is a lawman-for-hire who is hired to solve a kidnapping case, and the storytelling is notably fluid, with a clear focus on one main character, and with less extravagant exposition to pad out the running time (the Western *Imusi*, for instance, features several minutes of sheepherding). In comparison, crime movies such as *Impindiso* and *Black Crusader* are important insofar as they establish their statuesque hero, Popo Gumede, as a badass for the B-Scheme: a character of both Christian morality and state values, but also a recurring figure of athleticism, intelligence and combat expertise. Hardly surprising, one might argue, that Gumede became such a popular presence in the films of this period, with director van der Merwe also using him for his bigger budgeted, international co-production *Operation Hit Squad* in 1987. It could, perhaps *should*, also be mentioned that the more well-known figure of Johannes 'Panic' Themba Mzolo (Thomas Mogotlane) in *Mapantsula* might be deemed to fit the badass description. However, this study concludes with a close analysis of the film and its main character, primarily to initiate a wider discussion of why this text belongs *within* the ZAxploitation pantheon and perhaps symbolises the form's evolution from proverbial paracinematic 'trash' to arthouse 'treasure'. It does so, moreover, without – in purely generic terms – reinventing the presentation of a badass avenger. Indeed, Panic finally allows the presentation of the ZAxploitation hero to become *truly South African*.

From Van Peebles to Pretoria

Speaking about *Sweet Sweetback*, Yvonne Sims has mentioned how 'Van Peebles also used elements from the mythic street hero of urban, Black folklore – one skilled in performing sexually, evading the police, and fighting' (2006: 130). Instead of dialogue, Van Peebles displays physical superiority as his way of escaping emancipation; sexually, in terms of combat (he efficiently takes down two police officers) and also his character's endurance as he is depicted running night and day across the streets of Los Angeles. In the film's closing text, over a freeze frame of Van Peebles finally making his desperate but symbolic dash across the Mexican border, we are told 'Watch out. A Baad Asssss Nigger is coming back to collect some dues . . . ' Per an astute contemporary retrospective from critic Brad Stevens, a returning Sweetback could likely do very little 'except keep on running from the police' (2016) but Van Peebles' film contained a radical, revolutionary aesthetic and thematic reinvention of African American cinema and representation. At its heart is a refusal 'to reproduce Hollywood's cinematic grammar and syntax' (Yearwood 2000: 109) and to offer an alternative presentation of Black identity within the conservative narrative and stylistic confines of American cinema.

Ultimately, *Sweet Sweetback*, with its experimental, occasionally non-linear narrative and audacious, provocative, unfamiliar portrayals of race, gender and (perhaps just as importantly but less commented on) *white* savagery, grounded what became known as blaxploitation. Given that historically, exploitation cinema has focused on *Black* savagery – what authors Felicia Feaster and Bret Wood call the 'jungle-movie tradition' (1999: 163), any recourse to race-reversal, however cynical, can be viewed as subversive. Later blaxploitation films certainly took more from *Shaft* than the persona created by Van Peebles, but Sweetback and his tough, no-nonsense, hypermasculine and principled personality still cast an influence, even within the mainstream. Koven describes the badass character as one that emerges 'in those liminal spaces between the law, between illegality and vice on the one side and harmless decadence and pleasure-seeking on the other' adding that 'they cannot be the Man, or his representatives' (2010: 17). For Koven, this disqualifies John Shaft, but this study is less convinced.

Richard Roundtree's character might be a private detective, and his interest is certainly in battling New York City's endemic crime and corruption (regardless of race), but he is shown to perform and work at his own discretion and, most importantly, has little tolerance for the rules and regulations of white society. The Shaft personality has been described as 'He really doesn't care. He is a free man' (Briggs 2003: 127), and in his love and professional life, the character is shown, across the original three films, as navigating his individual and self-motivated course without obedience to the white world. Indeed, it is not too far-fetched to imagine that what appealed to audiences of *Shaft* in 1971 was that 'it depicted a black man kicking ass. The hero wins a personal victory and the narration emphasises a larger mythic theme of Blacks (the oppressed) triumphing over evil (their oppressor)' (Yearwood 2000: 91). In the first sequel, *Shaft's Big Score!* (Gordon Parks, 1972), when the character stands up to a burly white police officer abusing a young Black man, he adds the sarcastic line, 'Relax. Don't you know they are trying to rehabilitate you here?' This comment signifies a far larger power disparity between white authority and African American citizens, and whilst it is said with some comic timing, it is also tragic *but*, moreover, affirms Shaft as a badass: he does not tolerate injustice *in or out* of the law. This theme of oppressed against oppressor is part of what all blaxploitation cinema, even variants such as the horror film *Blacula*, have at the centre of their narrative causality. As such, it would be incorrect to ascertain that the badass has to be a Sweetback-style avenger on the run from white society as opposed to the tough lawman character that is found across the blaxploitation spectrum.

Perhaps inevitably, until *Mapantsula* we do not see the characters of ZAxploitation struggling *against* the apartheid state or engaged in any sort of righteousness that might be seen to subvert the settler claim to South African soil, but this does not mean there is no acknowledgement of discontent. The South African blaxploitation heroes of Joe Bullet, Simon Sabela's Lefty and Ken Gampu's journalist-turned-undercover-investigator Steve Chaka in *Death of a Snowman* (see next chapter), have their own ambiguities even if their politics do not stray from the state line. (Lefty's decision to use criminal means to gain personal wealth *might* be seen as an exception, his punishment notwithstanding; Chaka is consistently expected to be up to no good by his white colleagues). Bullet's employment is never mentioned, *he is just* a badass crime fighter, but most telling is the fact that Gampu's badass hero is never explicitly depicted as existing *within* South Africa itself. Sabela's Lefty is presented within Johannesburg, although his compromised movement is only alluded to, whilst Gampu's more standardised action persona in *Death of a Snowman* is as a principled, suave, serious-minded journalist battling against (implied) institutional racism. In neither *iKati Elimnyama* nor *Death of a Snowman* are we expected to know if these characters are the 'good guys' until towards the end of the narrative, but (and this is important to note) neither film indicates that apartheid, as a system, is to blame for the characters' actions or for their compromises. Whilst Gampu and Sabela, in these roles from the 1970s, offer interesting takes on American blaxploitation variants such as the private detective and the charismatic rogue criminal, the later B-Scheme films occasionally veer into badass portrayals that coexist in a broader understanding of life under apartheid itself.

The two characters played by Popo Gumede, in *Impindiso* and *Black Crusader*, are surprisingly closer to Sweetback in that they are accidental heroes: men who do the right thing within their community even if it means engaging in unlawful acts. Just as Simon Sabela teases audience familiarity with *Super Fly* in his *iKati Elimnyama*, so too does director Tony Cunningham acknowledge the Van Peebles film in *Black Crusader* – not just in the title but by introducing Gumede with his character, Marcus, a handsome middle-class family man, jogging across town. Cunningham's camera placement is, however, interesting: as Gumede jogs through a neighbourhood he is filmed *behind* the razor wire and metal netting that protects the suburban (most likely) Johannesburg houses from Black men such as himself. Tomaselli notes how (far superior) South African films such as *Mapantsula* and *My Country My Hat* draw attention to apartheid structures and how their protagonists

> do not exist as individuals, but as political subjects thrust between legal apparatuses, social practices and apartheid. They call attention to the invisible structures into which they have been born and within which they must live. Alternative courses of action occur within the relative spaces opened by the institutions that govern apartheid, or the contradictions caused by apartheid. (1992: 354)

Whilst it would be unwise to equate the tawdry, opportunistic exploitation of *Black Crusader* to either film, it should still be noted that the visual presentation of this opening sequence quite clearly draws attention to Gumede's outsider status upon entering a suburb of, one presumes, the white populace. In doing so, the same 'invisible structures' that exist in the more accomplished, highbrow examples of the ZAxploitation period, are exposed – even within this lowbrow framework. Marcus is also introduced as a badass character: his first act is to break up a fight between a shop owner and a local representative of a crime syndicate, which he does by greeting the criminal with a series of sharp punches. From this opening act of defiance, Marcus and his friend Terry become aware of a local crime racket that demands protection money from shop owners and the two make plans to infiltrate the ring, whose 'big man' crime leader is called Dlamini (Hector Manthanda).[1]

Speaking about 'populist' filmmaking, Clyde Taylor discusses cinema that

Figure 6.1 Popo Gumede sneaks up on a symbol of white authority in *Black Crusader* (Tony Cunningham, 1986)

can 'claim little gain in projecting any social dialogue or weight, or, less difficult to assess, in elevating group self-esteem, establishing positive images with dignity etc' (1995: 434). Nonetheless, appealing to populism – in the case of *Black Crusader* via audience familiarity with *Sweet Sweetback* and the structures of apartheid through a similar, localised tough hero – would at least mean initiating a wider dialogue with themes of contemporary concern. Take the depiction of (occasionally simulated) Black savagery in the notorious shock-documentary (or shockumentary) *Africa Addio* (Gualtiero Jacopetti, Franco Prosperi, 1966) which was 're-released soon after the 1976 Soweto disturbances' but screened only to white audiences (Tomaselli 1988: 21). *Africa Addio* documents the upheavals that took place in Kenya, Rwanda, the Democratic Republic of the Congo (aka Zaire) and Zanzibar shortly after the conclusion of European colonialism and juxtaposes chaos with the 'calm' of South Africa, depicted as a comparatively stable, democratic state. By screening *Africa Addio* after the events of Soweto, the apartheid government no doubt hoped that white liberals, perhaps becoming opposed to segregation, or undecided voters, would recognise the threat of majority rule as the old colo-

THE BADASS: STICKIN' IT TO APARTHEID?

Figure 6.2 Popo Gumede in trouble, as a badass for the B-Scheme in *Black Crusader* (Tony Cunningham, 1986)

nies fell into proxy conflict (one recalls Rhodesia's Ian Smith's famous quote of 'one man, one vote, one time'). The racist, *populist* exploitation cinema trope of Black savagery, then, was still being used politically because the images were made relatable to contemporary South African concerns.

Populism is certainly inseparable from older exploitation cinema and, within this relationship, race and racial conflict is heightened beyond any rational 'social dialogue or weight'; usually into more extreme and thus instantly accessible representations (such as the radicalised 'good' Black vs. 'bad' white narratives of many American blaxploitation films or the white farmer and the Mau-Mau). Given the transnational challenges of repositioning racially motivated blaxploitation narratives into the apartheid era, and for a local segregated audience, blatantly cynical representations are perhaps inevitable. *Black Crusader* does not make Marcus into a hypersexual Sweetback figure, but it does position the character *outside* of the law and thus the state. He and his friend Ken take matters into their own hands because the police are deemed to be disinterested and, in one scene, Marcus uses kung-fu to overpower and beat a villain – a nod to the popularity of martial arts imports in the townships (and a facet of these films that dates back to *Joe Bullet*). When Marcus and his friend Terry need to break into the house of their rival Dlamini, an armed white guard standing outside has to be distracted. 'What the bloody hell do you think you doing, man?' says the figure in clear English. 'Your day is coming. *Your days are numbered*, I'm telling you', says Terry, as he distracts the guard for Marcus to sneak into the house. Later, Marcus knocks the white guard unconscious. As a 'crusader', then, Marcus is evidently *not* subservient to the apartheid dictum and, in this moment, even the title – *Black Crusader* – becomes somewhat, surprisingly subversive. Moreover, briefly, the structures of apartheid that Tomaselli speaks about are no longer invisible – even in this cheapjack B-Scheme production. Certainly, corrupt police, a wealthy Black criminal protected by (white) authority and two men who overthrow a criminal with brute force does not sound unlike a plot for a seventies blaxploitation film: 'violent expressions of black manhood ... and a black-white confrontation that ends with the oppressed black coming out spectacularly victorious' (Guerrero 1993: 110). It is difficult not to conclude that, with Terry and Marcus standing up against a symbol of white force (himself depicted as brash and unpleasant), *Black Crusader* is making racial tensions *explicit* in a way that films from a decade earlier, such as *iKati Elimnyama*, could only make *implicit*. Finally, white savagery within the apartheid state *is* acknowledged on-screen, however minimal, limited or obnoxiously populist that might be.

Representations within *Black Crusader* still remain problematic, of course – when Marcus first meets Terry, his friend is shown picking bananas, and the conclusion of the film has the 'Black Crusader' and his compatriot agree to a date for a double wedding with their sweethearts (one of whom is called Princess). Despite being university-educated, Marcus also agrees to return to live at home with his mother and help her to rebuild her business: *family before aspiration*. He mentions how he does not want her to have to leave her property and seek employment far away – possibly attesting to the idea of *Black Crusader* being set in one of the Bantustans (one wonders if such an indication may have justified, to the South African censors at least, the provocative white vs. Black fight and dialogue exchange). Familiar tropes also resurface as, prior to breaking into the house of Dlamini, Terry voices his concern, to which Marcus reassures him 'we just have to believe in God'. The character of Marcus, then, is badass in the sense that he knows kung-fu, can overpower his enemies and even manages to take down a symbol of white authority (surely designed to draw cheers from a township audience, captive or otherwise), but he remains confined to the 'correct' sort of 'Black Crusader': one who is, in the long run, no threat to any sort of wider white power and understands that crime does not pay. As a tall, handsome, tough screen presence, Popo Gumede – who usually shows flair as an actor, even in these low-cost efforts – is a transnational badass or, as maintained at the opening of this chapter, a badass for the B-Scheme. He is tough, but he is also compromised as much by what he *cannot* do (bed multiple women, fight against apartheid) as what he *can*. *Black Crusader* is further limited by the fact it has been made for a small, localised, segregated audience. This factor has no precedence (even Nollywood films can be found on the streets of worldwide cities containing West African communities and, for some time, aired on British cable television). Nevertheless, Marcus standing up to white authority, and violently abusing it, is at least as subversive – on a purely symbolic level – as, for instance, when John Shaft is driven by a white chauffeur to a large stately home owned by a Black man in *Shaft's Big Score!*

Not Quite Spielberg

One of the most violent B-Scheme films is *Impindiso* – directed by a (probably pseudonymous) Carton Spielberg[2] and set in Durban. The hero is again Popo Gumede, playing a farm boy called David. In *Impindiso*, David lives on a farm with his father and his younger sister. However, as with the criminals in *Black Crusader*, David's father must pay protection money to a local mob in order to keep his business safe and his current transaction is overdue. Dumisani Shongwe, as Sam, leads a trio of thugs who harass the old gentleman and stab his daughter, Megan, to death. David arrives late on the scene and his father, seeing his daughter's dead body, has a heart attack and dies. Now without his family, David swears revenge, whilst Sam insists 'the Zulu culture says no healer can heal his own wounds'. Presumably, this statement (the film's only mention of localism) is meant to indicate that Sam has little intention to change his evil ways, but it also establishes Otherness – the character is not part of suburban Durban and exists on the fringes of the city (for which re: 'civilisation'). David, whilst never mentioning God (unusual for a B-Scheme hero) nor establishing any localised identity, is also depicted as 'at home' in the rural; the farm invasion not only costs him his family, but also his livelihood and he must venture into the city to take revenge. *Impindiso* then depicts David's wrath in a narrative structure that is similar to *Death Wish* (Michael Winner, 1974): he strangles one thug, he breaks into another's house and shatters a bedside lamp, electrocuting the man in the testicles. Finally, he kills Sam. A detective friend arrives and offers to clean up the mess, bizarrely assuring him that 'everything has turned out alright'. The two men part ways and David returns to his family's farm as a free man. Thus, despite the preceding violence, *Impindiso* falls quite comfortably into Tomaselli's genre of 'back to the homelands'.

It is worth mentioning that land invasion is a recurring story arc in many B-Scheme narratives including *Ambushed*, *Friday's Ghost*, *Mandla* and *Moyo Mubi*. Here again we see that these films do not exist in a mere bubble outside

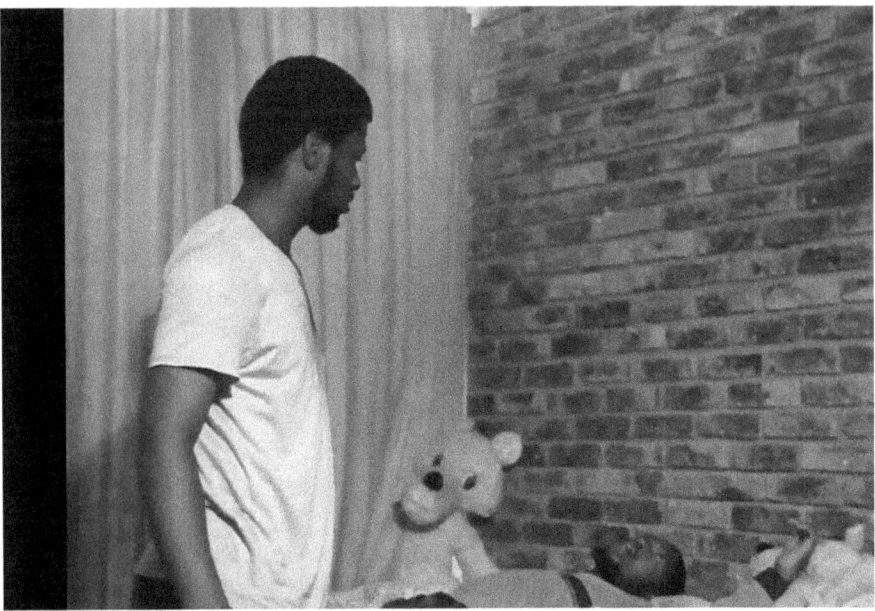

Figure 6.3 Popo Gumede avenges his sister and father by killing another member of a local criminal gang in *Impindiso* (or *Cold Justice*, Carton Spielberg, 1980s)

of the larger South African state. Indeed, Philip Bonner notes that in the formative years of apartheid, 'Squatter politics were not only parochial and introverted, they were also in many instances deeply sectional and divisive' (1991: 71). The author documents how infighting and squatters became a live political concern. According to Bonner, the seeds for this were sown in the 1920s with a Black influx into South African cities, an issue exacerbated by the election of the apartheid government two decades later, which lacked understanding of different tribal identities and languages. As seen from later Bantustans and townships, the land issue remained linked to population control as well as suppression of Black movement and, eventually, political activity across the apartheid state. *Impindiso*, by showing what might be interpreted as tribalism, and criminal control of sequestered land, is able to untangle the National Party from responsibility to the majority of its population and return the focus to a more primitive conflict around rural squatting and Black-on-Black violence.

Yearwood has noted how screen depictions of race, even within films directed/produced by African Americans, might be discussed within paradigms 'that have been constructed by the dominant society' (2000: 98). This factor is one that any analysis of exploitation films probably needs to account for too. Within the academy, there has been a tendency to argue that politicised Black agency is largely absent from blaxploitation and to maintain the viewpoint of the Western academic: audiences are/were free to *receive or reject*. One does not suggest disengagement with films from the past however problematic they might be, but per Austin Fisher's discussion of *Charley One-Eye* (Don Chaffey, 1973), a post-*Shaft* project for Richard Roundtree, it is probably healthy to be sceptical over claims that audiences of blaxploitation were 'critically aware of their own ambivalent relationship to the films, and were free to accept the connotations on offer . . . or not' (2016: 191). 'Freedom', even insofar as choosing to what to see at the cinema, is compromised by the very nature of an unequal state in which art and commerce retain the influence and control of the majority race, not to mention control on movement, price and all entertainment commodities. If this is true of American blaxploitation, then it goes without saying that it is maintained by ZAxploitation – in which township audiences were deliberately targeted by these morality stories, no matter how badass the leading man might be, not to mention forced into some screenings, and – as we see with *Impindiso* – exposed to stories that at least entertained tribalism (and indicated such differences were natural to Black citizens).

Therefore, if one is to argue that Gumede's character of David *is* a badass, it needs to be understood that such a persona is badass within the limited parameters of what the cheap B-Scheme films of this time usually present. David is

Figure 6.4 Sol Rachilo as the title character in *Charlie Steele* (Bevis Parsons, 1984)

a badass insofar as he is individualistic and tough and, unlike Marcus, does not have to diverge into discussions of God in order to decide that he is going to avenge his family. However, it would be naïve to suggest that the apartheid audience saw this sort of portrayal as 'liberating' any more than to assume that they saw Marcus brutalising a white man in *Black Crusader* beyond any basic, superficial, cognitive level. Nonetheless, it is improbable that a white man being disparaged by a 'Black Crusader' and then beaten by him could have been depicted outside of the less censorious environment that South African cinema experienced in the late 1980s.[3] Moreover, both personalities at least allow some agency to their actor, Popo Gumede, and give him the opportunity to showcase narrative concurrency with better-known and more holistic American blaxploitation figures. Finally, his badass persona involves working out problems for himself without lawful assistance.

In addition, might we assume that township audiences began to recognise these repetitive badass tropes in some of Gumede's characters as well? This question is inspired by a latter-day B-Scheme film from Tonie van der Merwe, *Moyo Mubi*, which casts Gumede as a stick fighter called Gambushe who, per a typical narrative, hears that his girlfriend has been kidnapped and her family house robbed by a small group of thieves. Unlike in his previous badass roles, however, here Gumede's lone hero is transformed into a comedy persona who uses his charisma and intelligence to outsmart his adversaries. Blaxploitation films had also veered into parody, most notably with motion pictures such as *The Mack* (Michael Campus, 1973) and *Black Shampoo* (Greydon Clark, 1976), but here the humour is drawn from Gumede's character subverting his own badass expectations. In a sequence where the unarmed actor looks set to battle a villain with a machete, played by the recurring B-Scheme figure Dumisane Shongwe, Gumede's hero, Gambushe, instead explains that the antagonist's blade is dirty and advises him to clean it at once lest he become infected, as only then, for the safety of his rival, can their fight commence. Shongwe nods along and agrees. 'Thank you for the information. Oil and soap – where can I get those?' he finally asks, and Gumede directs him to a nearby store that does not exist. This comical interlude finally allows Gumede to seize the moment and knock his adversary out with a blow to the head. In another sequence, a gang member – this time played by Hector Mathanda – is pinned down by Gumede, who proceeds to plant some grass around his bare feet and set fire to it.

In a late-day B-Scheme film such as *Moyo Mubi*, made and distributed just a year before Mandela's release, we begin to see exhaustion set into the narrative repetition of 'crime does not pay' and 'good citizenry' (itself usually concurrent with the urban-conditional demarcation), but also into the very limited flexibility that filmmakers had to portray *any* representations of Black power. Even within the clumsy, comical moments in *Moyo Mubi*, Gumede's character must still end the narrative by telling his girlfriend that, with the criminals caught and handed over to the police, 'We should go and see our parents ... The reward should be enough to start our life together'. Nonetheless, in its depictions of a comical badass and gullible, ridiculous villains (in one sequence Mathanda carries a rifle back-to-front because he is unsure of which end is which), the film appears to be passing commentary on the cheap, repetitive and exhausting nature of the B-Scheme cheapie itself. Murray also mentions that the B-Scheme meant that 'Several actors and actresses who had never been seen on television were widely known in rural areas where less quality was acceptable. Their popularity alone would have been a major contribution to the success of ethnic films' (1992: 262).[4] Discussing the American blaxploitation parody *Undercover Brother* (Malcolm D. Lee, 2002), Koven correctly mentions how parodies 'need to assume a degree of audience knowledge about the genre' (2010: 149) and without at least some understanding of Gumede and Mathanda's typical screen relationship (as quarrelling thieves or, respectively, suave hero and rotund buffoonish villain) the abrupt changes of tone in *Moyo Mubi* would probably seem puzzling.

Curator Darryl Els mentions, referring to the evolution in the B-Scheme representations:

> It is a changing tact – almost mimicking what radio was doing, where you incorporated that idea of separate development in a different medium, different languages broadcast in certain areas. So I think if you look at the very early films, there is that tension between the rural and the urban and tradition and modernity and if you follow that through to the 80s and 90s, the images start to change. The narrative starts to shift. (2016)

If *Black Crusader* is set within the urban, with an acknowledgement that Black-white relations are unequal, and *Impindiso* sustains its story within the rural (qualifying as 'back to the homelands' insofar as both antagonist and protagonist are depicted as sustaining ambition and existence outside of the city), whilst a later film such as *Moyo Mubi* even ridicules the repetitive simplicity of B-Scheme narratives and portrayals, then the better-made *Charlie Steel* suggests that a badass character, at the tail-end of apartheid, might come from a broader state service.

Charlie Steel replays the narrative of *Shaft* itself, but – in its prologue – also questions Black involvement with the South African armed forces. Steel, played by Sol Rachilo, and his military colleague Jimmy are shown to be surrounding a house in a jungle location that is unnamed (but probably representing Angola). Jimmy opts to open fire on everyone inside (in the tradition of the B-Scheme films we do not see anybody killed, we just hear the noise of a machine gun firing) even as Charlie warns him that women and children are present. 'Son of a bitch Jimmy', says Charlie,[5] 'One day I'll make you pay for this'. The film then cuts to an indoor shopping mall where Black and white alike mingle (with the camera making sure to detail this, which also makes *Charlie Steel* another rare gangster film exception from the urban-conditional category). The juxtaposition would seem to indicate that a different South African can emerge if an immediate rethink is given in regard to how the majority are identified: a state engaged in border conflict, co-opting Black citizens into an armed force that fights for white supremacy, is not destined to be a good neighbour or create confidence in its own longevity. This message is revisited in *Charlie Steel*, as the detective (whose office is in the city) discovers that, upon his return from warfare, Jimmy has built a small criminal syndicate that specialises in kidnapping and ransom. Rather than being the citizen of a shopping mall, living in a suburban area (as Charlie is – his office even has 'Charlie Steel, Private Detective' emblazoned on the doorway), Jimmy functions in the drug-dealing underground, addicted to the life of violence that he had become fond of in the army.

'The only time you got tough is when your victims were helpless', insists Charlie. This commentary (and this study is choosing to view it as such) is admittedly mild, but the prologue of *Charlie Steel* and the later admittance that Jimmy enjoyed the brutality of military life, anticipates similar – and admittedly far more powerful – depictions of Black labour being co-opted by the apartheid state in *Mapantsula* and *The Stick*. Jimmy in *Charlie Steel* is a rare example of a B-Scheme villain whose criminality has become formulated via serving the wills of the National Party. Whilst this representation on its own does not necessarily make *Charlie Steel* an anti-apartheid film, it does point to other key portrayals from blaxploitation cinema – most notably the idea that white America is to blame for the (glamourised) African American criminality that is seen in such benchmark texts as *Super Fly* as well as *Bone*, *Black Caesar* and many others. Unlike many of the other B-Scheme films which generally deny their characters any vice, Charlie Steel is allowed to inhabit more traditional aspects of the badass persona. For instance, we see him drinking whiskey, even at home, and he permits no nonsense from anyone – an armed local in a bar is taken down and stripped of his gun instantly whilst, at the narrative's conclusion, the detective uses a bow and arrow to shoot an adversary through the chest.

Charlie also gets to meet a young woman and romance her, albeit briefly – and the film concludes with the protagonist exclaiming 'oh shit' when he realises that, with his latest case solved, and the young woman receptive to his charm, he needs to prepare for the evening's date. *Charlie Steel* is still a cheap and often laborious undertaking – a scene where Jimmy takes the hero out to some bushland to murder him is recorded in ponderous real-time – but it also feels more like *Joe Bullet* insofar as it is less of an ensemble piece and there is no overriding message of state citizenship or Christian morality. As with Gampu's fictional detective, Charlie Steel is badass simply because his profession calls for it. In the later part of the 1980s, then, the badass persona introduced by Ken Gampu as *Joe Bullet* and built upon by Simon Sabela in *iKati Elimnyama* is given some further, if still limited, flexibility to be a little more like the lone avenger character of classic blaxploitation (as in *Charlie Steel*).

Wild, Wild, West, South Africa-style

There is a scene in Tonie van der Merwe's Zulu-language Western *Umbango*, perhaps the filmmaker's most technically accomplished film, in which a white man (played by the director) sits, quietly drinking, in a saloon. He is accosted by the film's antagonist, a Black bandit called KayKay (Fikile Majozi, from Tony Cunningham's *Gone Crazy*), who sizes up the bar and demands that everyone come to work for him. Finally, with no one daring to refuse, he turns to the white customer and – in language that indicates the transnational influence of ZAxploitation – he says: 'Hey Gringo, you going to work for me?' 'Not interested,' comes the response from the white man, in Zulu. 'Gringo, I'm going to kill you', KayKay responds, and throws a small glass of whiskey over the white man's face. A stand-off ensues and the white man is shot dead, but when the Black Sheriff arrives and takes KayKay in for questioning, it is not long before the violent gunslinger is released. The barman even gives the Sheriff an alternative story of what took place: 'The Gringo here tried to shoot this stranger. He was clearly drunk'.

In this brief moment, despite the setting of the Old West, *Umbango* reimagines the racial privilege of the old South Africa, giving B-Scheme audiences an opportunity to knowingly engage with the very real universe of apartheid that the action and dialogue is signifying. Of course, director van der Merwe might have been engaging with such commentary for sensationalistic reasons. His comments to Gus Silber during the apartheid period would certainly indicate little interest in Black welfare: 'Lucky there's no union for blacks', he would boast, whilst estimating that the B-Scheme initiative, and his own cinematic distractions, might have reduced 'the black birth-rate by a couple of hundred thousand a year' (1992: 271). However, this sequence in *Umbango* still, amazingly, emerged from a state in which Black detainees would find themselves 'falling down staircases or from windows, or slipping on soap' or described by the police as 'communists ... instructed by their commanders to commit suicide in detention' (van der Westhuizen 2007: 97). In this backdrop of police fabrications and brutality, one wonders just how a township audience responded to such a race-reversal, even one as brief, tawdry and (yes) populist as that seen in *Umbango*. Here, a cheap ZAxploitation film also engages with postmodernism – and not just the world of the Spaghetti Western itself (the scene is shot with Sergio Leone-style quick-cuts between close-ups of eyes), reimagined within predominantly Black frontiers, but one that evokes the modern South Africa. A reminder of a country which, in 1986, was under a state of emergency in which racial harmony seemed like a distant vision. A white man in an all-Black saloon was a provocative image.

It is perhaps for this reason that *Umbango* has been something of a revelation to modern viewers. In a 2020 retrospective, journalist Sihle Mthembu goes so far as to argue that van der Merwe used 'the apartheid government's money to make an allegorical film about' the 'have and have nots' and 'used the master's own tools to show what a monster it [apartheid] was'. The director, meanwhile, is quoted as regretting the lack of anti-apartheid politics in his work. Both conclusions seem unlikely as, by all accounts, van der Merwe was more attentive to narrative filmmaking than his B-Scheme contemporaries, peaking perhaps with *Umbango*, but to reposition him as an unrecognised liberation hero is not concurrent with his previous comments. With this said, it is evident that van der Merwe at least wanted the freedom to depict Black agency in his narratives, which makes his work deceptively easy to embrace from a more liberal perspective. For instance, Robert C. Allen and Douglas Gomery mention:

> The objection that films are merely a means of 'escape' for audiences is not a cogent one. Even if we assume that films have functioned as vehicles of escape from everyday woes, we must also assume that they have represented an escape into something. (1985: 158)

Thus, the escapism of *Umbango*, in this moment of Black-on-white dominance, is one of clear authority and revenge. Even within this depiction of the past, it is a powerful indication of the exploited rising up against the oppressor. The very least that can be said is that Van der Merwe was aware of what his audience wanted.

Koven draws on writing of Tarantino's *Django Unchained* (2012) that calls the film 'metacinematic' or 'cinema about cinema' (2016: 132) but, in reference to Allen and Gomery's questioning of the social history of film, I raise the idea of the South African Westerns as postmodernist satire in their own right. In his study of colonial audiences and cinemagoing in the old Zimbabwe, Burns speaks about how the British authorities across their Southern African colonies were concerned about the impact of Westerns, which in 'the 1930s and 1940s' had 'become the favourite films of audiences throughout Southern Africa' (2002: 152). Burns acknowledges Thelma Gutsche's affirmation of the American Western's popularity in South Africa and also maintains that 'in the postwar period ... the new censorship board took a decidedly dim view of Westerns' in what was then Southern Rhodesia (Ibid.: 133). It is difficult to know if the Boers' famously frosty attitude towards British authorities was in fact being explored in the Westerns of apartheid; perhaps in the form of a meta-*paracinematic* commentary – a cinema about cinema *about* political pastness *as well as* the political present. Depictions that flaunted Black cowboys shooting their kith and kin on the old frontiers, without any expectancy of exporting riots and violence from the townships to the cities and suburbs, displayed instead as a postmodern middle-finger to the censorious doubts of the paranoid old coloniser. Such conclusions certainly make for interesting consideration. Indeed, why else would it be in a Western, that old bugbear of the British authorities, that a Black antagonist would be given the opportunity to abuse and kill an innocent white settler without any ramifications from the law?

With this said, of all the countries in the sub-Saharan part of the African continent, perhaps none were more suited for a cycle of Westerns than van der Merwe's birthland. The story of the first Malan in South Africa, David Malan, as told by one of his descendants (Rian Malan) reads like the fodder for a classic Western – fleeing from the Cape, and the hangman's noose, with a Black lover to become a nomad in a still unexplored continent of rumoured 'wild beasts and savages and wild white men in animal skins' (1991: 21). Further attesting to this conclusion, one need only look back to early, silent cinema and one of the nation's first films, *De Voortrekkers* (Harold M. Shaw, 1916) or, as the opening English translation claims, *Winning a Continent*. Aptly described by Davis as a film in which the Boers are 'sympathetically-drawn individuals, whereas the Zulus are for the most part an ant-like mass' (1996: 133), the film romanticises the Great Trek and the Battle of Blood River, both events of key remembrance during the apartheid era. Christi van der Westhuizen mentions:

> Afrikaner nationalist mythology reinterpreted the motley groups of families that had left the Cape colony as a coherent nationalist action ... The Voortrekker victory over Zulu forces at the Battle of Blood River was immortalised in the Day of the Vow on 16 December. (2007: 23)

So ingrained were both events in the apartheid period that even *Africa Addio* would recreate the epic Boer trek, but for the modern day. This time, in glorious Technicolor, it was with (staged) white Kenyans, ousted from their colonial homestead following their adopted country's independence from the British, manoeuvring their packed stagecoach down the continent and to fairer lands (Pretoria). At this point in cinema, the Mau-Mau had not yet been replaced by the Zulus as the African celluloid 'bogeyman'.

Of course, the American Western was built on reimagining the old frontiers as part of a valiant conquest and civilising project. Even André Bazin, who quarrelled with the eroticised presentation of Jane Russell in *The Outlaw*

(Howard Hughes, 1941), would laud *Stagecoach* (John Ford, 1939) as an 'ideal example of the maturity of a style brought to classic perfection' (1971: 149). As with so many old Westerns, the representation of Native Americans in *Stagecoach* is problematic. Similarly, therefore, *De Voortrekkers*, arriving less than twenty years after the British had initiated a violent, traumatic conflict against the Boer settlers, offers some insight into how a South African Western might have evolved into an indigenous-minded cycle of 'blood and soil' nationalism. Perhaps surprisingly, this would not be the case. Instead, it is pistol-packing Black heroes who dominate the Wild West of Pretoria's B-Scheme cinema. In asserting this fact, one does not want to seem to be, to quote from Iain Robert Smith's work on transnational adaptation of popular foreign genres, 'misrepresenting the complex negotiations with global cultural flows and exchanges that are taking place' (2016: 190). Rather, this chapter is maintaining that whilst hybrid elements from Western iconography (notably cowboys, saloons, horses, deserts, gun fights, and banditry) exist in these films, they do so within the wider scope of B-Scheme presentations that in themselves are subsidised on account of their avoidance of state subversion. As such, whilst Smith chooses to analyse a series of Indian Westerns, any accounting of a ZAxploitation hybrid needs to clarify and account for the past and present of what land rights and even residency signifies in the old (and indeed present) South Africa. The same cannot be said of most other nations.

For instance, in *Revenge*, produced by Tonie van der Merwe, it is the character of Baba (Alex Ngubane) who finds himself having to defend his new land and family from a pair of vicious bandits. They rape his wife (as always, this takes place off-screen), light fire to his farmhouse and brutalise his young son, with intent to kill, but Baba takes gunslinging lessons from a local old man – even blowing the head off a (real) cobra – before heading into town to shoot it out with the antagonists. In *Imusi*, a similar landowner, Jeramiah (Pius Dladla), his wife and his two young sons have to face bandits who intend to take his livestock and his business. Jeramiah bemoans his existence in savage Africa: 'How long can we keep living like this?' asks his wife, to which he responds, 'We don't have a choice'. In the end, he concludes 'We will endure'. It is almost unthinkable to imagine such dialogue existing, completely irrelevant of, and unattached to, the apartheid struggle, but in the guise of the Western, this clearly symbolic dialogue can be transposed to another wistful pastness. In other words, the Western setting is used to commercially exploit a Black hero acting with independence and freedoms that contemporary settings compromise. We never see a B-Scheme Black hero walk freely around the streets of Cape Town, Durban, Johannesburg or Port Elizabeth (the closest we get is Charlie Steel in a vaguely identified Johannesburg bar, or a character called Moses, played by B-Scheme regular John Madala, who is briefly shown to be wandering around a middle-class suburb in *The Mobsters* [Ben du Plessis,

THE BADASS: STICKIN' IT TO APARTHEID?

Figure 6.5 The Wild West in South Africa in *Revenge* (Coenie Dippenaar, 1986)

1980s]). Such movement might be alluded to, temporarily tolerated or we may even have a scene where the city is shown as a backdrop (as in *Beware Tiger*), but the suggestion – per these Western variants – that the Black man or woman is free to straddle the entire plateau of South Africa is never formulated. Even here, in these visions of pastness, we still see the formation of Tomaselli's 'back to the homelands'. It is Black land for Black development.

Lee Broughton notes how, with only a few exceptions, 'Hollywood Westerns prior to the 1950s possessed stereotypical characteristics' – characters of parody or servants, for instance (2016: 105). Mel Brooks had even parodied the traditional absence of African American characters in the Hollywood Old West with *Blazing Saddles* (1974). However, the popularity of blaxploitation had resulted in a small cycle of Westerns that introduced tough, self-sufficient Black heroes to the frontier: *The Legend of Nigger Charley*, its sequel *The Soul of Nigger Charley* (Larry Spangler, 1973), *Adiós Amigo* (Fred Williamson, 1975), *Boss Nigger* (Jack Arnold, 1975) and *Joshua* (Larry Spangler, 1976), among others. Actor-director and former footballer Fred Williamson was the recurring star of these (often provocatively titled) motion pictures, including in some cases as writer and producer, attesting to his star power and influence within the blaxploitation cycle. The Westerns of ZAxploitation draw on the

Figure 6.6A Hector Mathanda looks on as actor Vincent Velekazi opens fire in *Umbango* (or *The Feud*, Tonie van der Merwe, 1986)

traditional Williamson toughness, but without the political undercurrents of slavery and race-tension, with the all-too-brief moment in *Umbango* aside. Van der Merwe's *Umbango*, as well as *Imusi* and *Revenge*, the latter two texts running for under an hour in length, are populated by all-Black casts and follow linear, classic, restorative three act narratives dealing with revenge and land protection in the Old (African) West.

In their introduction to the monograph, *The Western in the Global South*, editors MaryEllen Higgins, Rita Keresztesi and Dayna Oscherwitz mention, building on Giles Deleuze's post-war, postcolonial terminology of the so-called 'neo-Western', that 'the Western genre travels, becoming *more than* American, being both local *and* global, potentially "worlding" through borrowing and mutating the Western and turning it outward, redistributed, to the world' (2015: xvii). As an example, the authors cite how Quentin Tarantino's *Django Unchained* takes ideas from not just the classic Hollywood Western but also Sergio Corbucci's original Italian template *Django*, itself cited in the Jamaican gangster classic *The Harder They Come*,[6] thus offering a postmodern and transnational experience for learned cineastes.

THE BADASS: STICKIN' IT TO APARTHEID?

Figure 6.6B Director Tonie van der Merwe, playing a victim of a shoot-out, nurses his injuries in *Umbango* (or *The Feud*, Tonie van der Merwe, 1986)

Rarely commented upon is how South African cinema had itself already 'redistributed' the characters and narrative of a popular Spaghetti Western with the obscure but well-made, locally produced *Three Bullets for a Long Gun* (Peter Henkel, 1973) – a quasi-rehash of *The Good, The Bad and the Ugly* (Sergio Leone, 1966). The film may use South African locations (and there is at least one notable Afrikaner accent in the cast courtesy of actor Tullio Moneta) but its setting is Mexico and the characters are all white. Decades later and one might argue that a prominent filmmaker such as Tarantino is less concerned with using past cinematic sources for explicitly globalised and indeed contemporary political purposes, and more interested in his own brand of stylish postmodernism. However, there is no doubt that the Western has itself engaged in radicalised re-imaginings of the past for some time. Tarantino's own, impressive accomplishment is arguably as much formed in the heroics of blaxploitation badass characters, including those defined by Fred Williamson, as it is in any retrospective attempts to desirously reimagine Black-white power binaries in the old American West. This is an aspect that Koven picks up on as well, arguing that *Django Unchained* 'creates a veritable language of grindhouse cinema allusions' (2017: 134). It would therefore be naïve to assume that, given the mnemonic nature of the B-Scheme Black crime films – not quite *Shaft*, not quite *Sweetback*, not quite *Super Fly* – that the period's Westerns borrow *only* from the defining texts of John Ford or Howard Hawks.

Setting a Western in South Africa raises immediate questions, if not outright complications, perhaps the reason why the English-language *Three Bullets for a Long Gun* simply ignores and re-imagines its own setting entirely. In the advertising for *Imusi* and *Revenge* it is claimed that both are set in Kwa-Zulu Natal.[7] Both the cowboys and the bandits in *Imusi* and *Revenge* are Black, there are no white characters, and these are narratives clearly set in a period *before* apartheid (albeit not, it would seem, before European colonialism). Inevitably, Black-on-Black violence takes place in the narratives and localised Zulu-speaking heroes – in both instances the hero is a married, family man – solve these criminal conflicts by themselves. There is also an uncomfortable feeling of the notorious, rough-trodden homeland policies in these films: the so-called Bantustans of the National Party where local, nominally 'independent' government was promised to communities on scattered and sometimes unproductive land. The period setting obviously permits for this conclusion to be challenged, but these B-Scheme productions are not the epic, glorious South Africa depicted in even the films of Empire, such as *Zulu*, but rather dangerous, dusty, malevolent, pokey little satellites in a fictional 'Old West' where banditry erupts over land and women. These set-ups do permit for some impressive heroics – van der Merwe's *Umbango*, for instance, has some fierce shoot-outs and curious lines: 'If this place has wealth, whoever occupies that land will have to be strong' states Popo Gumede, adding later as he overlooks the plateau, 'A place like this gives a man ideas. A home . . . to call his own'. However, the notion of 'homeland' never goes further than the farm in these films – echoing the government line that the Black populace can maintain their own separate development in a ranch far removed from the hustle and bustle of any emerging modernity. The homelands, in other words.

Coenie Dippenaar, director of *Revenge*, mentions:

> You have to remember that if you said anything wrong [anti-apartheid] there would be no subsidy. We did not have the bad experience of apartheid, we had gone through the army and everything, but now we can see what the problems were . . . You really had to censor yourself. As a Christian, I never wanted to make a film I could be ashamed of. We just wanted to tell a good action story . . . I made the first Black cowboy film . . . I took a cowboy story, but it was all Black actors. We built a whole town, had bar fights, horses, gun draws – but with Black actors. We were trying to move away from the American blaxploitation films – [we did]

not want [to do something] like *Shaft*. We tried to copy *Shaft* in some of the films we did, but we also made children's fantasy films – everything . . . I'm proud of what we have made. (2016)

Dippenaar's *Revenge*, perhaps even more than *Imusi* or *Umbango*, is the most rounded portrayal of the B-Scheme badass in the Old West. The character of Baba gets to evolve into a tough, driven, individualistic figure who will protect his young son *and* what remains of his scorched land following the rape and murder of his wife. *Revenge* is one of the rare B-Scheme films that probably could have played on an imagined 42nd Street double-bill as part of a proverbial 'grindhouse nostalgia'.

Genre, then, or cycles within established formulas, were an important element when it came to offering Black actors a notable degree of screen agency within the B-Scheme. Even after the conclusion of the form, we can see the lineage of *Umbango* in a more acclaimed, upmarket, if still relatively obscure, effort such as *Jobman* (Darrel Roodt, 1990), which would also touch on land rights and race-conflict within a tangential Western framework and at a time when a new South Africa was beginning to seem vaguely possible. However, during the apartheid period, a small number of local productions also complicated the (general) all-Black B-Scheme/ZAxploitation set-up by initiating 'buddy' narratives in which racial harmony was 'won' by a mutual understanding between 'Africans' of all backgrounds. Surprisingly, this is one of the ZAxploitation tropes that sustained itself the longest, emerging in the mid-1970s and stretching on until the eventual release of Nelson Mandela in 1990. In the next chapter, I will deal with the buddy-blaxploitation film.

Notes

1. Dlamini is a common name for both villains and heroes across B-Scheme films. I'm not sure that the moniker has any real meaning, however. If it is a reference to the Dlamini royalty of Swaziland, it carries little relevance to the films of this study and their character namesakes. If it is a nod towards Sam Dlamini, the Deputy Mayor of Sharpeville, whose murder in 1984 was particularly famous for its brutality, or to Stephen Dlamini of the outlawed SACP (South African Communist Party) it also carries no immediate connection to the on-screen characters and their actions.
2. Judging by the cast, direction and music cues, I think that this could be Tony Cunningham, who is credited with the camerawork.
3. Tomaselli, for instance, mentions the unbanning of *The Rocky Horror Picture Show* (Jim Sharman, 1975) in South Africa (1988: 145)
4. It is also worth noting that this quote indicates Murray was aware that some B-Scheme films, and performers, had been popular and that not every motion picture that was made as a part of the incentive had to have unscrupulous distributors holding people 'captive'.
5. Tomaselli was apt to point out to me during the writing of this monograph that 'This phrase is a real Americanism, it is never used by South Africans, again pointing to American blaxploitation film influences'.

6. Author Kenneth W. Harrow also reads *The Harder They Come* as a Western in his monograph *Trash: African Cinema from Below* (2013: pp. 64–6). I would disagree and argue that it is a realist-musical, with director Henzell giving himself the challenge of using realist film techniques, including a Third Cinema approach, to tackle a genre that so clearly exists within not just generic unreality but the classical Hollywood structure of Bordwell, Staiger and Thompson.
7. Per the descriptions found on Gravel Road Entertainment Group's website: https://www.gravelroadafrica.com/retro-afrika-bioscope

7. FOR THE COMMON GOOD?

The ZAxploitation Buddy Movie

'We must fight for freedom! With the help of the American, who has proven himself to be our friend and our equal, we must finally rid ourselves of the powers of darkness!'

Ken Gampu as Dr Tamba, revolutionary fighter in an unnamed African country, *American Ninja 4: The Annihilation* (Cedric Sundstrom, 1990)

This chapter builds on discussion of the ZAxploitation badass by looking at how a selection of such on-screen personas interacted with various white counterpart(s) in a number of buddy films. Included in this chapter are some international co-productions, such as South African director Cedric Sundstrom's instalments in the *American Ninja* series, which one could consider to be an identifiable part of the ZAxploitation pantheon because of their placement within this multiracial buddy formula. It should be pointed out that prior to this monograph such films had also been considered by Trevor Taylor as part of South Africa's 'ethnic' cinema. The author was largely dismissive: 'None of the style Sundstrom brought to bear in his earlier work is apparent', he would write of *American Ninja 4: The Annihilation*, adding 'never aimed at South African distribution anyway... Targeted purely for video and cable television' for those who expect 'a certain tacky quality' (1992: 134). Nevertheless, a film such as *American Ninja 4* might also be contextualised as a clear evolution of the type of character that *Joe Bullet* first introduced to

Figure 7.1 Ken Gampu and Michael Dudikoff are 'buddies' in *American Ninja 4: The Annihilation* (Cedric Sundstrom, 1990)

South African audiences. Given that Ken Gampu plays major roles in both is testament to how the late actor navigated the storms of apartheid, including in some films that feature him as a blasé supporting player or a Sidney Poitier stand-in – what Bogle describes as 'the paragon of black middle-class values and virtues' (2016: 158). However, it is Gampu who might be seen, retrospectively, as bookending ZAxploitation via characters of badass action and revolutionary vigour even if his *American Ninja* film is, per Taylor, 'tacky' and targeted towards a VHS audience.

Mentions Sundstrom:

> Ken went to Hollywood and he was almost in [films such as] *The Scalp Hunters* [Sydney Pollack, 1968] and *The Professionals* [Richard Brooks, 1966]. But he always came back. There was a lot more work for him really, because of the local films. When we come to the tax haven that South Africa became in the 1980s, Ken Gampu was popular. In the 80s, Ken Gampu was in almost every film. (2016)

It was this tax haven that enticed such schlock-cinema producers as Cannon Films to establish a base, and even a theatre chain, in South Africa. Gus Silber quotes producer Edgar Bold as explaining, 'For the players in Hollywood ... South Africa was a joke. An easy ride, a quick buck, the bottom end of the movie industry barrel' (1992: 125). However, Sundstrom's *American Ninja* films fit into the ZAxploitation story (perhaps surprisingly) well and do not necessarily indicate that cheap genre cinema had to be bereft of radical ideas.

When *American Ninja 4* premiered on 8 March 1990, the late Nelson Mandela had been a free man for just under a month and the end of apartheid was a question of 'when' and not 'if'. At the time 'The economic crisis and the nature of civil upheaval meant the state could not suppress resistance absolutely' (van der Westhuizen 2007: 174) and the nature of a settlement remained in the air for four more years (particularly regarding live issues such as land rights and the dissolution of the Bantustans). One is tempted to ascertain that the more provocative representations of Black agency in the latter part of the decade may have been because the National Party government had far more pressing matters to deal with than film censorship. Sundstrom's *American Ninja 4*, the last in the popular franchise,[1] is an interracial buddy movie, but broken into two distinct acts. The first teams up a tough, wise, white secret agent, Sean Davidson (David Bradley), with his less experienced African American counterpart Carl Brackston (Dwayne Alexandre). Whilst Davidson is shown to be the more effective of the two in a brawl, there is no sense of racial inequality between them, and they arrive in (North) Africa (to an unnamed country) as a team. When the two are captured whilst on the field, series hero Joe Armstrong (action film veteran Michael Dudikoff) emerges from retirement to save his two American colleagues, in the process teaming up with local freedom fighter Dr Tamba (Ken Gampu). It is Gampu who leads the charge to victory, although – per franchise expectancy – Bradley and Dudikoff become the focus of the narrative's conclusion. Nonetheless, the sight of an African regime being toppled by a multi-ethnic force is difficult not to register and a first within the ZAxploitation pantheon. Admittedly, the country is not named, and the setting of North Africa allows for some confusion, but if Taylor could identify the on-screen location as 'definitely Lesotho' and point out that it is 'populated by very few Arabs' and instead hosts 'black comrades who speak Xhosa' (1992: 138) then one suspects that local viewers of the time (should there have been many) would have been able to understand the 'message' as well.

The sequel to Sundstrom's *American Ninja 3: Blood Hunt* (1989), *American Ninja 4* was produced by Cannon Films, who, much like South Africa's National Party, had once seemed unbeatable but would barely last into the decade ahead. Hitting a financial peak in 1986, in which shares in the company cost $45.5,[2] a typical Cannon formula was established: commercial genre films, B-level actors and actresses and garish marketing campaigns, often promising an abundance of sex and/or violence.[3] The 1980s had already seen an onslaught of commercially successful films headlined by a Black-white twosome, most notably *48 Hrs* (Walter Hill, 1982), *Beverly Hills Cop* (Martin Brest, 1984) and *Lethal Weapon* (Richard Donner, 1987), each inspiring sequels.[4] As such, it made sense that Cannon – a company that Andrew Yule, somewhat unfairly, would ascertain only ever engaged with public taste 'when they pandered to the lowest common denominator' (1987: 2) would want to ride the interracial buddy film bandwagon as well. With *American Ninja 4*, the film also offered at least one unique element: *two pairs* of interracial buddies, fighting for a good cause. Almost two decades after *Joe Bullet*, a South African director offered audiences two badass Black characters fighting against an oppressive police state, even if they were to be, by commercial dictates, overshadowed by white leading men.

Cannon's original interracial buddy film, *American Ninja* (Sam Firstenberg, 1985), which saw Dudikoff and erstwhile African American stunt man Steve James face-off against an elite and deadly Japanese army of martial arts experts in the Philippines, had been successful enough to lead to a sequel in 1987. *American Ninja 2: The Confrontation*, also directed by Firstenberg, took Dudikoff and James to an unnamed Caribbean Island (although actually Cape Town and Simon's Town in South Africa). As the rand plummeted in value, backdropped by the government's declaration of a state of emergency, the country became a popular location for B-movie filmmakers, beginning with *King Solomon's Mines*, which also brought in Sundstrom as the First Assistant Director. As mentioned by Martin Botha and Adri van Aswegen, following eight months of negotiations between Cannon Films and the Pretoria government, 'permission was given in October 1984 for Cannon to become part of the local film industry' (1992: 25).

Whilst Botha and Aswegen consider Cannon's *King Solomon's Mines* and other local productions from foreign filmmakers, such as *Alien from L.A.*, as films which do not offer representations of South Africa and thus cannot be seen as local cinema, Sundstrom's work with the company is unique. Not only does it represent the output of an indigenous filmmaker on the international stage, but his two *American Ninja* films pay clear lip-service to civil unrest within (fictional) African nations that only the most naïve viewer would not recognise as a stand-in for South Africa. Nonetheless, some actors were unwilling to risk their careers by breaking the cultural boycott against South Africa and *American Ninja*'s hero Michael Dudikoff, who had begun his (brief) rise to fame opposite Tom Hanks in *Bachelor Party* (Neal Israel, 1984), began to feel pressure from Hollywood. States Sundstrom:

> He made *Platoon Leader* [Aaron Norris, 1988] and *River of Death* [Steve Carver, 1989] in [South Africa] but it was becoming nasty. People were starting to picket outside Cannon's offices in Los Angeles. He had one more [film] in his contract. *American Ninja 3* was meant to be the end of Dudikoff [as a character] because we had a new one [actor], with David Bradley ... But Dudikoff said he would not come back to South Africa. That is why he never made the third film. (2016)

This nervousness around working in the country during the cultural boycott also meant misplacing the country of genesis. Thus, Silber mentions of *King Solomon's Mines*, an early starring role for Sharon Stone: 'For obvious political reasons prevailing at the time, Cannon was less keen to promote the movie's location as a holiday paradise. To the outside world, it was a purely Zimbabwean production, with South Africa's starring role conspicuously uncredited' (1992: 127).

For *American Ninja 3*, Sundstrom would introduce his new star, Bradley, opposite the returning Steve James, and also presented an Asian heroine (played by Michele Chan), who – in an especially subversive scene – goes undercover in white-face. The actress, who portrays a master-of-disguise named Chan Lee, is a tough kung-fu expert and devoid of such common cinematic Orientalism as the exotic girlfriend portrayal, which typified otherwise dominant franchise players such as Indonesian performer Laura Gemser in the previous decade.[5] Tellingly, the unnamed country that the heroes of *American Ninja 3* do battle in is typified by a flag that carries a Union Jack – symbolic, one would presume, of its presence in the old identity of South Africa itself. To entice Dudikoff back to the mythology, *American Ninja 4* would shoot in Lesotho with a South African crew. It would thus be Sundstrom's two films that tied together a number of recurring ZAxploitation elements within a new multiracial battle against tyranny: morality tales of 'crime does not pay', martial arts, a Black voice of common sense (offered to Gampu in the fourth film), localised corruption and the sense that good citizenship creates a better neighbourhood. Sundstrom, however, admits that he still felt the need to be cautious. Of Ken Gampu, the filmmaker states:

> He was not [out there] fighting with the struggle, he was actually a very placid man. When I did *American Ninja 4*, there were these people [in the film] who were rioting and going against the establishment in this African country and there was Ken shouting 'join us in our fight for freedom!' It was [done] so subtly, in a way, but there were a lot of references to here [South Africa] even though we shot it there [Lesotho] . . . There is a scene where a policeman jumps up and says 'this is an illegal gathering, you must disperse' – which at that time was not allowed [due to the state of emergency]. Those were the fun times – when you could subtly put in little comments about South Africa. (2016)

Writing about the interracial buddy film, a formula which the *American Ninja* series adheres to, Melvin Donalson mentions that it cannot be seen as a genre because it lacks an 'essential, connecting, and replicated foundation' (2006: 8). The author nevertheless sees recurring ideas and representations across a number of films, from the formative influence of *The Defiant Ones* through to *Lethal Weapon* and its sequels. In looking at the South African motion pictures of this chapter, we see two elements adapted from popular buddy film representations such as these. The first is that interracial bonding creates better human beings (and thus a more progressive and secure society). The second is more problematic and assures audiences that Black agency and aspiration are concurrent with, and even entirely dependent on, white approval. The former presentation, which is evident in the *American Ninja* films (and American templates such as *Lethal Weapon*), often results in 'teamwork' overcoming some form of criminality or duress and can be seen in such B-Scheme efforts as *Bona Manzi*, *Run for Your Life* and *One More Shot* or the independently financed and produced *Death of a Snowman* and *Kill and Kill Again*. However, just because a Black-white troupe is shown to overcome adversary through a dual effort does not mean that all of these films necessarily advocate a multiracial utopia.

Race Matters

Blaxploitation buddy films such as *Across 110th Street* (Barry Shear, 1972) and *Detroit 9000* would emerge only a few years after *In the Heat of the Night* (Norman Jewison, 1967) – with the interracial trend becoming so ingrained as part of the larger cycle of Black-centred cinema that even the famous sequel *Cleopatra Jones and the Casino of Gold* would offer star Tamara Dobson a sidekick. Speaking about *Detroit 9000*, Novotny Lawrence makes a convincing case about how the Black protagonist, an ambitious police detective called Sergeant Jesse Williams (Hari Rhodes), is less central to the story than his white partner, Lieutenant Danny Bassett (Alex Rocco), whose manoeuvring between the law and the criminal underground ultimately frames the entire narrative.[6] Nonetheless, one might also argue that in order for *Detroit 9000* to successfully execute its 'twist' ending (in which Bassett is revealed to be corrupt, albeit with some ambiguity) it needs to make the film *about* his seemingly 'straight' – albeit urbanised and out-of-shape – white detective vis-à-vis that of a university-educated, athletic Black do-gooder. The closest South African comparison to *Detroit 9000* is *Death of a Snowman*. Unlike *Detroit 9000*, however, which manipulates any audience racism by teasing the idea that the too-good-to-be-true Bassett could be involved in ghettoised crime, *Death of a Snowman* introduces Ken Gampu as a journalist and amateur sleuth, called Steve Chaka, who is immediately deemed to be unwelcome in a white man's world. Making Gampu's character a journalist is a far from decorous decision as 1976, the year *Death of a Snowman* was released, was also the time of the Soweto riots, following which a crackdown from Pretoria on the Union of Black Journalists ensued. The union was responsible for the liberal-leaning newspaper *The Bulletin* and it would be banned in August of

THE ZAXPLOITATION BUDDY MOVIE

Figure 7.2 Nigel Davenport and Ken Gampu as an unlikely crime fighting duo in *Death of a Snowman* (Christopher Rowley, 1976)

that year (Tomaselli and Louw 1991: 98). Conflict between the Union and the National Party government had been brewing for some time. As mentioned earlier in this study, exploitation films tend to be topical, so casting Gampu as a journalist during this period would have allowed South Africans to acknowledge his character's 'dangerous' nature (at least as regards the state line), which is essential to keeping his portrayal in this film politically ambiguous.

Introducing the interracial set-up of films such as *Detroit 9000*, Lawrence mentions:

> This interracial partnership changes one of blaxploitation's most essential characteristics – the black hero or heroine who was significant for three distinct reasons: (1) they cut against the stereotypical images that had traditionally circumscribed the black cinematic image; (2) they were capable of navigating the oppressive system while maintaining their blackness; (3) they were connected to and thus fought on behalf of the black community. (2016: 123)

Ironically, a South African variant such as *Death of a Snowman*, independently financed and shot by a British filmmaker, offers its Black star more agency than any of the B-Scheme portrayals introduced so far in this monograph and not least because of the provocation that comes from him being a Black journalist (and thus likely associated with the soon-to-be-banned UBJ). Opening with a focus on a pair of long, slender Black female legs, perched in a seat of the top deck of Johannesburg's famous Hillbrow Tower, and an accompanying (original) funk soundtrack, it is clear that *Death of a Snowman* has the international blaxploitation film market on its mind as well.

Released in America under the offensive moniker of *Black Trash* (acknowledging the film's transnational roots, the poster would boldly state 'From the USA to South Africa'), Gampu's Steve Chaka teams up with a genteel cop called Ben Deel (Nigel Davenport) to try and figure out who is behind a new war on crime in the city. Major drug dealers (Black, white, and Asian) are being executed across Johannesburg. Chaka is contacted by a crime boss who explains that he is behind the murders to try and avoid the poorest (re: Black) children becoming addicted to heroin. Meanwhile, Deel is told by the Captain of his precinct to be wary of Chaka, who he believes might be an informant or at least associated with criminal elements in Soweto. The 'snowman' of the title turns out to be a scurrilous but smart Black ringleader, slaughtering narcotics barons in order to claim their distribution networks as his own.

Donald Bogle talks about the 'huckfinn fixation' of American cinema in which:

> A good white man opposes the corruption and pretences of the dominant white culture. In rejecting society, he (like Huck Finn) takes up with an outcast. The other man (like Nigger Jim) is a trusted black who never competes with the white man and who serves as a reliable ego paddler. (2016: 126)

Such a conclusion, which Bogle also argues inspired later Hollywood films such as *In the Heat of the Night*, echoes similar words from Peter Davis on the interracial buddy set-up: 'some producers became convinced of the humanity of black people then, belatedly but not ineffectually, they began to [offer them] films ... whose message was anti-racist' (1996: 97). It is tempting to see Gampu, in *Death of a Snowman*, as this huckfinn representation: he might be best friends with a white man, but he avoids challenging him even as he (wrongly) becomes suspected of being an informer for a number of local gangsters. Nigel Davenport's underwritten character, in comparison, is only important to the narrative insofar as he tolerates his Black best friend to the chagrin of his boss and his colleagues. *Death of a Snowman* thus *becomes* a film in which Gampu has to prove his humanity; the 'goodness' of Davenport is never doubted, primarily because he is a white man in Johannesburg (this is also before the story of Donald Woods, which informs *Cry Freedom* [Richard Attenborough, 1987]).

It should also be noted that *Death of a Snowman* tries to avoid politicising 1970s Johannesburg, although it is telling that Chaka's favourite hangout is a local bar which has only Black staff and clientele. It is in this surrounding that he also gets some tough and typically macho lines; telling his on-off girlfriend, a heroin addict, 'If there's anything you know baby, it is how to make a man cum'. Nevertheless, the character still appeals to later B-Scheme presentations: Gampu must finally be the good citizen who brings down the (all-Black) crime syndicate himself. Gampu is set-up as the moral conscience early in the narrative as he tells Deel, 'There are thousands of kids in the city who could do with food and good clothes . . . I care about the kids'. This sort of characterisation is certainly no less subtle than that which is seen in later, Christian-themed, B-Scheme action films such as *Knockout Joe*. However, per Lawrence, fighting on behalf of the Black community is also a key element of American blaxploitation representation and Chaka is finally shown doing so alone, *without* the support of white authority. Moreover, when *Death of a Snowman* concludes, Gampu and Davenport sit playing chess, with the former turning down a weekend invite to socialise with the latter: ultimately, the white cop's distrust has cost him his friendship with an upstanding Black journalist. A sequence in which Gampu's Chaka shares fried chicken with Davenport's Deel is an especially tasteless visual 'joke' about Black-white bonding under segregation, but *Death of a Snowman* nonetheless successfully transports the urban upheaval of American blaxploitation cinema to the streets of Johannesburg and Soweto. More importantly, it shows a character 'navigating the oppressive system while maintaining their Blackness' – particularly given the outlet of Black journalism – even despite the fact Gampu never quite successfully escapes from his huckfinn persona.

Nevertheless, if the likes of *Across 110th Street* and *Detroit 9000*, not to mention *Assault on Precinct 13* (John Carpenter, 1976), are buddy films that highlight narratives of racial bonding under duress, then *Death of a Snowman*, surprisingly, offers a more unique spin on familiar presentations. There is no race-bonding at the conclusion, Gampu – much like in his two performances as Joe Bullet – is eventually forced to work alone and the badass action hero is contrasted with a weaker, more gullible white counterpart. Donalson has identified that interracial buddy films follow a typical character arc: 'inherent tension between reluctant partners suggests the improbability of any friendship, making the amelioration between the two more dramatic' (2006: 51). In contrast, *Death of a Snowman* begins with a tight, seemingly indestructible, interracial friendship where the two characters are bonded by trust and work. However, infiltration by the apartheid state draws them apart even when, as it turns out, it is the Black character and not the white 'hero' who belatedly proves to be the narrative voice of reason. Interestingly, this reinvention of the interracial buddy motif is repeated across other ZAxploitation films, including those of the B-Scheme. By all accounts, *Death of a Snowman* was influential.

Tommy Röthig's *Run for Your Life*, for instance, depicts a mixed-race friendship in which Roy, a young Black man, lives with his wife (of Indian descent, a unique presentation during this period) in a suburb near to Patrick – a white man – and Patrick's same-race spouse. *Run for Your Life* at least touches on multiculturalism in South Africa, and on the presence of Black economic mobility in the apartheid state. At first, Roy and Patrick are presented as close friends (as are their wives), but when they do go on their jog, things begin to change à la *Death of a Snowman* and its breakdown of Black-white ties. Roy is consistently shown to be less mobile and physically fit than Patrick. 'I thought you wanted to run, but you're killing me here', says an agitated Roy.[7] Patrick asks for time to rest and Roy berates and mocks him further, although skin colour is never referred to. Soon thereafter both men stumble upon a drug plantation and are captured, which takes *Run for Your Life* into another exploitation staple of the blaxploitation era: the banana republic prison film. Probably too short-lived and minor to be considered a demarcation in its own right, this trope would often star Pam Grier or another African American badass female to further the idea of a 'fish out of water' in a developing country: *The Big Doll House* (Jack Hill, 1971); *The Big Bird Cage* (Jack Hill, 1972); *Women in Cages* (Gerardo de León, 1972).[8] In *Run for Your Life*, one tortured female is shown tied-up and hanging from the ceiling by her arms, another is injected with heroin, others – we are told – will be killed for standing up to the drug lord who runs the establishment. It is up to Patrick – the white man – to save the day, however, because Roy proves too weak. Thus, Roy might exist within the urban elite, in his suburban house, but he does so awkwardly, and, in the end, he remains in the shadow of an athletic, heroic European. Nonetheless, *Run for Your Life* still normalises a Black-white friendship – despite emerging tensions, although the huckfinn persona is evident in Roy's kowtowing to Patrick's abuse.

In *One More Shot*, another B-Scheme film featuring a multiracial friendship, Chan, a Chinese martial arts expert, and his (Black) friend Johnny Tough, are called upon by a white man when his young daughter is kidnapped by a human smuggling ring. The operation is supported by mainly white criminals but owned by a rich foreign Arab (a dubious ethnic representation that repeats itself in *American Ninja 4*[9]). *One More Shot* – just like *Run for Your Life* – is far from radical, but these two films do choose to present a multiracial friendship and, in the case of the former motion picture, audiences of the mobile circuit were able to see a Black man battle and win against a small group of white mafioso.[10] Furthermore, on a purely surface level, *One More Shot* indicates how, historically, the apartheid regime's 'repression served to encourage unity and bring blacks, Indians and Coloureds together' (Welsh 2000: 446). It is, of course, open to conjecture if this was even the intention of the director, Ronnie Isaacs.

Isaacs made *One More Shot* in 1984, a decade before the first democratic election in South Africa. As cheap and meandering as much of the film might

Figure 7.3 Black and white team-up against criminal elements in *Run for Your Life* (Tommy Röthig, 1985)

be, it remains staggering to see a sequence in which a rotund Afrikaner is stripped of his weaponry and made, by Chan and Johnny, to enter a field full of hungry lions and left to his own devices. By all accounts, such scenes were cynically placed in the work of Isaacs to (not unlike Tonie van der Merwe) satisfy the understanding that Black audiences were increasingly unhappy under apartheid. One of the film's white actors, Stan Froom, is quoted as telling Silber:

> It was my idea to play this bad guy who walks around with a fly-swatter and tells people, 'Hey man, I even own the air that you breathe.' I think I was the first white guy in a black movie in their own language. (1992: 270)

Silber notes how white actors became (much like blaxploitation films) increasingly used as villains in B-Scheme cinema such as *One More Shot* as the 1980s progressed.

However, for all intents and purposes, those watching *One More Shot* in

Figure 7.4 Johnny Tough (Hector Rabotabi) takes on white authority in *One More Shot* (Ronnie Isaacs, 1984)

1984 were offered empowered, seemingly independent, non-white heroes to cheer. This multicultural ensemble is also central to the B-Scheme film *Bona Manzi*. With *Bona Manzi*, director Tonie van der Merwe returns to a common presentation of his work by introducing two child heroes, but the focal point of this story is on a pair of Black and white game wardens (Sipho and John) and their close friendship. When two white poachers (the villains, of course) begin to tread into their land, with the intention of killing rhino, the pair work together to foil their plans – and, in the concluding stand-off, Sipho even bludgeons one of the antagonists with a log. Both white and Black protagonists retain their friendship at the conclusion of the story.

Kill and Kill Again is an English-language, international co-production that, not unlike a cheap B-Scheme effort such as *One More Shot*, introduces martial arts experts and pits them against a small criminal empire. Although the narrative explicitly mentions South Africa as the location, only one Black character – 'Gorilla', played by Ken Gampu, is present here. The moniker of the character is obviously offensive, despite the narrative's attempt to indicate that Gampu's nickname comes from his large, statuesque frame and animalistic approach to combat ('every time I beat someone, I bite their ear off', he intones). In one scene, Gampu forces open the toilet door in an airplane. 'He's never flown in an airplane before', states one of his team. 'He's never been let out of the zoo before', replies the stewardess. 'Well, actually, we bribed his keeper', comes the retort. Whilst *Kill and Kill Again* does give Gampu authority to beat up on whitey, much like the American blaxploitation heroes, his depiction as a ferocious primitive is far more offensive than that of *Joe Bullet* or his triumph in *Death of a Snowman* and, later, *American Ninja 4*. Gampu is reduced to a human 'King Kong'.

Clifford T. Manlove mentions how 'All versions of *King Kong* use representations of Skull Island and New York City to portray the relationship between Africa and "Modernity", implicating narrative cinema, and Hollywood in particular, with the modern colonial project in Africa' (2012: 126). When Gampu's Gorilla is 'rescued' by his white cohorts from his humdrum manual labouring job in Johannesburg, and convinced to fly to Sun City (interestingly, the Bantustan of Bophuthatswana is presented here as a magnet for criminal activity) for a martial arts competition, he serves the same purpose as King Kong himself. Gampu's job is to act as the big, Black bogeyman and provide some muscle for an audience expecting extravagance and excess. The actor's Gorilla character shows how 'savage Africa' exists as a buddy film trope, a metaphor for the dangers of the dark continent and, when required, a useful force for good – at least if it can be controlled and used as such. Gampu is also thrown into a ragtag ensemble for Tonie van der Merwe's *Operation Hit Squad*, which is discussed as part of the border war cycle (see Chapter 9).

Escape from Africa

The presentation of Black agency and aspiration as concurrent with, and in some cases, entirely dependent on, white approval is as paternalistic as many of the B-Scheme portrayals of 'crime does not pay'. It might also be even more problematic and not just because this factor sustains the 'magic negro' stereotype. Rather, in a segregated state, there is the feel of a local Uncle Tom who provides the white man's servitude by guiding him towards some form of anti-colonial or postcolonial radicalisation. In a film such as *Shamwari* or the trashy (but more high-end, at least in terms of production values and notability) South African co-production *The Wild Geese*, white redemption (usually spiritual and moral) provides more story causality and narrative dominance than Black liberation, despite the spectre of segregation. Perhaps most obnoxiously, however, these are films about escape, where Africa returns to the savage netherworld of notorious old exploitation cinema such as *Mau-Mau* (Elwood Price, 1955). Exploiting the British struggle against uprising in Kenya, *Mau-Mau* boasted such lurid advertising campaigns as 'Crazed Mau-Mau Killers Slay Women and Children!' (Schaefer 1999: 114). It is in this Africa, however, that neither Black nor white are safe, but – in a buddy film such as *Shamwari* – each must depend on the other to find sanctuary. This is a different presentation from even Ken Gampu's bestial Gorilla in *Kill and Kill Again*, who makes the choice to join a white team in a white-run karate tournament in Bophuthatswana in his own right – including after throttling his racist boss. The presentation of Black-white 'bonding' and not-too-subtle commentary about South Africa as a rightful white settler safe space, in *Shamwari* and *The Wild Geese*, as well as their trashy gung-ho action theatrics, put even Sundstrom's two low budget *American Ninja* stories of liberation into a more progressive perspective. Speaking about the more recent blockbuster *Blood Diamond*, authors Bennetta Jules-Rosette, J. R. Osborn and Lea Maria Ruiz-Ade refer to 'a redemptive New Jack African film' (2012: 170). The authors use this term having built on the influential representations of inner-city toughness in the trendsetting *New Jack City* (Mario Van Peebles, 1991). The New Jack African film signifies the portrayal of Africa 'at once as a liminal space, a purgatory from which to escape, and a potential utopia' (Ibid.: 157). *New Jack City*, and the films it inspired (most notably from John Singleton), might be loosely labelled as post-blaxploitation 'hood' films. These are motion pictures that present Black urban aspiration but also introduce sympathetic characters who are involved in illicit means to escape from crime and/or poverty. White authority is not the immediate, daily threat in these narratives – rival gangs, comprising of local, young African American youths, surface as the prominent antagonists. *Blood Diamond* is seen as a reinvention of similar characterisations but within an exotic civil conflict (in Sierra Leone, complete with child mercenaries) rather than a localised urban one.

Whilst there is concurrency in the 'escape from the ghetto' films and the 'escape from Africa' films (such as *Blood Diamond*), the latter has its precedent in a film such as *The Wild Geese*. This commercially successful film has a group of mainly white, British mercenaries sent out to a fictional African country to save an ousted, revolutionary and (most importantly) Western-friendly Black leader called President Julius Limbani (played by South African actor Winston Ntshona). Although he was once in a powerful position as President, Julius Limbani cannot walk, so is shown to be figuratively castrated. Repeated across the Black representations in South African films, therefore, is a lack of sex and sexuality for the Black stars; perhaps typified by the previously acknowledged comments of Tonie van der Merwe to Silber: 'We try to stay away from nudity and sex, because our sex and the way they look at sex is entirely different' (1992: 271). Indeed, Black sexual agency is – it seems – a step too far for even cinema such as *The Wild Geese*, made for international consumption.

One of the squad members in *The Wild Geese* (Hardy Krüger with an attempt at an Afrikaans accent) is a racist South African. Pointing to the further kindship between B-Scheme portrayals and those of the more main-

THE ZAXPLOITATION BUDDY MOVIE

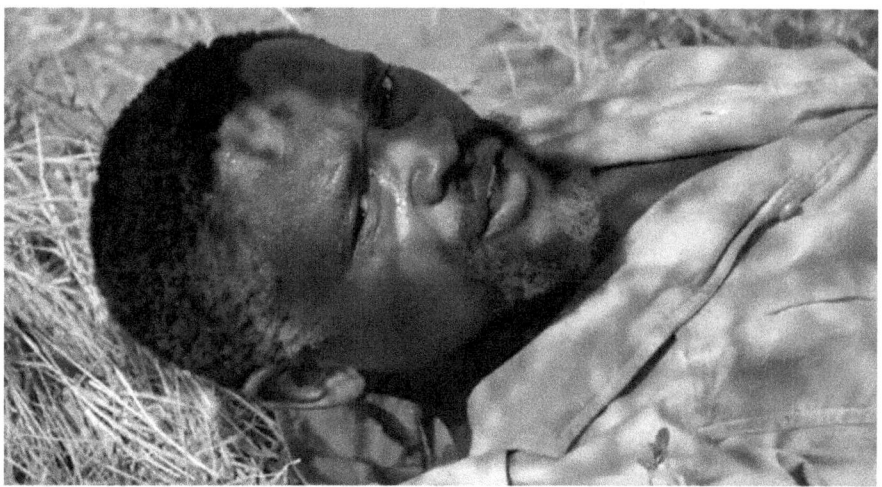

Figure 7.5 Actor Winston Ntshona in *The Wild Geese* (Andrew V. McLaglen, 1978)

stream co-productions lensed in South Africa, *The Wild Geese* returns to the same trope of van der Merwe's *Umbango* and numerous other stories in and about the country: land. State Tomaselli and van Zyl:

> In *Wild Geese*, the Afrikaner mercenary has joined the invading force simply to make enough money to buy a farm. The counter-migration, however, was an ambition which, in reality, was realised by only a few. The image of 'the farm' nonetheless remains encoded in South African linguistic patterns. (1992: 417)

Krüger wants his land so badly that he spends much of the film carrying the injured Limbani on his back across the African bush, despite referring to him repeatedly as 'kaffir' – as if the symbolism of a Black leader, symbolically castrated and requiring the assistance of white guidance, was not semiotically offensive enough. Naturally, the two eventually come into conflict. Argues the South African:

> Whites have carried you people on our backs ever since we came to this country. You need me to save your miserable black life right now don't you? Man, we have built your countries and now you are kicking us out of almost all of them. You are living on foreign aid, robbing your own people blind and crying about outside oppression, while you are killing each other in great big bleeding batches. Once you have something better to offer come talk to us and the white South.

Keeping himself calm and collected, the President argues:

> We need each other, white man, and that's the way it should be. We have the world using us right now, setting group against group, destroying Africa. Our new freedom is just another label for their brand of slavery and the final bloodbath is coming. First between black and white and then between black and black when you whites have left Africa for good ... We have got to learn to care for each other or there will be nothing left of our Africa ... We have to forgive you for the past and you have to forgive us for the present. If we have no future together white man, then we have no future. That is what I believe in. That is what I'm willing to die for.

Despite insisting just seconds earlier that 'we whites were born here, we are just as African as you are and don't make a mistake because we are going to stay', the young white mercenary finds himself taken by the President's words. 'You are beginning to sound good to me, maybe we need you. Maybe you are just the man,' he declares, later running in front of gun-fire to sacrifice his own life and protect the man he was earlier demeaning as a 'kaffir'. He dies, hand-in-hand with his new Black saviour, another Savimbi figure – the Mr Right of the dark continent.[11] This is Hollywood's Africa, a savage land navigated by the brave and the foolhardy. *The Wild Geese*'s version of the continent is one where a racist but well-meaning white South African would lay down his life for a forgiving Black man,[12] literally carried on his Aryan back, having touched his heart with a story about future relations based on 'forgiveness' for centuries of colonial plunder and exploitation. Tomaselli would also note how *The Wild Geese* had to 'obtain official clearance at the script stage' in order to procure the official involvement of the South African Defence Force (1988: 21). For actor Roger Moore, being advised against performing in another coup for Pretoria's propaganda 'was becoming a bit of a bore' (2008: 216), attesting to how South Africa had managed to normalise apartheid to considerable sections of the population abroad.

Whilst this study is cautious of speaking about mainstream and/or Hollywood studio representations of South Africa, outside of comparisons such as those of Sabela in his *iKati Elimnyama* and the previous year's *Gold*, it is worth noting how the buddy representations of (the particularly racist) *The Wild Geese* dominate other, similar presentations aimed at a wide audience as opposed to a small indigenous one or even a film with limited (at best) cult appeal (per *Death of a Snowman* or *Kill and Kill Again*). Boasting A-list stars, films such as *The Wilby Conspiracy* and the later, famous anti-apartheid narrative in *Cry Freedom* – which was shot in Zimbabwe – also equate Black liberation as equal to some kind of white moral or spiritual awakening.[13] Although not a buddy film *per se*, star Donald Sutherland undergoes a similar transformation in *A Dry White Season* (Euzhan Palcy, 1989); playing a life-long South African citizen who has his awakening after a Black colleague is tortured to death under police custody. *A Dry White Season* was groundbreaking for featuring a female Caribbean director behind the camera of a major studio production, although (typical for Hollywood's Africa) the film itself is still mediated through the perspective of white characters. One might also include at least two films from Jamie Uys in this company: his formative *Dingaka* and his most famous blockbuster, *The Gods Must be Crazy*.

In defining ZAxploitation within the parameters of, first and foremost, exploitation films and their relationship to similar, concurrent low budget, trashy genre cinema, this book has excluded the Uys productions from more detailed analysis. However, Davis identifies *Dingaka*, in which Ken Gampu plays opposite Stanley Baker, as representing the genesis of the buddy trend for South African film producers. The author dismisses *Dingaka* as 'a syncretising of apartheid's delusions' (1996: 66). However, *Dingaka*'s presentation of separate development, between savage tribesman (Gampu) and European professional (Baker as an attorney), forced into a circumstantial bond, introduces the same uneven power binaries that exist even in later mainstream work such as *Cry Freedom*, attesting to its thematic influence. Acknowledging this factor perhaps initiates why a film such as *Death of a Snowman*, for all its faults (as documented earlier), is especially underrated given the period from which it emerged. Thus, ZAxploitation, as a *cinema* of the old South Africa, can also be defined within low budget, clearly exploitative (*Death of a Snowman* features copious violence and even some sex) presentations which are nonetheless occasionally provocative and even subversive.

Prior to *Cry Freedom* and *The Wild Geese* there was also *The Wilby Conspiracy*, which has Michael Caine and Sidney Poitier on the run from South African forces. 'You two have got to stay together,' insists Caine's white love interest (Prunella Gee), as the two attempt to avoid police attention, having scuffled with the force in Johannesburg, as they travel by road to Cape Town and then (by plane) to Botswana. Davis notes how the writers of *The Wilby Conspiracy* deliberately set out to avoid politics despite the backdrop of apartheid (1996: 74). As such, whilst Caine and Poitier – particularly given their dual star power – are presented in a far more racially equal power binary than actors Winston Ntshona and Hardy Krüger in *The Wild Geese*, a problem remains: the white man can only understand Africa and its political fragility by escaping from her soil. *The Wilby Conspiracy* concludes with a horde of 'savages' appearing from the Botswanan bush to chop and kill some South African racists, as Caine and Poitier look on in bemused horror. A similar scene in *The Wild Geese*, featuring machete-wielding 'Simbas' (as they are identified by the victims), was perhaps inspired by this showstopping grand guignol finale. In the case of *The Wilbur Conspiracy*, we are clearly in the same continent of Ntshona's speech in *The Wild Geese*: *the final bloodbath is coming. First between black and white and then between black and black.* Despite the supposed intention to be apolitical about apartheid, a foolhardy goal in its own right, *The Wilbur Conspiracy*, like *The Wild Geese*, can finally only maintain that Africa is no place for a white man. At least until the decent, democratised, eloquent and well-spoken likes of Ntshona or Poitier can provide a paradise of multiracial bonding (albeit in which settler rights are equal with those of the selfish non-white majority, *who just really need to learn how to share*). In the meantime, as Kevin Cline finds out in *Cry Freedom*, Africa is a continent that the white man *can* at least escape from with moral conscience. Providing encounters with the *proper* sort of Black saviour radicalise him against continued minority rule in the continent. This hokey old trope returns us to the colonial depiction of Mr Right.

The less well-known *Shamwari*[14] is perhaps the most problematic of all the 'escape' films. The film was made for the South African market, but shot in Rhodesia with local financing (Tomaselli 1988: 135). Despite being arguably *the* post-Kenya hotspot for pan-African liberation movements, there was surprisingly little genre cinema to emerge from Rhodesia during the country's fifteen-year period of UDI – with only the historical action film *Shangani Patrol* (1970) from South African filmmaker David Millin, who also remade *Die Voortrekkers* (1973 – this time spelled as *Die Voortrekkers*), and the more obnoxious international co-production *Whispering Death* (AKA *Albino*, Jürgen Goslar, 1976) of note. By the time *Shamwari* was released, the country no longer existed.[15] The narrative's adaptation of *The Defiant Ones* into a white settler state is thus further complicated by the events of the period. By the time *Shamwari* was debuted in South Africa in 1982, Mugabe's Zimbabwe had already emerged with a cease in Black-white hostilities, and the film must have seemed dated. Mugabe's success in Zimbabwe's first majority elections, in February 1980, had been followed by a surprising television address on 4 March of that year, in which the new leader offered the hand of reconciliation to the country's white minority.

Stephen Chan notes how 'foreboding among the Rhodesians' at the former liberation hero's rise to high office soon led to 'not an unimpressed person in Whitehall and the dying Rhodesia' (2019: 17). For most onlookers, Mugabe's apparently multicultural Zimbabwe had begun on the right foot and, despite the generally underreported Matabeleland atrocities, the country would be at least fourteen years away from the beginning of its freefall into a national financial crisis, hurried land redistribution and political and racial violence by the time *Shamwari* was released. Thus, setting the film in a country that no longer existed (Rhodesia), in the midst of a battle that had concluded (the Bush War), cannot help but make the film feel like an imagined prophecy

THE ZAXPLOITATION BUDDY MOVIE

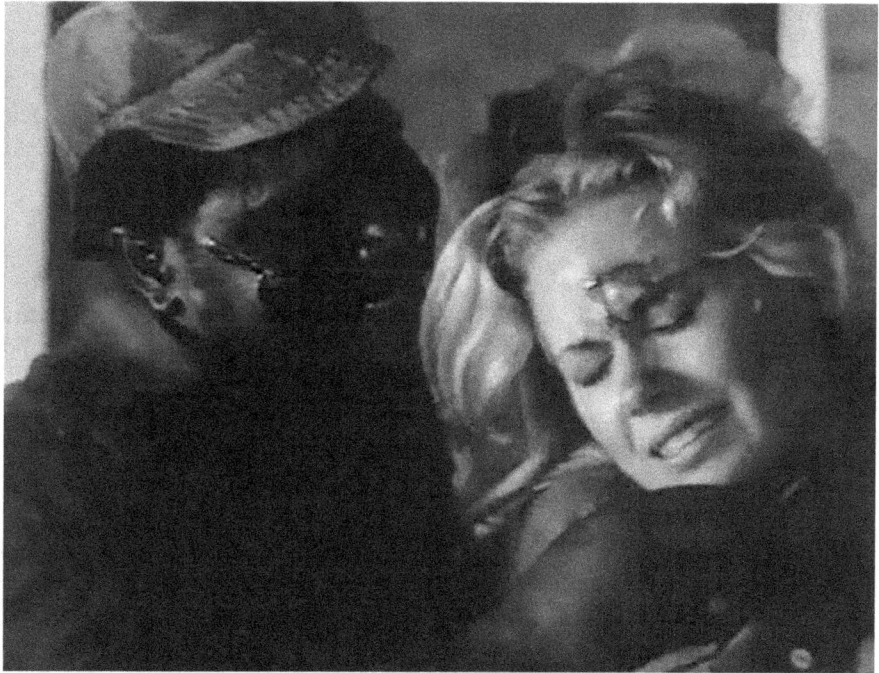

Figure 7.6 White nightmare – a Black communist guerrilla takes a hostage in *Shamwari* (Clive Harding, 1982)

for the South Africa to come. As such, for its initial theatrical run, Tomaselli describes Ian Yule and Ken Gampu 'persuaded to walk chained together the 400 miles from Durban to Johannesburg' (1988: 143). This stunt must have seemed like either a bad joke at the expense of the neighbouring white minority in Zimbabwe or a bizarre call for unity in Pretoria's fast-declining apartheid state. Either way, it certainly indicates how ZAxploitation had its own sense of Kroger Babb-style 'carny' trickery to attract audiences and to heighten sensationalism.

Gampu plays a Rhodesian police officer who executes his own son and a local witchdoctor because of their 'terrorist' activities, while Yule portrays a racist local man who slaughters some Black residents after his daughter is killed by a guerrilla insurgent. Both men are arrested and chained together but they escape and go on the run à la *The Defiant Ones*, teaming up with a young white woman who they save from being raped (Tamara Franke). Whilst Ian Smith's Rhodesia is shown to be populated by the sort of trigger-happy, backwoods thugs who also antagonise the more civilised heroes of *Deliverance* (John Boorman, 1972), Yule's character is so obnoxiously racist that it is difficult to feel any sympathy for him. In the film's most ludicrous scene, Yule has

167

to think twice about saving his own life by taking Gampu's hand and boarding a speeding train because, as established in a previous moment, he fears even sharing a cup of water with him. Yule and Gampu eventually stumble across some Chinese arms in a field and use them to infiltrate and kill a local Black guerrilla army, symbolic one presumes of Mugabe's ZANU (which had been backed by Beijing) or Joshua Nkomo's ZAPU (which had enjoyed Soviet support).[16] Yule is shot dead, leading Gampu to decry 'my Shamwari' but it is difficult to understand how or why he has such sympathy for the fallen white man outside of performing the narrative role of the 'magic negro' who, in the end, has shown that not all Black Rhodesians were on the 'bad' side of the war.

With its huckfinn representation of Gampu, a character consistently on the retreat from his co-star's venom, *Shamwari* seems like a film that is decades more out-of-sync with contemporary race relations than one made just a few years before Sundstrom had the same actor trample an authoritarian state in *American Ninja 4*. Yet, by looking at such a formulaic production, the thread of South African buddy-films becomes evident. These are productions which, until Sundstrom's boisterous *American Ninja* sequels, fail to shatter the ingrained roles of Black men (and it is always Black men) under apartheid. The B-Scheme buddy films, particularly *Bona Manzi* and *One More Shot*, go some way to celebrating Black-white or Black-Asian friendships, but they are also careful not to define their Black characters within cityscapes. *Run for Your Life* even opens with a lengthy credit sequence establishing that the Black-white friendship of the narrative involves two people living in different parts of town. It is a damning comment indeed that a film aimed at the international market but produced locally, such as *Death of a Snowman*, could offer Gampu so much more authority than a Hollywood co-production such as *The Wild Geese* could give to its flagship Black hero. However, it is arguably even more shocking than when the mainstream did attempt to address apartheid. In such instances it would be white liberation (from ingrained racism) that was deemed to be important to the narratives of *The Wilby Conspiracy*, *Cry Freedom* and others. Nevertheless, it is through the buddy films discussed in this chapter that we perhaps see images of apartheid at their most cinematically provocative.

NOTES

1. Whilst there was an *American Ninja 5* (Bobby Jean Leonard, 1993), it was a retitling of an unrelated film, *American Dragons*.
2. See: Yule 1987: 2.
3. Among the most famous examples are the excessively violent sequels the company made to *Death Wish*. To this day, *Death Wish II* (Michael Winner, 1982) remains censored in the UK. Cannon was also lambasted for its sleazy, violent films at the time – *The Delta Force* (Menahem Golan, 1986) for instance was dubbed 'a flagrant attempt to celebrate irrational racial hostility' (Yule 1987: 109).

4. I had the opportunity to arrange an on-camera interview with director Richard Donner in March 2020. When the topic of *Lethal Weapon* came up he gave an interesting explanation for the casting of Danny Glover, indicating that the film – despite its influence and success – was never actually meant to be a racial-buddy film: 'A great woman, [casting director] Marion Dougherty, she said "How about Danny Glover?" And my first reaction was "He is Black" and she said "So what?" And there I am, this liberal-thinking New York sophisticated liberal, and I said "Yeah, where did that come from?" And I realised that if it was not written on paper, this character is Black, you just assume he has to be white. And it shocked me – I had to look into my own past and my own attitude and that was a real learning curve'.
5. See Gemser's recurring role as *Black Emanuelle* and my own commentary: 'Cinethetic Racism and Orientalism in Early Italian Exploitation Films' in *Mise-en-scène: The Journal of Film & Visual Narration*, 5:1, pp. 2–15, 2020.
6. See: Lawrence 2016: pp. 114–36.
7. This depiction of the white man as more athletic than the Black man is most likely wish-fulfillment, but it may also be presumption on the part of the European settler community. For instance, writing about the end of minority rule in neighbouring Zimbabwe, author Christina Lamb notes how the arrival of Black students at the Prince Edward high school in Harare sent some pupils into a spin, with one commenting of cross-country running (which he found himself challenged at for the first time), 'my main motivation was that there was no way I was going to be beaten by a black boy' (2007: 113).
8. The political and racial threads of this short-lived cycle continue into the *Penitentiary* (Jamaa Fanaka, 1979) series as well as, arguably, *Mapantsula*.
9. One of Pretoria's last remaining Western allies was Israel, which even helped the National Party develop nuclear weapons (Dowden 2008: 414). However, I'm not sure it is quite so easy to connect these dubious presentations with the country's geopolitical alignment – although one should probably note that producer Menahem Golan, who had launched the *American Ninja* franchise, also directed *The Delta Force*, a film that author Andrew Yule argues is 'Brainlessly concocted to inspire vengeful hatred towards Arabs and Palestinians' (1987: 109). Nonetheless, it could be that with *One More Shot* and *American Ninja 4*, the screenwriters, wishing to avoid an international villain that represented the sub-Saharan area of the continent (and thus being Black), opted for a North African representation instead.
10. Per Palekar, Ronnie Isaacs, director of *One More Shot*, ran his own mobile circuit (2010: 94).
11. Perhaps the greatest irony of Pretoria's support for the 'Mr Right' figure of Savimbi and his UNITA movement in Angola is that, as recorded by Matloff, by 1993 the same South African mercenaries who had fought *against* the communist MPLA government were now stationed in Luanda, protecting it against their former ally (1997: 209).
12. 'The fact that actor Winston Ntshona bears a passing resemblance to the Rhodesian nationalist leader Joshua Nkomo is probably coincidental', states James Chapman (2009: 93), albeit incorrectly identifying ZAPU (Zimbabwe African People's Union) leader Nkomo as a leader with the intention of liberating Rhodesia.
13. Despite this criticism of *Cry Freedom*, one should not ignore the controversy it stirred up in South Africa at the time. Christie van der Westhuizen discusses how security force members would even phone bogus 'bomb threats' into cinemas showing the film so that it would be pulled under the drastic state of emergency laws (2007: 163).

14. The title means 'my friend' in Shona, the majority African language of Zimbabwe.
15. Katrina Daly Thompson has *Shamwari*'s date of completion as 1980 (2013: 209). Using Tomaselli as an additional source, and the narrative of the film, it seems most likely the film began pre-production in 1978 and was filmed in 1979, hence my (cautious) use of 'Rhodesia' instead of Zimbabwe in this instance.
16. This fear of guns falling into the hands of Black citizens might have had some popular basis, ironically, in the British experience of the Anglo-Zulu War. Aware of the forthcoming conflict, King Cetshwayo began to prepare: 'Between 1872 and 1877, 60,000 guns had been legally imported into Natal, 40,000 of which had been re-exported, and 20,000 of these shipped to Mozambique – the main point of entry for firearms into Zululand'. Whilst the weapons were of poor quality, this was doubtlessly a formidable image for the enemy (Knight 2010: 284).

8. BE MORE LIKE MIRIAM

The Women of ZAxploitation

'Men and women will never be the same. Women just want to talk all the time. That's not how a man is.'
    Popo Gumede as Alex in *Umbango* (Tonie van der Merwe, 1986)

Picture the scene: a drug-pusher is shot and left for dead. However, he lives and returns to the streets – in good health – to find out that the person who double-crossed him, and put a bullet in his stomach, is now dating his wife, Miriam. One by one he finds and slaughters his perceived enemies, leaving a threatening note on their bodies, until finally he finds his ex-wife, ties her up, threatens her and questions her about her loyalty. Then, in a twist finale, it is revealed that she is actually an undercover policewoman playing a long-game and expertly pitting both sides against one another. In the process she has brought down the city's two biggest drug traders, including her ex-husband, the last man standing, who ends the narrative with a gun pointed at his head, led to the police to await his fate.

    This story will be familiar to anyone who has seen *Yojimbo* – or its most famous European adaptation *A Fistful of Dollars* – but with its all-Black cast and Johannesburg location, *Johnny Dlamini* is unique in its own right. In addition, its inclusion of a smart, independent female character, Miriam (played by Dominique Tyawa), who fights to solve crime, makes *Johnny Dlamini* equally rare within the ZAxploitation pantheon. At the start of the film, which runs for slightly under fifty-eight minutes, the title character (Hector Rabothapi) claims,

IMAGES OF APARTHEID

Figure 8.1A Dominique Tyawa as Miriam in *Johnny Dlamini* (Robert van de Coolwijk, 1986)

'I am Johnny Dlamini, no one betrays me'. Yet, in the end, it is a female who double-crosses him, causing his eventual imprisonment and humiliating him in the process. This example might not be the sort of 'feminist' film presentation that Tomaselli suggested when he spoke of more progressive post-apartheid routes for South African cinema and the general lack of 'gender issues' from Third Cinema in and out of the continent (1992: 359). However, within its ZAxploitation placement, *Johnny Dlamini* – and this may be regarded as faint praise – stands out for even *considering* the notion of a brave, individual, intelligent female character.

In contrast, *Black Crusader* – that rare B-Scheme movie which allows the Black world of apartheid to engage in a brief, armed fight against a white representative of the state – has a scene in which the main character's mother is dismissively told, by the film's hero no less, 'You're a woman. You wouldn't understand this'. In *The Hobo* (Tony Cunningham, 1980), a female character called Pretty tries to outsmart two men, stealing their briefcase full of cash at gun point. Only moments later, however, and the male protagonists track her down to Durban's beachfront and shoot her dead on the streets. 'She thinks she's smart', laughs one of the heroes, dismissively, prior to the end

THE WOMEN OF ZAXPLOITATION

Figure 8.1B Dominique Tyawa's Miriam is a rare B-Scheme heroine who outsmarts the male characters in *Johnny Dlamini* (Robert van de Coolwijk, 1986)

credits. It goes without saying that not every apartheid-era filmmaker offered their actresses the same opportunity that was given to performer Dominique Tyawa when she had the chance to craft and portray that rare thing: a *female* B-Scheme badass.

Speaking about the relationship that is shared between Kurosawa and Leone, Rachael Hutchison argues that stylistic comparisons between the Japanese original – itself inspired by a classic American Western – and its conversion into an Italian blockbuster (predominantly seen in English) risks 'reducing Kurosawa to a "national cinema" model – only interesting as an example of a Japanese director, in binary opposition to Hollywood, and thus marginalised' and could 'lead to Orientalist misreading' (2007: 176). What then of a cheap Zulu-language B-Scheme spin-off that features an all-Black cast and female 'Yojimbo' but made by a white filmmaker under a subsidy from the old apartheid government? One might be forced to conclude that as English (rather than Japanese or Zulu) is the dominant language, and Clint Eastwood is a global brand name, *A Fistful of Dollars* is likely to maintain itself as the most recognised and viewed text of the three.

Of course, it is in the nature of the more dedicated cineaste to seek out transnational adaptations or groundworks and, in this regard, *Yojimbo*'s template for *Johnny Dlamini* (even if it was also by way of Leone) initiates a dialogue about cinema's ability to transition not only narrative, but also race and gender, into localised representations. These are representations that, in the case of *Johnny Dlamini*, at least unsettle conscripted notions of place and time. Equating this to a 'national cinema model' is, however, certainly not to pander to Orientalism, in which Kurosawa's film becomes a distant Other, marginalised as the start of a recurring, popular, modified story conception. Instead, what we might discover is that some films are more comprehensible if understood within the market that they were made and marketed for and, in turn, the original text can be increasingly celebrated as a formative work – permitting itself to be reimagined and reconfigured outside even its own borders and iconography. In this regard, Miriam is not just a rare apartheid cinema heroine; her journey begins in Japan. This factor is perhaps an argument for why no post-war developed society can, could or should resist multiculturalism – even one as dogmatic about eugenics as the old South Africa. It also attests to why, even when considered through the flimsy paradigm of B-Scheme adaptations, apartheid was on borrowed time.

From the 'mammy', described by Donald Bogle as 'closely related to the comic coons' or 'the aunt Jemima, derogatively referred to as "handkerchief head"' (2016: 6–7) to the more sexualised blaxploitation heroines of the 1970s, mainstream cinematic representations of Black women have undoubtedly evolved but remained frequently controversial. Stephanie Dunn critiques Pam Grier's best-known characters: 'it is "pussy power" that proves her ultimate resource' (2010: 108) – whilst Bogle notes that, in the present day, Viola Davis – despite having won an Oscar – remained a fixture of 'big pictures with big stars but without having much to do' (2016: 466). Hollywood stars from the period prior to blaxploitation, such as Dorothy Dandridge, faced similar struggles.[1] Given that such contemporary debate questions the agency, authority and integrity offered to even prominent African American actresses in Hollywood, it is possible to view the presentations of the B-Scheme females, grounded as they are in the 1980s, as problematic, if still emblematic of a state undergoing gradual reform and even an identity crisis in relation to its own sustainability. Moreover, if the blaxploitation badass still had to be contained within narratives which promoted good citizenship and the family, then it will serve as little surprise to reveal that their female counterparts are often cast as the token girlfriend or budding, lovelorn, dependent wife. At least part of the reason for this presentation may be that the apartheid state had long experienced female-led protest, even in the early days of its reign. Christi van der Westhuizen, for instance, discusses how 'In the 1950s, women conducted protests that temporarily upset the state's efforts at imposing passes on black women' reaching a peak of 26,000 in 1956 (2007:

73). Better, no doubt, that such mobilisation was, on the cinema screen at least, reimagined in more traditional binaries of (dominating) husband and (subservient) partner.

Another aspect that should be noted is that whilst Dobson and Grier would become notable sex symbols, the women of ZAxploitation are not usually concurrent to the statuesque glamour that their blaxploitation counterparts presented. The actresses of the B-Scheme films are almost always presented with a degree of androgyny: short hair and modest clothing (skirts are usually worn down to below the knees) are common and, with very few deviations (Abigail Kubeka in *Joe Bullet*, for instance, or the female leads of *Mapantsula*, *Mine Boy*, *uDeliwe* and *Uthemba*), rotund figures. One could make an argument that this at least means the various actresses are not presented as sex (or sexualised) objects. However, their male co-stars will burst into declarations of adoration for their wives or girlfriends, urging elopement, or swear that no one in the world is more beautiful, and usually without any foreshadowing to such bombast. Despite showcasing no chemistry and with the narrative and dialogue providing no opportunity to anticipate the occasion, actor Popo Gumede suddenly confirms his undying love for co-star Lungi Mdlada in Tonie van der Merwe's *Rich Girl*: 'I can't hide my feelings. I love you Charlotte ... The Lord himself knows I love you', he reveals, having only met her a day before. When she dismisses his proclamations, he slights her: 'Carry on being pompous, you'll never find a real man'. Such moments are obviously difficult to take seriously even if viewed within a trash cinema lexicon.

This chapter began by highlighting the role of Miriam in *Johnny Dlamini*, a female Yojimbo who, thematically at least, does not divert too far from the narrative arc afforded to her American blaxploitation counterparts. However, Miriam's contemporaries mediate aspects of the latter days of a state that probably hoped, against odds, that its policy of separate development might maintain some degree of harmony among (exploited) races. In discussing representations of femininity in these films, this chapter questions how these portrayals interact with, and sometimes *against*, the images of Black masculinity that have been established so far in this monograph.

Hollywood's Badass Heroines

It might be worth diverging, slightly, to discuss the 'badass' heroine as she surfaced and appeared in blaxploitation cinema, a decade prior to such B-Scheme representations as *Johnny Dlamini*. It was in 1973 that two commercially successful films arrived in American theatres, both helmed by white directors, that changed the face of American action cinema and the genre's depiction of women. *Coffy*, from Jack Hill – a protégé of Roger Corman – was released by the dominant indie-house American International Pictures and gave actress Pam Grier her first leading role. In a review in *The Monthly Film Bulletin*, critic Verina Glaessner dubbed *Coffy* to be a 'superficially rough and routine effort' but nonetheless praised the film's 'all-embracing grimness. Its moral blackness in fact. Coffy is shown to inhabit a world where exploitation, both sexual and political, is simply the norm' (1974: 145). As noted by Christopher Sieving, *Coffy* would later reach the 'number one position on *Variety*'s August 22nd listing of the nation's top moneymakers' (2005: 16). In the film, Grier plays a nurse, satirically entitled Miss Coffin, who infiltrates a heroin racket in Los Angeles following the addiction and overdose of her younger sister. In the interim, she also discovers that her politician boyfriend, a respected figure in the local African American community, is a driving force behind the local narcotics industry. *Coffy*'s immediate contemporary, *Cleopatra Jones*, starring the former model Tamara Dobson, came from Warner Bros. and was directed by another low budget veteran in Jack Starrett, who had been working in the blaxploitation field for American International Pictures just one year earlier with *Slaughter*. The film was another commercial hit and, as noted by authors James Robert Parish and George H. Hill, grossed over three million dollars in American rentals and half a million in soundtrack sales. Unlike Grier's character, Dobson's statuesque screen persona works as an undercover agent for the FBI – although, like Miss Coffin, her goal is to destroy a heroin syndicate. Thanks to the success of these films, the short-lived era of the Black action heroine had begun.

Both *Cleopatra Jones* and *Coffy* permitted a lone African American female avenger to drive the narrative causality and, moreover, to come out on top – although Grier's Coffy was more proudly 'R' rated, with plenty of nudity, brutal violence and a concluding sequence in which she castrates a corrupt Black politician, also her former lover, with a shotgun blast to the crotch. Copycat titles emerged fast: *Foxy Brown* (Jack Hill, 1974), *Lady Cocoa* and *Sheba Baby* among the best known. However, if ever a key component of the American blaxploitation film failed to translate to ZAxploitation, it is this one, which the author Stephanie Dunn dubbed '*Baad Bitches*' *and Sassy Supermamas*. Images of strong, tough, liberated Black females taking back the streets at gun point and challenging white privilege is not a part of ZAxploitation mythology. Miriam even has to wait until the closing moments of *Johnny Dlamini* to reveal her true identity and cause.

Discussing *Coffy*, Joseph S. Valle draws on Linda Williams and her discussion of 'film body genres', particularly melodrama. Williams talks about melodrama as a genre of cinema 'deemed excessive for the gender-and-sex linked pathos, for their naked displays of emotions' (1991: 3), a factor Valle links to blaxploitation and its frequent depiction of female suffering:

melodrama is rarely acknowledged for contributing to the success of blaxploitation cinema, yet as Williams argues, it is the most popular mode for addressing race in American popular culture ... Blaxploitation cinema, then, is the cinematic representation of this predicament, and melodrama cannot erase the groundbreaking, edgy, and at times radical aim of blaxploitation cinema. In fact, it historicises the movement's most progressive qualities by pointedly countering and parodying long-held racist stereotypes about African Americans circulating within American popular culture. Arguably, melodrama, with its special emphasis on emotionality and the spectacular, is one of the reasons why blaxploitation cinema initially became popular with black and white audiences in the 1970s and for its nostalgic resurgence in American popular culture at the dawn of the twenty-first century. (2016: 140)

The female body, particularly in the action-heroine films of blaxploitation, has been subject to other recent retrospection. Sims, for instance, questions whether Dobson, Grier and their contemporaries 'replaced the mammy, the exotic other, Aunt Jemima and Sapphire with alternate sexual stereotypes of African American women' (2006: 22). However, Valle's discussion of the *Coffy* character, specifically as mediating the 'agonised suffering' (2016: 151) that one would expect from melodrama, misses another factor at work in the blaxploitation mythology; that of heteronormative redemption. Grier's Foxy Brown, for instance, shatters a bar stool across the body of an obese lesbian character in the 1974 film of the same name, whilst Dobson's Cleopatra Jones is depicted not just as racially more appealing to the overweight, aggressive lesbian (patronisingly named Mommy) in her adventure but sexually more civilised. Shelley Winters as Mommy, for instance, is shown to be obsessed with teenaged, white servant women, whereas Cleopatra Jones has a hunky, muscular African American male lover.

Whilst Valle sees the suffering endured by Grier's Miss Coffin and Foxy Brown – who are molested, raped and tortured, and often by white, gap-toothed criminals (a role picked up by Hector Mathanda in films such as Tonie van der Merwe's *Impango* and *Impango II*, indicating the influence the South African director) – it may also be argued that these depictions are not just about bodies 'under constant peril' (2016: 15) but bodies that *seek to do the right thing*. No drugs, no same-sex relations and certainly no hesitation at annihilating any form of dissent from acceptable beauty standards (a final battle between Winters and Dobson, in *Cleopatra Jones*, where the latter drops the former to her doom, has aged especially badly due to the ableist, ageist and sizeist connotations), films such as *Coffy*, *Foxy Brown* and *Cleopatra Jones* are forms of melodrama but not necessarily radicalised ones. Indeed, for all of the bullets and bluster, Miss Coffin is ultimately fighting a battle of family values, Foxy Brown takes to the streets to avenge her dead lover and Cleopatra Jones is hired by *the man* to instigate 'ten miles of bad road' across criminal entities in the area. These *are* melodramatic stories about conserving a good, wholesome society (although it is worth noting that the character Foxy Brown finally entails the assistance of some Marxist revolutionaries to assault a drug cartel). Valle tends to focus, as does Williams, on the body's role in melodrama, in this case under duress, finally recovered to triumphantly restore order and maintain equality for local, exploited Black communities.[2] The melodrama element, as indicated by the depictions of 'perverse' sexuality in these films, also functions as a way to reclaim the blaxploitation heroine as a fighter of values that even conservative white viewers may relate to – a basic good against bad, 'straight' against 'queer'. Admittedly, *Coffy* – with its haunted lone vigilante – is the more thematically leftfield example of the three, but it still retains a somewhat redemptive conclusion when the character kills her former lover (after dropping her guard and briefly expressing her feelings) for finding a white woman in his beachside penthouse. In this moment, although played for humour, the overriding message is of race-betrayal, which could be interpreted as an especially conservative punchline, a pan-Africanist *femme castratrice*, in which to end a film that at least flirts with (or exploits) a pistol-packing Angela Davis-style Marxist avenger.

As such, affirming that the role of women in ZAxploitation is also one of melodrama, albeit often with values that could be interpreted as synonymous with the apartheid state, is to confirm a continuity with the cycle of old. Take the example of *Zero for Zep*, a B-Scheme effort which begins by indicating that a young female, Caroline, will represent the crux of the story. Caroline, a college student, is pregnant and her teen boyfriend Zep wants nothing to do with it: 'I told *you* to use contraception', he tells his girlfriend (emphasis mine). 'It's over, I won't date a stupid girl', he concludes (of all the B-Scheme films researched in this book, only *Mine Boy* deals with the urgency and necessity of safe sex and the AIDS problem in South Africa. Perhaps tellingly, it comes from a female director). Caroline seeks sympathy from her mother but is given a frosty reception: 'How could you disappoint me like this? You have hurt me'. Distraught, Caroline slits her wrists in the bath and dies, instigating the idea that this will be a family-centred melodrama rather than a typical B-Scheme gangster outing. However, the narrative of *Zero for Zep* then focuses on her lover, who embarks on a crime spree out of frustration and guilt, although in the end he turns himself in to the police. Caroline, however, is forgotten by this stage and male guilt and trauma has become the sole focus of the narrative – before finally deciding to give himself up to the law, Zep is even permitted to tell the audience, in monologue, that he has to do the right thing. It is not his cruelty towards his girlfriend that he regrets, however, but rather his criminal

Figure 8.2 Zep (So Mhlanga) argues with his pregnant girlfriend Caroline (unidentified actress), who later kills herself in *Zero for Zep* (Steve Hand and Laurens Barnard, 1980s)

rampage. For this he does not repent, and the filmmakers clearly saw no need to offer such a resolution.

Another example of this representation – not far removed from what Bogle labels as 'the exotic, doomed mulatto' (2016: 157) – is *Uthemba*. This is a Soweto-based film which plays unlicensed Bob Marley music across its unusually long ninety-five-minute running time (the opening credits, close to six minutes, take place over a static shot of a car garage, a strange decision given that the project clearly meets the B-Scheme parameters for length). In this film, a young woman called Thandi is in a romantic relationship with two car thieves – but unlike Miriam, she fails to play each criminal against one another and is instead stabbed to death in her Soweto home. One of her lovers, Themba, upon release from jail, beats and admonishes her in the back garden of her house – 'So because he bought you drinks you decided to have sex with him? Are you that cheap?' – and then throws dirty water over her head as she breaks down and sobs. Her other suitor, Vusi, states 'Don't you come back you bitch' and calls her a 'stupid farm girl'.

When Thandi finally chooses a side, and approaches Themba to try and win him back, she is called a 'bloody whore' and dismissed. Frustratingly, like Miriam, Thandi is one of the few B-Scheme heroines to have any agency at all. She wears sexy clothing when we first see her, dressed in a slinky red dress, and she is seen freely interacting with the city, albeit casually involved in crime (such as petty shoplifting). Her eventual death, when compared to the more redemptive arc given to Themba (who ends the story in an upmarket Johannesburg restaurant), should indicate that *Uthemba* belongs in the 'urban-conditional' genre. Director Mayer would tell Silber that Black audiences did not understand film language (1992: 172). However, according to a cinema owner also speaking to the author, Mayer and his contemporaries made products that would 'far exceed' the returns of Hollywood movies (Ibid.). Perhaps the illegal use of Bob Marley songs throughout *Uthemba* might go some way towards explaining this, although it should be noted that the film is – despite Mayer's claims – constructed in the basic language of a Hollywood thriller (Thandi is even stalked by her attackers as she walks home, just before she is killed) in order to muster some basic suspense.

The narrative of *Uthemba* is certainly conservative. Thandi mentions that she might not be satisfied with just one man and is killed. Themba, despite his misogyny, is framed as a hero: a wronged man, sent to prison for a crime he did not commit and now seeking to expose his former friend Vusi as a thief. When Vusi organises for Thandi to be killed, there is a sense of 'she asked for it' because Themba has consistently rejected her attempts to re-enter his life and, when she does receive the 'privilege' of the urban, she steals. Despite his violence towards Thandi, it is Themba who ends the narrative as a free man, toasting to a crime-free existence with a new, glamourous girlfriend. 'Crime does not pay', he says, 'We will have a beautiful life . . . Let's celebrate like the whites do'. As he concludes the story as part of the urban-conditional, Marley's 'No Woman, No Cry' surfaces again, accompanying the end credits.

Hence, female suffering in B-Scheme cinema generally comes from two factors: 1) a character who is involved in activities that compromise Christian values (sex before marriage, two-timing, narcotics, vice or even basic theft) or 2) has become intimately involved with a 'badass' boyfriend or husband whose good citizenship compromises her safety (but only insofar as buffoonish criminals are rife in Black neighbourhoods). The former character trope is also central to the narrative of *Double Deal* (Tonie van der Merwe, 1985). In this film, which nods to its influence from the blaxploitation arena by having a sound credit for a clearly pseudonymous 'Foxy Hand', we are introduced to a frustrated housewife called Mary. She is upset that her husband, George, is always distracted by his business ('all you think of is work, work, work' she bemoans) so she goes on a short vacation to Cape Town to visit her friend Anne. In the hotel bar, she meets a local man called Andrew and they embark on a brief affair, but upon returning home to her husband, Mary decides she will try and make her marriage work after all. A disappointed Andrew hires a white assassin to kill George but, when Mary walks into her house at the time of the killing, she is shot through the head. The narrative ends, in melodramatic fashion, with Andrew sobbing, drunk, in his bedroom.

The racial tensions of *Double Deal* are unavoidable as, prior to hiring the hitman, a depressed and dejected Andrew begins a brawl with some white men in a bar, perhaps alluding to the idea that 'separate development' is best for both races. *Double Deal* straddles both the urban-conditional and the back to the townships genres. Mary is well-to-do and urbanised, so she can remain in the city. Andrew, however, is shown to be bad for her and he concludes the narrative back in his threadbare township bedroom, where the film decides he, as the wrong kind of Black character, belongs. However, the noir-style story and unresolved conclusion of *Double Deal* are unique within the wider B-Scheme tradition – specifically, we have no idea what will come of Andrew or his for-hire white gangster colleague. Nonetheless, there remains the message (common in most of van der Merwe's work) that loyalty to the family unit and good husbandry are the key to positive living and (conditional) Black upward mobility. Mary is shot dead *because* she dared to have an affair and throw away the privileged but conditional urban life that she had with her hardworking husband.

Empowerment Against Apartheid?

As noted at the beginning of this chapter, women played a prominent part in opposing the apartheid state (MP Helen Suzman is perhaps the most famous white example, whilst activist Lilian Ngoyi also plays an important role in the history of the ANC). Historian Frank Welsh mentions how this opposition continued throughout the decades of National Party rule, but not always with the same sort of brutal crackdown that would take place against organised resistance from men:

> Women were increasingly active in confronting official repression. However brutal police and other state servants might be, they acted within their own traditions, which held women in great disrespect (and generally underestimated them) ... Women of different races often showed a better capacity for cooperation than did their men. (1998: 452)

One imagines that the female presentations of cheap B-Scheme films such as *Double Deal*, *Uthemba* or *Zero for Zep* were an attempt to indicate that 'bad' (Black) women are concurrent with 'bad' men. Yet, as also seen with *Double Deal*, it would be incorrect to assume that every film from this period promoted imagery of barbarism vis-à-vis South Africa's more 'genteel' and chivalrous European settlers.

In writing about Simon Sabela's *uDeliwe*, itself a melodrama and from which one could argue many of the later B-Scheme female characters evolved from, Litheko Modisane notes that the presentation of the character Deliwe (Cynthia Shange), whose journey as an aspiring local beauty queen moves her from the rural (Soweto) to the urban (Johannesburg), 'is concerned with the tension between the moral structures of family and the freedom that urban social life promises, especially for young women' (2013: 73). Whilst *uDeliwe* was produced by the apartheid state – and at the height of its interest in making cinema (and certainly better quality cinema) for Black audiences – actress Shange had previously reached international attention as a controversial symbol of the state's soft power, even becoming South Africa's entry to the 1972 Miss World contest. In her best-known role, as Deliwe, she anticipates the later, limited agency that is given to some women in apartheid cinema, such as in *Johnny Dlamini*. Modisane's argument that Deliwe's (apparent) free movement across Johannesburg is, fundamentally, subversive because of the 'real world' understanding that – during this time – cities were not *for* the vast bulk of South Africa's population (hence she becomes one of the earliest examples of the urban-conditional), is worth acknowledging. Indeed, this argument is consistent with a similar approach to 'film Blackness' from Michael Boyce Gillespie: 'a conceptual reframing' of cinematic representations of race that takes into account wider-reaching aspects and influence of genre, gender, time, place and production' (2016: 118). Modisane chooses to see progressive ideas in *uDeliwe*, even whilst acknowledging its place as a film of its time and, of course, of the apartheid state. In doing so, however, the author is able to provide much-needed insight into why it resonated so well with township audiences, becoming another huge commercial success for director and co-star Sabela.

In his reading of *Medicine for Melancholy* (Barry Jenkins, 2008), Gillespie speaks about what the dialogue and interactions between the two young male and female Black characters of the film tells us about their (and by extension the film's) approach to ethnic belonging in San Francisco – a city whose African American diaspora has continued to dwindle. Gillespie argues, convincingly, that the interplay between these characters permits a channel for us, the audience, to gain insight into what the Californian metropolis means to non-white residents (both in the past and present). Similarly, Modisane's discussion of Shange's Deliwe persona offers an enticing perspective: namely that *uDeliwe*'s depiction of her opportunity *within* the urban – and her interactions with the city (however subtle or minimal) – may represent Sabela's acknowledgement of a South African state in slow (inevitable) transition. Likewise, Thandi – in *Uthemba* – in the few scenes where she is depicted in Johannesburg, is identified by a transaction with a criminal friend (someone who steals a dress for her), foreshadowing her later death in Soweto as a 'bad' girl. Unlike the hero,

Themba, her criminal behaviour in Johannesburg indicates that she is not deserving of the privilege of the city, 'like the whites do', and therefore lives and dies in her homeland – never making it into the aspirational B-Scheme category of the urban-conditional. Whilst *Uthemba* is, fundamentally, still a B-Scheme film about how 'crime does not pay', the way it portrays its main female character points to problematic ideas – inherent in many of these motion pictures – about gender; namely an apparent dislike of sexually or financially independent young Black women. The presentation of Themba's journey also indicates how subtly the genres identified by Tomaselli within the B-Scheme could be conveyed to audiences. Apartheid thus never needs to be explicitly mentioned in *Uthemba*; it already dictates the lives of its characters and it exists in even the meagre aspirations of Themba to be accepted into the city (or the urban-conditional).

Another recurring figure in these films is the kidnapped woman, a crucial part of the narrative in *Ambushed, Beware Tiger, Charlie Steel, Gone Crazy, Hostage, Impango, Impango II, One More Shot, Ransom, Rich Girl* and *Under Cover*. All of these films share the same monotonous premise: a young, conservatively dressed, short-haired female, usually with a boyfriend, husband or fiancée, is taken to a rural shed or house by a group of two or three criminals and held captive in order to extort money from her family. Women in B-Scheme films are, thus, frequently victim or victimised. In *Charlie Steel*, a male-on-female rape also takes place, whilst in *Ambushed* an armed guerrilla, played by Hector Mathanda, molests his female captive before leaving her in a shabby, makeshift prison with her young son. In most instances, the narrative ends with the distraught woman reunited with her male partner who has managed to foil the local villain. With Tonie van der Merwe's *Impango* and *Impango II*, the character of Joyce Dlamini (Gugu Mhlanga), the wife to a wealthy Black South African businessman and philanthropist, is kidnapped and raped. However, Joyce has a more provocative representation insofar as she is permitted to fight back: in the first film she hides a brick in a pillow and knocks out her two attackers. In the second film she uses a brick again to bludgeon one of her kidnappers and beats another with a saucepan. In this regard, the *Impango* films seem to be more influenced by the American rape-revenge cycle, such as the notorious *I Spit on Your Grave* (Meir Zarchi, 1978). Perhaps the biggest key difference between *I Spit on Your Grave* and the B-Scheme, however, is not even in the kidnapping and the extent of the abuse itself but in the outcome: whilst the heroine in the American film ends her story as a lone avenger, Joyce concludes *Impango* and its sequel in the arms of her husband, with the family unit restored. Whereas van der Merwe's *Impango* films are at least grittier and less monotonous than some of his B-Scheme contemporaries, indicating the director's willingness to push some boundaries, his *Rich Girl* (which is shot by B-Scheme regular Tony Cunningham) is a particularly frustrating melodrama-thriller. The film initiates some of the most radical moments in the entire cycle, but ultimately subverts these instances in order to reinforce the more typical B-Scheme narrative about the 'right kind' of Black aspiration.

The story focuses on the daughter of a millionaire, Charlotte Dlamini (Lungi Mdlala). Charlotte's father is worried that she might be kidnapped, so he hires a local heavy, Robert (Popo Gumede) to be her guardian. In one sequence, Charlotte is shown to employ a white driver, who takes her wherever she wants. In another scene, she buys out the stock of a local white-owned art gallery ('You'll end up owning your own gallery', intones Robert). Hence, Charlotte seems, at first glance, to be a character who is of the urban and with no conditions attached, even if she admits 'respect ends when you run out of money'. Gumede's Robert then begins to fall in love with Charlotte and this becomes the focus of *Rich Girl*'s second act, before they too are kidnapped and held for ransom. 'You know what? I enjoy freedom', insists Charlotte. 'But my whole life I haven't been allowed to be who I want to be', she adds – ordering Robert to fetch her slippers. 'I don't want him to think I'm depending on him', Charlotte later bemoans, referring to her father.

Figure 8.3 Charlotte Dlamini (Lungi Mdlala) meets her bodyguard, Robert (Popo Gumede)

However, it is not long before we learn what the *Rich Girl* narrative really expects of Charlotte: to find love with Robert and to discover her 'freedom' by way of marriage to a good, protective husband. It does not matter that Robert will refer to her as a 'spoilt brat' or insist 'your father trusts me, is that not enough?' when trying to convince her that he will be a devoted partner. Before long Charlotte will be smitten. Upon being kidnapped, she will even beg their captors, 'Don't kill him, kill me instead', and tell Robert, 'I'd rather die here than be treated like a prisoner', referring to her life as the daughter of a millionaire.

Love is the ultimate 'victory' of *Rich Girl*, not wealth. Indeed, the villainous Hector Mathanda is shown scowling and muttering, 'I love money so much... If I get this money, I'll be so happy'. Of course, it is Charlotte and Robert who end the narrative together, and happy, having foiled such criminality. Whilst *Rich Girl* does not introduce Charlotte as part of the urban-conditional, it concludes by initiating the concept – common to the B-Scheme – that such fortune (meaning a good life in the city) can only come to someone who is pure of heart and willing, against any initial hesitation or judgement, to succumb to the wishes and desires of a devoted and clean-living man. At the end of van der Merwe's film, we understand that these characters deserve to be together because they are heroic, kind, just, respectful and – above all else – content with a life that involves little more than each other. Aspiration, or money, is not what Charlotte needed after all. She finds 'respect' in the arms of her suitor.

Speaking about using film as a source, author Sian Barber mentions:

> even films which deal with the past in farcical, comical and irreverent ways are not useless or unworthy of study, nor can it be said that such films simply present 'bad' history. *Carry on up the Khyber* (1968) may say little about British India, but says a great deal about attitudes towards British imperialism, colonialism, race, gender and ideas of comedy and national identity in late 1960s Britain. Sometimes it is the treatment of the historical subject that is more interesting, rather than historical accuracy. (2015: 9)

Viewing *Rich Girl* is curious because it suggests that the South Africa of 1985 was one in which Black mobility had – in some cases – improved to such an extent that white labour was now (presented on-screen as) available for hire. It is difficult to conclude how a township audience *might* have reacted to *Rich Girl*'s heroic female character, pictured with a white servant. Such a depiction indicates at least some awareness from the filmmakers that race relations in South Africa were changing or were going to have to change. Hence, when Silber concludes that in the B-Scheme cinema 'there's no Soweto' (1992: 272), he is not necessarily correct. Soweto exists as the (unmentioned) alternative to the more affluent Black lives that these films transition into presenting. Moreover, Soweto exists in *Uthemba*; it is the place where Thandi lives and dies. It is also where Themba escapes, in order to live 'like the whites do' in Johannesburg. In *Rich Girl*, van der Merwe goes even further: proposing that a life outside of Soweto can be attained, complete with a white servant, for the 'right kind' of Black citizen. Such a presentation allows the apartheid system to seem adjustable, balanced, and even fair. Perhaps, through such narratives, the directors were reassuring themselves.

'A lot of the producers took advantage of the B-Scheme and they were pushing things out just to get a buck,' admits Cynthia Hlanguza of Gravel Road Entertainment Group. 'But *Rich Girl* is undervalued. It is a play on *The Bodyguard* and that was a nice one for me [to discover]'. Film curator and festival programmer Darryl Els adds:

> *Rich Girl* is interesting because it is this story of a young Black woman, who is wealthy, and there is this scene of a white man cleaning her car and she goes out and drives away [but without him] and he is impressed. And that is quite subversive for an image from 1985. (2016)

Unfortunately, as with so many B-Scheme heroines, Charlotte in *Rich Girl* – who even gets a tough, sexually provocative line when she teases Popo Gumede by saying 'tell me have you ever used your gun?' – must finally revert back to stock. She will be kidnapped, and she will admit her undying love to her new bodyguard, promising to spend her life with him if only they can escape to safety. At the conclusion of *Rich Girl*, her initial upward mobility – itself the result of a wealthy family – is forgotten; she is merely another wife for a dashing hero.

Dunn mentions: '

> One-dimensional contemporary portraits of black femaleness, the historical imagery of the Sapphire-like bitch, the amoral jezebel, and subsequently the demonisation of black women's bodies and cultural personality have created dominant notions of a loud, socially uncouth, and even dangerous or violent black female type that upsets public space. (2010: 23)

One could argue that Dunn is being unfair to (particularly) Pam Grier's screen personas, given the longevity of the actress, which indicates that her presence in the 'public space' was far more progressive than her 'loud, socially uncouth' and 'dangerous' characters might have suggested, even on their initial appearance in cinemas. Indeed, the comparison between Grier's screen body – even if one were to argue that she represents a 'Sapphire-like bitch', who sheds her clothes (for the audience) and takes no nonsense from whitey or from two-timing boyfriends – and that of the B-Scheme heroine, indicates quite how transgressive her presentations were. In being depicted as a liberated woman, racially and sexually, and driven to come out of her confrontations as the victor, Grier tangentially transcends the needs of her exploitation films (nudity, castration, bloody shoot-outs) despite the race-provocations that she faces. Or as maintained by Sims:

> In spite of criticism, Grier provided a face and voice to a new type of heroine that was subsequently appropriated by the action genre, and that was significant. Her heroines (particularly her early portrayals in *Coffy* and *Foxy Brown*) redefined African American beauty, sexuality, and womanhood, and subsequently led to alternative images of African American actresses onscreen. (2006: 79).

In contrast, the women of the B-Scheme are victims who remain victims – and the message is usually that victimhood is avoided only by protection from a good man.

In the more satirical *Moyo Mubi*, a secret love affair is revealed between two characters – Gambushe (Popo Gumede) and Sally. The latter is kidnapped and Gambushe uses his stick-fighting skills and smarts to beat an unruly pack of villains, finishing the narrative with Sally in his arms and stating 'We should go and see our parents ... The reward should be enough to start our life together'. The entire arc of Sally's character is to be introduced, captured, and fall into the arms of her (secret) lover who she agrees immediately to marry. Such a presentation is obviously melodramatic and compromises the B-Scheme woman as a figure of blaxploitation. Even a less action-based film, such as *Lola* (Tony Cunningham, 1985), a 'feel good' teen-sports drama, is about a high school student using her skills at netball to win over a slacker from a group dubbed 'the thugs' and to conclude the film with him affirming, 'Lola, I love you'.[3] Earlier in the film, Lola is heard discussing her plans to go to university, possibly to study physical education (she also interacts freely with her white teacher, again perhaps a nod to 'changing' times[4]), but the story is more interested in her ability to 'win' a boyfriend than an education. A film such as *Lola* indicates that the love of a good woman can stop an aspiring young male criminal in his tracks and convert him to a more positive lifestyle. Given the history between Black students and the National Party government, focusing the story of *Lola* on a 'thug' who changes his way when he finds love might make sense – especially given the fact that even in the late 1980s, the government was still finding ways to infiltrate ANC sympathisers in high schools and colleges.[5]

The final chapter of this monograph focuses on *Mapantsula*; however it is

Figure 8.4 Thembi Mtshali as Pat, girlfriend of Panic and political activist in *Mapantsula* (Oliver Schmitz, 1988)

also briefly worth introducing the character of Pat, played by Thembi Mtshali, into this discussion. Pat is the good-looking, politically active, Soweto-based lover of a local small-time gangster, Panic (Thomas Mogotlane). Nonetheless, despite her clear radicalism and apparent awareness of the apartheid state's vulnerability, her placement in the story remains as a token love interest, whose beauty and intelligence places her outside of the more dangerous and unpredictable world inhabited by her new partner. Discussing *Mapantsula*, Maingard mentions how 'Under apartheid the representation of race in the cinema is obviously a primary issue but, increasingly, gender issues are being placed on political and cultural agendas' and goes on to describe Pat as 'useful for the development of the narrative' but 'nevertheless represented as a victim of Panic's abuse' (1994: 236). As one of the most acclaimed films of the apartheid era, it needs to therefore be noted that if (in Maingard's words) *Mapantsula* features characters, perspectives and dialogue that are 'stereotypically male' then it is surely worth noting that the females of the trashier, action-based formula films of this chapter are also of their time. Against this backdrop, contemporaries in lesser quality motion pictures such as *Rich Girl* and *Johnny Dlamini* can at least be seen as products of the state that offered little emancipation for female characters in its cinema. Whilst the films of this chapter give little evidence of strong-willed females fighting to defend a wider political cause, that does not mean that such presentations do not also exist in other demarcations that emerged as part of South Africa's low budget, exploitation filmmaking. As such, this study will discuss the Border War cycle next.

NOTES

1. Author Donald Bogle notes: 'Producers and directors seemed unable to think of her in any terms but that of the exotic, doomed mulatto' (2016: 157).
2. Valle claims: 'Melodrama above all other modes, fully reveals the blaxploitation hero/heroine's suffering and why it is important to recognise not only their price and physical prowess but also the emotions that make them vulnerable and soulful' (2016: 49).
3. Despite seeming inoffensive, *Lola* has some notable (likely racist) political commentary. In one scene Lola says 'I hear UNISA's staff is incompetent' when the cast are discussing universities in the area. UNISA was, notably, the first university in South Africa to employ a Black professor: Deuteronomy Bhekinkosi Zeblon Ntuli.
4. I need to repeat here that I am the proverbial 'outsider looking in' so later B-Scheme films that feature harmonious or at least 'equal' presentations of exchange between white and Black characters are surprising and must indicate, in some regard, that filmmakers were aware multiculturalism was becoming increasingly acceptable to their audience. However, Richard Dowden argues, regarding apartheid, that 'the whole project was already in retreat' as early as 1979 (2008: 399).
5. See: van der Westhuizen 2007: 162.

9. ARMED AND DANGEROUS

The Border War

In January 1976, the start of the same year in which the Soweto riots signalled the beginning of the (slow) end of apartheid, South Africa began full transmission of television (Omond 1985: 199). However, whereas the Vietnam War was famously deemed to be America's first televised conflict, the full extent of Pretoria's long, complex war with Angola (and, to a lesser extent, Mozambique) remained in the shadows, despite the enlistment of young white men to fight in the country's army (military service was mandatory in the old South Africa). States Ian-Malcolm Rijsdijk of the University of Cape Town:

> Half the time the government was promoting the idea that it was not even there, because they were not supposed to be in Angola. They were trying to promote the idea that our borders were safe and that they were [successfully] fighting against communism and Black insurgency. And at the same time, they were trying to downplay how bad that war was because they wanted to indicate South Africa was safe. (2016)

Nevertheless, even with such secrecy, South African cinema presented and *exploited* this shadowy battle between Cold War proxies, including in Tonie van der Merwe's little-seen lowbrow B-Scheme film *Ambushed*, released in 1988. Perhaps more motion pictures, similar to *Ambushed*, have yet to be restored, or perhaps they are lost forever, but van der Merwe's film represents the culmination of frequently exploitative 'border war' cinema that was all-too-often aimed at an international market.[1]

As such, we once again see the spectre of adaptation in cheap South African filmmaking during the apartheid era. Indeed, sleazy genre cinema existed alongside highbrow and/or mainstream-orientated motion pictures in the wake of the Angola conflict, even giving rise to what Tomaselli and van Zyl describe as 'a new kind of white male hero. Because war is perceived as a male activity, women are usually portrayed "at home". The men pair up as twins, one tough and hard, the other sensitive and soft' (1992: 442). The authors acknowledge the racism of this presentation in such previously discussed buddy films as *Shamwari* and *The Wild Geese*; however what might be considered most interesting about the Border War cycle of this chapter is that it encompasses, however clumsily, the unlikelihood of apartheid's survival. Even in *The Wild Geese* the heroes end their story fleeing, helplessly, from the warzone, outnumbered and having failed at their mission, their idealised postcolonial Black Mr Right, who they were supposed to save, shot dead. The narrative is certainly jingoistic, but in its futile ode to Empire, it also acknowledges (and this is doubtlessly not the intention) that such days are gone because colonial rule was unsustainable against well-organised opposition.

This new 'white male hero' emerged from a period in South Africa where conflict was sustained and secretive. President Reagan had labelled South Africa 'a friendly country, a wartime ally, and a country of strategic importance to the free world' shortly after taking office in 1980 (Welsh 1998: 480). William Minter adds that in 1982, Washington 'was still eagerly feeding carrots to the Botha regime' as Pretoria battled against leftist administrations in Angola and in Mozambique (1994: 149). Of course, several African countries had previously become proxies for Cold War conflict, most notoriously perhaps in the Democratic Republic of the Congo (Zaire), and by the mid-1970s, South Africa was surrounded by unfriendly neighbours. There was the threat of Marxist Robert Mugabe and his Chinese-backed ZANLA guerrillas in neighbouring Rhodesia (prior to independence as Zimbabwe in 1980) and communist governments in Angola and Mozambique, which had become independent from Portuguese rule in 1975 following nearly fifteen years of armed resistance. Almost immediately, Angola – which bordered Pretoria's satellite of South West Africa (now Namibia) – began to fall into civil war, one complete with horror film elements if Ryszard Kapuściński is to be believed: 'Corpses with hearts and livers cut out' (1976: 113) and 'drunken cannibals' waging war against the new government in Luanda (Ibid.: 114).

Cuban soldiers were welcomed into the new independent Angola by President Agostinho Neto, who represented the People's Movement for the Liberation of Angola (MPLA). The USA favoured, and supplied arms to, the more Western-friendly National Liberation Front of Angola (FNLA) and – most famously or infamously – Jonas Savimbi of the National Union for the Total Independence of Angola (UNITA), the perceived Mr Right of the struggle, despite his training in China. When South Africa itself took the initiative, with the backing of Washington, to invade Angola on 14 October 1975 (Gleijeses 2013: 29), on the pretext of limiting communist excursion into its South West Africa territory (which had an electricity supply maintained close to the border), it is doubtful that anyone could have imagined that what became known as the Border War would last until the end of the 1980s.[2] Summarising the initial outbreak of war between Pretoria and Luanda, journalist and author Judith Matloff writes:

> When Portugal withdrew, foreign meddlers jumped into the vacuum. South Africa wanted a base from which to strike at SWAPO (South West African Peoples' Organisation) guerrillas in what later became Namibia. Pretoria also wanted to destabilise any leftist thread in nearby black states ... South Africa occupied large parts of the Cunene and Cuando Cubango provinces from 1981–88, creating a buffer zone between Namibia and the rest of Angola. (1997: 36)

It is upon this backdrop that *Terrorist*[3] (Neil Hetherington, 1978), which exploits the grisly horror film elements of the crisis, and *The Stick* (or *Platoon Warrior*) emerged, as well as the far less ambitious B-Scheme cheapie *Ambushed*, which boasts a cast of just six players. Even after Namibian independence and the transition towards full democracy in South Africa, horror film frameworks would be used by South African director Richard Stanley to address the barren hellscapes of legend, memory and war in *Dust Devil* (1992).

The Border War is also prevalent in the influential South African blockbuster *The Gods Must Be Crazy*, a film which slyly maintains its European perspective by, as noted by Barry Keith Grant, a 'voice-of-god narrator' who speaks for the narrative's primitive Bushman but not – of course – for 'any of the white characters' (2008: 85). *The Gods Must Be Crazy*, which was so successful it even inspired unofficial spin-off sequels from producers in Hong Kong,[4] introduces Ken Gampu as the leader of an unnamed African nation facing a potential coup from terrorists. The main narrative, however, focuses on a lovelorn white African, based in Botswana, who falls in love with a (white) English teacher who has left the hustle and bustle of Johannesburg for a job educating children in the Kalahari. Keyan Tomaselli believes that the film's armed (if incompetent) guerrillas could be interpreted as Cuban-led, which 'mobilized the myth that Cuba was then an "exporter of revolution", and that even Black governments were not safe from communism' (2006: 182). Certainly, the likelihood of Angola's Neto sustaining his communist govern-

ARMED AND DANGEROUS: THE BORDER WAR

Figure 9.1 Actor Ken Gampu, playing a tough African dictator, in the controversial but commercial *The Gods Must Be Crazy* (Jamie Uys, 1980)

ment's hold on Luanda without Cuban assistance was unlikely, so Tomaselli's reading of *The Gods Must Be Crazy* makes sense.

The (unnamed) Angolan conflict also plays a minor part in the B-Scheme film *Charlie Steel* – as discussed in Chapter 6 – with private detective Charlie's main antagonist, Jimmy, becoming involved in crime after returning from an unnamed conflict in which he is heard opening fire on women and children. This sense of post-traumatic stress disorder (PTSD) and a protracted war following its people home is, of course, a familiar theme from such American Vietnam films as *Coming Home* (Hal Ashby, 1978) and *The Deer Hunter* (Michael Cimino, 1978). Perhaps *because* the extent of the Border War was kept secret, this portrayal of trauma is largely absent from other South African variants. For the definitive discussion of Border War cinema, Tomaselli and van Zyl offer an insightful analysis of the cycle in both international co-productions and Afrikaans-language films, arguing that 'In contrast to the American experience in Vietnam, the South African film industry followed the troops into action with no qualms at all' (1992: 442).

With the risk of treading across familiar ground, then, it is useful to mention such Broederbond-orientated, Afrikaans-language films as *Grensbasis 13* (Elmo de Witt, 1979), which thanks the South African police in both its opening *and* closing credits, the local hit *Boetie Gaan Border Toe* (Regardt van den Bergh, 1984) and its similarly popular, rushed follow-up *Boetie Op Maneuvers* (Regardt van den Bergh, 1985). ZAxploitation has been redis-covered as a new part of an old exploitation film network and, as a result, it is doubtful that readers interested in pursuing the texts further will also be aware of these better-known but influential Afrikaans motion pictures. The coming-of-age border war films generally play the conflict 'straight' (despite

193

Figure 9.2 Arnold Vosloo as a soldier of the apartheid state in *Boetie Gaan Border Toe* (Regardt van den Bergh, 1984)

some initial comedy) whereas *The Gods Must Be Crazy* – a stylish and well-made adventure which continues to encourage considerable discussion about its representation of bushmen – carries an irreverent, slapstick tone. Apartheid, and related state abuses, however, are never highlighted so as to maintain a privileged, localised and most importantly *white* perspective (some Black characters, predictably representing largely incompetent enemy forces, are introduced in *Grensbasis 13* but they are infiltrated and defeated by the whites in a fiery conclusion).

Tomaselli acknowledges that both *Boetie Gaan Border Toe* and its sequel were produced with the assistance of the South African Defence Force and 'exhibit a new generation of technical, textual and propagandistic competence' (1988: 219), offering further context to where its sympathies lie. The author also acknowledges how the sense of a 'Border' war played into wider local politics: 'The Border stands for the imperialist world onslaught ... which, like the British war on the Boers, seeks to take away what belongs to Afrikanerdom: its wealth, its culture and its God-given privilege in life' (1992: 439). Or, to quote a character in *Ambushed* – who may as well be speaking as a settler himself – 'Death is never easy. One minute you are here. The next you are gone.

Unbelievable'. If war cuts young lives short, then, the solution is to prevent it and, as such, the Border emerges in some South African genre films as a character in its own right, a force which separates not only civilisation from savage Africa but life from death.

It is worth discussing *Boetie Gaan Border Toe* (*Buddy Goes to the Border*) so as to establish how an example of mainstream South African cinema presented this threat of infiltration from dark Africa into white Africa (*Ambushed*, despite its all-Black cast, does not veer too far from the same theme, attesting to the influence). The film follows character actor Arnold Vosloo as Boetie – a handsome, easy-going youth, transfixed by the challenges of puberty and women, who joins the army and matures whilst in training and on the battlefield, particularly in a brutal and protracted action-packed finale. Well-directed by van den Bergh, and featuring a contemporary chart soundtrack, *Boetie Gaan Border Toe* is interesting because it anticipates (and possibly even inspired) similar 'drill sergeant' scenes as that later found in *Full Metal Jacket* (Stanley Kubrick, 1987).[5] Moreover, it features no Black characters – even on the battlefield (the Angolans remain 'invisible'). Tomaselli labels these films as 'jeep operas', contrasting their tough-guy army heroes with the shattered-adolescence melodrama that the respective narratives present. *Boetie Gaan Border Toe* certainly offers a taut character arc for Vosloo, and goes some way to equating masculinity with nationalism, even though the war scenes are (strangely) without any sense of jubilance.

Tomaselli also mentions how the 'jeep opera' cycle might be aligned with 'mercenary films' such as *The Wild Geese*, which share their own dubious visions of (older) white men in Africa: 'These kinds of films reveal clear racism on the part of their directors, as a handful of usually ageing American and British actors playing mercenaries wipe out hundreds of pursuing blacks' (2016: 113). Whilst *The Wild Geese* is discussed in Chapter 7 (and it is also worth noting its patronising, if not outright racist, theme song 'The Flight of the Wild Geese' by Joan Armatrading[6]), its emergence during two notable and extensive conflicts in white-governed Africa – the Bush War in Ian Smith's Rhodesia and Pretoria's ongoing conflict with the MPLA in Angola – is telling. *The Wild Geese* shares common space with other films presenting the same sort of story of white mercenaries battling against Black communist insurgency – most notably *Dogs of War* (John Irvin, 1980), which also places its gung-ho theatrics in a fictional African country, and the low budget, VHS-orientated *Operation Hit Squad* (Tonie van der Merwe, Kathy Viedge, 1987). As with *The Wild Geese* and *Dogs of War*, *Operation Hit Squad*, which co-stars the ubiquitous Ken Gampu (who gets to battle B-Scheme hero Popo Gumede, synonymous with the cinema of van der Merwe and here cast as a guerrilla), plays it safe for the international market by never mentioning where it is set.

As with *The Wild Geese*, this is simply a return to savage Africa, a fictional

Figure 9.3 Vera Johns is terrorised in *Operation Hit Squad* (Tonie van der Merwe, Kathy Viedge, 1987)

country called Lanseria,[7] during a guerrilla insurgency that has taken a beautiful blonde woman (Vera Johns) hostage. Although produced by the American mini-major studio New World Pictures, *Operation Hit Squad* – despite its higher production values and more expansive cast and locations – follows the same formula as a number of van der Merwe's B-Scheme stories: women are kidnapped and raped and it is up to a do-gooder figure to save the day. *Operation Hit Squad* is racially less problematic than *The Wild Geese* because the enemy fighters comprise mainly white guerrillas and the rescuing ensemble is headlined by Gampu, whose national allegiance is never mentioned or questioned. One presumes that van der Merwe and his South African crew knew that depictions of African savages were not only problematic but likely passé for an international audience of 1987. *Operation Hit Squad* is a mix of the *Boetie* 'Boy's Own' adventure spectacle, where war is exciting before it becomes hell, and the more noxious politics of *The Wild Geese*, where proxy conflicts are diluted into depictions of 'us' (the urban) against 'them' (the rural).

Speaking about the American Vietnam War film, author Leo Cawley notes how many of the more outlandish entries in the field – beginning with *The*

Green Berets (John Wayne/Ray Kellogg, 1968) and including post-war entries *Missing in Action* (Joseph Zito, 1984), *Rambo: First Blood Part II* (George P. Cosmatos, 1985) and *The Hanoi Hilton* (Lionel Chetwynd, 1987) feature the 'use of overage stars'. The author notes how this factor 'depicts war as the business of "real" men, mature men rather than the star-crossed adolescents who fight it' (1990: 76). In this regard, the Border War films can, not too dissimilar from the Vietnam variant made in Hollywood, also be seen to split into two kinds. Gaylan Studlar and David Desser mention how American cinema presented both a 'right-wing revisionism' of the conflict (Stallone's John Rambo and Chuck Norris as James Braddock) and a 'more realistic strain', such as *Platoon* (Oliver Stone, 1986) or *Full Metal Jacket* (1990: 104). *The Wild Geese* and similar mercenary films, involving actors far too old for combat but eliciting images of Empire and imperialism, are Africa as fantasy: a savage land into which (not unlike Rambo's Vietnam) the white man should never have been forced to retreat. This study also introduced *Shamwari* in Chapter 7 – starring South African performers Ken Gampu and Ian Yule as two convicts handcuffed together at the height of the Rhodesian Bush War. Gampu also appears, alongside *Shaft*'s Richard Roundtree, in *Game for Vultures* (James Fargo, 1979), playing a hard-line Mugabe-Leninist liberation leader, as quick to kill white sympathisers as he is to lead men into battle. Roundtree is shown to be concerned with the liberation struggle but more willing to give the whites (and middle-class Black people) a chance in a new nation (it is probably worth mentioning that *Game for Vultures* was completed around the time the affable Abel Muzorewa was installed as the Prime Minister of the short-lived Zimbabwe-Rhodesia). As noted by Cameron, *Game for Vultures* – which was adapted from a pulp novel – was 'made with the cooperation of the South African Defence force, so its killing of Blacks, its fear of racial mixing, and above all its paranoid hatred of Black terrorists, are its real meanings' (1994: 154). Nonetheless, as with *The Wild Geese*, the film also indicates that white Africa is on borrowed time: as the narrative reaches its bullet-ballet conclusion, imperialist fantasies are put into harsh perspective even if the producers believed otherwise. Indeed, it is not the Black mercenaries trying to escape from colonial Rhodesia come the final act.

Effectively repeating the character that he played in *The Wild Geese*, Richard Harris plays a mercenary and arms dealer in *Game for Vultures*, although he ends the film in the trenches with Roundtree, fighting for a country that he cannot possibly salvage from terrorism, but united with his (gradually less radicalised) Black compatriot in briefly battling against leftist insurgency. This sort of presentation is what Tomaselli and van Zyl describe, albeit with reference to *The Wild Geese*, as 'racial moralising where black and white solve their differences in terms of the dominant apartheid discourse', one in which the 'white mercenaries "save the black man from himself"' (1992:

Figure 9.4 Richard Roundtree takes aim, as a Zimbabwe liberation fighter, in *Game for Vultures* (James Fargo, 1979)

443). In comparison, *Boetie Gaan Border Toe* – which still sympathises with white South African dominance in the region – has more in common with an American film such as *Platoon* in that it at least depicts armed conflict as a gruelling experience in which close friends not only bond during a time of war, but die together as well.

Darrell Roodt's better known *The Stick*, which presents war as even more inhumane, as well as monotonous, suffers from the same problems that Hollywood's 'more realistic strain' of Vietnam War films encounter, namely that the narratives are told from the perspective of the invading soldiers. The result of this approach made the Hollywood depiction of the conflict in Indochina, even the Oscar-winning likes of *Platoon*, an *American* tragedy rather than a *Vietnamese* one. Therefore, whilst *Boetie Gaan Border Toe* and *The Stick* do not share the same political perspective, they both suffer from treating South African aggression against Angola as a localised catastrophe, for handsome young white men, rather than as contributing to the destabilisation of a newly independent country.

Furthermore, one of the things that becomes most notable about the Border War films is that they are not even sure what Africans are fighting *for*. In

Game for Vultures, for instance, Roundtree's guerrilla hero argues with a remark from a Black schoolteacher ('things are changing, it's a question of time and talking'): 'Yeah changes, now I can sleep with a white girl without being arrested for it, but I cannot vote'. Thus, for the film, the liberation fight is about democracy (which Mugabe's Zimbabwe quickly and efficiently stifled anyway), not land or capital redistribution or freedom of movement or residence. For British director Neil Hetherington, in *Terrorist*, there is another purpose altogether. A white American asks a local about the Border War in South West Africa and is told, 'Under this sand and rocks are the richest minerals in the world. We are sitting on the bloody jackpot . . . That's what we are fighting for'. In the case of *Terrorist*, then, an African war of liberation is about recovering the land's wealth from the white settlers and *not* democracy. Roodt's *The Stick* is perhaps more honest by having its young, haunted cadet Cooper (Greg Latter) begin the film with the following voice-over:

> Things got so bad, they — the generals and politicians — didn't even know how to control us anymore. It wasn't enough to give speeches about patriotism, hand out medals or talk about the invasion of communism. We were too busy trying to stay alive to worry about our mothers and sisters being raped by homesick Cubans.

Cooper, still recovering from PTSD, the only survivor from his platoon, ends the film by proclaiming 'The war was a lost cause. But they knew that anyway'. For Roodt, the conflict with Angola is at least framed as part of a confusing, never-ending proxy nightmare – what travel writer Daniel Metcalfe would later dub a 'horrible pointless war' (2014: 125) – rather than one which South Africa needed to involve itself with in the first place. By the time van der Merwe's *Ambushed* appeared, at least the urgent issue of conservation is introduced to explain why two game wardens are willing to go into battle. As mentioned by Metcalfe, the Angolan War depleted the nation of its livestock, 'the rebel movements overran the national parks . . . machine-gunning the animals for food' (Ibid.: 218). Matloff also acknowledges empty game parks in Angola in the 1990s (1997: 184). Perhaps surprisingly, *Ambushed* is the only Border War film to address the likely impact of proxy conflict on the environment: a B-Scheme adventure with a social conscience.

Strangers in a Strange Land

Whether based in fictional lands, as was the case with *The Wild Geese* and *Dogs of War*, or neighbouring Zimbabwe – where the writing was on the wall for the white minority by the mid-1970s, but which made a suitable alternative locale for films designed for release in South Africa – the mercenary films cast

Figure 9.5 Hector Mathanda as a guerrilla and poacher in *Ambushed* (Tonie van der Merwe, 1988)

an indelible bogeyman on the apartheid state by way of indicating that 'this could happen here'. *Terrorist*, for instance, shares threads with these films but also with home-invasion and rape-revenge cinema, which became popular following the exploitation-horror classic *The Last House on the Left* and the more mainstream (if still frequently censored) thriller *Death Wish*. *Terrorist* is the Border War film that, of all the texts explored in this study, feels like a 'grindhouse' exploitation effort. It is a different style of ZAxploitation: its Black characters are savage, its white characters are noble, and the violence includes attempted rape, an elderly lady who has her throat cut and a young child threatened and abused by one of the Angolan guerrilla fighters. Whilst Vietnam lingered in the background of the American blaxploitation films – including characters such as Jim Brown's iconic *Slaughter* and *Mean Johnny Barrows* (Fred Williamson, 1976) – the closest American exploitation cousin to *Terrorist* is *Fight for Your Life* (Robert A. Endelson, 1976). Pitting a civilised Black family against some poor white trash home invaders, Bill Landis labelled *Fight for Your Life* as 'the racism exploitation movie to end them all ... it would also be suitable entertainment for a Ku Klux Klan barbecue' (2002: 103). In comparison, *Terrorist* simply reverses the roles: the violent, unkempt Black characters – who never discuss exactly what they are doing or why (attesting, perhaps unwittingly, to how confusing the Angolan conflict was) – arrive by sea in South West Africa to harass and murder a wealthy white family. Unlike in *Fight for Your Life*, where the Black characters finally 'win', *Terrorist* shows a small group of four (white) people failing to kill all of the antagonists. One even struggles away into the sea, picked up by his comrades in a speedboat and ready for another day of looting and murdering. One imagines that this conclusion was far from welcome to the South African audiences of the time; Tomaselli confirms that *Terrorist* met with censorship problems (2016: 30), leading to some changes for local audiences. Writing with Mikki van Zyl, the author notes how the film 'was granted censorship exemption when the director altered the ending to state that terrorists will be apprehended and punished [which] encapsulates the dominant discourse on terrorism in order versus anarchy terms' (1992: 443).

States the director, Neil Hetherington:

> Originally it was called *Freedom Fighters* . . . I was asked to make a film about 'now' and 'now' [in 1978] was South West Africa . . . And at one point the producers said, 'You can't call it *Freedom Fighters*'. 'Well why

Figure 9.6 The Angolan conflict spills into Namibia in *Terrorist* (Neil Hetherington, 1978)

not?' 'Because they are terrorists!' 'Alright, we will call it *Terrorist*'. It was a 19-day shoot, in Namibia, South West Africa, up in Henties Bay, in a hotel where the lights went out at 8pm every night. We would film in the desert, where there were guys with lights going past, the real terrorists, and we cast Miss South Africa [Vera Johns], who was actually Rhodesian [and] who was terrified what this might do to her family because this was a film she wanted to make and of course Miss South Africa goes through the entire movie in a jump suit. It was not romantic or glamourous or anything and I think that is why she wanted to do it. So we did it and once we made it, we put it into the censor board and they said 'bugger off, this is banned'. And that was frightening. It seemed insane . . . It hit the front page of *The Sunday Express* . . . about this film that was going to split South Africa in half. We thought, 'Well that is a bit ropey. How can a film do that?' but that is what they believed. They said it was more violent than *Taxi Driver* . . . 'Well, I wish it was'. There were four or five sequences that were pretty bloody but today it is nothing. At the same time, one could understand that there were a percentage of people, maybe 70 percent of the white population, who would have burned us alive.

Reputedly based on true events, *Terrorist* emerged from a pivotal year: 1978 was when South West Africa held its first 'democratic' elections, famously boycotted by the main liberation party SWAPO (South West African People's Organisation, still in government in Namibia today). The result meant that Namibia would need to wait until 1990 for its independence, whilst on 4th May of that year, Pretoria all but guaranteed the continuation of the armed struggle in its satellite when it launched its well-documented attack on the Cassinga refugee camp (Gleijeses 2013: 96). Of all the films to deal with the Border War, then, *Terrorist* is not just the most paranoid but also the most violent and offensive. The small group of Black guerrilla fighters seem to have no aim other than disorganised mass-murder. They break into the lavish house of an elderly white man and his wife, brutally kill them, and take a young local boy, Pete, hostage. The child's young, beautiful mother, Anna (Vera Johns, later in *Operation Hit Squad*) teams up with an American friend, Brad (Robert Aberdeen), a Scottish settler, Mac (Howard Connell), and a gas station owner and budding mercenary, Joe (Allan Granville) to find the child. Whilst some of the comparable projects from this era, even *The Wild Geese*, at least pay lip-service to multiculturalism in an imagined, all-is-forgiven postcolonial South Africa or Zimbabwe, where white capital and rights are protected, *Terrorist* contains some of the most inflammatory dialogue from the cinema of this period. Take this exchange between the unapologetically racist Joe and his new American acquaintance Brad (Robert Aberdeen), who explains that he has just visited Africa as part of the peace corps:

Joe: The black bastards.
Brad: You really hate the blacks, don't you?
Joe: You can say that again and with a very good reason.
Brad: Oh, I'm sure everybody has a good reason...
Joe: How long have you been here in Africa?
Brad: Eight weeks.
Joe: You know nothing about living with these bastards. I was born in Kenya. We had a strong army and police force there. What happened? One day the Mau-Mau got my old man on his farm. After he slaved to give us all a good life.
Brad: I'm sorry to hear that. It's a different thing here. The writing is on the wall.
Joe: What do you want us to do? Share with them? They don't want to share with us. Did you share with the Indians in America?
Brad: That's not the same thing.
Joe: I've heard it all before. You and your peace corps.

All through this 'discussion' Joe calmly and 'rationally' explains his point (plus acknowledging the Black cinematic bogeyman of old – the dreaded Mau-Mau, providing *Terrorist* with a further link to old exploitation cinema). At the end of *Terrorist*, in which Joe is blown-up in a final attack on the last Angolan communist (who escapes to safety), Brad is shown to be astounded and emotionally distraught – finally realising, it would appear, that his dead contemporary was right all along: majority-rule would destroy South West Africa and South Africa with it. 'You see how they treat their own people. How the hell do you think they would treat us?' screams Joe at Brad, just moments before Hetherington has two of the insurgents stop a car (driven by a young Black couple), kill the driver and attempt to rape his girlfriend. Whilst the Black representations in *Terrorist* are undoubtedly offensive,[8] the director nonetheless insists that when the film was finally released it played to non-white audiences in South Africa:

> Eventually it went out independently and did very well. But it was a bit old by then. It was made in 1976 and only went out in 1979. I went to a screening in an Indian cinema in Johannesburg and it played with a Kris Kristofferson movie and it was packed. It was loud and [there was] screaming. But they did not object to the storyline... I [also] went to cinemas that only had Black audiences and I was well looked after. (2016)

Figure 9.7 Vera Johns tries to survive in *Terrorist* (Neil Hetherington, 1978)

Alternative Takes

Tonie van der Merwe's B-Scheme project *Ambushed* is an example of how the initiative would respond to even successful, localised cycles of genre cinema. *Terrorist* undoubtedly deserves a place among global exploitation trends of the time, including those within South Africa, but *Ambushed* is a curious attempt to rectify the race-panic of the Angolan monster by returning to the old Mr Right against Mr Wrong of Black Africa. *Ambushed* features an all-Black cast of just six and, although there is no acknowledgement of where it is set, it exploits the mythos of land, livestock and border protection as concurrent with social (in this case the family unit) and political stability. A local game ranger (played by Popo Gumede) – accompanied by his best friend – has to save his wife and son when they are kidnapped by a local guerrilla insurgency led by a pair of armed thugs from across the border (Hector Mathanda is once again cast as a villain). With *Ambushed*, the usual dialogue about good, clean living is exchanged between Popo and his young son: 'You must do well at school', states the proud father. His son, hearing about raids on similar farms in the area, mentions 'I'll protect us from bad guys'.

But who are these bad guys? South Africa in 1988 certainly had reason to be concerned about communism at home and in nearby countries: in Lesotho, a North Korean embassy had arrived in 1982, the Cubans remained in Angola and Robert Mugabe had unleashed his notorious Gukurahundi onslaught with the assistance of the 5th Brigade from Pyongyang (Chan 2019: 23). Feared ANC figures such as Mzwandile Piliso had 'tortured suspects' in the party's infamous Morris Seabelo Rehabilitation Centre in Angola (Johnson 2010: 33). According to journalist Roger Omond, writing in the mid-1980s, 'The South Africa Defence Force estimates that the ANC has up to 7,000 guerrillas' (1985: 185). Even as late as 1989, the ANC had been talking of 'building East Germany in Africa' (Johnson 2010: 75). The communists of *Ambushed* are possibly *even more* evil, however, because they are seeking to make some additional money in poaching.

Mathanda, dressed in military uniform (albeit without alignment to any actual countries) imprisons the kidnapped woman in a makeshift wooden jail and attempts to rape her, with only her young son's screaming finally distracting him from the act and convincing him not to bother (as much for censorship reasons, one presumes). Maingard mentions how the remake of the seminal South African film *De Voortrekkers* in 1973 visualises 'the threat posed by Black people on South Africans and especially white Afrikaners', often by 'using close-up imagery' (2007: 134). Whilst there are no white characters in *Ambushed*, there is Gumede in his recurring role as the family-orientated, handsome, muscular B-Scheme hero. Close-ups are reserved for the portly Mathanda and his sweaty face, complete with missing teeth, particularly in the scenes where he harasses Gumede's wife and son and transforms into an obese, debased caricature of the communist spectre. Whilst *Ambushed* lacks the technical competence of *Terrorist*, and appears threadbare even by the thin standards of the B-Scheme, the film contains similar vitriol towards those armed enemies of the state and their potential to destabilise the perceived hard-fought for gains of apartheid, such as the upstanding, land-owning, peaceful Black husband and his devoted family.

Perhaps the most famous of the Border War films is *The Stick*. Director Darrell Roodt, supported by producer Anant Singh, had already used genre to at least touch upon the crimes of the apartheid state: his *Tenth of a Second* (1987) might be described as a 'nightmare movie' about entrapment and coercion. Roodt's first low budget horror film was *City of Blood* (1983), which features a largely white cast, although Ken Gampu emerges in the final reel as a mysterious and shadowy figure, responsible for a city-wide murder spree of prostitutes. Gampu gets some fierce lines: 'Do you know what it is like to be black in this country? Do you? A black is not a man, he is a dog,' but he is underrepresented and his motives for murder are unclear. More curious is the film's prologue: a witchdoctor sinisterly attacks and kills some Black bushmen in 'Africa' two thousand years earlier, which anticipates Roodt's later, similar use of local legends in *The Stick*.

Figure 9.8 The war in Angola becomes horror film nightmare in *The Stick* (Darrell Roodt, 1988)

Discussing some of the B-Scheme representations, Paleker notes the use of witchdoctors: 'While African people make a distinction between (evil) witchdoctors and (therapeutic) sangomas, many of the B-Scheme films blur or ignore this distinction' (2010: 96).[9] Roodt's *The Stick* features only two Black characters with any agency (dialogue or character name). One is a 'black tracker' (Dixon Malele) who joins the platoon on their infiltration into Angolan territory and refuses orders to kill innocent civilians (leading to his own demise). The other is a witchdoctor (Winston Ntshona, of *The Wild Geese*), who is part of a hamlet that the crew destroy out of paranoia and frustration early in the film, My Lai style. The story of *The Stick* is also told via expository voice-over from star, and leading man, Greg Latter, which all-too-often verges on the comic book (sample dialogue: 'I hoped that he was dead so that he didn't have to live with that nightmare for the rest of his life').

Whilst Roodt uses war to make a horror film, not unlike Michael Mann with *The Keep* (1983), *The Stick* also draws on local legend with its witchdoctor presentation. When Latter's men approach the hamlet, the tribesman, for all intents and purposes, appears to be a healer – a sangoma – *not* a figure of evil, although the troops identify him as a witchdoctor. Noting the Ovimbundu ethnic group of Angola, Matloff acknowledges a traditional belief in spirits and ancestors. The tradition passed down during the generations is that when a person dies the soul leaves the body and becomes a ghost, or *ocimbanda*. The *ocimbanda* can be very badly behaved. Illness or death can result if it is not appeased with a feast or treated with proper respect. (1997: 259)

Roodt appears to be aware of this mythology and draws upon it, but in doing so he skates on thin ice. During the Angolan War of liberation from Portugal, the MPLA would burn opponents for 'witchcraft' (Metcalfe 2014: 268). Depicting superstition as a (literal) *reality* of Africa could be seen as an attempt to justify such horrors. Ryszard Kapuściński would opine that 'The spiritual world of the "African" (if one may use the term despite its gross simplification) is rich and complex' (2001: 15). Roodt reduces this complexity to something that is literally black and white, benefitting his horror film framework but offering little context to the Angolan conflict.

Indeed, one is reminded of author Nicky Arden, a white woman who wrote her book, *African Spirits Speak*, about her journey of becoming a sangoma. The tale includes hallucinations of leopards and concludes with ritualism and animal sacrifice, in which the author has convinced herself that a cow permitted its own death: 'She had lowered her head to me', claims the writer, as she recalls stabbing the beast in the throat (1999: 253). This association of tradition and violence, of *us* and *them*, raises complicated arguments about how the white 'outsider' depicts, normalises, or even engages with what they deem as Africanness, albeit one framed in pastness and superstition, not to mention complexities dating back centuries. In doing so, this approach also maintains a continent oppositional to 'our' own modernity, even inadvertently. Roodt offers a similar presentation with *The Stick*: as the white soldiers begin to hallucinate, walk in circles around the Bush and fall prey to mysterious booby traps, the unfolding horror is the work of an *ocimbanda*. By utilising such folklore, Roodt highlights the foreignness of Black Africa to the white man. Given that his audience is most likely the latter rather than the former, he risks falling into the same, almost century-old cinematic presentation of the 'dark continent' as one of the tribal macabre: *unchanged* and *unchangeable*, but reduced to a fight between the 'civilised' world and the primitive. *The Stick*'s Angola gradually becomes less of a warzone and more of a terrifying maze in which the white man is shown to be misplaced and unwelcome, not through his own imperialistic actions but because ghouls and ghosts – deemed phoney but proven to be genuine – compromise his presence.

The director veers into similarly problematic ground with *City of Blood*, similarly initiating the idea that Black Africa is a place of mysticism and magic, as unfamiliar to the white progressives as it is to racist policemen and politicians. Tomaselli, noting that *The Stick* was banned until 1990, sees the film as 'a semi-autobiographical account of Darrell Roodt's alienation from the army and the psychopathic tendencies caused by apartheid. The story concerns eight men who, while on patrol against unseen odds, psychologically destroy themselves, each other and whole black villages' (2016: 35). Botha also reads the film along similar lines, maintaining how the white protagonists 'have destroyed an indigenous lifestyle' by killing 'a village of blacks and a witchdoctor. The film becomes a surreal and nihilistic work – that which is incomprehensible to the white protagonists, namely Africa, is portrayed as sinister and irrational' (1992: 72).

The Stick remains a powerful horror film, but it has its own 'magic negro' figure. The witchdoctor is, narratively, the crux upon which the audience comes to terms with the barbarity of the film's white men. He is a mystical figure that, per Matthew Hughey, 'has become a stock character that often appears as a lower class, uneducated black person who possesses supernatural or magical powers' (2009: 544). Roodt also disappoints by ending his film with sole survivor, Latter, encountering the same witchdoctor but this time as an everyman on the city streets. Botha exclaims that this moment is symbolic because, for the white man, 'Africa still surrounds him – he cannot destroy it. To fight against it means self-destruction' (1992: 72). It also symbolises the sense of exotic Africa – a place in which spells and witchcraft remain, despite colonialism, and where the white man can be seduced, confused or victimised by practices which he does not understand and should not have interfered with. R. W. Johnson has written about Thabo Mbeki 'cultivating the sangomas' during his disastrous response to South Africa's AIDS epidemic in the post-apartheid years (2010: 208). Perhaps it is this clash of the traditional with the harsh reality of modernity, third world practices against the first world war machine, that Roodt attempts to present in his film. Yet one is left with the impression, from *The Stick*, that the white man in Africa can only ever be spiritually at rest if he experiences such 'primitive' nativism up close and personal. Ritualism and sacrifice included.

Therefore, in its own way, *The Stick* represents the old cinema of Tarzan, the savage Africa (also initiated by Roodt's witchdoctor of *City of Blood*) that is sustained through only a modicum of Black characters who we never become familiar with. *The Stick* might be best summarised vis-à-vis the experience of Lara Pawson in her investigation of the failed 1977 coup against President Agostinho Neto in Angola. As she searches for the rumoured mass grave of the perpetrators, four decades later, she describes herself wondering, 'Am I stuck in my own othering of the African continent as a site of catastrophe?' (2014: 158). The characters of *The Stick* search for Angola, and by extension the 'enemy' that is Black Africa, as just such a 'site of catastrophe'. When they cannot find it, they inadvertently create it for themselves, unleashing forces too foreign for the big city kids in the 'privileged' South.

Writing about such major American studio films as *Tears of the Sun* (Antoine

Fuqua, 2003) and *Black Hawk Down* (Ridley Scott, 2001), MaryEllen Higgins speaks about 'their evocation of the classic Hollywood Western, this time with its outlaw heroes discovering a new "Wild Wild West" on African frontiers' (2012: 69). Roodt's *The Stick*, the most prominent and certainly the best made Border War film of the period, plays to the same tune – presenting the Angola conflict from the perspective of defeated, dislikeable white men, venturing onto new plains that they can never hope to understand nor modernise. Whilst Roodt avoids the trap of 'new' African films such as *The Last King of Scotland* (Kevin Macdonald, 2007), in which 'colonial exploitation is scorned, but the complete withdrawal of dominant Western influence is projected as dangerous, unconscionable, and cowardly' (Ibid.: 8), by suggesting that Angola was and is a lost (and aimless) cause, his depiction of a symbolically haunted – and *haunting* – Africa veers close to sensationalism.

As with Hollywood's Vietnam films, even those which attempted to critique America's defence of its satellite state in the South, the Border War cycle was routinely played out in terms of Otherness: undefined African opponents, with undefined ideology, challenging Pretoria's dominance in the continent or seeking to make spoils from her wealth (including even her animal life). Whilst *The Stick* maintains that the war is wrong, its refusal of a Black voice is telling – an acceptance, perhaps, from producers, that cinema's Africa only works with audiences when the endangered white minority are under threat in unfamiliar frontiers. By analysing *Mapantsula* in the final chapter of this monograph, this study indicates how other oppositional voices, even those working within genre frameworks, struggled to have their voices heard when presenting a different kind of African story.

Notes

1. During the research of this book, Coenie Dippenaar, whose Western *Revenge* is a standout from the B-Scheme, told me that he was most proud of a film he produced called *Endangered* (Mark Engels, 1989), which is about ivory poaching during a time of revolution. Dippenaar would mention how its pro-conservation message pre-dated Clint Eastwood's *White Hunter Black Heart* (1990). Unfortunately, I have been unable to find a copy of *Endangered*.
2. The Civil War in Angola would, however, stretch on until 2002, despite intermittent ceasefires.
3. Per Tomaselli the film was re-released as *Black Terrorist* for maximum sensationalism in 1985 (2016: 162).
4. See: Tomaselli, Keyan G. and McLennan-Dodd, Vanessa (2005) 'The Gods Must be Crazy in China', *Visual Anthropology*, 18: 199–228.
5. With its initial scenes of pretty women and glorious adolescence, eventually compromised by the need to serve one's government and the related ideology, one might even see some interesting and curious parallels between *Boetie Gaan Border Toe* and the Israeli conscription comedy *Sapiches* (or *Private Popsicle*, Boaz Davidson, 1982), part of the classic *Eskimo Limon/Lemon Popsicle* series.

6. Sample lyrics: 'Time is running out/So much to be done/Tell me what more/What more/What more can we do/There were promises made/Plans firmly laid/Now madness prevails/Lies fill the air'.
7. Lanseria is, however, an airport in Johannesburg – possibly indicating that *Operation Hit Squad* is initiating its fictional war as 'close to home' and pointing to an assumption that local viewers would understand that this was about the war with Angola.
8. Despite not featuring a single positive portrayal of a Black character, Hetherington does feel differently, stating: 'I think the whole point of the film was to say not all Black people are bad and not all white people are good. It was a morality play made in 19 days about a situation that was dangerous and which we objected to. Anyway, the film got banned, our phones got tapped, they came and put lovely little devices in our offices, posing as toilet repair people, and it really was a mess. It killed my career' (2016).
9. An especially tawdry B-Scheme film such *The Mobsters* even goes so far as to integrate such local mysticism into a plot involving fraud and gangsterdom, culminating in the ridiculous sight of an evil, cackling, rural sangoma being impaled with a spear, thrown by an urban 'Mr Right' Black character.

10. A DIFFERENT KIND OF GANGSTER CINEMA?

Mapantsula *and a state of 'Panic'*

Perhaps no motion picture from the apartheid era has been given more coverage than *Mapantsula*.[1] Co-written by, and starring, Thomas Mogotlane as the small-time hooligan and crook 'Panic', the film was released when the country was still under a state of emergency, which had been introduced on 20 July 1985. Journalist Roger Omond would report that 'By the end of July 1985 more than 1,200 people had been detained without trial and at least 15 people killed in clashes with the police and army' (1985: 211). Three years later and there was little sense that the country's turmoil was concluding. Christi van der Westhuizen notes how five thousand people were arrested in 'unrest related incidents' in 1988 (2007: 144), the same year in which *Mapantsula* presents the younger, politically-motivated inhabitants of Soweto refusing to pay rent whilst its lead character, Panic, concerns himself with little more than booze, sex and petty theft. Jacqueline Maingard mentions first seeing *Mapantsula* during this tumultuous time and notes the 'euphoric intensity of the small audience, present at what felt like the first truly South African film' (1994: 235). Such commentary offers valuable insight into how revolutionary *Mapantsula* must have seemed back in 1988, a period in which intense resistance – especially within the townships – against the National Party government was at a peak.

Videographer and producer Brian Tilley, who documented the unrest but also worked on locally-made genre fare such as the B-Scheme gangster farce *Upondo & Nkinsela* (Bernard Buys, 1984)[2] and the slightly more notable

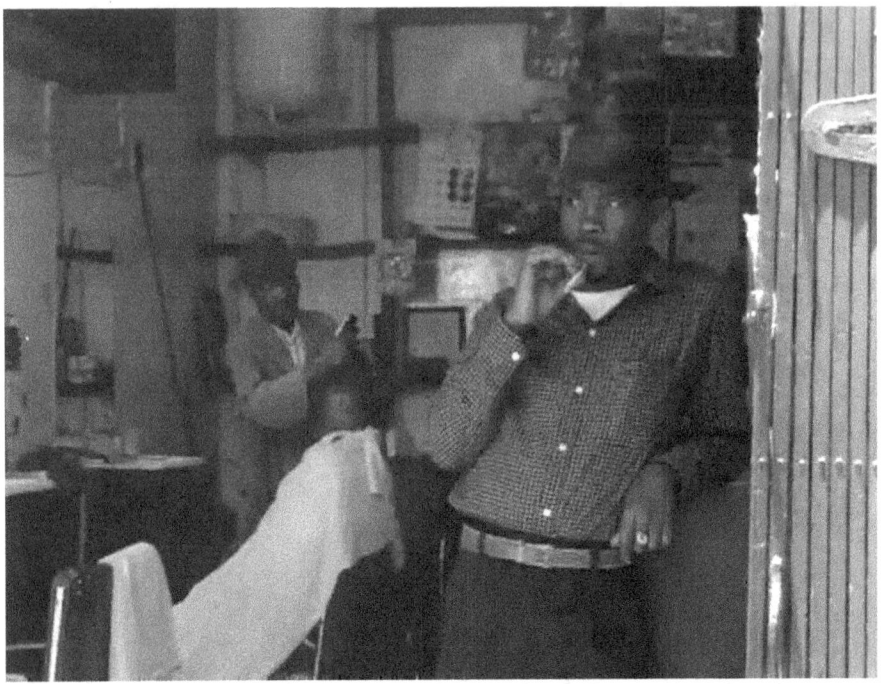

Figure 10.1 Thomas Mogotlane as Johannes 'Panic' Themba Mzolo in *Mapantsula* (Oliver Schmitz, 1988)

Survival Zone (Percival Rubens, 1983), which was aimed at the global VHS market, notes that

> the most intense period of mass struggle in South Africa was the 1980s. In 1987, the mass struggle was not tapering off; it was building to its crescendo ... Even in the early nineties it did not seem like there was going to be a settlement in South Africa. The world was shocked when we came to a settlement. It was an intense struggle, every day, in the streets of the poorest areas of the country people were being killed and abused. And if anyone says it was not happening, they are not telling the truth. (2016)

It was from this environment that *Mapantsula* emerged.

However, the B-Scheme initiative also played a (largely unacknowledged) part in the film's genesis. Tomaselli and Jeanne Prinsloo have mentioned how Mogotlane had learned his craft as an employee of Heyns Films. Indeed, the film company allowed Mogotlane and Schmitz to use their backlot, where *Mapantsula* was shot (1992: 134). Gugler further details how the filmmakers had crafted 'a dummy script' to avoid suspicion whilst, in perhaps the greatest irony surrounding the *Mapantsula* controversy, its nearly all-Black cast meant that it also qualified for the B-Scheme subsidy after completion and release (2004: 91). As also noted by Tomaselli and Prinsloo, the same had previously happened with David Bensusan's anti-apartheid drama *My Country My Hat* (belatedly released in 1983), which was 'refused distribution' by the major South African cinema chains and was finally 'classified "black" by the Department of Industries' and 'eventually distributed by the conservative Afrikaner-dominated "black" mobile cinema arm' (1992: 332).

Botha affirms that *Mapantsula* 'has been one of the first truly South African films made from a black African point of view' (2012: 133), although – drawing on similar comments from the director Spike Lee – Keyan Tomaselli has charged that

> *Mapantsula* was a collaboration between a white director, Oliver Schmitz, and a black actor/co-scriptwriter, Thomas Mogotlane. Of *Mapantsula*'s fifty-person crew, only thirteen were black; none except Mogotlane were key technicians. What, then, makes this film "black" while [Lee's] *Malcolm X* becomes unacceptably "white" if directed by equally-talented white directors? (2016: 101)

This debate is worth acknowledging because at the time of its release, and in the years since, *Mapantsula* has been seen as an authentic *Black* representation of apartheid and an example of belated, contemporary South African Third Cinema. This monograph began by raising the question of race and *Africanness* in the stories of cheap, often tawdry, ZAxploitation films. Tomaselli, however, suggests that Schmitz's far more potent anti-apartheid text is no less radical because of the director's whiteness, although one might reply that *Mapantsula* is *itself* a complex and even confusing gathering of cinematic identities, no matter how powerful its message and on-screen depiction of state brutality is. Unpacking these identities is, therefore, the primary focus of this concluding chapter.

Gugler labels *Mapantsula* 'the first militant anti-*apartheid* feature film to be produced in South Africa' (2004: 91). Despite this acclaim, in the years since its debut, *Mapantsula* has become increasingly obscure. There exists no official Blu-ray or DVD release in Europe or the USA and, despite gaining a theatrical release in the UK and elsewhere, it remains absent from many important studies of global Black cinema representation.[3] Through establishing some comparison between *Mapantsula* and the cheap and tawdry gangster cinema of the B-Scheme, perhaps some new light can be shed on the former, which is generally analysed by way of its politics rather than of its genre. However, per the discussion that follows – authors have repeatedly introduced (sometimes

Figure 10.2 Thomas Mogotlane as Johannes 'Panic' Themba Mzolo in *Mapantsula* (Oliver Schmitz, 1988)

conflicting) terminology to describe the film. This challenge of semantics surely signifies confusion about what or where *Mapantsula* might be (mis)placed. For instance, Cameron argues that the film 'used the gangster genre to show the life of Soweto's streets and the police state that surrounds them' (1994: 160). However, in conclusion, the author later describes *Mapantsula* as 'melodramatic' (Ibid.: 163), which could be taken to insinuate that it does not, in fact, operate within the trappings of an easily identifiable generic framework.

Discussing the film within the wider representations of Black life in the nation at the time, Davis notes that 'the importance of *Mapantsula* lies in its breaking free of the Buddy genre' (1996: 112). Whilst the author maintains that the film refuses some of the established representations of lower budgeted South African crime cinema, *Mapantsula* benefits from being understood as a genre project in its own right. Maingard analyses the scene in which Panic, whose lover Pat has been forced to leave her job as a maid for a wealthy white family, smashes a window in the former employer's spacious Johannesburg house. In the lead-up to this scene, the author notes how Panic is shown taking a bus ride across the city and into the suburbs:

The camera deliberately pans left from its window picture of the world beyond the bus, to incorporate Panic within the frame, thereby iterating and re-iterating his point-of-view. There is a sense of the excessive in this act as if the point has to be made that the film represents a definitively black point-of-view. And by embracing Panic in this image, in this way, *Mapantsula*, and so too South African cinema, marks a point of 'cutting away' from cinema before it. (2007: 154)

Maingard's sensing of a proverbial 'ground zero' for South African cinema within *Mapantsula* ('cutting away' from the past) and, by extension, Black representation is astute. This is not least because the film might be viewed as an *international* example of what blaxploitation cinema could have been had the revolutionary zeal and turbulent, jarring, experimental aesthetic foundations and racial point-of-view seen in *Sweet Sweetback's Badass Song* been built upon nearly two decades prior. Van Peebles introduced a powerful and unusual Black hero, finally forced to confront the exploitative nature of the local state police force, presented within a non-linear narrative (albeit offering plentiful sex and violence) which aesthetically challenged Hollywood presentations. So too does *Mapantsula* present the possibility for a *new* kind of South African cinema (one that was arguably – much like *Sweetback* – never really built upon, including by Schmitz himself). By noting that Panic evokes similar rebellious and trendsetting Black heroes of cinema's past, one is not arguing against *Mapantsula*'s place as a radical anti-apartheid narrative but rather indicating that – for a film intended to also reach an international market – it works *within* identifiable referents, despite Maingard's conclusion that it also breaks with traditional Black South African cinema.

Gugler notes that 'In some respects, *Mapantsula* is indeed a gangster movie', although the author qualifies this, somewhat confusingly, by affirming that 'it is anything but a regular gangster movie' (2004: 91) and later makes a comparison to *The Harder They Come*. With this said, one might argue that the author is correct and that this is another key comparison because *The Harder They Come*, whilst likely inspired by the early blaxploitation films from the United States, reimagines the gangster-on-the-run narrative to an indigenous locale (Kingston) and provides audiences with a reinvention of familiar, troubled, criminal characters. In this regard, identifying *Mapantsula* as a tangentially transnational adaptation of popular American blaxploitation films, such as *The Harder They Come*, which – not unlike *Super Fly* et al – uses soundtrack as a dictate of narrative progression and character symbolism (and it is worth noting that Maingard also points out *Mapantsula*'s use of soundtrack in the key scene that she analyses) is not overly ambitious or wishful. *Mapantsula* is a film that acknowledges its own grounding in the past, whilst looking to a new future of Black South African representation and concerns. Even from a purely stylistic perspective, it – much like *Sweet Sweetback* or *The Harder They*

Come – feels *exciting* – in spite of (or maybe even because of) its hard-hitting subject matter. Part of this excitement, however, comes from Panic's increasing strength in the face of adversity – which, much like *Sweet Sweetback* or Jimmy Cliff's Ivanhoe Martin, allows for the forward direction of the narrative, no matter how non-linear the presentation – and its representation of white characters as the real 'savages' in sub-Saharan Africa. As with *Sweet Sweetback*, this means that *all* white characters are loathsome: a typical (and exploitative) trope of blaxploitation cinema in general (it is also worth pointing out that *The Harder They Come* uses paler-skinned characters as its antagonists, including a vulgar record label owner, to comment on Jamaica's own postcolonial problems with race).[4]

Modisane further argues that '*Mapantsula* is made in the gangster genre and Third Cinema register' (2013: 99), a comment echoed by Tomaselli, who labels it as 'South Africa's first film that could be categorised stylistically as Third Cinema' (2016: 23). Can genre thematic and Third Cinema aesthetic co-exist? Discussing the liberation cinema of Mozambique (when still under Portuguese rule), Diawara mentions how the films, such as Sarah Maldoror's *Sambizanga* (1972), whilst militant in their anti-colonial messages, adapted their messages into cinematic frameworks that could provide both a 'cultural and entertainment purpose' (1992: 90). It is here that, one could argue, another clue to *Mapantsula*'s impact emerges. Whilst the non-linear narrative and (predominantly) Zulu-language, as well as the verité approach, makes *Mapantsula* more *avant-garde* than most other South African cinema from the apartheid years, it *is* still a gangster film. It is also not without its own postmodern references (which also confuses, however slightly, the Third Cinema charge), such as when Panic's landlady accuses him of dressing up 'like a gangster', nodding to the outside universe of 'badass' characters that the knife-carrying hoodlum and thief imagines himself as.

Maingard mentions, also referring to *Mapantsula*'s ambiguous ending, that

> the film draws on the gangster genre. But it does not attempt to present rounded, holistic characterisations; rather, because its task is to represent its sociopolitical context, its narrative and its realism is used for that purpose and not to provide a closed text. (1994: 239)

However, just because the *Mapantsula* narrative refuses closure for Panic – a street hustler and thief who ends the film refusing to admit to political activity under police duress and torture – does not mean that the production only (as in minimally) 'draws on the gangster genre'. Mogotlane's Panic actually points to Van Peebles' Sweetback creation, who himself was 'just' a common hustler or Youngblood Priest, the scummy low-time pimp and pusher of *Super Fly*, neither of which offers clear narrative resolution either or 'rounded, holistic characterisations'. At the start of the film, Panic is shown to be interested only in himself and his criminal, gangster lifestyle (which also includes alcoholism and a local lover, Pat, played by Thembi Mtshali). As such, it is not a huge stretch to claim that Panic is a character rooted in the more radical American blaxploitation representations of the past but, unlike the cheap and opportunistic B-Scheme variations of these tropes, he is presented within a distinctly indigenous location and situation as well as a time and place that is not just politically urgent, but also transient.

This confusion of time, place, character and genre would lead Cameron to conclude that foreign audiences might also consider *Mapantsula* 'inaccurate and melodramatic' but qualifies this comment by arguing that South Africa 'with its killings and burnings, its government-sponsored murder and its anarchy', means the film might even approach 'reportage' (1994: 163). Although this conclusion is muddled, Cameron touches on the film's powerful actuality but *seems* to be maintaining that the use of character and – particularly – violence results in a conflict between aesthetic (realist) and thematic (genre). In response, one could argue that, as a gangster film, *Mapantsula* takes a form that had been misused by filmmakers such as Tonie van der Merwe for the purpose of projects presented within the dominant apartheid discourse and offers deliberate subversion. Primarily this might be because the story of *Mapantsula* demands a more neorealist or Third Cinema approach. Unfortunately, but perhaps attesting to the confusion over its identity, *Mapantsula* not only failed to gain much of a release in South Africa, but it struggled to reach a wider international audience. After a screening at The New York Film Festival, critic Janet Maslin wrote how 'it feels more authentic and less contrived than other South African films that have been shown here' (1989: 89), yet a general theatrical release in the United States was not forthcoming. This aspect is worth discussing further because it indicates how apartheid itself had perhaps been compromised by its integration into Hollywood's Africa, reimagined as just another aspect of just another African failed state.

The Struggle to the Screen

Author Johan Blignaut quotes the late producer and activist Laurence Dworkin as bemoaning the South African cinema of the apartheid years: 'If South Africa ever enjoyed a hint of an original and distinct film identity it has now been fully smothered by a plethora of no-name-brand schlock' (1992: 104). Dworkin would become involved in the cultural boycott of South Africa and its related arts. It is worth quoting his retrospection of this period as it offers some insight into how difficult it was for even anti-apartheid cinema, such as *Mapantsula*, to find a foreign audience during the years leading up to the fall of the National Party government:

Once again, it was not a case of black and white. Some people came out and genuinely thought they were trying to bring about change through the project they were involved with ... take Paul Simon and [his music album] *Graceland*. He came out to make music with some South African groups that had not had any exposure and the product was fantastic ... Remember, the cultural boycott meant we could not take stuff out here either. So people from a leftist, progressive viewpoint could not show their film in London. There was a lot of ambiguity and it did give people a space to use counter arguments ... We were involved with a set-up called The Film and Allied Workers Organisation where we had to police the cultural boycott. We were given the task of saying which projects were okay. And it was not a pleasant experience. We had people even like Darrell Roodt who had to come to us for a stamp of approval and we were seen as Stalinists, who said 'yes, you can have a stamp but you have to do this or this'. I did not enjoy being the political commissar who had to approve projects [*laughs*]. And some filmmakers today still pass me and spit in my face for not approving their projects – including Darrell Roodt. (2016)

In light of this aspect, it may be easy to see why *Mapantsula* struggled to find its audience (it was unsuccessfully entered into the Academy Awards as the South African nominee for Best Foreign Film). Schmitz does not offer a white mediated narrative – in fact, almost the entire story is filtered through Panic's point-of-view. However, nor does the director offer a depiction of the 'savage'/'primitive' Africa that wider audiences of this period had responded to – i.e. *The Wild Geese* or *The Gods Must Be Crazy*. This factor led Cameron to claim that audiences 'will probably not recognise their movie Africa' (presumably referring to wildlife and tribes) in *Mapantsula* (1994: 163). It is also worth noting that Hollywood's shot-in-Zimbabwe films about apartheid, such as *Cry Freedom* or *A World Apart* (Chris Menges, 1988), both of which are mentioned for the purpose of comparison on the British quad poster for *Mapantsula*,[5] and *A Dry White Season* – *were* told via white protagonists *and* had not been box office successes. These are films which connect apartheid's tragic impact on Black lives to the well-being of South African whites who also become aware of the tyranny of segregation.

Modisane argues that *Mapantsula*'s 'failure to observe the mass-market convention of translating a radical South African narrative into a white mediated one resulted in its failure to draw a major distributor' (2013: 123). This conclusion is not necessarily true. Not only had these stories of white South Africa failed to capture the attention of international audiences, but they had faced additional accusations of using the country's privileged minorities to express the inequalities of apartheid. These factors may have led major distributors to proceed carefully with a (grittier) comparable film in a foreign language – even if an added attraction was a mainly Black cast. Writing about the release of *A Dry White Season* in *Playboy* magazine, critic Bruce Williamson acknowledged that 'Similar polemical films (e.g. *Cry Freedom*) have been condemned for concentrating on the awakened consciences of white characters instead of spreading black Africa's story' but the writer felt that 'Weighed against the topical urgency and dramatic power of *Dry White Season* [sic], such arguments won't wash' (1989: 24). Nonetheless, as with other examples of Hollywood's anti-apartheid cinema, *A Dry White Season* would also be a box office failure. One might also conclude that apartheid was such a live issue in newspapers and on television during the late 1980s that audiences cared little to engage with the topic in the guise of cinematic 'entertainment', regardless of whether the protagonist was white or Black. *Mapantsula*, by using genre as a framework through which to tell its story, was at least attempting to do something unique.

Schmitz also presented audiences, unfamiliar with South Africa, with an Africa that international audiences rarely even saw: one of modernist cityscapes juxtaposed with township squalor and multiple languages. Speaking about *Shaft in Africa*, Tomaselli rightly notes 'its blaxploitation characters' to 'which Africa was merely a convenient backdrop to American storylines' (2016: 118). Part of what makes *Mapantsula* so refreshing (as well as radical) is that location is central to the evolving character arc of Panic – something that cannot be said of even the more provocative portrayals that ZAxploitation cinema had previously presented (*Black Crusader*, *Death of a Snowman*, *One More Shot* – motion pictures that acknowledge apartheid, however subtly, but do not allow it to influence the direction of the typical and repetitive 'crime does not pay' narrative). The opening of *Mapantsula*, in which Panic casually mugs a white businessman who – realising his wallet has been taken, approaches the criminal, only to be greeted with the threat of a pocket-knife – is pivotal in establishing the streets of Johannesburg as a key part of Mogotlane's character and, by extension, the film's universe. Cinema's African jungle is now replaced with a (more dangerous) concrete jungle. With this (newfound) freedom to move around the city, *Mapantsula* subtly introduces Panic as an apolitical character – his interest in the racial struggles still ongoing in South Africa is non-existent. This element becomes increasingly clear when Panic has to spend time with arrested activists in crowded prison cells. In these moments, Panic is stripped of the minor power that he has in Johannesburg, whereby he can plan efficient hit-and-run thefts on the white middle classes.

Behind bars, however, the character is shown to be insecure – his gangster persona demystified and Schmitz aptly identifying how such wider cinematic personalities become compromised by a change of location. There is, of course, good reason why a character such as Sweetback is never captured and interrogated: *it is not that kind of film* and yet there is still a shared space between these two radicals. Just as Sweetback reaches physical freedom thanks to the work of a united Black community, so too does Panic experience his mental emancipation by finally, belatedly (after pretending, upon lock-up, to be part of the liberation movement) realising his loyalty to the struggle and not to his own lifestyle. Hence, Tomaselli states that '*Mapantsula* looks like a "black" movie, when it is really an anti-apartheid film. *Mapantsula* questions not just black exploitation, but implicitly indicts the larger system of capitalism itself' (2016: 104). It is surely most clear, with the scenes in which Panic is imprisoned and interrogated, that this aspect of *Mapantsula* most efficiently surfaces. It is in such sequences that Rivers also argues that the film firmly 'rejects the racial reconciliation themes of "buddy" films like *Cry Freedom* (1987) and *The Power of One* (1992), where the "good" white guy allies himself with a black junior partner in order to redeem South Africa' (2007: 20). Whilst Rivers sees *Mapantsula* as oppositional entirely to genre constructs, it is possible to argue that even in the scenes of Panic's interrogation, where we witness his humiliation and the threats to his life, Schmidt still veers into expected gangster film framework, namely the police procedural.

When *Mapantsula* was finally released in the UK, it also arrived with typical exploitation (genre) film carny: 'Life and death on the streets of Soweto', screamed the poster, which added 'Banned in South Africa!' In its marketing, as well as its mix of Third Cinema aesthetics, localised narrative and gangster film violence, *Mapantsula* remains difficult to label, but through the discussion offered in this chapter, and having acknowledged the considerable writing that has been produced on the production, it is possible to see Schmitz's groundbreaking achievement as that most unique of entities: a postmodern political gangster film. It is South Africa's own *Sweet Sweetback's Badass Song* and an attempt to reimagine Black portrayals within the country's cinema as something less concerned with the mythos of Africa in general and more symbolic of a place, time and people that had – within the B-Scheme and other ZAxploitation examples – been merely Black characters in mythical, undefined cities and countries. Modisane mentions how *Mapantsula* would be banned from theatre screenings of over 200 people in South Africa, although it was permitted to be rented on videotape (2013: 105). The film remains provocative and highly disturbing – perhaps because of its realism it feels (for the first time in South African cinema) as if Panic's fate lies outside the narrative structures of the screen – and, stylistically, it is an exceptional guide to how genre can be subverted and used for militant, political radicalism. Whilst some will no doubt baulk at such a statement, it also brings ZAxploitation full circle. Indeed, it is not too far-fetched to describe *Mapantsula* as *Joe Bullet* with a social and political pulse. As well as featuring superior filmmaking skills, *Mapantsula*'s

Panic is the belated badass character that South African cinema needed, and township audiences had perhaps always wanted.

OTHER TRENDSETTING TALES

It would be incorrect, of course, to assume that *Mapantsula* was the first anti-apartheid film to be made in South Africa and with the (limited) awareness or later support of state funding. As the final decade of complete National Party rule surfaced, experimental motion pictures began to emerge. Darrell Roodt's *The Stick* lies in the periphery, although its director previously made the more forthright *A Place of Weeping* (1986), which – despite featuring white-on-Black violence – Tomaselli notes was the first film to open simultaneously in the townships and cities and escaped the wrath of South African censors (2016: 39). Unlike Schmitz, Roodt would usually frame his stories through the experiences of South African whites (as seen in *Tenth of a Second*), indicating his attachment – intentional or not – to the 'Hollywood'/mainstream South Africa of *Cry Freedom* et al. Tomaselli has also noted the work of director Ross Devenish (such as *A Chip of Glass Ruby* from 1982) as part of South Africa's 'Second Cinema' movement in the 1980s (2016: 30). The more experimental, and little-commented upon, *Shot Down* (Andrew Worsdale, 1987), which Tomaselli also briefly mentions, is as heavy-handed as it is outlandish and provocative. A sample scene, for instance, involves a low-rent white agitprop performance group who sing:

> *I don't want to live in South Africa*
> *Nobody free in South Africa*
> *Emergency in South Africa*
> *ANC in South Africa*
> *Don't want to die in South Africa*
> *Government lie in South Africa*
> *Children cry in South Africa*
> *Everyone fry in South Africa*

If the brutally forthright *Shot Down* is anything to go by, inciting the censorship board into action seemed to be a cause célèbre for some independent South African filmmakers during the final years of apartheid and, true to form, *Mapantsula* itself would be cut by forty seconds for its local release (Tomaselli and Prinsloo 1992: 332).

Even more obscure than *Shot Down* is the fact that, not long after the production of *Mapantsula*, a young film student and activist, Karen Thorne – who has gone without notice[6] – made the Zulu-language *Mine Boy*, co-written by and also featuring an Assistant Director credit for a Black South African (Bexi

IMAGES OF APARTHEID

Figure 10.3 Xuma (Phinda Mazibuko) and Stella (Lungi Mkwanazi) in *Mine Boy* (Karen Thorne, 1989)

Nxumalo). This project is even more experimental than Schmitz's *Mapantsula*, with the film's opening sped-up into a jarring collision of scenes depicting Johannesburg's city bustle, a group of young budding actors in Soweto ad-libbing most of the dialogue and even the breaking the fourth wall. In addition, the film features random, but effective, jump cuts that eliminate days and even weeks from the narrative. In some moments during the film, *Mine Boy* feels more like a documentary than a work of fiction, especially in its travelogue footage of Kliptown poverty – attesting to Thorne's use of verité filmmaking methods. Whilst less explicitly political than *Mapantsula*, *Mine Boy* is a provocative, and occasionally disturbing, mediation of aspiration and poverty in the dying years of apartheid. Indeed, of all the films discussed in this monograph, it is *Mine Boy* which most effectively depicts township squalor, and evokes the minimal distraction and pleasure found in makeshift bars and parties.

The story concerns a young man, Xuma (Phinda Mazibuko), who travels from KwaZulu-Natal into Johannesburg to find work. After initially encountering and befriending some drug addicts, he meets Stella (Lungi Mkwanazi), who has relocated to the township from near where he grew up. A divorced alcoholic, Stella is a loudmouthed but good-hearted owner of an illegal bar (known as a Shebeen Queen), who also makes money on the side selling watered-down spirits. Xuma falls in love with a beautiful prostitute called Pinki (Olga Mothi), who he meets at Stella's 'bar'. Many weeks into their meetings and Xuma finds out that Pinki has become pregnant and is going to have an abortion. Despite Xuma being willing to raise another man's child as his own, Pinki goes ahead with her plan and dies, alone in an outhouse, after drinking a local-made concoction recommended by Stella. Xuma is distraught but makes a decision to stay in Soweto so that he can continue working in the mines, but Stella decides to leave and return to KwaZulu-Natal, convinced that her party lifestyle led her to make a disinterested, snap decision on Pinki's pregnancy. A final shot sees Xuma join a small gang of young boys, sitting on a hill, looking over at the vast, tempting cityscape of Johannesburg in the distance as night begins to fall. Just another young Black labourer in a metropolis that he can probably never fully call his own. *Mine Boy* may not feature any white characters, but with the depiction of cramped workers' accommodation and the general hopelessness of Kliptown, as well as its matter-of-fact presentation of desperation, drug addiction and alcoholism in Soweto, the film paints a depressing image of the time. The humanising of the characters, played by actors who are uniformly excellent in their roles, results in a hard-hitting and occasionally naturalistic mimesis of township life.

Thorne mentions:

> I was not in control of the process. I am sure I brought a lot of my baggage as a white South African even though I was an activist [but] I thought 'okay this is your film. [I want] you to make this film'. I'm quite proud of it ... I had become an activist at university and when I left I got involved in the Film and Allied Workers Organisation which was an anti-apartheid cultural formation. It was about uniting filmmakers against apartheid. (2016)

Despite benefitting from the state subsidy (and the film uses the same canned music as the earlier B-Scheme production *Doomsday*) and maintaining a narrative that is structured around criminal activity, *Mine Boy* indicates how more experimental cinema captured at least some of the day-to-day challenges, not to mention the abjection and depression, of township life. Furthermore, Thorne did not experience censorship with the film – *Mine Boy* does not carry any obvious anti-apartheid message; instead, its visuals speak for themselves. In particular, the film comes to life in the scenes where Stella hosts her alcohol-infused gatherings. Without patronising her audience, or wallowing in the despair of township existence, Thorne gives poverty a human and relatable face and shows that in even the worst of times, good people still aspire to

IMAGES OF APARTHEID

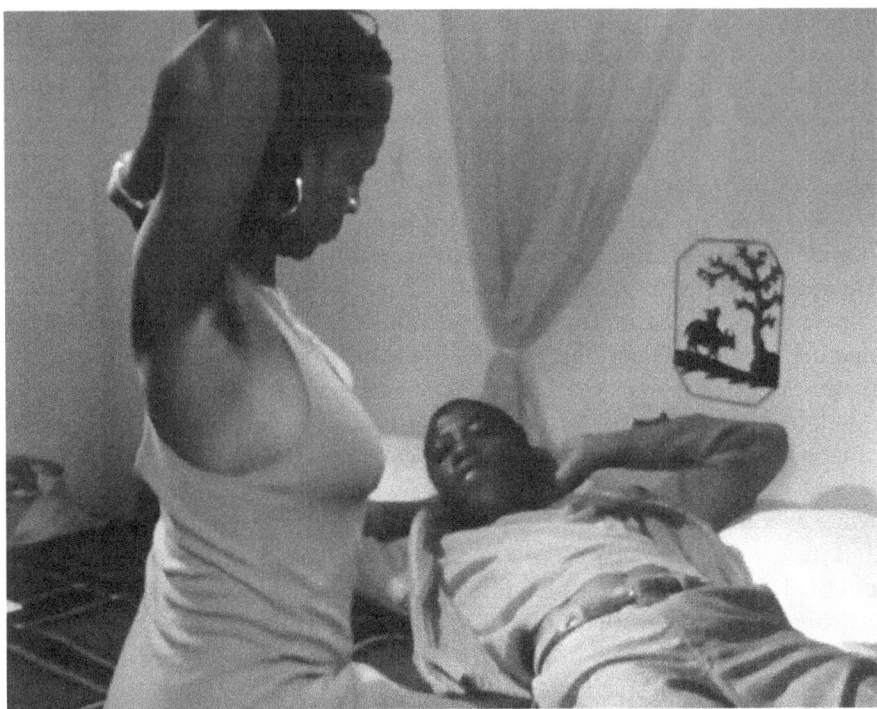

Figure 10.4 Xuma (Phinda Mazibuko) and Pinki (Olga Mothi) in *Mine Boy* (Karen Thorne, 1989)

good times. Most effective of all is the fact that it is difficult to imagine anyone watching *Mine Boy* and feeling that these characters exist in a Comic Relief stereotype of sub-Saharan African incompetence or impoverishment. Instead, Thorne offers a well-rounded presentation of Black life under a system that compromises opportunity, and her characters are all the stronger for it.

Arguably the most notable, pre-*Mapantsula* film of opposition, however, is the aforementioned *My Country My Hat*, which is shot in English and splits its running time between a racist white family in suburban Johannesburg and a local Black worker, James Fingo (Peter Sephuma), who lacks the residency pass needed to gain employment in the city. The film is placed within 'second cinema' by Tomaselli, referring to the category of projects which are 'not explicitly political. Where criticism is practiced through form and content, films exhibit an ambiguity of genre' (2016: 30). Nonetheless, *My Country My Hat* is arguably still identifiable as a crime film: a wealthy white homeowner runs over a Black man he assumes burgled his house and struggles to cover the scene. He takes the body for a makeshift burial but, in a fluster, fails to notice his hat has fallen off. James, illegally wandering the local estate, knocks on

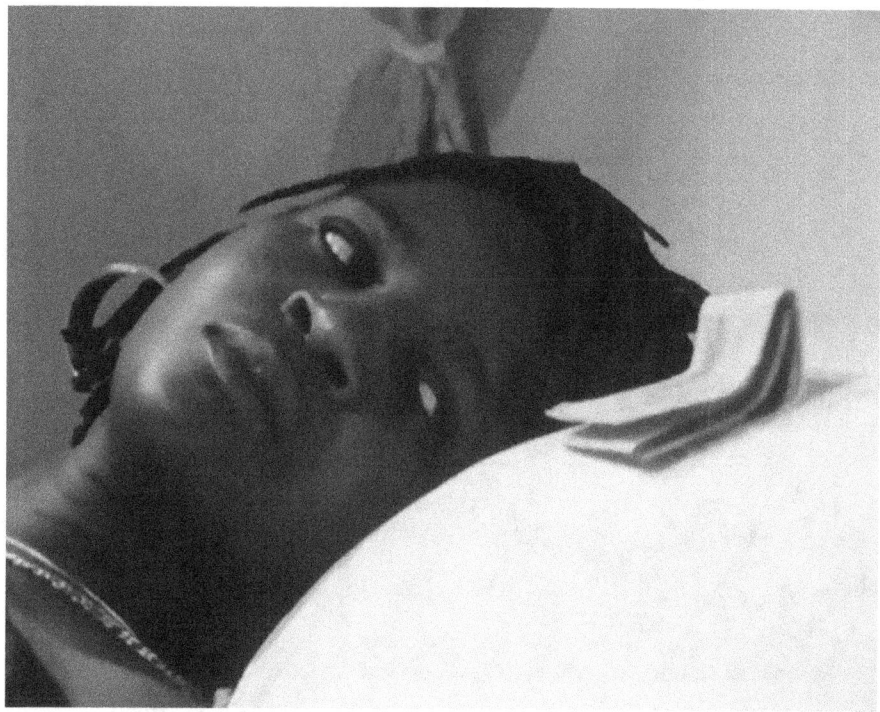

Figure 10.5 Kliptown prostitute Pinki (Olga Mothi) awakes to money on her pillow in *Mine Boy* (Karen Thorne, 1989)

the man's door seeking work – having stolen the hat for himself. The two lives then collide, with James finally being given the dead man's pass in exchange for a promise to leave the (increasingly paranoid) family alone. At the end of *My Country My Hat*, James is chased and caught by two local policemen, who only let him go when he produces the pass he has finally acquired – his limited freedom finally available to him, albeit through the preposterous networks of the apartheid state. The film closes with James crying tears of relief. For anyone familiar with the B-Scheme, of course, the great irony is that – for once – *crime does pay* in the apartheid dystopia, it just takes a white person to light the initial spark.[7]

Modisane mentions how, prior to making *Mapantsula*, Schmitz had been working for 'Video News Service, an outfit that gathered news for foreign media, but was actually involved in underground political work' (2013: 98). Brian Tilley, who formed a video collective with the late Laurence Dworkin – who like Tilley, was involved with the production of *My Country My Hat* – acknowledges that such radical filmmaking began to emerge from such video ensembles:

Figure 10.6 Peter Sephuma in *My Country My Hat* (David Bensusan, 1983), an anti-apartheid film that found its audience on the B-Scheme network.

I think the film industry in the 1980s was a lot like the society. It was very separated. In the feature film industry, there were films being made and there were films getting onto television and into the cinema. But they reflected white life and what white people wanted to see, predominantly Afrikaners. At the start, when we were trying to get our video collective funded, we worked doing jobs in that industry. Laurence Dworkin was a film editor; I did some boom swinging and camera assisting. We worked for a guy Tony Bensusan who was a sound engineer and then we made *My Country My Hat* ... We saw ourselves as opposition, not just in society but in the film industry too. There were a couple of alternative films made, such as *Mapantsula*, which was made in the 1980s as well. Like-minded people tended to gravitate towards one another, so there was alternative stuff starting to happen in the 80s in fiction, but it overlapped with the opposition documentary movement which was small. Towards the mid to late 80s there were other groupings that got together, and we all worked very closely with *Mapantsula*. I think being part of a political movement, we saw our film work as part of that. Our political movement was absolutely urgent and necessary at that time. It was life and death. People were being killed on the streets and we felt that was much more urgent in the development of a country than films that didn't reflect life and, frankly, were not very good. (2016)

My Country My Hat was also distributed with the help of recognisable names. 'It is a film that retroactively qualified for the subsidy,' affirms curator Darryl Els. 'The [producers] had problems getting the film out and distributed so Tonie van der Merwe and Ronnie Isaacs approached [director] David Bensusan to put it out on the mobile circuit under the B-Scheme. And that is definitely a subversive anti-apartheid film. *Mapantsula* was made through the scheme as well' (2016). Hence, *My Country My Hat*, *Mine Boy* and *Mapantsula* came to either exist or to gain a release *because* – rightly or wrongly – pioneers of comparatively lowbrow cinema such as Heyns Films and then Tonie van der Merwe had sought to establish a 'not very good' B-Scheme film culture. Certainly, part of *My Country My Hat*'s less problematic reception might be that, as identified by Tomaselli, 'there were criticisms about its conventional narrative that were alleged to prefigure a return to the apartheid *status quo*' (2016: 32). Whereas Panic concludes *Mapantsula* by refusing to sign paperwork regarding an illegal political gathering, frustrating the police force (which is mixed with Black and white officers), who have tortured him over several days, James concludes *My Country My Hat* without standing up to race supremacy, locally or otherwise. The character is simply glad that he can avoid arrest within the privilege of free movement in the glamorous white suburbs (making him, finally, part of the familiar urban-conditional). Regardless, *My Country My Hat* is a powerful reminder of the racial power binaries that existed under apartheid and how such relationships kept the majority of the South African population living in fear.

In future studies of Black film, including the legacy of the early blaxploitation years, one hopes that *Mapantsula* will no longer be absent. Similarly, as approaches to African cinema have begun to focus on film services and distribution methods, particularly with the explosion of Nollywood and the format's gradual progression onto the international stage (including Netflix), one hopes that the mobile circuit – and little-discussed but stylistically inventive cinema such as *My Country My Hat* and *Mine Boy* – may also obtain a new lease of life. The discussion of this chapter has largely focused on *Mapantsula*, but it has done so because the film is remarkably subversive when reappraised (perhaps, one is tempted to admit, even reimagined) within the larger 'schlock' of the B-Scheme. As previous discussion has attested, other scholars have placed the film within a genre identity. However, what Schmitz may ultimately have succeeded at doing is indicating that radicalism need not be the enemy of commercial storytelling. As such, the baby-steps taken by *Joe Bullet* are, fifteen years later, fulfilled by the first truly *South African* genre movie.

NOTES

1. Per Maingard: 'The title of the film refers to a particular type of township gangster, represented by Panic in the film, modelled on the Hollywood gangster of the 1950s – dressed in smart suits, with wide trouser legs, a stetson hat, and brogue shoes' (1994: 236).
2. *Upondo & Nkinsela* certainly shows the crossover between the B-Scheme and a more 'legitimate' film scene in South Africa – director Buys had plied his trade on such films as *The Demon* (1979) and would go on to edit the South African teen-slasher film *The Stay Awake* (1987) and produce the made-for-video thriller *Sweet Murder* (Percival Rubens, 1990).
3. For instance, Bogle, Donald (2016), *Toms, Coons, Mulattoes, Mammies and Bucks*. New York: Bloomsbury, Guerrero, Ed (1993), *Framing Blackness: The African American Image in Film*. Philadelphia: Temple University Press, or Koven, Mikel (2010), *Blaxploitation Films*. London: Kamera Books.
4. As discussed by Ian Thomson, 'white Jamaicans still wield huge (if uncontested) power; the Jamaica created by the merchant-capitalists of slavery has survived. So anxious are some Jamaicans to "whiten up" that they use skin bleaches – a sad after-effect of the aristocracy of skin nurtured by the British during slavery' (2009: 5).
5. 'A Terrific Movie . . . Even more remarkable than *Cry Freedom* and *A World Apart*'
6. Tomaselli mentions the 'overdue' need to recognise more of South Africa's female filmmakers (2016: 11).
7. The 1986 Urban Areas Act finally removed the pass laws, hence the comparative freedom of movement enjoyed by Panic in *Mapantsula* (Welsh 1998: 491).

CONCLUSION

The intention of embarking upon this monograph was to try and make sense of new terms in the global exploitation film pantheon, namely 'Sollywood' or its more recognised and repeated moniker 'ZAxploitation'. The discovery of fresh, potentially enlightening and exciting, genre cinema – however 'schlocky' or 'trashy' or 'excessive' or even likely to fall into the elastic parameters of Jeffrey Sconce's influential 'paracinema' bracket – is difficult not to respond to for those of us who relish the study of what could be deemed 'marginal film-making'. Certainly, it does not get much more marginal, or 'on the fringe', than a network of hitherto largely disregarded or dismissed low, *low* budget, genre cinema, mainly involving gangsters and crime, made for segregated audiences during the period of apartheid in South Africa.

This study was given the title *Images of Apartheid* for a reason. Despite the protests from many of the interviewees who offered fascinating insight during the summer of 2016, when research on this monograph began, there *are* clear socio-political representations from the pre-rainbow nation period in even the lowliest of B-Scheme cheapies. It is not difficult to see, in these poverty row productions, the National Party mantra of the late 1970s and 1980s, in which Black South Africans might be 'kept apart by class and economics' with new immigration laws to 'keep the unskilled poor away from urban, wealth-making centres' where only 'if blacks had a skill and a job they could come into the white-controlled economy' (Dowden 2008: 412). Stories of good citizenship and able, Christian, family-orientated, Black heroes, even in the Westerns, act as a propaganda arm of the same state that supported the films and their (often nationalistic) filmmakers. Nevertheless, the proverbial 'winds of change' are difficult not to see expressed as some of the stories evolve to incorporate images of Black-white co-operation, friction and even exploitation, however paternalistic or patronising the wider character or narrative arcs might be.

From Simon Sabela's *iKati Elimnyama* to the radical *Mapantsula*, the bulk of this study has been focused on the output of the B-Scheme. However, ZAxploitation has also been categorised as films that are generally seen to follow tropes of blaxploitation cinema and/or present low budget, generic presentations of Black identity in South Africa or, at least, a local or 'imagined' stand-in for the 'beloved country'. As such, this study has also drawn on other international co-productions and cycles that have chosen to – in their own admittedly esoteric manner – use the country (or in some cases default into Zimbabwe) for formulaic stories of savage Africa and simultaneous Black-white reconciliation, albeit with the on-screen power-binary heavily stacked in favour of the latter. Despite being bigger-budgeted, international co-productions, films such as *Game for Vultures*, *Gold* and *The Wild Geese* fall into the same ideology as much of the B-Scheme – in which good Black men, the Mr Rights, are rare and should be cherished, their time might even come to run a country, but it is through the European – and usually British (despite the obvious historic friction between Anglo and Boer) – perspectives that these stories unfold. Even *The Stick*, which makes its opposition to Pretoria's decade-and-a-half conflict with Angola explicit, does so via a white leading man, haunted by the spirit of a magical Black villager who was gunned down by bored soldiers.

Speaking about the classic age of exploitation and related exotic cinema, Eric Schaeffer opines how 'Nineteenth-century discourse had constructed Africa and Africans as savages by "negative comparison" with Europe' (1999: 271). *The Stick*, even given its powerful atmospherics from director Darrell Roodt, comes perhaps a little too close to revamping this savage Africa mantra, despite its intention to oppose the National Party's most famous proxy war. Whilst *Mapantsula* would belatedly offer Black agency to a story that challenged the apartheid state, the *genre* cinema of apartheid is remarkable insofar as it forbids its characters to vocalise the inevitable. The National Party's shambolic approach to the opposition they faced in the townships and Bantustans, particularly after the other European Empire countries left South Africa's bordering states, would guarantee its demise. This point might be easy to conclude in retrospect, but it seems clear that Prime Minister John Vorster's détente policy was never going to placate the Black majority and that unfriendly neighbours in Angola, Mozambique and Zimbabwe threatened the very existence of a white minority government in Pretoria. A film such as *Shot Down*, whilst featuring a narrative that is largely expressed via white characters, is a rare exception – it feels prophetically confident about the collapse of the ruling government. Nonetheless, even a film as moving and powerful as *My Country My Hat* fails to initiate any dialogue about the idea of apartheid disappearing, perhaps attesting to why Tomaselli is correct to label it as 'second cinema'.

The state, as depicted in *Mapantsula*, is omnipresent and powerful; it has grown in the years since *My Country My Hat*: the opening scene of the film features a heavily armoured police truck trundling through Soweto – probably the most evocative and upsetting image from the entire period – but one that evidently leaves little room for the likelihood of majority rule, in actual fact *just six short years away*. As such, perhaps the finest discoveries from this period have been the tough blaxploitation films, transported to South Africa, that provide popcorn thrills and only minimal, if any, political dialogue: *Joe Bullet, Death of a Snowman, Bullet on the Run, Umbango*. These are films set in a universe where apartheid only tangentially exists – perhaps the easiest way to approach making cheap genre fare during the days of white rule. The most rewarding discovery from the B-Scheme lot, however, is undoubtedly *Mine Boy*, a verité approach to documenting life in Soweto, and a youth's aspiration to find wealth in Johannesburg – 'the city of gold', mainly told through the prism of a teenage labourer and a young prostitute. The jump-cut edits, which allow for the film to unfold in a time mimesis that is made unclear and is genuinely confounding but also compelling, makes clear the monotony of life within township squalor – perhaps even more effectively than in *Mapantsula*, with Panic's one-bedroom squat, in which he sleeps until late afternoon and drinks beer.

This study has also argued that ZAxploitation, beginning with *Joe Bullet*, a film which casts its influence onto the B-Scheme, is an identifiable *cinema* of South Africa. Although it is understandable that this will be a statement that may cause further discussion, this conclusion arrives, not as part of a clearly evident and recurring South African national film identity, but rather as a cinema that should be – as mentioned in the introduction to this study – integrated into wider discussion of global exploitation trends and related networks. In the fan sphere, we can already begin to see this dialogue taking place and it would be somewhat churlish to ignore it. A review of the recent, violent South African Western, *Five Fingers for Marseilles* (Michael Matthews, 2017), on the IndieWire website, mentions Tonie van der Merwe's *Umbango*, dubbed 'coincidentally a South African Western that predates "Five Fingers," [which] was produced during the last days of Apartheid' (Obenson 2018). As Benjamin Cowley's Gravel Road Entertainment Group continues to make inroads in unearthing older films of the B-Scheme, it is inevitable that further connections will be made between South Africa's tawdrier past genre cinema and its present. To date, such comparisons have in fact been widely ignored. For instance, the British promotional poster for *Fools* (Ramadan Suleman,

Figure C.1 Popo Gumede in *Umbango* (or *The Feud*, Tonie van der Merwe, 1986)

1997) advertised the film in screaming capital letters as 'South Africa's first black feature film' (Gugler 2003: 98). Whatever one's conclusions about Simon Sabela's relationship with Heyns Films, this statement is, of course, factually untrue.

The ZAxploitation cinema of this monograph is comprised of buddy films, cheapjack Westerns, savage terrorists; low budget, formulaic stories, usually focused on crime and gangsters, girls and their infatuated captors, and even some provocative portrayals of small-time street hustlers, Black heroes and middle-class aspiration. At its most ribald, we see authoritarianism battled against by the heroes of Cedric Sundstrom's underrated *American Ninja* sequels, Ken Gampu as a Black journalist searching for facts in *Death of a Snowman* or guerrilla hideouts destroyed by the heroes of the surprisingly inoffensive popcorn actioner *Operation Hit Squad*, a rare international achievement from the influential Tonie van der Merwe. However, at its most dubious, we are exposed to gurning Black antagonists presented as a threat to civilised European modernity in what remained of the minority-ruled countries on the continent – as in Neil Hetherington's *Terrorist*, Clive Harding's *Shamwari* or the postcolonial nostalgia for white rule in *The Wild Geese*. In each case, Black representation plays a central, defining part of the respective narratives and the B-Scheme subsidy could even be argued as having provided, at the very least, less explicitly fascist entertainment by comparison.

Through this approach and an admittedly flexible policy of containment, this study has chosen not to acknowledge some of the international genre productions that were shot on location in South Africa during apartheid – from trashy horror efforts such as *Headhunter* (Francis Schaeffer, 1988) or *Hellgate* (William A. Levey, 1989) to the minimalist thriller *The Shadowed Mind* (Cedric Sundstrom, 1988) or the popcorn actioner *City Wolf* (Heinrich Dahms, 1988). These films, and many like them, do not ascertain that they are South African cinema and, moreover, offer no racial representations of note.[1] Aimed primarily at the VHS market, these are motion pictures that – watched today – for all intents and purposes seem little different from the typical genre fare that could be found straining video rental shelves throughout the 1980s. Nonetheless, their future study within wider South African genre filmmaking, particularly the country's largely unacknowledged and surprisingly vast legacy of horror cinema, should undoubtedly be encouraged. This aspect is noted because one of the better-known films from the period of apartheid-exploitation cinema, *Snake Dancer* (Dirk De Villiers, 1976),[2] gained a surprise DVD release in 2006 from the fringe label Mondo Macabro with a back-cover strapline of old-time carny:

> The movie that proves little girls shouldn't play with snakes is now on video for the first time anywhere! Mondo Macabro has proudly brought you classic exploitation films from places all over the world that people never expected to see. Indonesian action films? We gave them to you. Bollywood Horror? Uh, didn't you see the September release? Pakistani vampires? That was THE LIVING CORPSE, my friend. And now we bring you a first for Mondo Macabro, something we've never done before. Can your heart stand a sexploitation film about the true-life story of a SNAKE DANCER from South Africa?

What is perhaps most interesting about the hyperbole accompanying *Snake Dancer*'s re-release is that it pre-empts later attempts to place (or displace) ZAxploitation within transnational paracinematic activity of yesteryear. The strapline of *Snake Dancer* initiates South African genre cinema within a wider unknown exotic world of 'Indonesian action' and 'Bollywood horror' – appealing to fans of obscure global exploitation, or what David Church discusses as a dedicated subculture within the wider cult film market. Drawing on work by Thomas Elsaesser and Elena Gorfinkel, Church discusses how DVD, and more recently Blu-ray, has seen reflections on cinema's past collide

Figure C.2 Woman meets snake in *Snake Dancer* (Dirk De Villiers, 1976)

with a hip, globalised, postmodern audience seeking out wild examples of outlandish old films:

> The cultist and the cinephile who similarly search for fleeting, fragmentary moments of excess and profilmic revelation may have begun to blur during the midnight-movie era but have since become increasingly indistinguishable in the home video era, with cultism operating as a historical subcategory of cinephilia when films can be endlessly replayed. (2015: 17)

This resulting contextualisation of low budget generic cinema within the home video market as something unique and hitherto undiscovered – and as in the case of *Snake Dancer*, as an exoticised 'Other' that conflicts with more traditional and recognisable low budget excess – fails to do the film itself justice because it offers only displacement. Anyone seeking 'fleeting, fragmentary moments of excess' would likely be disappointed by how *Snake Dancer* merely repositions Johannesburg into a Soho-style burgh of striptease clubs and middle-class debauchery (the film is about a young striptease artist whose act, involving full nudity, falls foul of the law). In Chapter 1 I mentioned how author Novotny Lawrence maintained 'There is no such thing as a white exploitation film' – something I dispute, particularly given the 'white trash' (or hillbilly) horror cinema that emerged after *Deliverance* and the low budget exploitation classic *The Texas Chain Saw Massacre* (Tobe Hooper, 1974), films also made without any Black crew. *Snake Dancer* thus falls into a hybrid form of exploitation cinema – part poor-white-trash and part softcore sexploitation rather than, as per the film's later DVD advertising, a wild mish-mash of transnational excess. John Fiske speaks about how 'the accumulation of knowledge is fundamental to the accumulation of cultural capital' in marginal cult film circles – occasionally used to 'rewrite' the meaning and context of the original motion picture (2008: 452). However, lest it seem that this last-minute intention of introducing *Snake Dancer* within a wider discussion of Black South African representation is to somehow reimagine the film, let it instead be maintained that some of the same moral values regarding women within the B-Scheme retain themselves in the narrative: decency, marriage, family and God.

As such, whilst the worlds of Black and white were clearly separated, it bears stressing that the overreaching idea of good citizenship was, in terms of cinematic presentations, not an entirely different world. *Snake Dancer* is a unique depiction of whitesploitation cinema in the purest sense: only one ethnicity is ever depicted on the screen and only one race is 'sold' back to its South African audience. Whilst Church argues that after-the-fact retrospection of obscure exploitation cinema, particularly on DVD, results in texts that 'increasingly become lost chunks of film history, complicating one's imagined connection to past audiences' (2015: 22), placed within the wider gender representations of the B-Scheme output, *Snake Dancer* makes sense as both cinema of exploitation *and* cinema of apartheid. In addition, by eliminating any Black voices, never mind depictions of Black sexuality, whilst at the same time being reflexive enough to openly condemn state repression and censorship *in the narrative*, the story could even be read as meta-ZAxploitation fable – a self-aware commentary on white female privilege which itself struggles to maintain a profile within a nation of secret police and contraband gatherings.

The all-white Johannesburg and all-white South Africa imagined in *Snake Dancer* places it outside the canon of ZAxploitation defined in this monograph. However, the film's after-the-fact discovery on DVD, many years since it was first released in its country of origin, does raise questions about what else might have been missed by scholars of the country's filmmaking. Whether trashy, exploitative or even inept, it is clear South Africa was a base for a number of low budget endeavours that have, for all intents and purposes, been lost to time. If this monograph serves a place then, one hopes that it is to initiate a discussion about how the academy, and even fandom, incorporates what might be dubbed 'trash' film, but also marginal, fringe cinema activity and interesting, if lowbrow, depictions of genre, into wider discourse about 'national' identity for unashamedly populist attempts at representing a state and its peoples. How and when, for instance, do we decide if a certain type of cinema fails to register with our imagined histories of a country? Moreover, if we are mere spectators – proverbial cinematic tourists looking in – can we also make our own decisions about an exploitation of ideas and images from a pastness that excludes our own experiences?

Whilst one does not doubt the 'grindhouse nostalgia' that has been, perhaps rightfully, critiqued among some academics, one is also prepared to argue that South African exploitation cinema is at least as rich as some of its better-known global counterparts. This is not to maintain that most of the films discussed in this publication are what might be objectively labelled as 'good', but rather to argue that there is a variety of transnational adaptations and engagements that indicate a filmmaking period that was not entirely dismissive of the concept, at least, of a blaxploitation industry on the Cape. In addition, much like how nostalgia for New York's old 42nd Street has given iconic status to a number of old-time, carny distributors (Terry Levene's Aquarius Films, Bryanston Pictures, the infamous Jerry Gross, Canada's Cinepix, Independent-International Pictures), so too does South Africa's variant hint towards a market dominated by a tight clique. Michelle Hartslief directs for 'Conlyn Films', also the label Mitch Dyter produces under, and Tony Cunningham is responsible for 'Take Two Films'. Others have more localised-sounding names such as 'Afro TV & Films' (for *Uthemba*) or 'Coastal Films' (for *Thunder Valley*). Tonie van der Merwe, meanwhile, as the most prolific of all, directs under a variety of labels (examples: 'Royal Films' for *Rich Girl*, 'Taurus Films' for *Ambushed*, 'Tempo Films' for *Double Deal*, 'Tugela Films' for *Impango* and *Impango II*, 'United Films Release' for *Bullet on the Run*) presumably liquidating each after retrieving a profit. Many films are made by one-shot labels or do not have a production company listed at all, indicating scant attention to even a professional presentation during a time that has, in filmmaking terms, only recently come to wider public notice.

Whilst the images in many of these films are problematic – they also (and this is not a defence) point to a white South Africa that was at least willing, per the government line, to entertain, even tolerate, the concept of an upwardly mobile Black middle-class as neighbours and colleagues. This factor may have served a commercial dictum in the first instance, but its very presence as part of narrative cinema during the apartheid years may surprise many. These stories were made to connect with the Black audiences of the time because there seemed to be a clear understanding, even from paternalistic white producers, that aspiration remained a part of apartheid's downtrodden majority. In viewing the large number of B-Scheme films that this monograph has demanded, it

Figure C.3 Thomas Mogotlane as Johannes 'Panic' Themba Mzolo in *Mapantsula* (Oliver Schmitz, 1988), the crowning achievement of 'filmmaking on the fringe' in the old South Africa.

also becomes clear that Black heroes follow the demands of the state: to live quietly with family, but also to be prepared to avoid and tackle corruption, criminality and the temptation of 'bad' living (usually illustrated by alcohol, drugs, embezzlement, occasionally even sex outside of marriage or adultery). Nonetheless, even these ideas of a 'permissible' Black citizenship, within the old South Africa, stretching as far as black policemen in *Mapantsula* who are loyal to the apartheid status quo or a Black soldier in *The Stick*, could be deemed provocative.

In my previous work, *The Style of Sleaze*, I argued that exploitation films belong to the past. This is as true of the groundbreaking American templates as it is of the shoddier variant that emerged in South Africa following the success of imported (and sometimes illicitly distributed) blaxploitation and kung-fu films in the country's townships, particularly via their adaptation into Ken Gampu's trendsetting *Joe Bullet*. New South African cinema cannot and will not recapture the flood of cheap genre product that existed thirty or forty years ago – but nor, as tempting as it might be, is it ideal that the older texts be reconfigured into a proto-Nollywood set-up. Filmmaking on the fringe in the old South Africa was about fraud, populism and even cynicism – but it was also about, as all exploitation cinema is, appeasing and also aggravating censors. In the interviews that were conducted for this monograph, some of the filmmakers of the period bemoaned not being given the support, budgets, or freedom to make stronger content; however some of what exists is still remarkable given the era. An all-white film such as *Snake Dancer* has scenes of implied bestiality that shock even today, whilst the controversies around *Joe Bullet*, *Terrorist* and *Mapantsula* – all very different motion pictures and made for a different audience – show that occasionally South African producers were willing to push the boundaries of perceived 'good taste' within the apartheid state. The B-Scheme runt are, inevitably, trickier to admire but, even in this pantheon, a few surprises still emerge. Certainly, we might never know if an all-Black audience really did cheer an obese Afrikaner thug being kung-fu kicked into submission by principled youngster and karate expert Johnny Tough in *One More Shot*, as is shown to us in *Mapantsula*. However, even accounting for the racist comments of director Ronnie Isaacs to Gus Silber, it is an appealing vision.

The old South Africa is thankfully gone but, in engaging with its exploitation films, and particularly the schlock, we might need to accept that, just as the remnants of the fallen National Party would eventually and ironically be integrated into the ANC, its most audacious images are better placed and discussed in the context of other lowbrow blaxploitation adaptations. Through this approach, we can see a South African cinema of evocation, usually with threadbare production values, and a pastness that aspires for legitimacy – a 'Shaft in Africa' that hinders its badass in order to keep the state onside – until, finally, radical filmmakers produce a *Mapantsula* or a *Mine Boy* and try to challenge or destabilise the status quo. South Africa was a global news story for so long that it is incredible to look back at its cinema and see the real lives that were rebelling against a tyrannical state reimagined and depicted in harmony with the time, place and wider surroundings across government-subsidised presentations of 'crime does not pay'. It is through this aspect, however, that we also see what all global exploitation cinema does: produce a mythology that capitalises and commercialises its time period but without necessarily acknowledging or even admonishing the wider real-time universe of destabilising factors that exist behind-the-scenes.

Critiquing South Africa's apartheid variant for generally avoiding the sociopolitical realities of race segregation is akin to lambasting Hong Kong horror for not addressing British colonial rule, Maoism or the Chinese Communist Party's approach to Taiwan or Tibet; bemoaning Filipinos Cirio H. Santiago or Eddie Romero for failing to present screen opposition to the Marcos regime or even admonishing Nollywood's many cheapjack genre outings for avoiding discussion of the country's persecuted LGBTQ community.[3] Exploitation cinema certainly flirts with – nay, *exploits* – realities of national identity and discourse but, as a wider movement of cinema, it has little precedence in making explicit political noise or (outside of tabloid-fuelled 'video nasty' scandals) reaching and concerning the political class. Even *Sweet Sweetback's Baadasssss Song* was, and still is, received by some critics as less of a radical analogy, an independent American example of racialised Third Cinema, and more of a sleazy, softcore porn project, produced for profit first and political provocation second. South Africa's output, then, is mostly about localised heroes, doing the right thing, family and friendships, the bond of marriage and – at its grittiest – maintaining strength under adversity and comfort in community, rather than necessarily finding a way to 'smash' the entire system. That challenge had to come later, outside of the safety of the cinema screen.

In other words: that's ZAxploitation.

Notes

1. Work on Afrikaans-language film and female representations during the apartheid era is lacking (and outside the scope of this monograph). Keyan Tomaselli has also noted this in a recent online article: http://rozenbergquarterly.com/imaging-africa-gorillas-actors-and-characters/
2. The director of *Snake Dancer*, Dirk De Villiers, is also responsible for the racist silliness of *The Virgin Goddess* (1974), another South African obscurity from this era that I have had some difficulty finding placement for. The film, which has decent production values for the time, stars Ken Gampu and Isabel Sarli as the title character – who is swept up from a shipwreck by a besotted African tribe in the 13th century. She can 'retain her exquisite beauty through the centuries' so long as she remains a virgin, which is easier said than done when a hunky white explorer (Victor Bo) discovers her. 'She never knew what it was to be a real woman', intones the narrator of this cheap but surprisingly tame adventure film (Sorli never even undresses for her love scene), which looks to have been partly inspired by the exotic-erotic chicanery of the Italian shocker *Man from Deep River* (Umberto Lenzi, 1972) despite its basis in H. Rider Haggard's *She*.
3. A 2013 article in *The Guardian* newspaper addressed this issue: https://www.theguardian.com/film/filmblog/2013/aug/01/nollywood-lgbt-community

FILMOGRAPHY

The following are films mentioned in this book which qualified for the B-Scheme subsidy:
Abathumbi (or *The Kidnapper*, Tonie van der Merwe, 1985)
Beware Tiger (Michelle Hartslief, 1986)
Black Crusader (Tony Cunningham, 1986)
Bona Manzi (or *Look, Water*, Tonie van der Merwe, 1989)
The Boxer (Michelle Hartslief, 1986)
Charlie Steele (Bevis Parsons, 1984)
The Comedians (Japie van der Merwe, 1980)
Doomsday (Abie Hattingh, 1986)
Double Deal (Tonie van der Merwe, 1985)
Ezintandaneni (or *Orphans*, Tonie van der Merwe, 1987)
The Faceless Man (Carl Bleakley, 1985)
Fishy Stones (Tonie van der Merwe, 1989)
Friday's Ghost (Marcel Joubert, 1980)
Gone Crazy (Tony Cunningham, 1980s)
The Hobo (Tony Cunningham, 1980)
Hostage (Michele Hartslief, 1986)
iKati Elimnyama (or *Black Cat*, Simon Sabela, 1975)
Impango (or *The Marked One*, Tonie van der Merwe, 1986)
Impango II (or *The Marked One II*, Tonie van der Merwe, 1987)
Impindiso (or *Cold Justice*, Carton Spielberg, 1980s)
Imusi (or *Smoke*, Carton Spielberg, 1980s)
Isiboshwa (or *Prisoner*, Tonie van der Merwe, 1989)
Isiqalekiso (or *Gold Fever*, Tonie van der Merwe, 1980s)
Ivondwe (Louis De Witt, 1986)
Johnny Dlamini (Robert van de Coolwijk, 1986)

Knockout Joe (Laurens Barnard, 1984)
Lana Pirana (no director noted, 1985)
Lola (Tony Cunningham, 1985)
Mandla (Tonie van der Merwe, 1980s)
Mapantsula (Oliver Schmitz, 1988)
Mine Boy (Karen Thorne, 1989)
The Mobsters (Ben du Plessis, 1980s)
Moyo Mubi (or *The Evil Ones*, Tonie van der Merwe, 1989)
My Country My Hat (David Bensusan, 1983)
One More Shot (Ronnie Isaacs, 1984)
The Priest and the Thief (Wanna Fourie, 1980s)
Ransom (Tony Cunningham, 1980s)
Revenge (Coenie Dippenaar, 1986)
Rich Girl (Tonie van der Merwe, 1985)
Run for Your Life (Tommy Röthig, 1985)
Strikeback (Ronnie Isaacs, 1980s)
Thunder Valley (Marcel Joubert, 1985)
uDeliwe (Simon Sabela, 1975)
Ukuzingela (or *Treasure Hunter*, Tonie van der Merwe, 1989)
Umbango (or *The Feud*, Tonie van der Merwe, 1986)
Umgulukudu (or *Thieves*, Marcel Joubert, 1980s)
Under Cover (Tony Cunningham, 1989)
Upondo & Nkinsela (Bernard Buys, 1984)
Uthemba (Rudi Mayer, 1980)
The Witchdoctor (no director noted, 1985)
Zero for Zep (Steve Hand and Laurens Barnard, 1980)

The following list represents other films made in, or co-produced with, South Africa, and mentioned in this book:
Alien from L.A. (Albert Pyun, 1988)
American Ninja 2: The Confrontation (Sam Firstenberg, 1987)
American Ninja 3: Blood Hunt (Cedric Sundstrom, 1989)
American Ninja 4: The Annihilation (Cedric Sundstrom, 1990)
Boetie Gaan Border Toe (Regardt van den Bergh, 1984)
Boetie Op Maneuvers (Regardt van den Bergh, 1985)
Bullet on the Run (Tonie van der Merwe, 1982)
A Chip of Glass Ruby (Ross Devenish, 1982)
City of Blood (Darrell Roodt, 1983)
City Wolf (Heinrich Dahms, 1988)
Cry, the Beloved Country (Zoltan Korda, 1951)
Death of a Snowman (Christopher Rowley, 1976)
The Demon (Percival Rubens, 1979)
Dingaka (Jamie Uys, 1965)
Endangered (Mark Engels, 1989)
Five Fingers for Marseilles (Michael Matthews, 2017)
Fools (Ramadan Suleman, 1997)
Game for Vultures (James Fargo, 1979)
The Gods Must Be Crazy (Jamie Uys, 1980)
Gold (Peter R. Hunt, 1974)
Golden Rendezvous (Ashley Lazarus, 1977)
Grensbasis 13 (Elmo de Witt, 1979)
Headhunter (Francis Schaeffer, 1988)

IMAGES OF APARTHEID

Hellgate (William A. Levey, 1989)
House of the Living Dead (Ray Austin, 1974)
How Long (Gibson Kente, 1976)
I Am Not a Witch (Rungano Nyoni, 2017)
Jannie Totsiens (Jans Rautenbach, 1970)
Jobman (Darrel Roodt, 1990)
Jim Comes to Jo'burg (or *African Jim*, Donald Swanson, 1950)
Joe Bullet (Louis de Witt, 1973)
Karate Olympiad (Ivan Hall, 1977)
Kill and Kill Again (Ivan Hall, 1981)
King Solomon's Mines (J. Lee Thompson, 1985)
Last Grave at Dimbaza (Chris Curling, Pascoe Macfarlane, 1974)
Livia AKA *Amor de Assassino* (Bill Prout-Jones, 1977)
Operation Hit Squad (Tonie van der Merwe, Kathy Viedge, 1987)
The Native Who Caused all the Trouble (Manie van Rensburg, 1989)
Ngomopho (Tonie van der Merwe, 1975)
A Place of Weeping (Darrell Roodt, 1986)
Platoon Leader (Aaron Norris, 1988)
Quest for Love (Helena Nogueira, 1988)
River of Death (Steve Carver, 1989)
The Shadowed Mind (Cedric Sundstrom, 1988)
Shamwari (Clive Harding, 1982)
Shot Down (Andrew Worsdale, 1987)
Skeleton Coast (John Carlos, 1987)
Snake Dancer (Dirk De Villiers, 1976)
Song of Africa (Emil Nofal, 1951)
The Stay Awake (John Bernard, 1987)
The Stick (Darrell Roodt, 1988)
Survival Zone (Percival Rubens, 1983)
Sweet Murder (Percival Rubens, 1990)
Target of an Assassin (or *Tigers Don't Cry*, Peter Collinson, 1976)
Tenth of a Second (1987)
Terrorist (Neil Hetherington, 1978)
Three Bullets for a Long Gun (Peter Henkel, 1973)
Trompie (Tonie van der Merwe, 1975)
The Virgin Goddess (Dirk De Villiers, 1974)
De Voortrekkers (Harold M. Shaw, 1916)
Die Voortrekkers (David Millin, 1973)
The Wilby Conspiracy (Ralph Nelson, 1975)
The Wild Geese (Andrew V. McLaglen, 1978)
Zonk! (Hyman Kirstein, 1950)
Zulu (Cy Endfield, 1964)

The following is a list of the non-South African films referenced in this study:
48 Hours (Walter Hill, 1982)
Abby (William Girdler, 1972)
Across 110th Street (Barry Shear, 1972)
Adiós Amigo (Fred Williamson, 1975)
After the Fall of New York (Sergio Martino, 1983)
Africa Addio (Gualtiero Jacopetti, Franco Prosperi, 1966)
American Ninja (Sam Firstenberg, 1985)

FILMOGRAPHY

American Ninja 5 (Bobby Jean Leonard, 1993)*Assault on Precinct 13* (John Carpenter, 1976)
Bachelor Party (Neal Israel, 1984)
Beverly Hills Cop (Martin Brest, 1984)
The Bicycle Thieves (Vittorio De Sica, 1948)
The Big Bird Cage (Jack Hill, 1972)
The Big Doll House (Jack Hill, 1971)
Black Caesar (Larry Cohen, 1973)
Black Dynamite (Scott Sanders, 2009)
Black Emanuelle (Bitto Albertini, 1975)
The Black Gestapo (Lee Frost, 1975)
Black Hawk Down (Ridley Scott, 2001)
Black Mama White Mama (Eddie Romero, 1973)
Black Shampoo (Greydon Clark, 1976)
Blacula (William Crain, 1972)
Blazing Saddles (Mel Brooks, 1974)
Blood Diamond (Edward Zwick, 2006)
Bone (Larry Cohen, 1972)
Boss Nigger (Jack Arnold, 1975)
Bucktown (Arthur Marks, 1975)
Bruce Almighty (Tom Shadyac, 2003)
Carry on up the Khyber (1968)
Charley One-Eye (Don Chaffey, 1973)
Cleopatra Jones and the Casino of Gold (Charles Bail, 1975)
Coffy (Jack Hill, 1983)
Coming Home (Hal Ashby, 1978)
Coonskin (Ralph Bakshi, 1975)
Cotton Comes to Harlem (Ossie Davis, 1970)
Cry Freedom (Richard Attenborough, 1987)
Death Wish (Michael Winner, 1974)
Death Wish II (Michael Winner, 1982)
The Deer Hunter (Michael Cimino, 1978)
Deliverance (John Boorman, 1972)
The Delta Force (Menahem Golan, 1986)
Detroit 9000 (Arthur Marks, 1973)
The Devil in Miss Jones (Damian Damiano, 1973)
Django (Sergio Corbucci, 1968)
Django Unchained (Quentin Tarantino, 2012)
Dogs of War (John Irvin, 1980)
Dolemite (D'Urville Martin, 1975)
Don't Go in the House (Joseph Ellison, 1980)
A Dry White Season (Euzhan Palcy, 1989)
Dust Devil (Richard Stanley, 1992)
Enter the Dragon (Robert Clouse, 1973)
Escape from New York (John Carpenter, 1981)
Fight for Your Life (Robert A. Endelson, 1976)
A Fistful of Dollars (Sergio Leone, 1964)
For Y'ur Height Only (Eddie Nicart, 1981)
Foxy Brown (Jack Hill, 1974)
The French Connection (William Friedkin, 1971)
Friday Forster (Arthur Marks, 1975)
Ganja and Hess (Bill Gunn, 1974)

The Good, The Bad and the Ugly (Sergio Leone, 1966)
G.O.R.A. (Ömer Faruk Sorak, 2005)
The Green Berets (John Wayne/Ray Kellogg, 1968)
Hammer (Bruce D. Clark, 1972)
The Hanoi Hilton (Lionel Chetwynd, 1987)
The Harder They Come (Perry Henzell, 1972)
Hell Up in Harlem (Larry Cohen, 1973)
I Drink Your Blood (David E. Durston, 1970)
Ilsa, She Wolf of the SS (Don Edmonds, 1975)
In the Heat of the Night (Norman Jewison, 1967)
I Spit on Your Grave (Meir Zarchi, 1978)
Joshua (Larry Spangler, 1976)
Karate Warrior (Fabrizio De Angelis, 1987)
The Keep (Michael Mann, 1983)
King Kong (Merian C. Cooper, Ernest B. Schoedsack, 1933)
Lady Cocoa (Matt Cimber, 1975)
The Last House on the Left (Wes Craven, 1972)
The Last Hunter (Antonio Margheriti, 1980)
The Last King of Scotland (Kevin Macdonald, 2007)
The Legend of Nigger Charley (Martin Goldman, 1972)
Lethal Weapon (Richard Donner, 1987)
The Little Shop of Horrors (Roger Corman, 1960)
The Mack (Michael Campus, 1973)
Man from Deep River (Umberto Lenzi, 1972)
The Matrix (Lana Wachowski, Lilly Wachowski, 1999)
Mau-Mau (Elwood Price, 1955)
Mean Johnny Barrows (Fred Williamson, 1976)
Medicine for Melancholy (Barry Jenkins, 2008)
Missing in Action (Joseph Zito, 1984)
Moonraker (Lewis Gilbert, 1979)
The Muthers (Cirio H. Santiago, 1976)
New Jack City (Mario Van Peebles, 1991)
Oasis of the Zombies (Jesús Franco, 1981)
The Outlaw (Howard Hughes, 1941)
Penitentiary (Jamaa Fanaka, 1979)
Platoon (Oliver Stone, 1986)
The Professionals (Richard Brooks, 1966)
Rambo: First Blood Part II (George P. Cosmatos, 1985)
The Rocky Horror Picture Show (Jim Sharman, 1975)
Sambizanga (Sarah Maldoror, 1972)
Sapiches (or *Private Popsicle*, Boaz Davidson, 1982)
The Scalp Hunters (Sydney Pollack, 1968)
Shaft (Gordon Parks, 1971)
Shaft's Big Score (Gordon Parks, 1972)
Shaft in Africa (John Guillermin, 1973)
Shangani Patrol (David Millin, 1970)
Sharon Stone (Adim Williams, 2002)
The Shawshank Redemption (Frank Darabont, 1994)
Sheba, Baby (William Girdler, 1975)
The Slams (Jonathan Kaplan, 1973)
Slaughter (Jack Starrett, 1972)
Smokey and the Bandit (Hal Needham, 1977)

Song of the South (Wilfred Jackson, 1946)
The Soul of Nigger Charley (Larry Spangler, 1973)
Stagecoach (John Ford, 1939)
The Strange Vice of Mrs. Wardh (Sergio Martino, 1971)
Sugar Hill (Paul Maslansky, 1974)
Super Fly (Gordon Parks Jr., 1972)
Sweet Sweetback's Baadasssss Song (Melvin Van Peebles, 1971)
Tears of the Sun (Antoine Fuqua, 2003)
The Texas Chain Saw Massacre (Tobe Hooper, 1974)
The Texas Chainsaw Massacre 2 (Tobe Hooper, 1986)
Thunderball (Terence Young, 1965)
TNT Jackson (Cirio H. Santiago, 1975)
Tom Dollar (Marcello Ciorciolini, 1967)
Truck Turner (Jonathan Kaplan, 1974)
The Two Farmers (Stephen Peet, 1948)
Undercover Brother (Malcolm D. Lee, 2002)
Upperseven (Alberto De Martino, 1966)
Whispering Death (AKA *Albino*, Jürgen Goslar, 1976)
White Cannibal Queen (Jesús Franco, 1980)
White Hunter Black Heart (Clint Eastwood, 1990)
Wolf Warrior (Wu Jing, 2015)
Women in Cages (Gerardo de León, 1972)
Women in Cellblock 9 (Jess Franco, 1977)
A World Apart (Chris Menges, 1988)
Yojimbo (Akira Kurosawa, 1961)

BIBLIOGRAPHY

Allen, Robert and Gomery, Douglas (1985), *Film History: Theory and Practice*. New York: McGraw-Hill.
Altman, Rick (1999), *Film/Genre*. London: BFI.
Arden, Nicky (1999), *African Spirits Speak: A White Woman's Journey into the Healing Tradition of the Sangoma*. VT: Destiny Books.
Armes, Roy (2006), *African Filmmaking North and South of the Sahara*. Edinburgh: Edinburgh University Press.
Bakari, Ishaq Imruh and Cham, Mbye B. (1996), *African Experiences of Cinema*. London: BFI.
Balseiro, Isabel and Masilela, Ntongela (2003), *To Change Reels: Film and Film Culture in South Africa*. Detroit: Wayne State University Press.
Barber, Sian (2015), *Using Film as a Source*. Manchester: Manchester University Press.
Baschiera, Stefano (2016), 'The 1980s Italian Horror Cinema of Imitation: The Good, the Bad and the Sequel', in S. Baschiera and R. Hunter, *Italian Horror Cinema*. Edinburgh: Edinburgh University Press.
Bazin, André (2005 [1971]), *What Is Cinema? Vol 2*. Los Angeles: University of California Press.
Bennett, Lerone, 'The Emancipation Orgasm: Sweetback in Wonderland', *Ebony*, 26, pp. 106–18.
Blignaut, Johan and Botha, Martin (eds) (1992), *Movies-moguls-mavericks: South African cinema, 1979–1991*. Johannesburg: Showdata.
Blignaut, Johan (1992), 'Lights! Camera! . . . Shelve It!!! – The Distribution Dilemma of South African Films', in J. Blignaut and M. Botha (eds), *Movies-moguls-mavericks: South African cinema, 1979–1991*. Johannesburg: Showdata.
Bogle, Donald (2016), *Toms, Coons, Mulattoes, Mammies, and Bucks: An Interpretive History of Blacks in American Films*. New York: Bloomsbury Academic.

Bonner, Philip (1991), 'The Politics of Black Squatter Movements on The Rand, 1944–1952', in J. Brown, P. Manning, K. Shapiro, J. Wiener, *History from South Africa: Alternative Visions and Practices*. Philadelphia: Temple University Press.
Botha, Martin (2012), *South African Cinema 1896–2010*. Chicago: University of Chicago Press.
Botha, Martin and van Aswegen, Adri (1992), *Images of South Africa: The Rise of Alternative Film*. Pretoria: Human Rights Research Council.
Briggs, Joe Bob (2003), *Profoundly Disturbing: Shocking Movies that Changed History!*. London: Plexus Publishing.
Burns, James McDonald (2002), *Flickering Shadows: Cinema and Identity in Colonial Zimbabwe*. OH: Ohio University Research in International Studies.
Butters, Gerald R. (2016), 'Sweetback in Chicago', in N. Lawrence and G. Butters, *Beyond Blaxploitation*. Detroit: Wayne State University Press.
Cameron, Kenneth M. (1994), *Africa on Film: Beyond Black and White*. New York: Continuum.
Canby, Vincent (1975), 'Now For a Look at Some Really Bad Movies', *The New York Times*, New York, 30.11.1975.
Cawley, Leo (1990), 'The War About the War: Vietnam Films and the American Myth', in L. Dittmar and G. Michaud, *From Hanoi to Hollywood: The Vietnam Film*. New Brunswick and London: Rutgers University Press.
Chan, Stephen (2019), *Mugabe: A Life of Power and Violence*. London: LB Tauris & Co. Ltd.
Chapman, James (2009), 'Action, Spectacle and the *Boy's Own* Tradition in British Cinema', in R. Murphy, *The British Cinema Book*. London: BFI/Palgrave.
Chaffin-Quiray, Garrett (2002), '"You Bled My Mother, You Bled My Father, But You Won't Bleed Me': The Underground Trio of Melvin Van Peebles"', in X. Mendik and S. J. Schneider (eds), *Underground U.S.A.: Filmmaking Beyond the Hollywood Canon*. London and New York: Wallflower Press.
Church, David (2016), *Grindhouse Nostalgia: Memory, Home Video and Exploitation Film Fandom*. Edinburgh: Edinburgh University Press.
Cooke, Paul (2007), 'From Caligari to Edward Scissorhands: The Continuing Meta-Cinematic Journey of German Expressionism', in P. Cooke, *World Cinema's 'Dialogues' With Hollywood*. New York: Palgrave MacMillan.
Cripps, Thomas (1977), *Slow Fade to Black: The Negro in American Film, 1900–1942*. New York: Oxford University Press.
Davis, Peter (1996), *In Darkest Hollywood: Exploring the Jungles of Cinema's South Africa*. Johannesburg: Ravan Press, Johannesburg.
De Klerk, Frederik Willem (1998), *The Last Trek: A New Beginning*. London: MacMillan.
Diawara, Manthia (1992), *African Cinema: Politics and Culture*. IN: Indiana University Press, Indiana, 1992.
Diawara, Manthia (1995), 'Black American Cinema: The New Realism', in M. Martin, *Cinemas of the Black Diaspora: Diversity, Dependence and Oppositionality*. Detroit: Wayne State University Press.
Donalson, Melvin (2006), *Masculinity in the Interracial Buddy Film*. NC: McFarland & Company.
Dowden, Richard (2008), *Africa: Altered States, Ordinary Miracles*. London: Portobello Books.
Du Bois, W. E. B. (1903 [1994]), *The Souls of Black Folk*. New York: Dover Publications.
Dunn, Stephane (2008), *Baad Bitches and Sassy Supermamas: Black Power Action Films*. Chicago: University of Illinois Press.
Eshun, Kodwo (2005), 'Escaping the Genre Ghetto', *Sight and Sound*, 15:6, BFI.

Feaster, Felicia and Wood, Brett, *Forbidden Fruit: The Golden Age of Exploitation Film*. Baltimore: Midnight Marquee Publishing, Baltimore.

Fisher, Austin (2016), 'Go West, Brother: The Politics of Landscape in the Blaxploitation Western', in A. Fisher and J. Walker (eds), *Grindhouse (Global Exploitation Cinemas)*. London: Bloomsbury Academic.

Fisher, Austin and Walker, Johnny (eds), *Grindhouse (Global Exploitation Cinemas)*. London: Bloomsbury Academic.

Gaines, Mikal J., 'Strange Enjoyments: The Marketing and Reception of Horror in the Civil Rights Era Black Press', in R. Nowell, *Merchants of Menace: The Business of Horror Cinema*. London: Bloomsbury.

Garritano, Carmela (2013), *African Video Movies and Global Desires: A Ghanaian History*. OH: Ohio University Press.

Gavshon, Harriet (1983), 'Levels of intervention in films made for African audiences in South Africa', *Critical Arts*, 2:4, pp. 15–21.

Gavshon, Harriet (1991), '"Bearing Witness": Ten Years Towards an Opposition Film Movement in South Africa', in J. Brown, P. Manning, K. Shapiro, J. Wiener, *History from South Africa: Alternative Visions and Practices*. Philadelphia: Temple University Press.

Gillespie, Michael Boyce, *Film Blackness: American Cinema and the Idea of Black Film*, Durham and London: Duke University Press.

Glaessner, V. (1974), 'Coffy Review', *Monthly Film Bulletin*, 41:486, p. 116.

Gleijeses, Piero (2013), *Visions of Freedom: Havana, Washington, Pretoria and the Struggle for Southern Africa, 1976–1991*. Chapel Hill: The University of North Carolina Press.

Grainge, Paul, Jancovich, Mark and Monteith, Sharon (2007), *Film Histories: An Introduction and Reader*. Edinburgh: Edinburgh University Press.

Guerrero, Ed (1993), *Framing Blackness: The African American Image in Film*. Philadelphia: Temple University Press.

Gugler, Josef (2003), *African Film: Re-Imagining a Continent*. IN: Indiana University Press.

Gutsche, Thelma (1972), *The History and Social Significance of Motion Pictures in South Africa, 1895-1940*. Cape Town: Howard Timmins.

Hake, Sabine (2001), *Popular Cinema of the Third Reich*. Texas: University of Texas Press.

Harrow, Kenneth W. (2013), *Trash: African Cinema from Below*. IN: Indiana University Press.

Hartmann, Jon (1994), 'The Trope of Blaxploitation in Critical Responses to "Sweetback"', *Film History*, 6:3, Indiana University Press, pp. 382–404.

Hawkins, Joan (2007), 'The Anxiety of Influence: Georges Franju and the Medical Horrorshows of Jess Franco,' in E. Mathijs and X. Mendik (eds), *The Cult Film Reader*. London: Open University Press.

Haynes, Jonathan (2011), 'African Cinema and Nollywood: Contradictions', *Situations*, 4:1, pp. 67–90.

Higgins, MaryEllen (2012), *Hollywood's Africa After 1994*. OH: Ohio University Press.

Higgins, MaryEllen (2012), 'Hollywood's Cowboy Humanitarianism in Black Hawk Down and Tears of the Sun', in M. Higgins, *Hollywood's Africa After 1994*. OH: Ohio University Press.

Hughey, Matthew W. (2009), 'Cinethetic Racism: White Redemption and Black Stereotypes in "Magical Negro" Films', in *Social Problems*, 56:3, pp. 543–77.

Hunt, Leon (2000), 'Han's Island Revisited: *Enter the Dragon* as Transnational Cult

Film', in X. Mendik and G. Harper, *Unruly Pleasures: The Cult Film and its Critics*. London: FAB Press.

Hutchison, Rachael (2007), 'A Fistful of Yojimbo: Appropriation and Dialogue in Japanese Cinema', in P. Cooke, *World Cinema's 'Dialogues' With Hollywood*. New York: Palgrave MacMillan.

Johnson, R. W. (2010), *South Africa's Brave New World: The Beloved Country Since the End of Apartheid*. New York: Overlook.

Jules-Rosette, Benetta, Osborn, J. R., Ruiz-Ads, Lea Marie (2012), 'New Jack African Cinema: Dangerous Ground; Cry, the Beloved Country; and Blood Diamond', in M. Higgins, *Hollywood's Africa After 1994*. Ohio: Ohio University Press.

Kapuściński, Ryszard (1976 [2001]), *Another Day of Life*. London: Penguin, London.

Kapuściński, Ryszard (2001), *The Shadow of the Sun: My African Life*. London: Penguin.

Kenney, Henry (2016), *Verwoerd: Architect of Apartheid*. Cape Town and Johannesburg: Jonathan Ball Publishers.

Knight, Ian (2010), *Zulu Rising: The Epic Story of Isandlwana and Rorke's Drift*. London: MacMillan.

Koven, Mikel J. (2010), *Blaxploitation Films*. Hertfordshire: Kamera Books, Herts.

Koven, Mikel J. (2016), 'Corbucci Unchained: Miike, Tarantino and the Postmodern Discursivity of Exploitation Cinema', in A. Fisher, *Spaghetti Westerns at the Crossroad: Studies in Relocation, Transition and Appropriation*. Edinburgh: Edinburgh University Press.

Kraidy, Marwan M. (2005), *Hybridity, or the Cultural Logic of Globalisation*. Philadelphia: Temple University Press.

Lamb, Christina (2007), *House of Stone*. London: Harper Perennial.Landis, Bill (2002), *Sleazoid Express*. New York: Plexus Publishing.

Lawrence, Novotny (2005), 'The Detective Film as Genre', in *Screening Noir: Journal of Black Film, Television, & New Media Culture*, 1:1, pp. 32 48.

Lawrence, Novotny (2008), *Blaxploitation Films of the 1970s: Blackness and Genre*. New York: Routledge.

Lawrence, Novotny (2016), 'A White Film for a Blaxploitation Audience? The Making and Marketing of Detroit 9000', in *Beyond Blaxploitation*. Detroit: Wayne State University Press.

Lott, Tommy L. (1995), 'A No-Theory Theory of Contemporary Black Cinema', in M. Martin, *Cinemas of the Black Diaspora: Diversity, Dependence and Oppositionality*. Detroit: Wayne State University Press.

Lovell, Julia (2020), *Maoism, a Global History*. London: Vintage.

Maingard, Jacqueline (1994), 'New South African Cinema: *Mapantsula* and *Sarafina*', *Screen*, 35:3, pp. 235–43.

Maingard, Jacqueline (2007), *South African National Cinema*. London: Routledge.

Malan, Rian (1991), *My Traitor's Heart*. London: Vintage.

Mangcu, Xolela (2012), *Biko: A Biography*. Cape Town: Tafelberg.

Manlove, Clifford T. (2012), '"An Image in Africa": Representations of Modern Colonialism in Peter Jackson's *King Kong*', in M. Higgins, *Hollywood's Africa After 1994*. OH: Ohio University Press.

Maslin, Janet (1989), 'A Black South African's Radicalization', *The New York Times*, New York, 03.12.1989.

Matloff, Judith (1997), *Fragments of a Forgotten War*. London: Penguin Books.

McCluskey, Audrey Thomas (2009), *The Devil You Dance With: Film Culture in the New South Africa*. Chicago: University of Illinois Press.

McKendry, Rebecca (2010), 'Fondling Your Eyeballs Watching Doris Wishman', in

J. Cline and R. Weiner, *From the Arthouse to the Grindhouse: Highbrow and Lowbrow Transgression in Cinema's First Century*. PA: Scarecrow Press.

Meintjies, Frank (1992), 'In the Townships', in J. Blignaut and M. P. Botha (eds), *Movies-moguls-mavericks: South African Cinema, 1979–1991*. Johannesburg: Showdata.

Metcalfe, Daniel (2014), *Blue Dahlia, Black Gold, A Journey into Angola*. London: Arrow Books.

Minter, William (1994), *Apartheid's Contras, An Enquiry into the Roots of War In Angola and Mozambique*. Johannesberg: Zed Books and Witwatersrand University Press.

Mitchell, Edward (2012), 'Apes and Essences: Some Sources of Significance in the American Gangster Film', in K. B. Grant, *Film Genre Reader IV*, Austin: University of Texas Press.

Modisane, Litheko (2013), *South Africa's Renegade Reels: The Making and Public Lives of Black-Centred Films*. New York: Palgrave MacMillan.

Moore, Roger (2008), *My Word is my Bond*. London: Michael O'Mara Books.

Morse, L. A. (1989), *Video Trash and Treasures*. Toronto: Harper & Collins.

Morse, L. A. (1990), *Video Trash and Treasures II*. Toronto: Harper & Collins.

Murray, James (1992), 'Ethnic Cinema – How Greed Killed the Industry', in J. Blignaut and M. P. Botha (eds), *Movies-moguls-mavericks: South African Cinema, 1979–1991*. Johannesburg: Showdata.

'*Night of the Living Dead* review', 16 October 1968, Variety Media, CA – no author credited.

Nixon, Ron (2015), *Selling Apartheid: South Africa's Global Propaganda War*. South Africa: Jacana Media.

Nowell, Richard (2011), *Blood Money: A History of the First Teen Slasher Film Cycle*. New York: Continuum International Publishing.

Omond, Roger (1985), *The Apartheid Handbook: A Guide to South Africa's Everyday Racial Policies*. London: Penguin Books.

Paleker, Gairoonisa (2010), 'The B-Scheme Subsidy and the "Black Film Industry" in Apartheid South Africa, 1972–1990', *Journal of African Cultural Studies*, 22:1, pp. 91–104.

Parish, James Robert and Hill, George H. (2019), *Black Action Films*. Los Angeles: Encore Film Books.

Pawson, Lara (2016), *In the Name of the People: Angola's Forgotten Massacre*. London: I. B. Taurus.

Ritzer, Ivo (2016), 'Spaghetti Westerns and Asian Cinema: Perspectives on Global Cultural Flows', in A. Fisher, *Spaghetti Westerns at the Crossroads: Studies in Relocation, Transition and Appropriation*. Edinburgh: Edinburgh University Press.

Rivers, Patrick Lynn (2007), 'Governing Images: The Politics of Film and Video Distribution in Late-Apartheid and Postapartheid South Africa', *Journal of Film and Video*, 59:1, University of Illinois Press, pp. 19–31.

Robinson, Cedric J. (1998), 'Blaxploitation and the Misrepresentation of Liberation', *Race and Class*, 7:40.

Saks, Lucia (2010), *Cinema in a Democratic South Africa: The Race for Representation*. Indiana: Indiana University Press.

Schaefer, Eric (1999), *"Bold! Daring! Shocking! True!" A History of Exploitation Films, 1919–1959*. Durham and London: Duke University Press.

Sconce, Jeffrey (1995), '"Trashing" the Academy: Taste, Excess, and an Emerging Politics of Cinematic Style', *Screen*, 36:4, pp. 371–93.

Sieving, Christopher (2011), *Soul Searching*. CT: Wesleyan University Press.

Silber, Gus (1992), 'Dream Factory', in J. Blignaut and M. P. Botha (eds), *Movies-moguls-mavericks: South African Cinema, 1979–1991*. Johannesburg: Showdata.
Silber, Gus (1992), 'Tax, Lies and Videotape – Who Killed the South African Film Industry?', in J. Blignaut and M. P. Botha (eds), *Movies-moguls-mavericks: South African Cinema, 1979–1991*. Johannesburg: Showdata.
Sims, Yvonne D. (2006), *Women of Blaxploitation: How the Black Action Film Heroine Changed American Popular Culture*. NC: McFarland Publishing.
Smith, Iain R. (2016), 'Cowboys and Indians: Transnational Borrowings in the Indian Masala Western', in A. Fisher, *Spaghetti Westerns at the Crossroad: Studies in Relocation, Transition and Appropriation*. Edinburgh: Edinburgh University Press.
Smith, Iain R. (2017), *The Hollywood Meme*. Edinburgh: Edinburgh University Press.
Ssali, Ndugu (1996), 'Apartheid and Cinema', in I. Bakari and M. Cham, *African Experiences of Cinema*. London: BFI.
Steadman, Ian (1988), 'Popular Culture and Performance in South Africa', in K. G. Tomaselli, *Rethinking Culture*. Belville: Anthropos Publishers.
Studlar, Gaylyn and Desser, David (1990), 'Never Having to Say You're Sorry: Rambo's Rewriting of the Vietnam War', in L. Dittmar and G. Michaud, *From Hanoi to Hollywood: The Vietnam Film*. New Brunswick and London: Rutgers University Press.
Taylor, Clyde (1995), 'The Paradox of Black Independent Cinema', in M. Martin, *Cinemas of the Black Diaspora: Diversity, Dependence and Oppositionality*. Detroit: Wayne State University Press.
Taylor, Trevor S. (1992), 'Genres in Accented English – There's a Killer on the Road . . . Voodoo Killings on the Brow of the Hill . . . Ninjas in the Third World . . . ', in J. Blignaut and M. P. Botha (eds), *Movies-moguls-mavericks: South African Cinema, 1979–1991*. Johannesburg: Showdata.
Thompson, Katrina Daly (2013), *Zimbabwe's Cinematic Arts: Language, Power, Identity*. IN: Indiana University Press.
Thomson, Ian (2009), *The Dead Yard, A Story of Modern Jamaica*. London: Faber and Faber.
Tomaselli, Keyan G. (1988), *The Cinema of Apartheid: Race and Class in South African Film*. Chicago: Smyrna/Lake View Press.
Tomaselli, Keyan G. (1992), 'The Cinema of Jamie Uys – From Bushveld to Bushmen', in J. Blignaut and M. P. Botha (eds), *Movies-moguls-mavericks: South African Cinema, 1979–1991*. Johannesburg: Showdata.
Tomaselli, Keyan G. (2006), 'Re-reading "The Gods Must be Crazy" Films', *Visual Anthropology*, 19:2, pp. 171–200.
Tomaselli, Keyan G. (2016), *Encountering Modernity: Twentieth Century South African Cinemas*. Pretoria: UNISA Press.
Tomaselli, Keyan G, and Louw, Eric (1991), *The Alternative Press in South Africa*. South Africa: Anthropos Publishers.
Tomaselli, Keyan G. and McLennan-Dodd, Vanessa (2005), 'The Gods Must be Crazy in China', *Visual Anthropology*, 18.
Tomaselli, Keyan G. and Prinsloo, Jeanne (1992), 'Third Cinema in South Africa – The Anti-Apartheid Struggle', in J. Blignaut and M. P. Botha (eds), *Movies-moguls-mavericks: South African Cinema, 1979–1991*. Johannesburg: Showdata.
Tomaselli, Keyan G. and Shepperson, Arnold (2003), 'Le cinéma sud-africain après l'apartheid: la restructuration d'une industrie', *CinémAction*, 106, pp. 199–228.
Tomaselli, Keyan G, Teer-Tomaselli, Ruth E. and Muller, Johan (1987), *The Press in South Africa*. Belville: Richard Lyon and Company.
Tomaselli, Keyan G., and Ureke, Oswelled (2017), '"African Cinema" to Film Services Industries: A Cinematic Fact', *Journal of African Cinemas*, 9/1:18, pp. 75–92.

Tomaselli, Keyan G. and van Zyl, Mikki (1992), 'Themes, Myths and Cultural Indicators – The Structuring of Popular Memories', in J. Blignaut and M. P. Botha (eds), *Movies-moguls-mavericks: South African Cinema, 1979–1991*. Johannesburg: Showdata.
Toye, Richard, *Churchill's Empire*. London: Pan MacMillan.
Uradike, N. Frank (1994), *Black African Cinema*. Los Angeles: University of California Press.
Valle, Joseph S. (2016), 'As Foxy as Can Be: The Melodramatic Mode in Blaxploitation Cinema', in N. Lawrence and G. Buttes, *Beyond Blaxploitation*. Detroit: Wayne State University Press.
Van der Westhuizen, Christi (2007), *White Power & The Rise and Fall of the National Party*. Cape Town: Zebra Press.
Von Doviak, Scott (2015), *Hick Flicks: The Rise and Fall of Redneck Cinema*. NC: McFarland Publishing.
Waddell, Calum (2018), *The Style of Sleaze: The American Exploitation Film 1959–1977*. Edinburgh: Edinburgh University Press.
Ward, Glenn (2016), 'Grinding out the Grind House: Exploitation, Myth and Memory', in A. Fisher and J. Walker (eds), *Grindhouse (Global Exploitation Cinemas)*, London: Bloomsbury Academic.
Welsh, Frank (1998), *A History of South Africa*. London: HarperCollins.
Williams, Linda (1991), 'Film Bodies: Gender, Genre, and Success', *Film Quarterly*, 44:4.
Williams, Linda (2008), *Screening Sex*. NC: Duke University Press.
Williamson, Bruce, 'Review of *A Dry White Season*', *Playboy* magazine, 12, Playboy Press, p. 40.
Witt, Emily (2017), *Nollywood: The Making of a Film Empire*. New York: Columbia Global Reports.
Yearwood, Gladstone (2000), *Black Film as a Signifying Practice: Cinema, Narration and the African American Aesthetic Experience*. NJ: Africa World Press.
Yule, Andrew (1987), *Hollywood A Go-Go: The True Story of the Cannon Film Empire*. London: Sphere Books Ltd.

ONLINE RESOURCES

(All URLs last accessed Dec 2020–Jan 2021)

Brown, Ryan Lenora (12 March 2017), 'Blaxploitation Movies, South Africa style? A Lost Era of Film Sees New Light': https://www.csmonitor.com/World/Africa/2017/0312/Blaxploitation-movies-South-Africa-style-A-lost-era-of-film-sees-new-light

Cousins, Mark (5 March 2018), 'African Cinema: Open Your Eyes': https://www2.bfi.org.uk/news-opinion/sight-sound-magazine/comment/africa-lost-classics-uk-tour-open-your-eyes

Foster, Tyler (23 October 2018), '*Gone Crazy* Review': https://www.dvdtalk.com/reviews/73478/gone-crazy-retro-afrika/

Gravel Road Entertainment web site – 'Retro Afrika Bioscope': https://www.gravelroadafrica.com/retro-afrika-bioscope

Haynes, Gavin (14 April 2015), 'Sollywood: The Extraordinary Story Behind Apartheid South Africa's Blaxploitation Movie Boom': https://www.theguardian.com/film/2015/apr/14/apartheid-south-africa-black-cinema-blaxploitation-b-scheme-subsidy

Hoad, Phil (1 August 2013), 'How does Nollywood picture its LGBT community?': https://www.theguardian.com/film/filmblog/2013/aug/01/nollywood-lgbt-community

Lelyveld, Joseph (19 July 1981), 'Bringing a Bit of Vegas to South Africa's "Homelands"', *The New York Times*, https://www.nytimes.com/1981/07/19/business/bringing-a-bit-of-vegas-to-south-africa-s-homelands.html

Mthembu, Silhe (16 November 2020), 'Umbango', South Africa's first Western was part of Apartheid's scheme to keep township dwellers docile': https://www.news24.com/arts/culture/umbango-south-africas-original-Western-20201116

Obenson, Tambay (5 September 2018), '"Five Fingers for Marseilles": How a Couple of South African Filmmakers Recreated the Western': https://www.indiewire.com/2018/09/five-fingers-for-marseilles-Western-south-africa-film-industry-1201999004/

253

Onishi, Norimitsu (29 July 2014): 'Honoring a Filmmaker in the Shadow of Apartheid': https://www.nytimes.com/2014/07/30/world/africa/honoring-a-filmmaker-in-the-shadow-of-apartheid.html

Stevens, Brad (18 Oct 2016): 'Why *Sweet Sweetback's Baad Asssss Song* is a radical blaxploitation classic', BFI, https://www2.bfi.org.uk/news-opinion/sight-sound-magazine/comment/bradlands/sweet-sweetback-s-baadasssss-song

INTERVIEWS CONDUCTED

Benjamin Cowley: 24 August 2016 (Cape Town)
Coenie Dippenaar: 19 August 2016 (Johannesburg)
Laurence Dworkin: 23 August 2016 (Cape Town)
Mitch Dyter: 19 August 2016 (Johannesburg)
Darryl Els: 22 August 2016 (Cape Town)
Neil Hetherington: 20 August 2016 (Port Elizabeth)
Cynthia Hlanguza: 24 August 2016 (Cape Town)
Abigail Kubeka: 19 August 2016 (Johannesburg)
Litheko Modisane: 22 August 2016 (Cape Town)
Gairoonisa Paleker: 18 August 2016 (Pretoria)
Ian-Malcolm Rijsdijk: 22 August 2016 (Cape Town)
Clive Scott: 19 August 2016 (Johannesburg)
Cedric Sundstrom: 17 August 2016 (Johannesburg)
Trevor Taylor: 17 August 2016 (Johannesburg)
Karen Thorne: 21 August 2016 (Cape Town)
Brian Tilley: 23 August 2016 (Cape Town)
Tonie van der Merwe: 24 August 2016 (Cape Town)
Christie van der Westhuizen: 18 August 2016: (Pretoria)
Ntshavheni Wa Luruli: 17 August 2016 (Johannesburg)

INDEX

2019: After the Fall of New York, 37
48 Hrs, 151

Abathumbi, 92
Abby, 44
Aberdeen, Robert, 202
A Chip of Glass Ruby, 221
Across 110th Street, 154, 157
Adamson, Al, 105
Adiós Amigo, 143
A Dry White Season, 165, 218–19
Africa Addio, 130, 141
African Jim; see *Jim Comes to Jo'burg*
Albertini, Bitto, 37
Albino; see *Whispering Death*
Alexandre, Dwayne, 151
Alien from L.A., 8, 152
Allen, Robert C., 140
Altman, Rick, 87
Ambushed, 30, 95, 133, 183, 190, 192, 194, 199–200, 204–6, 236
American Dragons; see *American Ninja 5*
American Ninja, 73, 162, 232
American Ninja 2: The Confrontation, 152
American Ninja 3: Blood Hunt, 32, 151–3
American Ninja 4: The Annihilation, 15, 40n, 149–51, 153, 158, 161, 168, 169n
American Ninja 5, 168n
Amin, Idi, 52

Amor de Assassino; see *Livia*
A Place of Weeping, 221
Arden, Nicky, 207
Armatrading, Joan, 195
Armes, Roy, 31
Arnold, Jack, 143
Ashby, Hal, 193
Assault on Precinct 13, 157
Aswegen, Adri van, 46
Attenborough, Richard, 156
Austin, Ray, 78
Avildsen, John G., 123
A World Apart, 218, 228n

Babb, Kroger, 167
Bachelor Party, 152
Bail, Charles, 81
Baker, Stanley, 39, 165
Bakshi, Ralph, 44
Balseiro, Isabel, 19
Banda, Hastings, 57n
Barber, Sian, 185
Barnard, Laurens, 32, 99, 179
Baschiera, Stefano, 83
Bazin, André, 141
Bennett, Lerone, 40n
Bensusan, David, 6, 15, 213, 226–7
Bensusan, Tony, 226
Bernard, John, 8

INDEX

Beverly Hills Cop, 151
Beware Tiger, 80–1, 92–3, 101, 110, 143, 183
The Bicycle Thieves, 21
The Big Bird Cage, 158
The Big Doll House, 158
Biko, Steve, 5
Binder, Maurice, 55
Black Caesar, 33, 62, 65, 70, 109, 124, 138
The Black Cat; see *iKati Elimnyama*
Black Crusader, 32, 83, 111, 126, 129–33, 136, 172, 219
Black Dynamite, 66
Black Emanuelle, 37, 169n
The Black Gestapo, 102
Black Hawk Down, 209
Black Mama, White Mama, 113, 115
Black Shampoo, 136
Black Terrorist; see *Terrorist*
Black Trash; see *Death of a Snowman*
Blacula, 44, 128
Blazing Saddles, 143
Bleakley, Carl, 85–6
Blignaut, Johan, 3, 8, 22, 217
Blom, Paul, 4
Blood Diamond, 32, 162
The Bodyguard, 186
Boetie Gaan Border Toe, 193–5, 198, 209n
Boetie Op Maneuvers, 193
Bogle, Donald, 24, 39, 43, 150, 156, 174, 179, 189n, 228n
Bold, Edgar, 150
Bona Manzi, 83, 85, 91–2, 154, 160, 168
Bone, 44, 138
Bonner, Phillip, 134
Boorman, John, 167
Bordwell, David, 148n
Boss Nigger, 143
Botha, Martin, 3, 22, 25–6, 46, 82, 85, 152, 208, 213
Botha, Pieter Willem (or P. W.), 51, 111, 191
Botha, Pik, 50, 76
Bourdieu, Pierre, 61
The Boxer, 11, 35, 121–3
Bradley, David, 151–3
Brest, Martin, 151
Briggs, Joe Bob, 128
Brooks, Mel, 143
Brooks, Richard, 150
Broughton, Lee, 143
Brown, Jim, 200
Bruce Almighty, 71
Brugués, Alejandro, 88
Bucktown, 44
Bullet on the Run, 15, 31, 36, 44, 54–7, 82, 126, 231, 236

Burns, J. M., 19, 41, 120–1, 140
Burton, Richard, 73
Butters Jr, Gerard R., 23
Buys, Bernard, 107n, 211

Caine, Michael, 165
Cameron, Kenneth M., 9, 31, 125, 214, 217
Campus, Michael, 136
Canby, Vincent, 23, 102
Candy Tangerine Man, 62
Carlos, John, 30
Carpenter, John, 37, 157
Carry on up the Khyber, 185
Carver, Steve, 152
Castle, William, 80
Cawley, Leo, 196
Chaffey, Don, 135
Chan, Michele, 153
Chan, Stephen, 166, 205
Chapman, James, 169n
Charley One-Eye, 135
Charlie Steel, 39, 48, 88, 126, 135, 137–9, 183, 193
Chetwynd, Lionel, 197
Church, David, 20, 39n, 233–5
Churchill, Winston, 14
Cimino, Michael, 193
Cimber, Matt, 33, 62, 87
Ciorciolini, Marcello, 65
City of Blood, 205, 207
City Wolf, 233
Clark, Bruce, D., 33
Clark, Greydon, 136
Cleopatra Jones, 176–8
Cleopatra Jones and the Casino of Gold, 81, 154
Cliff, Jimmy, 14, 20, 216
Cline, Kevin, 166
Clouse, Robert, 13
Coffy, 86, 175–8, 187
Cohen, Larry, 33, 44, 81
Cold Justice; see *Impindiso*
Collinson, Peter, 66
The Comedians, 94–6, 114, 121
Coming Home, 193
Connell, Howard, 202
Connery, Sean, 37
Coonskin, 44
Cooke, Paul, 11, 34
Corbucci, Sergio, 65, 126, 144
Corman, Roger, 7, 80, 175
Cosmatos, George P., 197
Cotton Comes from Harlem, 23–4, 32–3, 49, 80
Cousins, Mark, 46

Cowley, Benjamin, 4, 13, 81, 101, 104–5, 123–4, 231
Crain, William, 44
Craven, Wes, 4
Cry Freedom, 156, 164–6, 168, 169n, 218–19, 221, 228n
Cry, the Beloved Country (1951 film adaptation), 64, 111
Cunningham, Tony, 32, 90–1, 96, 98–9, 119–20, 129–31, 139, 147n, 172, 183, 187, 236
Curling, Chris, 85

Dahms, Heinrich, 233
Damiano, Gerard, 77
Dandridge, Dorothy, 174
Darabont, Frank, 71
Davenport, Nigel, 155–6
Davidson, Boaz, 209n
Davis, Angela, 178
Davis, Ossie, 24
Davis, Peter, 27, 60, 64, 71, 111, 113, 115, 125, 141, 156, 165, 214
Davis, Viola, 174
Dawson, Anthony M.; *see* Antonio Margheriti
De Angelis, Fabrizio, 93
Death of a Snowman, 15, 55, 83, 128, 154–8, 161, 164–5, 168, 219, 231–2
Death Wish, 133, 168n, 200
Death Wish II, 168n
The Deer Hunter, 193
The Defiant Ones, 113, 115, 153, 167
de Klerk, F. W., 109, 119
Deliverance, 167, 235
de León, Gerardo, 158
Deleuze, Giles, 144
De Martino, Alberto, 65
The Delta Force, 168n, 169n
The Demon, 78–9, 228n
De Niro, Robert, 12
Desser, David, 197
De Sica, Vittorio, 21
Detroit 9000, 109, 154–5
The Deuce, 28
The Devil in Miss Jones, 77
Devenish, Ross, 221
De Villiers, Dirk, 233–4, 239n
de Witt, Elmo, 45, 193
de Witt, Louis, 4, 34, 36, 41–3, 47, 94, 118
Diawara, Manthia, 61, 216
Dingaka, 38, 165
Dippenaar, Coenie, 15, 17, 27–8, 85, 126, 143, 146–7, 209n
Django, 65, 144
Django Unchained, 140, 144–5

Dladla, Pius, 142
Dlamini, Sam, 147n
Dlamini, Sizwe, 121
Dlamini, Stephen, 147n
Dobson, Tamara, 16, 101, 175–7
Dogs of War, 195, 199
Dolemite, 116
Donalson, Melvin, 55, 153, 157
Donner, Richard, 151, 169n
Doomsday, 29, 85, 119, 124, 223
Double Deal, 180–1, 236
Dougherty, Marion, 169n
Dowden, Richard, 18n, 50, 119, 168n, 189n, 229
Du Bois, W. E. B., 88
Dust Devil, 192
Dudikoff, Michael 80, 150–3
Dunn, Stephanie, 31, 174, 186
du Plessis, Ben, 142
Durston, David, E., 23
Dworkin, Laurence, 109, 217–18, 225–6
Dyter, Mitch, 90, 103, 105, 236

Eastwood, Clint, 173, 209m
Edmonds, Don, 102
Eisner, Lotte, 108
Els, Darryl, 48, 137, 186, 227
Elsaesser, Thomas, 108, 233
Endangered, 209n
Endelson, Robert A., 200
Endfield, Cy, 9
Engels, Mark, 209n
Enter the Dragon, 13
Escape from New York, 37
The Evil Ones, see *Moyo Mubi*
Ezintandaneni, 87, 92, 113

The Faceless Man, 85–6
Fanaka, Jamaa, 43, 116
Fargo, James, 197–8
Feaster, Felicia, 127
The Feud; see *Umbango*
Fight for Your Life, 200–1
Firstenberg, Sam, 152
Fisher, Austin, 11, 102–3, 107n, 135
Fishy Stones, 81, 91–2, 110, 114
A Fistful of Dollars, 15, 171, 173
Fiske, John, 235
Five Fingers for Marseilles, 231
Fools, 231–2
Ford, John, 142, 146
For Y'ur Height Only, 37–8
Fourie, Wanna, 87
Foxy Brown, 176–8, 187
Franco, Jesús, 83, 102, 104
Franke, Tamara, 167

Freedom Fighters; see *Terrorist*
Freeland, Cynthia, 6
The French Connection, 25
Friday Forster, 33
Friday's Ghost, 44, 111, 121, 133
Friedkin, William, 25
Frost, Lee, 102
Fulci, Lucio, 83, 104
Fuqua, Antoine, 208–9
Full Metal Jacket, 195
Furie, Wanna, 107n

Gaines, Mikal J., 80
Game for Vultures, 197–9, 230
Gampu, Ken, 5, 25–6, 31, 33–6, 38–9, 41–6, 48–58, 67, 76, 79, 96, 101, 128–9, 139, 149–51, 153–7, 160–2, 165, 167–8, 192–3, 195–7, 205, 232, 237, 239n
Ganja and Hess, 87
Garritano, Carmela, 90
Gavshon, Harriot, 5, 7, 25, 66, 68
Gee, Prunella, 165
Gemser, Laura, 153
Gilbert, Lewis, 55
Gillespie, Michael Boyce, 21, 44, 182
Girdler, William, 44
Glaessner, Verina, 176
Gleijeses, Piero, 192, 202
Glover, Danny, 169n
The Gods Must Be Crazy, 83, 113, 165, 192–4, 218
Golan, Menahem, 168n, 169n
Gold, 16, 32, 59, 70–2, 164, 230
Golden Rendezvous, 73
Gold Fever; see *Isiqalekiso*
Gomery, Douglas, 140
Gone Crazy, 90, 94–6, 118–19, 121, 139, 183
The Good, The Bad and the Ugly, 145
G.O.R.A., 33–7
Gorfinkel, Elena, 233
Goslar, Jürgen, 166
Grange, Paul, 108–9
Grant, Barry Keith, 192
Granville, Allan, 202
The Green Berets, 197
Grensbasis 13, 193–4
Grier, Pam, 16, 87, 101, 157, 174–7, 186
Griffith, D. W., 126
Gross, Jerry, 23, 236
Guerrero, Ed, 62, 228n
Guess Who's Coming to Dinner?, 49
Gugler, Josef, 89, 212–13, 232
Guillermin, John, 31
Gumede, Innocent; see Popo Gumede

Gumede, Popo, 21, 25, 54, 81–2, 89, 92–3, 95, 113–14, 116–18, 126, 129–31, 133–7, 146, 171, 175, 184, 186–7, 195, 204–5, 232
Gunn, Bill, 87
Gutsche, Thelma, 19–20, 35, 39n, 140

Haggard, H. Rider, 239n
Hake, Sabine, 18n
Hall, Ivan, 79
Hammer, 33–4, 55
Hand, Steve, 99, 179
Hanks, Tom, 152
The Hanoi Hilton, 197
The Harder They Come, 14, 20–1, 35, 144, 148n, 215–16
Harding, Clive, 76, 167, 232
Hark, Tsui, 14
Harris, Richard, 73, 197
Harrow, Kenneth M, 12, 48, 123, 148n
Hartmann, Jon, 40n
Hartslief, Michelle, 11, 80, 90, 92, 110, 121–22, 236
Hattingh, Abie, 29
Hawkins, Joan, 83
Hawks, Howard, 146
Haynes, Jonathan, 79
Headhunter, 233
Hellgate, 233
Hell Up in Harlem, 81
Henkel, Peter, 145
Henzell, Perry, 14, 148n
Hetherington, Neil, 8, 199, 201–4, 210n, 232
Higgins, MaryEllen, 106, 144, 209
Hill, George, H., 87, 176
Hill, Jack, 86–7, 158, 175
Hill, Walter, 151
Himmelman, Natasha, 106
Hlanguza, Cynthia, 186
The Hobo, 172
Hooper, Tobe, 7, 235
Hostage, 90, 98–100, 110, 183
House of the Living Dead, 78
How Long, 73n
Hughes, Howard, 142
Hughey, Matthew, 71, 208
Hunt, Leon, 13
Hunt, Peter, R., 16, 72
Hutchison, Rachael, 173

I Am Not a Witch, 40n
I Drink Your Blood, 23
If…., 105
iKati Elimnyama, 15, 57, 59–72, 74n, 75, 102, 110, 128–9, 132, 139, 164, 230

Ilsa, She Wolf of the SS, 102
Impango, 110, 177, 183, 236
Impango II, 110, 177, 183, 236
Impindiso, 126, 129, 133–5
Imusi, 126, 142, 144, 146–7
In the Heat of the Night, 154
Irvin, John, 195
Isaacs, Harry, 4
Isaacs, Ronnie, 15, 22–3, 77, 158–60, 169n, 238
Isiboshwa, 92–3, 125
Isiqalekiso, 118
I Spit on Your Grave, 183
Israel, Neal, 152
Ivondwe, 36, 89, 93–4, 96, 121

Jackson, Michael, 98, 107n
Jackson, Wilfred, 71
Jacopetti, Gualtiero, 130
James, Steve, 32, 152–3
Jancovich, Mark, 108–9
Jannie Totsiens, 78
Jenkins, Barry, 172
Jewison, Norman, 154
Jing, Wu, 3
Jim Comes to Jo'burg, 26–7
Jobman, 147
Joe Bullet, 4–5, 8–9, 13, 15, 22, 26–7, 33–6, 38–9, 40n, 41–59, 61–3, 75, 79, 82, 101, 103, 118, 125–6, 128, 132, 138–9, 149, 152, 161, 175, 220, 231, 237–8
Johnny Dlamini, 15, 171–5, 182, 188
Johns, Vera, 196, 202, 204
Johnson, R. W., 118
Joshua, 143
Joubert, Marcel, 44, 107n
Juan of the Dead, 88
Jules-Rosette, Bennetta, 162

Kaplan, Jonathan, 33, 87, 116
Kapuściński, Ryszard, 191, 207
Karate Olympiad, 79
Karate Warrior, 93
Kar Wai, Wong, 14
The Keep, 206
Kellogg, Ray, 196
Kenney, Henry, 51, 91
Kente, Gibson, 73n
Keresztesi, Rita, 144
The Kidnapper; see *Abathumbi*
Kill and Kill Again, 79, 154, 160–2, 164
King Cetshwayo, 170n
King Kong, 161
King Solomon's Mines (1985 film adaptation), 31, 152–3
Kirstein, Hyman, 26

Knockout Joe, 32, 36, 111–13, 115–16, 118–19, 157
Korda, Zoltan, 64
Kotto, Yaphet, 95
Koven, Mikel, 41, 62, 72, 127, 140, 145, 228n
Kracauer, Siegfried, 6, 108
Kraidy, Marwan M., 11
Kramer, Stanley, 49, 113
Kristofferson, Kris, 203
Krüger, Hardy, 162–3, 165
Kubeka, Abigail, 25, 35, 42, 47–9, 52–4, 175
Kubrick, Stanley, 195
Kurosawa, Akira, 15, 173–4

Lady Cocoa, 33, 109, 176
Lamb, Christina, 169n
Lana Pirana, 75
Landis, Bill, 200
Last Grave at Dimbaza, 85–6
The Last House on the Left, 4, 200
The Last Hunter, 8
The Last King of Scotland, 209
Latter, Greg, 199, 206
Lawrence, Novotny, 17, 33, 38–9, 49, 62, 154–5, 157, 169n, 235
Lazarus, Ashley, 73
Lee, Malcolm D., 137
Lee, Spike, 213
The Legend of Nigger Charley, 102, 107n, 143
Lelyveld, Joseph, 40n
Lenzi, Umberto, 239n
Leonard, Bobby Jean, 148n
Leone, Sergio, 15, 126, 140, 145, 173–4
Lethal Weapon, 151, 154, 169n
Levene, Terry, 236
Levey, William A., 233
The Little Shop of Horrors, 80
Livia, 79
Loach, Ken, 14
Lola, 187, 189n
Look, Water; see *Bona Manzi*
Lopez, Joe, 25
Louw, Eric, 154
Lovell, Julia, 10

Mabizela, Pepsi, 95–8, 107n
McCluskey, Audrey Thomas, 2
Macdonald, Kevin, 209
Macfarlane, Pascoe, 85
The Mack, 136
McLaglen, Andrew V., 30, 163
McLennan-Dodd, Vanessa, 209n

Madala, John, 142
Magubane, Kay, 95
Magubane, Khulikani, 111
Maingard, Jacqueline, 1, 21, 26, 41, 59–62, 64, 67–9, 188, 205, 211, 214–16, 228n
Majozi, Fikile, 139
Makhathini, Sylvia, 97
Malan, David, 141
Malan, Rian, 10, 141
Malcolm X, 213
Maldoror, Sarah, 216
Malele, Dixon, 206
Manaka, Matsemela, 49, 53
Mandela, Nelson, 8, 10, 74n, 109, 118, 136, 147, 151
Mandla, 92, 133
Man from Deep River, 139n
Manhattan Baby, 104
Manlove, Clifford T., 161
Mann, Michael, 206
Mapantsula, 6, 10, 15–16, 36, 60, 89, 128–9, 138, 169n, 175, 187–8, 209, 211–22, 224, 227, 228n, 230–1, 237–8
Marcos, Ferdinand, 3, 113, 238
Margheriti, Antonio, 8, 83
Marins, José Mojica, 89
The Marked One; see *Impango*
The Marked One II; see *Impango II*
Markov, Margaret, 113
Marks, Arthur, 33, 44, 87, 109
Marley, Bob, 179–80
Martin, D'Urville, 43, 116
Martin, Goldman, 102
Martino, Sergio, 37, 79
Masilela, Ntongela, 19–20
Maslansky, Paul, 44
Maslin, Janet, 217
Mathanda, Hector, 25, 54, 81, 92–6, 114, 118, 121, 129, 136–7, 144, 177, 183, 185, 200, 204–5
Matloff, Judith, 169n, 192, 206–7
The Matrix, 71
Matthews, Michael, 231
Mau-Mau, 161
Mayer, Rudi, 94, 101, 180
Mazibuko, Phinda, 222, 224
Mbeki, Thabo, 208
Mdlada, Lungi, 175, 184
Mean Johnny Barrows, 200
Medicine for Melancholy, 182
Melville, Jean Pierre, 15
Meintjies, Frank, 65
Menges, Chris, 218
Metcalfe, Daniel, 199
Metsing, Simon, 67
Mhlanga, Gugu, 183

Mhlanga, So, 179
Mkwanazi, Lungi, 222
Millin, David, 166
Mine Boy, 10, 12, 15, 47, 53, 83–5, 175, 178, 221–5, 227, 231, 238
Minter, William, 191
Missing in Action, 197
Mitchell, Edward, 20–1
The Mobsters, 142, 210n
Modisane, Litheko, 7, 22, 32, 58–9, 65–6, 73n, 95, 182, 216, 220, 225
Modise, Joe, 74n
Mogotlane, Thomas, 126, 188, 211–12, 214, 237
Moneta, Tullio, 145
Monteith, Sharon, 108–9
Moonraker, 55
Moore, Roger, 32, 59, 70–2, 164
Moore, Rudy Ray, 5
Morse, L. A., 79, 83
Mothi, Olga, 223–5
Moyo Mubi, 38, 133, 136–7, 187
Mr. T, 55
Mthembu, Sihle, 1
Mtshali, Thembi, 188, 217
Mugabe, Robert, 106n, 166, 168, 191, 199, 205
Muhammed, Rashid, 13
Muhammed, Richie, 13
Murphy, Eddie, 55
Murray, James, 1, 6–8, 18n, 27–8, 39, 66–7, 77, 79, 85, 91, 101, 105, 123, 137, 147n
The Muthers, 3
Muzorewa, Abel, 106n, 197
My Country My Hat, 15, 129, 213, 224–7, 231

The Native Who Caused all the Trouble, 6
Needham, Hal, 39
Nelson, Ralph, 10
Neto, Agostinho, 191–2, 208
New Jack City, 162
Ngomopho, 2, 78
Ngoyi, Lilian, 181
Ngubane, Alex, 142
Nicart, Eddie, 37
Nixon, Ron, 10
Nkomo, Joshua, 168, 169n
Nofal, Emil, 26
Nogueira, Helena, 6
Norris, Aaron, 152
Norris, Chuck, 197
Nowell, Richard, 43
Ntshona, Winston, 162–3, 165–6, 169n, 206

Ntuli, Deuteronomy Bhekinkosi Zeblon, 189n
Nxumalo, Bexi, 221–2
Nyidi, Zanela, 99
Nyoni, Rungano, 40n

Oasis of the Zombies, 83
Omond, Roger, 108, 190, 205, 211
O'Neal, Ron, 62–3
One More Shot, 15, 22, 50, 80, 83, 88–9, 91, 154, 158–60, 168, 169n, 183, 219, 238
Onishi, Norimitsu, 1
Operation Hit Squad, 54, 126, 161, 195–6, 202, 210n, 232
Orphans; see *Ezintandaneni*
Osborn, J. R., 162
Oscherwitz, Dayna, 144
The Outlaw, 141

Palcy, Euzhan, 165
Paleker, Gairoonisa, 7, 22, 26, 45, 51, 56, 58, 68, 75, 77–8, 82, 88, 97, 100, 105, 106n, 109, 169n, 206
Parish, James Robert, 87, 176
Parks, Gordon, 4, 25, 128
Parks Jr., Gordon, 4, 63, 110
Parsons, Bevis, 39, 135
Pawson, Lara, 18n, 208
Peet, Stephen, 19
Penitentiary, 116, 169n
Piliso, Mzwandile, 205
Platoon, 197–8
Platoon Leader, 152
Platoon Warrior; see *The Stick*
Poitier, Sidney, 49, 64, 113, 165–6
Pollack, Sydney, 150
The Power of One, 220
Price, Elwood, 161
The Priest and the Thief, 88, 107n, 111
Prinsloo, Jeanne, 212–13, 221
Prisoner; see *Isiboshwa*
Private Popsicle, 209n
The Professionals, 150
Prosperi, Franco, 130
Prout-Jones, Bill, 79
Pyun, Albert, 8

Quest for Love, 6

Rabotabi, Hector, 80, 160, 172
Rachilo, Sol, 135, 137
Rambo: First Blood Part II, 197
Ransom, 90, 120, 183

Rautenbach, Jans, 78
Reagan, Ronald, 191
Reid, Mark A., 110
Revenge, 15, 126, 142–4, 146–7, 209n
Rhodes, Hari, 154
Rich Girl, 83, 175, 183–6, 188
Rijsdijk, Ian-Malcolm, 48–9, 190
River of Death, 152
Rivers, Patrick Lynn, 220
Robinson, Cedric, J., 24–5
Rocco, Alex, 154
Rocky, 123
The Rocky Horror Picture Show, 147n
Romero, Eddie, 113, 238
Romero, George, 88
Roodt, Darrell, 6, 8, 147, 198–9, 205–9, 218, 221, 230
Röthig, Tommy, 36, 157–9
Roundtree, Richard, 24, 33–4, 53, 55, 61, 83, 128, 135, 197–9
Rowley, Christopher, 15, 155
Rubens, Percival, 78, 212, 228n
Ruiz-Ade, Lea Maria, 162
Run for Your Life, 36, 76, 91, 119, 154, 157–9, 168
Russell, Jane, 141
Rutherford, Eric, 27

Sabela, Simon, 6, 15, 24, 26, 31, 53, 58–75, 96, 101, 103, 105, 125, 128–9, 139, 164, 182, 230, 232
Sambizanga, 216
Sanders, Scott, 68
Santiago, Cirio H., 3, 17, 238
Sarli, Isabel, 239n
Savimbi, Jonas, 50, 76, 164, 169n, 192
The Scalp Hunters, 150
Schaefer, Eric, 29, 39n, 161, 230
Schaeffer, Francis, 233
Schmitz, Oliver, 6, 188, 212, 214–15, 218–22, 225, 237
Sconce, Jeffrey, 12, 61, 123, 229
Scott, Clive, 66–7
Scott, Ridley, 209
Seko, Mobutu Sese, 52
Sephuma, Peter, 224, 226
The Shadowed Mind, 233
Shadyac, Tom, 71
Shaft, 4, 32–4, 42–3, 49, 55, 59, 61, 63, 66, 83, 86–7, 95, 97, 126–8, 135, 137, 146, 197
Shaft in Africa, 31, 219
Shaft's Big Score!, 128, 133
Shamwari, 76, 113, 161–2, 166–8, 170n, 232
Shangani Patrol, 166

Shangase, Emmanuel; *see* Shongwe, Dumi/Dumisani
Shange, Cynthia 65, 182
Sharman, Jim, 147n
Sharon Stone (Nollywood film), 48
Shaw, Harold M., 141
The Shawshank Redemption, 71
She, 239n
Shear, Barry, 154
Sheba, Baby, 44, 176
Shongwe, Dumi/Dumisani; 86, 95, 97, 99–100, 118, 120, 133, 136
Shot Down, 221–2, 230
Sieving, Christopher, 49
Silber, Gus, 2, 22, 50, 77, 79, 139, 150, 153, 159, 162, 180, 185, 238
Simon, Paul, 218
Sims, Yvonne, 110, 127, 177, 187
Singh, Anant, 205
Siswe, Hector, 93
Skeleton Coast, 30–1
The Slams, 116
Slaughter, 176, 200
Smith, Ian, 131, 167, 195
Smith, Iain Robert, 2, 11, 33–7, 142
Smoke; see *Imusi*
Smokey and the Bandit, 39
Snake Dancer, 233–5, 238, 239n
Song of Africa, 26
Song of the South, 71
The Soul of Nigger Charley, 143
Sorak, Ömer Faruk, 34
Spangler, Larry, 143
Spencer, Bud, 92
Spielberg, Carton, 126, 133–4
Stagecoach, 142
Staiger, Janet, 148n
Stallone, Sylvester, 12
Stamp, Terence, 92
Stanley, Richard, 192
Starrett, Jack, 176
The Stay Awake, 8, 228n
Steadman, Ian, 49
Stevens, Brad, 127
The Stick, 8, 16, 138, 192, 198, 205–9, 221, 230, 237
Stone, Oliver, 197
Stone, Sharon, 153
The Strange Vice of Mrs. Wardh, 79
Strikeback, 22–3
Ssali, Ndugu Mike, 75
Studlar, Gaylan, 197
Sugar Hill, 44
Suleman, Ramadan, 231

Sundstrom, Cedric, 15, 32, 40n, 73, 80, 149–53, 168, 232–3
Super Fly, 4, 9, 11, 15, 43, 62–5, 68, 70, 86, 110, 129, 138, 146, 215–16
Survival Zone, 212
Sutherland, Donald, 165
Suzman, Helen, 181
Swanson, Donald, 26
Sweet Murder, 228n
Sweet Sweetback's Baadasssss Song, 4, 9, 14–15, 23–4, 33, 43–5, 55, 61–2, 77, 127, 130, 146, 215–16, 219–20, 239

Tarantino, Quentin, 3, 23, 140, 144–45
Target of an Assassin, 66, 73
Taxi Driver, 202
Taylor, Clyde, 129
Taylor, Trevor, 13, 66, 82–3, 104–5, 149–51
Tears of the Sun, 208–9
Tenth of a Second, 205, 221
Terrorist, 8, 16, 192, 199–205, 209n, 232, 238
The Texas Chain Saw Massacre, 235
The Texas Chainsaw Massacre 2, 7
Thieves; see *Umgulukudu*
Thompson, J. Lee, 31
Thompson, Katrina Daly, 170n
Thompson, Kristin, 148n
Thomson, Ian, 228n
Thorne, Karen, 10, 84, 221–5
Three Bullets for a Long Gun, 145–6
Thunderball, 37–8
Thunder Valley, 107n, 236
Tiger Don't Cry; see *Target of an Assassin*
Tilley, Brian, 211–12, 225–7
TNT Jackson, 3
Tomaselli, Keyan, 4, 6–7, 9, 14, 20, 26–7, 33–4, 38, 45–6, 49, 57n, 58, 62, 66–8, 78, 89, 103, 106n, 111–12, 117, 129, 132–3, 139, 142–3, 147n, 155, 163–4, 166–7, 170n, 172, 183, 191–5, 197, 201, 207, 209n, 212–13, 216–17, 219–21, 224, 227, 228n, 231, 239n
Tom Dollar, 65
Towers, Harry Alan, 30
Toye, Richard, 14
Treasure Hunter; see *Ukuzingela*
Trompie, 78
Truck Turner, 33, 87
The Two Farmers, 19
Tyawa, Dominique, 171–3

uDeliwe, 58, 65–6, 175, 182
Ukadike, Nwachukwu Frank, 14, 83
Ukuzingela, 91, 95, 109, 116–18, 121

Umbango, 1–2, 15, 107n, 126, 139–40, 144–7, 163, 171, 231–2
Umgulukudu, 107n, 111, 118
Under Cover, 90, 96–102, 111, 118, 121, 183
Undercover Brother, 137
Upondo & Nkinsela, 107n, 211, 228n
Upperseven, 65
Ureke, Oswelled, 30, 38, 58–9, 103
Uthemba, 94, 175, 179–83, 236
Uys, Jamie, 38, 83, 113, 165, 192

Valle, Joseph S., 176–8, 189n
van Aswegen, Adri, 152
van de Coolwijk, Robert, 15, 172–3
van den Bergh, Regardt, 193–4
van der Merwe, Japie, 94, 114
van der Merwe, Tonie, 1–3, 15, 25, 27–8, 30–1, 37, 45, 50, 52–6, 65–6, 77–83, 85, 87, 91–2, 95, 109–10, 113, 116–18, 126, 136, 139–41, 144–6, 159–62, 171, 175, 177, 180–1, 183, 185–6, 190, 195–6, 199–200, 227, 231–2, 236
van der Westhuizen, Christi, 8, 51, 106n, 111, 116–17, 119, 139, 141, 151, 169n, 174, 189n, 211
Vanishing Point, 105
Van Peebles, Mario, 162
Van Peebles, Melvin, 4–5, 14, 22, 25, 43–4, 61, 110, 125, 127, 215–16
van Rensburg, Manie, 6
van Zyl, Mikki, 6, 57n, 163, 191, 193, 197, 201
Velekazi, Vincent, 144
Verwoerd, Hendrik, 91
Viedge, Kathy, 195–6
Viljoen, Gerrit, 115
The Virgin Goddess, 239n
Von Doviak, Scott, 40n
De Voortrekkers, 141, 205
Die Voortrekkers, 166
Vorster, John ("B. J."), 57n, 116–17, 230
Vosloo, Arnold, 194–5

Wachowski, Lana, 71
Wachowski, Lilly, 71
Walker, Johnny, 88, 102–3
Wa Luruli, Ntshaveni, 12, 60–1, 72–3, 85

Ward, Glenn, 27
Watson, Paul, 76
Wayne, John, 196
Welsh, Frank, 85, 111, 120, 158, 181, 228n
Weng Weng, 37–8
Whispering Death, 166
White Cannibal Queen, 83
White Hunter Black Heart, 209
The Wilby Conspiracy, 10, 30, 164–6, 168
The Wild Geese, 30, 38, 73, 161–6, 168, 191, 195, 197, 199, 202, 206, 218, 230, 233
Williams, Adim, 48
Williams, Linda, 9, 50, 176–8
Williamson, Bruce, 219
Williamson, Fred, 34, 70, 81, 95, 109, 143–5, 200
Winner, Michael, 133, 168n
Winning a Continent; see *De Voortrekkers*
Winters, Shelley, 177
The Witchdoctor, 75
Wolf Warrior, 3
Women in Cages, 158
Women in Cellblock 9, 83
Woo, John, 13
Wood, Bret, 127
Wood, Robin, 6
Woods, Donald, 156
Worsdale, Andrew, 221

Xaba, Isaac, 111

Yearwood, Gladstone L., 13, 127–8, 134
Yojimbo, 15, 171, 174
York, Susannah, 59
Young, Terence, 37
Yule, Andrew, 151–2, 168n, 169n
Yule, Ian, 76, 167–8, 197

Zarchi, Meir, 183
Zedong, Mao, 10
Zero for Zep, 99, 119, 178–9, 181
Zimbert, Richard, 87
Zonk!, 26
Zulu, 9, 146
The Zulu's Heart, 126
Zulu, Shaka, 93, 125
Zwick, Edward, 32